The Cambridge Companion to Electronic Dance Music

Electronic dance music is increasingly the focus of a multitude of academic research projects around the world but has been drastically under-represented in accessible core published material. This innovative scholarly collection provides an important 'first stop' for researchers and students wishing to work in this area. It examines the key features of numerous electronic dance music scenes and (sub) genres alongside discussions of the musical, social, and aesthetic experiences of participants to consider how these musical practices create purpose and cultural significance for millions around the world. At the same time, it introduces diverse theoretical approaches to the understanding of electronic dance music cultures and addresses the issues and debates in the study of electronic dance music cultures. Adopting an interdisciplinary approach drawn from both music and cultural studies – including music aesthetics, technologies, venues, and performativity – from a broad geographical perspective, the volume sheds fresh light on electronic dance music.

HILLEGONDA C. RIETVELD is Professor Emerita at London South Bank University. She has published extensively on electronic dance music cultures, including the monograph *This is Our House: House Music, Cultural Spaces and Technologies* (1998/2021) and the co-edited collection *DJ Culture in the Mix: Power, Technology and Social Change in Electronic Dance Music* (2013).

TOBY YOUNG is Professor of Composition at Guildhall School of Music & Drama, and Research Lead in Digital Performance. He is Music Supervisor for leading immersive theatre company Punchdrunk and has collaborated with pop and jazz artists including Chase & Status, the Rolling Stones, Duran Duran, Florence Welch, Kano, Snow Ghosts, MOKO, and Jacob Banks.

Cambridge Companions to Music

Topics

The Cambridge Companion to Ballet
Edited by Marion Kant

The Cambridge Companion to Blues and Gospel Music
Edited by Allan Moore

The Cambridge Companion to Caribbean Music
Edited by Nanette de Jong

The Cambridge Companion to Choral Music
Edited by André de Quadros

The Cambridge Companion to Composition
Edited by Toby Young

The Cambridge Companion to the Concerto
Edited by Simon P. Keefe

The Cambridge Companion to Conducting
Edited by José Antonio Bowen

The Cambridge Companion to Eighteenth-Century Opera
Edited by Anthony R. DelDonna and Pierpaolo Polzonetti

The Cambridge Companion to Electronic Dance Music
Edited by Hillegonda C. Rietveld and Toby Young

The Cambridge Companion to Electronic Music, second edition
Edited by Nick Collins and Julio D'Escriván

The Cambridge Companion to the 'Eroica' Symphony
Edited by Nancy November

The Cambridge Companion to Film Music
Edited by Mervyn Cooke and Fiona Ford

The Cambridge Companion to Folk Music
Edited by Ross Cole

The Cambridge Companion to French Art Song
Edited by Stephen Rumph

The Cambridge Companion to French Music
Edited by Simon Trezise

The Cambridge Companion to Global Rap
Edited by Richard Bramwell and Alex de Lacey

The Cambridge Companion to Grand Opera
Edited by David Charlton

The Cambridge Companion to Hip-Hop
Edited by Justin A. Williams

The Cambridge Companion to Jazz
Edited by Mervyn Cooke and David Horn

The Cambridge Companion to Jewish Music
Edited by Joshua S. Walden

The Cambridge Companion to K-Pop
Edited by Suk-Young Kim

The Cambridge Companion to Krautrock
Edited by Uwe Schütte

The Cambridge Companion to the Lied
Edited by James Parsons

The Cambridge Companion to *The Magic Flute*
Edited by Jessica Waldoff

The Cambridge Companion to Medieval Music
Edited by Mark Everist

The Cambridge Companion to Metal Music
Edited by Jan-Peter Herbst

The Cambridge Companion to Music and Romanticism
Edited by Benedict Taylor

The Cambridge Companion to Music in Australia
Edited by Amanda Harris and Clint Bracknell

The Cambridge Companion to Music in Digital Culture
Edited by Nicholas Cook, Monique Ingalls and David Trippett

The Cambridge Companion to the Musical, third edition
Edited by William Everett and Paul Laird

The Cambridge Companion to Opera Studies
Edited by Nicholas Till

The Cambridge Companion to Operetta
Edited by Anastasia Belina and Derek B. Scott

The Cambridge Companion to the Orchestra
Edited by Colin Lawson

The Cambridge Companion to Pop and Rock
Edited by Simon Frith, Will Straw and John Street

The Cambridge Companion to Recorded Music
Edited by Eric Clarke, Nicholas Cook, Daniel Leech-Wilkinson and John Rink

The Cambridge Companion to Rhythm
Edited by Russell Hartenberger and Ryan McClelland

The Cambridge Companion to *The Rite of Spring*
Edited by Davinia Caddy

The Cambridge Companion to Schubert's 'Winterreise'
Edited by Marjorie W. Hirsch and Lisa Feurzeig

The Cambridge Companion to Serialism
Edited by Martin Iddon

The Cambridge Companion to Seventeenth-Century Opera
Edited by Jacqueline Waeber

The Cambridge Companion to the Singer-Songwriter
Edited by Katherine Williams and Justin A. Williams

The Cambridge Companion to the String Quartet
Edited by Robin Stowell

The Cambridge Companion to the Symphony
Edited by Julian Horton

The Cambridge Companion to Tango
Edited by Kristin Wendland and Kacey Link

The Cambridge Companion to Twentieth-Century Opera
Edited by Mervyn Cooke

The Cambridge Companion to Video Game Music
Edited by Melanie Fritsch and Tim Summers

The Cambridge Companion to Wagner's *Der Ring des Nibelungen*
Edited by Mark Berry and Nicholas Vazsonyi

The Cambridge Companion to *West Side Story*
Edited by Paul R. Laird and Elizabeth A. Wells

The Cambridge Companion to Women Composers
Edited by Matthew Head and Susan Wollenberg

The Cambridge Companion to Women in Music since 1900
Edited by Laura Hamer

Composers

The Cambridge Companion to Bach
Edited by John Butt

The Cambridge Companion to Bartók
Edited by Amanda Bayley

The Cambridge Companion to Amy Beach
Edited by E. Douglas Bomberger

The Cambridge Companion to the Beatles
Edited by Kenneth Womack

The Cambridge Companion to Beethoven
Edited by Glenn Stanley

The Cambridge Companion to Berg
Edited by Anthony Pople

The Cambridge Companion to Berlioz
Edited by Peter Bloom

The Cambridge Companion to Brahms
Edited by Michael Musgrave

The Cambridge Companion to Benjamin Britten
Edited by Mervyn Cooke

The Cambridge Companion to Bruckner
Edited by John Williamson

The Cambridge Companion to John Cage
Edited by David Nicholls

The Cambridge Companion to Chopin
Edited by Jim Samson

The Cambridge Companion to Debussy
Edited by Simon Trezise

The Cambridge Companion to Elgar
Edited by Daniel M. Grimley and Julian Rushton

The Cambridge Companion to Duke Ellington
Edited by Edward Green

The Cambridge Companion to Gershwin
Edited by Anna Celenza

The Cambridge Companion to Gilbert and Sullivan
Edited by David Eden and Meinhard Saremba

The Cambridge Companion to Handel
Edited by Donald Burrows

The Cambridge Companion to Haydn
Edited by Caryl Clark

The Cambridge Companion to Liszt
Edited by Kenneth Hamilton

The Cambridge Companion to Mahler
Edited by Jeremy Barham

The Cambridge Companion to Mendelssohn
Edited by Peter Mercer-Taylor

The Cambridge Companion to Monteverdi
Edited by John Whenham and Richard Wistreich

The Cambridge Companion to Mozart
Edited by Simon P. Keefe

The Cambridge Companion to Arvo Pärt
Edited by Andrew Shenton

The Cambridge Companion to Ravel
Edited by Deborah Mawer

The Cambridge Companion to the Rolling Stones
Edited by Victor Coelho and John Covach

The Cambridge Companion to Rossini
Edited by Emanuele Senici

The Cambridge Companion to Schoenberg
Edited by Jennifer Shaw and Joseph Auner

The Cambridge Companion to Schubert
Edited by Christopher Gibbs

The Cambridge Companion to Schumann
Edited by Beate Perrey

The Cambridge Companion to Shostakovich
Edited by Pauline Fairclough and David Fanning

The Cambridge Companion to Sibelius
Edited by Daniel M. Grimley

The Cambridge Companion to Richard Strauss
Edited by Charles Youmans

The Cambridge Companion to Stravinsky
Edited by Jonathan Cross

The Cambridge Companion to Michael Tippett
Edited by Kenneth Gloag and Nicholas Jones

The Cambridge Companion to Vaughan Williams
Edited by Alain Frogley and Aiden J. Thomson

The Cambridge Companion to Verdi
Edited by Scott L. Balthazar

The Cambridge Companion to Wagner
Edited by Thomas S. Grey

Instruments

The Cambridge Companion to Brass Instruments
Edited by Trevor Herbert and John Wallace

The Cambridge Companion to the Cello
Edited by Robin Stowell

The Cambridge Companion to the Clarinet
Edited by Colin Lawson

The Cambridge Companion to the Drum Kit
Edited by Matt Brennan, Joseph Michael Pignato and Daniel Akira Stadnicki

The Cambridge Companion to the Electric Guitar
Edited by Jan-Peter Herbst and Steve Waksman

The Cambridge Companion to the Guitar
Edited by Victor Coelho

The Cambridge Companion to the Harpsichord
Edited by Mark Kroll

The Cambridge Companion to the Organ
Edited by Nicholas Thistlethwaite and Geoffrey Webber

The Cambridge Companion to Percussion
Edited by Russell Hartenberger

The Cambridge Companion to the Piano
Edited by David Rowland

The Cambridge Companion to the Saxophone
Edited by Richard Ingham

The Cambridge Companion to Singing
Edited by John Potter

The Cambridge Companion to the Violin
Edited by Robin Stowell

The Cambridge Companion to Electronic Dance Music

Edited by

HILLEGONDA C. RIETVELD
London South Bank University

TOBY YOUNG
Guildhall School of Music & Drama

Shaftesbury Road, Cambridge CB2 8EA, United Kingdom

One Liberty Plaza, 20th Floor, New York, NY 10006, USA

477 Williamstown Road, Port Melbourne, VIC 3207, Australia

314–321, 3rd Floor, Plot 3, Splendor Forum, Jasola District Centre, New Delhi – 110025, India

103 Penang Road, #05–06/07, Visioncrest Commercial, Singapore 238467

Cambridge University Press is part of Cambridge University Press & Assessment, a department of the University of Cambridge.

We share the University's mission to contribute to society through the pursuit of education, learning and research at the highest international levels of excellence.

www.cambridge.org
Information on this title: www.cambridge.org/9781009215824

DOI: 10.1017/9781009215817

© Cambridge University Press & Assessment 2026

This publication is in copyright. Subject to statutory exception and to the provisions of relevant collective licensing agreements, no reproduction of any part may take place without the written permission of Cambridge University Press & Assessment.

When citing this work, please include a reference to the DOI 10.1017/9781009215817

First published 2026

Cover image: Image created by Hillegonda C. Rietveld

A catalogue record for this publication is available from the British Library

A Cataloging-in-Publication data record for this book is available from the Library of Congress

ISBN 978-1-009-21582-4 Hardback
ISBN 978-1-009-21578-7 Paperback

Cambridge University Press & Assessment has no responsibility for the persistence or accuracy of URLs for external or third-party internet websites referred to in this publication and does not guarantee that any content on such websites is, or will remain, accurate or appropriate.

For EU product safety concerns, contact us at Calle de José Abascal, 56, 1°, 28003 Madrid, Spain, or email eugpsr@cambridge.org

Contents

List of Figures [*page* xii]
List of Contributors [xiii]
Acknowledgements [xvii]

Introduction [1]
HILLEGONDA C. RIETVELD AND TOBY YOUNG

PART I SETTING THE SCENE [15]

1 Raves as Aesthetic Experience: The Blackburn Parties [17]
   BEATE PETER

2 The 'Affective Charge' of the 'Inexistent' Dance Floor: Exploring Nightclub Architecture and Design [30]
   CATHARINE ROSSI

3 Sound System Legacies [50]
   CASPAR MELVILLE

4 Let the DJ Tell the Story: Thoughts on Archiving and Genre Formation in the Age of Electronic Dance Music [71]
   KAI FIKENTSCHER

PART II LOCAL AND GLOBAL CONTEXTS [81]

5 Party as Protest: Free Party, Teknivals, Early Rave Scenes, and Berlin's Hardcore Techno [83]
   BIANCA LUDEWIG

6 Angolan Kuduro in the Context of Sound System Cultures of the Black Atlantic [109]
   STEFANIE ALISCH

7 Chinese Electronic Dance Music Cultures: An Analysis of Their Local Cultural and Social Characteristics [128]
   MATTHEW MING-TAK CHEW

8 Taking the Mix to Twitch: Streaming DJ Culture during and after the Pandemic   [146]
TOBIAS C. VAN VEEN AND BERNARDO ALEXANDER ATTIAS

PART III GENRE AESTHETICS   [165]

9 Drum and Bass as Cultural Accelerator: Underground Resistance or Ecstatic Concession to Speed?   [167]
CHRIS CHRISTODOULOU

10 Chill Out: Seeking Ecstatic Trance in Low-Tempo EDM   [182]
RUPERT TILL

11 Genre Classification in Electronic Dance Music Culture: From Localised Histories to the Bandcamp Underground   [205]
BOTOND VITOS

PART IV SONIC SUBJECTIVITIES   [229]

12 Timbre and Gesture at the Threshold of Meaning   [231]
MARIA PEREVEDENTSEVA

13 Pulse Trains: An Autoethnography of Techno Production in Berlin   [254]
NICOLAS BOUGAÏEFF

14 EDM's Secret Technologies   [276]
ROBERT FINK

15 Dance Music and Flow   [295]
TAMI GADIR

PART V DANCE FLOOR IDENTITIES   [311]

16 Feminine Subjectivities: Gender in Electronic Music Production and Performance   [313]
SAMANTHA PARSLEY

17 The Divisiveness of the Bass Music Drop in the North
   American Festival Setting [337]
   ED KATRAK SPENCER

18 Ageing Provocateurs: Responding to Older People's
   Participation in Electronic Dance Music Culture [353]
   ALICE O'GRADY AND ALINKA GREASLEY

   Index [368]

Figures

2.1 Inside the upper level of Space Electronic, designed by Gruppo 9999. Visible are furnishings including salvaged washing machine drums turned into seating, a parachute suspended from the ceiling, the stage and bridge for audio visual equipment. Space Electronic, Florence, 1969. 9999 Archive, Courtesy Elettra Fiumi. [*page* 31]

2.2 The main dance floor at Studio 54, showing the theatrical lighting designed by Paul Marantz and Jules Fisher, including the vertical chase poles and horizontal 'flying ceilings' suspended from ceiling rigging. Studio 54, New York, 1977. Photographer: Jaime Ardiles-Arce. Photograph courtesy of Scott Bromley. [42]

8.1 DJ tobias (left) and DJ Professor Ben (right) DJing vinyl back-to-back on PANDEMiX! using Streamyard, 20 November 2020. [147]

8.2 DJ tobias (left) and DJ Professor Ben (right) DJing vinyl back-to-back on PANDEMiX! using VDO.Ninja, 2 August 2023. [156]

10.1 Chillout Classics Spotify Playlist BPM, 2023. [196]

13.1 'Pulse Train' bassline. [261]

13.2 'Pulse Train' chords. [262]

13.3 'Cognitive Resonance' rhythmic structure. [265]

13.4 'Cognitive Resonance' track structure. [268]

Contributors

STEFANIE ALISCH leads the DFG-funded research group 'Sound System Epistemologies: Knowledge Engendered through Practice' at Humboldt University of Berlin. As a musicologist she investigates and theorises music and dance of the Black Atlantic, focusing on the Portuguese-speaking realm and pleasure politics, as well as DJ and dance cultures.

BERNARDO ALEXANDER ATTIAS is Professor of Communication Studies at California State University, Northridge. He co-edited the collection *DJ Culture in the Mix: Power, Technology and Social Change in Electronic Dance Music* (2013), and publishes on topics in cultural, rhetorical, and performance studies. He co-edited special issues of *Dancecult: Journal of Electronic Dance Music Culture* and *Women & Language*. He is also an accomplished DJ.

NICOLAS BOUGAÏEFF is a Canadian-born, Berlin-based artist and researcher. Bougaïeff released his debut album for Mute, *The Upward Spiral* (2020), following his 2017 12" *Cognitive Resonance*, which formed part of the NovaMute relaunch. His recent productions feature a distinct use of polytemporality.

MATTHEW MING-TAK CHEW is Associate Professor at the Department of Digital Arts and Creative Industries of Lingnan University in Hong Kong. His research interests include cultural sociology, social theory, media sociology, and political sociology. His work is published in journals including *Sociology*, *Cultural Studies*, and *New Media & Society*.

CHRIS CHRISTODOULOU's academic work concerns the links between sound, moving image practice, and emerging/interactive media. His publications focus on the impact of accelerationism across media culture and in electronic dance music subcultures inflected by Black British and UK working-class experiences, especially jungle drum and bass.

KAI FIKENTSCHER holds degrees in jazz studies from Berklee College of Music and Manhattan School of Music. He received his PhD in Ethnomusicology from Columbia in 1996. He has taught at Columbia,

NYU, Tufts University, Amherst College, Rhode Island School of Design, and Ramapo College of New Jersey. He published his book *'You Better Work!' Underground Dance Music in New York* in 2000 and is a member of the international advisory board for *Dancecult: Journal of Electronic Dance Music Culture*.

ROBERT FINK is Professor of Musicology and Music Industry at the UCLA Herb Alpert School of Music. He has published widely on contemporary and popular music, including the monograph *Repeating Ourselves: American Minimal Music as Cultural Practice* (2005), and the co-edited collection *The Relentless Pursuit of Tone: Timbre in Popular Music* (2018), which was awarded the American Musicological Society's Ruth Solie Prize.

TAMI GADIR is a lecturer in music industry in the School of Media and Communication at RMIT University in Naarm/Melbourne. Gadir's research addresses the social and political mechanisms of musical participation, with a specialisation in the study of DJ cultures and the social life of labour choirs.

ALINKA GREASLEY is Professor of Music Psychology at the University of Leeds. Her research focuses on the role of music in everyday life, with expertise in musical preferences and listening behaviour. She is a DJ with a passion for investigating the benefits of musical participation for health and wellbeing.

BIANCA LUDEWIG is a cultural anthropologist, journalist, and record collector. She studied philosophy, cultural anthropology, and European ethnology in Hamburg and Berlin and completed her PhD at the University of Innsbruck with a study on Transmedia Festivals. She researches ambivalences of post-modern life in audio-social communities, art, and culture.

CASPAR MELVILLE was Senior Lecturer in Global Creative and Cultural Industries at SOAS, University of London. Educator, journalist, and editor, he is author of the book *It's A London Thing: How Rare Groove, Acid House and Jungle Remapped the City* (2020). His work bridges decades and genres of dance music but ties them together into a single narrative of Black musical scenes of the city, from ska, reggae, and soul in the 1970s, to rare groove and rave in the 1980s and jungle and its offshoots in the 1990s, and on to dubstep and grime.

ALICE O'GRADY is Professor of Applied Performance at the University of Leeds. With a background in arts education, her research investigates the efficacy of participatory performance across a range of cultural and subcultural contexts, including underground club cultures, burlesque communities, and festival spaces. She has both published in and edited for *Dancecult: Journal of Electronic Dance Music Culture*.

SAMANTHA PARSLEY is Professor of Organization Studies at the University of Portsmouth, and is investigating gender inequality in electronic music production funded by a Leverhulme Fellowship 2019–2022. As well as her academic role, Samantha is Diversity and Inclusion Co-Chair at the Association for Electronic Music and is currently writing a monograph from her research, to be published by Bristol University Press.

MARIA PEREVEDENTSEVA researches electronic dance music, timbre, cognition, and online discourse, and is a co-founder of the Music and Online Cultures Research Network. Her work appears in edited collections and journals such as *Dancecult: Journal of Electronic Dance Music*, *Sound Studies*, and *Journal of Popular Music Studies*.

BEATE PETER is a cultural sociologist at the University of Groningen, Netherlands. She is interested in the role that music plays for the formation of communities. With a specialism in electronic dance music, Beate has researched the rave scene in the north-west of England for the past ten years.

HILLEGONDA C. RIETVELD is Professor Emerita at London South Bank University, was Chief Editor of *IASPM Journal*, and pioneered electronica with Quando Quango for Factory Records. She has published extensively on electronic dance music cultures, including the monograph *This is Our House: House Music, Cultural Spaces and Technologies* (1998/2021), the co-edited collection *DJ Culture in the Mix: Power, Technology and Social Change in Electronic Dance Music* (2013), and a co-edited special issue for *Dancecult: Journal of Electronic Dance Music Culture*.

CATHARINE ROSSI is Professor of Architecture at UCA Canterbury. Her interests include post-war Italian design and architecture, craft, club culture, and feminism. Publications include *Designing Craft in Italy: from Postwar to Postmodernism* (2015). Exhibitions include *Night Fever: Designing Club Culture 1960 to Today* (Vitra Design Museum, 2018).

ED KATRAK SPENCER is Assistant Professor of Screen and Music Cultures at Utrecht University. His research concerns electronic dance music in the social media era, the politicisation of music via audiovisual web content, and music-related conspiracy theories. He is a co-founder of the Music and Online Cultures Research Network.

RUPERT TILL is Professor of Music at the University of Huddersfield, Series Editor of *Elements in Popular Music* for Cambridge University Press, and Associate Editor of *Dancecult: Journal of Electronic Dance Music Culture*. His PhD (2000) pioneered practice-based composition with recordings of original downtempo electronica, chill out music. He has published on a range of popular music subjects, including the monograph *Pop Cult: Religion and Popular Music* (2010).

TOBIAS C. VAN VEEN holds doctorates in communications and philosophy from McGill University. His research addresses technology and race in media studies. He is series co-editor of *Afrofuturism & the Speculative Arts* for Rowman & Littlefield, editor of special issues at *Dancecult: Journal of Electronic Dance Music Culture* and *TOPIA*, and author of *Afrofuturism and Abolition: Exodus, Music, and MythScience*.

BOTOND VITOS is a cultural anthropologist with research interests in popular music studies, event-cultures, electronic dance music culture, genre classification in machine learning, and the Burning Man movement. He is a member of the editorial team for *Dancecult: Journal of Electronic Dance Music Culture*.

TOBY YOUNG is Professor of Composition at Guildhall School of Music & Drama, and Research Lead in Digital Performance. He previously contributed to the editorial work of *Dancecult: Journal of Electronic Dance Music Culture*. Toby's work draws on popular musicology, composition, philosophy, and cultural sociology to explore the blurred space between classical and popular music, with a particular focus on opera. As an award-winning composer and producer, Toby has co-written with pop and jazz artists including Chase & Status, the Rolling Stones, Duran Duran, Florence Welch, Kano, Snow Ghosts, MOKO, and Jacob Banks. He is also the Music Supervisor for leading immersive theatre company Punchdrunk.

Acknowledgements

We thank the contributors to this volume on electronic dance music for their generosity, as well as Kate Brett of Cambridge University Press for her support and patience. We are grateful to Jess Far-Cox for indexing and grouping the multi-layered terminologies used throughout this collection of essays that draw on a wide range of connections and approaches. In addition, we thank the editorial team at Cambridge University Press for their assistance, including Senior Editorial Assistant Abi Sears, Production Manager Nigel Graves, and copy-editor Maria Whelan.

We further thank the authors for giving and gaining permission to reprint images for illustrative purposes, in particular: 9999 Archive, courtesy Elettra Fiumi for Fig. 2.1 Space Electronic, designed by Gruppo 9999, Florence, 1969; and Jaime Ardiles-Arce courtesy of Scott Bromley for Fig. 2.2, Studio 54, New York, 1977.

This project has been a few years in the making, and much has shifted in both personal and professional dimensions since we first approached it. We especially mourn the loss of Caspar Melville and are grateful to his family for their permission to include his work.

Introduction

HILLEGONDA C. RIETVELD AND TOBY YOUNG

What is electronic dance music and its abbreviation, EDM? The simple answer would be that it is electronic music you can dance to. Yet this would be too general, as the term mostly relates to post-disco and post-rave dance musical forms that emerged from a transatlantic exchange. Electronic dance music could arguably be understood as dance music made by and for DJs, characterised by repetitive phrases, electronic production methods, and an electronic sonic palette in which timbre and rhythm are foregrounded, as discussed in this collection by Maria Perevedentseva. Commonly, the tempo of recordings ranges between 120 BPM (beats per minute) and 180 BPM, often further manipulated by the DJ. Early examples, can be found in the electronic dance music recordings of Chicago house music of the mid-1980s, quickly expanding into a globalised dance phenomenon during the early 1990s, leading to a diversity of sub-genres that ranges from club anthems to psytrance, and from drum and bass to dubstep. Fundamental to the ontology of EDM is an aesthetic that lies in abstraction and challenge as much as in reconciliation and celebration, in which the audio components of historical recordings are recast. In some cases, like New York's Club Music (also understood by British readers as garage or deep house), this is to pay homage to those who came before, as an oral history of dance music. Elsewhere, machine aesthetic of techno and trance enables dancers to negotiate rapidly developing and accelerating technological developments and increasing cybernetic connectivity.[1] In other words, we argue that EDM's musical language is inextricably intertwined with electronic, digitalised culture. As shown by Vitos' and van Veen & Attias' contributions to this collection, dance music is firmly embedded in mainstream popular culture, with the interconnectivity of social media allowing this music to be made available to a wide audience.

Music genres are continually contested within a living music culture and evolve during their use in their contexts of time and locality. McLeod notes that 'electronic/dance music in the 1990s has yielded a metagenre that is constantly breaking apart, recombining, and making obsolete numerous subgenres on a yearly basis'.[2] As a form of communication within the context of a specific political economy,[3] music genres are subject to the power dynamics of classification.[4] For example, in Germany, most electronic dance music is understood as 'techno', while in the Netherlands the tag 'house' was adopted as a general term during the 1980s and 90s, regardless of whether the tags 'techno' or 'house' referred to a vocal club anthem or to industrial techno. In the process, the importance of marginalised, queer, and African-American dance cultural spaces, which have been essential to the formation of underground disco and club culture and concomitant forms of dance music, seems to have been forgotten in popular cultural memory.[5] Music genres are produced discursively within the fluid inner-circle debates by DJs, dancers, fans, and producers, and solidified in music industry definitions by journalists, record shops, streaming services, and sales platforms. Together, these discursive spaces delineate a porous set of stylistic descriptors[6] that are validated and reinforced within networks of overlapping dance music scenes,[7] which raises questions regarding what is included and excluded. While there are attempts to fix unstable meanings, it is useful to wonder who benefits from a particular representation.[8]

Since the late 1980s, the term 'dance culture' has been used in the UK to indicate the post-rave electronic dance music scene, which may be understood as 'electronic dance music culture', or 'EDMC', in line with the specialist research journal *Dancecult: Journal of Electronic Dance Music Culture*. The abbreviation 'EDM' is used as an umbrella term for many subgenres. However, since the early 2010s, in the USA the term 'EDM' has been claimed to narrowly indicate a pop dance subgenre. As Spencer's contribution on EDM festivals shows, such festivals seem to utilise the collective language of togetherness of yesteryears' raves but instead offer a ruptured spectacle in which the power politics of identity differentiation are embraced. Overall, you will find that the terms 'electronic dance music' and 'EDM' are used in slightly different ways by the contributors to this collection, which are clarified within the contexts of their case studies. Fikentscher foregrounds the importance of the DJ's record archive in music genre formation. A case study regarding online genre definition is further explored by Vitos, while van Veen and Attias address this format off and on the dance floor in the context of screened live DJ shows. As part of a music cultural form that circulates globally, electronic dance music genres are reworked and hybridised locally, which is illustrated in this volume by, for example, Chew's study of dance culture in China, in Alisch's observations of kuduro in Angola, Peter's theorisation of the rave concept in Blackburn, UK, and Ludewig's investigation of the hardcore techno scene in Berlin. Music genre can also be regarded as a social process in the production of social identity, a position that is particularly prominent in contributions by Parsley,

Spencer, and by O'Grady and Greasley. As a music genre, it also produces a range of subjectivities through technological manipulation in music production – as can be read in contributions by Bougaïeff and Perevedentseva – and within the contexts of musicking[9] on the dance floor, as discussed by Gadir. In this way, electronic dance music shapes an affective response to lived experience, as Christodoulou explains in relation to accelerated culture in drum and bass, and Till does in a discussion of chill out music. As these contributions show, although electronic dance music may on the surface seem easily recognisable, its genealogy is rich, and its cultural meanings are varied. Avoiding an exhaustive encyclopaedic approach, the purpose of this collection is to give insight into potential understandings, offering a multidisciplinary and interdisciplinary set of approaches, ranging from architecture and geography to media studies and musicology.

During the 1990s, when the notion of 'electronic dance music' was increasingly used, we heard much about 'global dance culture'. There was a sense amongst dancers that the dance floor offered an unspoken lingua franca, a cosmopolitan space that would become the place to just be. We acknowledge this can be an oversimplification, criticised by some of the contributors here, including Gadir, Parsley, and Spencer, as well as O'Grady and Greasley. Yet, there is a kernel of truth if one considers the wider context of the emergence of electronic dance music, in response to a shift to a post-industrial neoliberal economic paradigm that emerged during the 1970s in New York and rapidly spread across the globe accompanied by an economic crisis.[10] On the margins of the economy, we see the development of disco and hip-hop during the 1970s in NYC, house music in Chicago and forms of techno music in both Detroit and Frankfurt during the 1980s, and, since the late 1980s, rave culture in the UK. The development of information and communication technologies accelerated during the 1990s, enhancing a sense of being a global citizen with shared relationships to an emerging digitally coded network society. The formation of electronic dance music helped dancers to ritually make sense of a new way of being in relation to a newly technologically enhanced existence, in the context of financial nomadism and enhanced entrepreneurship. Those closer connected within this globally networked world – at first in the USA, Western Europe, and Japan – acutely needed forms of music and movement to articulate what felt like a new cyborgian subjectivity.[11] Electronic dance music soon became the party soundtrack of choice in places as far apart as South Africa, Israel, India, Australia, and Brazil.

The genealogy of electronic dance music not only includes early dance music years in New York's underground disco scene during the 1970s and

Chicago's house music scene during the 1980s; post-industrial, post-punk synthesiser music and electro; and de-territorialised electronic funk of Afro-futurist Detroit techno.[12] For example, Melville shows in his contribution that Jamaican reggae sound system culture gave the UK part of its 'rave' dance party template, which is further developed in Peter's chapter. In turn, this helped to shape the sound system logistics of teknivals and dance parades. Also, 1960s hippie music festivals and the civil rights movement concept of P.L.U.R. (Peace, Love, Unity, Respect), shaped the DIY ideology of teknivals, later commodified in the form of huge EDM festivals. Enabled by the availability of relatively affordable music technologies, geographically spread post-war zones developed their hard-hitting, minimalist styles, from gabber to kuduro. Add to this mix a general attitude of hedonism in hard times. Such formative contexts and influences, and more, have fed into what we now recognise as electronic dance music and its associated dance cultures. Such a rich family tree illustrates some of the ways in which electronic dance music and its cultural contexts may be understood. As a recorded music, especially within the promiscuous musical practices of DJ-mixes, its sounds eventually move into new contexts, leading to new interpretations, processes that are intensified by the global spread of the internet.

The convergence of various music-cultural trajectories into EDM has led to ways in which the terms 'clubbing' and 'raving' are often used interchangeably. Historically, raves are large dance parties that initially took place in London's deserted post-industrial workspaces during the 1980s, using mobile sound systems inspired by the reggae sound systems that were imported as a concept by migrants from Jamaica during the 1970s, as Melville explains in his chapter. They offered an alternative to nightclubs in terms of music policy and, operating in a semi-legal territory, allowing for alternative opening times, which can be explored further in Peter's chapter on the development of the UK rave concept with a case study from Northern England. A moral panic gripped the UK in relation to this party format during the late 1980s and early 1990s, during which a proliferation of acid house tracks from Chicago became the music of choice. By 1989 some rave organisations moved their sound system-based dance parties to rural settings to avoid police surveillance, where it met and merged with the party calendar of travellers.[13] Eventually, this set the scene both culturally and politically for the development of teknivals around nomadic sound system party crews, such as Spiral Tribe and Bedlam, which spread from the UK across Europe and beyond. Ludewig shows in her chapter how such parties partly inspired Berlin's Love Parade and its spin-offs, while elsewhere St John traces their lineage to DIY parties in the Australian outback, known as 'Doofs'.[14] As rave organisations struggled with police actions and new anti-rave legislation in the UK, raving once again became clubbing; going to a dance club became a form of raving, as shown in Malbon's late 1990s study of UK club culture.[15] According to Rief, the term 'clubbing' not only 'refer(s) to dance and music events in nightclubs of variable sizes and capacities', but also to 'open-air parties in the open countryside, on beaches or in the mountains'.[16] Just as the terms 'clubbing' and 'club culture' are associated with DJ-led nocturnal dancing events, regardless of setting, so is 'raving'. Due to a cultural heritage based in reggae sound system culture, dance club nights associated with breakbeat genres such as jungle, drum and bass, and its hybrid club music sound UK garage are sometimes considered 'raves' by their participants; yet the music played at those club nights is not understood as 'rave music', itself an electronic dance music subgenre that has its own, recognisable style that is partly hardcore techno, partly accelerated breakbeat.

The sonic worlds created by EDM producers are a product of the musical material they both craft and re-use within the creative relationships they forge with the music technologies they engage with. According to Strachan, '(e)ach network of creativity ... is distinct and relational according to the particular make-up of a given network. ... technologies are active in the production of experience for the human actor'.[17] In other words, the affordances of the music production and performance technologies are important actors within the creative processes. This is why certain pieces of equipment are associated with the sound of certain subgenres and even with iconic tracks, just as the analogue 12-inch vinyl dance single remains in the imagination as a residual medium within the digital DJ hardware and software, from CDJs (CD players designed for turntable manipulation) to digitally coded vinyl interfaces and digital audio workstation (DAWs).[18] The early production equipment may well be obsolete, but their affordances have made an important impact on the musical aesthetic of electronic dance music; their residual versions live on in the form of digital plug-ins for DAW computer software. In brief, at various points, electronic technology, whether in production, performance, or dissemination, has acted towards exponentially driving musical change while challenging and rupturing perceived notions of authorship, distributed creativity, and *liveness* in performativity.

In this collection, insights are shared from first-hand ethnographic and archival research on how rapid developments in digital communication technologies also impacted the production and performance of electronic dance music. Up to the mid-1980s this had depended on analogue tools and media, such as vinyl records, turntables, and reel-to-reel tape, as discussed in Fikentscher's chapter in relation to the importance of the DJ's physical music archives. This development accelerated with the introduction of digital music tools.[19] At its foundation, electronic dance music originated with DJs 'hacking' vinyl record players to keep people dancing – whether this meant mixing between tracks on multiple turntables or experimenting with innovative techniques to overcome the limitations of the DJ equipment. Also, during the early 1980s, house music DJ Frankie Knuckles used reel-to-reel tape machines to remix tracks to suit his queer, mostly African-American and Latinx, dance crowd at his weekly club, The Warehouse in Chicago, by adding a heavier 'foot' (kick drum) and slightly increasing the tempo.[20]

Through miniaturisation of electronic circuits, electronic music production technologies became increasingly accessible in the form of synthesisers, sequencers, effects processors, and drum machines, allowing producers, remixers, and DJs a new range of creative freedom and, eventually, merging the roles of DJ, remixer, producer, and composer together to form what is now known as 'the artist' or 'the producer'. It was during the early 1980s that iconic drum machines such as Roland's TR-808 Rhythm Composer and the bass sequencer TB-303 Bassline (initially discontinued due to poor sales), and later the TR-909 Rhythm Composer gained popularity, forming a sonic backbone to most of the emergent electronic dance music forms, with the 808 and 303 combination initially more popular with the electro crowd in New York, and the 909 gaining popularity in the Chicago house scene, followed by the Detroit techno scene and related subgenres in the UK and elsewhere. The 303 experienced a re-appreciation in 1987, addressed by Fink here, with the accidental creation of acid house, its machine-generated, random sequences enhanced by the squelching sound of its resonance control, dominating electronic dance music subgenres from acid house to psytrance and everything in between.

Important to the rise of electronic dance music during the 1980s was the introduction of MIDI (musical instrument digital interface), which allowed components such as synthesisers to communicate with each other, rather than to rely on analogue control voltage (CV) for sequencers to trigger a synthesiser. The 909, released in 1983, was one of the first instruments fitted with this connection. In 1985, the Atari 520ST was one of the first home computers kitted out with an inbuilt MIDI connection, making it the PC of choice for the so-called bedroom producer, music producers who compose and record electronic music at home, much of which was, and still is, dance music. The availability of MIDI to PC connections started the development of sequencing software, such as Notator in 1987 (which later morphed into Logic Pro) and Steinberg's Cubase in 1989, the forerunners of what are now known as software-based DAWs. By the start of the new millennium, Ableton Live was introduced, a DAW that enables DJs to create music sets for live performance as well as to produce music, further blurring the line between stage and the music studio, and between the DJ, remixer, and producer.[21] Illustrating this technological context in our collection, producer and performer Bougaïeff presents examples from his techno music making practices.

The digital miniaturisation of audio technology enabled the introduction of relatively affordable digital audio samplers during the 1980s and 90s, which were basically digital audio recorders with very small memory allocation. Initially used as a recording engineering tool,[22] partly to replace analogue echo effects and partly because the sampler was adopted by remixers and producers with a DJing background as an extension of their mixing practices. For example, its use can be heard extensively in both electro and house music recordings. For house music, which offers a foundation for electronic dance music, the sampler enabled DJ-producers to remake hard-to-obtain older disco classics, and to also produce crude remixes on cassettes and vinyl cuts as an alternative to Knuckles' studio remixes on reel-to-reel audio tape. Meanwhile, the Amiga 500 home computer, introduced in 1986, used audio samples for its media content, offering a potential that was exploited by young working-class jungle producers in the UK during the early 1990s, when this classic PC became available as second-hand gear. By 1991, Akai had released its iconic MPC60 sampler, which offered an interface that allowed for rhythmical programming that became popular with producers in house music, drum and bass, and hip-hop in the 1990s and later, during the early 2000s, with the West London broken beat (bruk) scene. And, by the mid-1990s, time stretching became a possibility in audio sampling, allowing for an (albeit crude) tempo deceleration in an audio sample without losing its original pitch, a feature that became especially popular with drum and bass and underground garage producers in the UK.

The accessibility of music production technologies enhanced the ability to respond within local cultural crossroads and specific music scenes, heralding the development and splintering of local sub genres, micro-labels, custom-ripped mix tapes and, since the turn of the millennium, online mixes. The affordances of these music technologies broadened the potential for an authentic DIY model of creativity, and also enabled the tightening of a developing neo-liberal gig economy in which major record companies no longer invest in individual music careers but instead incorporate successful music labels. The signature of the individual music maker became less important than the trademark of their company, while the DJ emerged from the shadows onto the stage as the live music performer, re-embodying studio-generated recordings that no longer represent live events, making them appear like a magician, even a god-like entity.[23] The DJ as spectacle became a marketable entity, presented on the front pages of club magazines and headlining as the main music act rather than as the stop-gap entertainer at music events. Studio producers take their music to their audiences in the role of DJ, even if they only play their own music during pre-programmed sets, leading to a rethinking of *liveness* of the performance and of the DJ as necessarily being an improvising performer.[24]

The sound of electronic dance music showcases the dynamic relationship between human and machine. Producers and DJs pursue increasingly immersive and complex machine–body interactions with their music. Indeed, dance club anthems often feature strong vocal performances, while vocal samples from older dance and movie classics can be heard throughout EDM production work. Disembodied and reprogrammed samples of the human voice are common, as are pitch-shifted vocal samples.[25] During performances, especially those with a genealogy in sound system culture, the voice and embodied presence of the MC is of importance in bringing together the crowd at drum and bass and hardcore dance events. Yet, to enable the sonic space for the MC's voice, the actual music recording is an instrumental production, meaning it is usually devoid of vocals. Within the production aesthetics of dominant subgenres, such as techno and trance, the sounds of the music production technologies are foregrounded within the sonic quality of the music. This can contribute to a trance-like virtuality that, perhaps paradoxically, enables dancers to counter or process the isolation that capitalism brings by using its technological innovations to provide the means for a concentrated form of embodied communality between fellow human beings. Where a DJ performs their skill in collecting, selecting, and programming, they simultaneously act out their experience as participant in the machine-made party, often empathic with the vibe of the crowd and sharing in its communal affect. In this way, a feedback loop develops between dancers and the DJ.[26] A blurring of function occurs between the producer and their audience, replacing the creative agency of an artist with a 'living text that resulted from the collaborative performance of DJs and ravers and existed only in the moment of their interaction with the music'.[27] Where for some a seeming lack of *liveness* is not an issue, for others the challenge of being seen to perform their music has encouraged DJs to manipulate controllers as part of their live performance.[28] The DJ-producer performance has become a spectacle even though the intertextuality of mixing tracks and of using music samples should be sufficient to sonically validate the curatorial prowess of the DJ-performer, in the virtuosity of mixing, blending, arrangement, and presentation of found and pre-existing sounds. Within the resulting whirlwind of machine sounds, human embodiment and the DJ's relationship to the dance floor are crucial.

The complex entanglement of human and non-human actors is crucial to the study of electronic dance music. As Wiltsher puts it, 'dance music involves fluid, fully human engagement with music that flaunts its distance from the human; a relentless, repetitive and robotic act'.[29] Electronic dance music is music to be danced to – where the teleological and processual use of looping is designed to prolong pleasure with an almost spiritually trance-like potential for ritual and psychological expansion. The relentless four-to-the-floor beat that characterises many subgenres, including house and techno, may lead one to think that this is 'machine-made music that turn[s] you into a machine',[30] and thereby enables a cyborgian subjectivity.[31] However, from a musicological perspective, Young observes that

it is not the regular thuds of the kick drum that drives dance music's creation and perception but rather the continual stream of cycles of desire and fulfilment ... demarcated in the sonic space with indicators of accumulation (such as multi-tracked build-ups, drum-roll effects and filter sweeps/uplifters) and arrival (the characteristic bass drop).[32]

We can find the negotiation of potentially robotic affects at a broader generic and stylistic level as well. As the marketing of hardware was initially associated with a shiny utopianism of cybertechnology, this is now redundant against the miniaturised processing power of modern computer chips. Similar to the fate of vinyl records, the music-making hardware has been re-signified as 'nostalgic' and 'authentic', referring to a time when hopeful optimism for the future of humanity lay in the cybernetic pleasures of a nascent digital posthumanism, articulated in the shiny aesthetics of digital art. This has been largely replaced by a renewed search for organic, analogue, material, and human aspects in electronic dance music – found, for example, in the aesthetics of rhythmic imperfection and vinyl lo-fi sonorities, or the inclusion of acoustic instrumentation.

The dance floor offers a space outside the everyday rules of social engagement and temporalities of daytime society, a temporary 'escape from the objective drudgery of life'.[33] Being thrust into an intimate, pulsating space with strangers engenders a certain sort of openness and release, only possible by surrendering to the sonic and haptic intensity of the experience. Melechi even suggests that '(t)o understand the pleasures of the dance floor we must move to a different logic of tourism where one comes to ... [relocate] into the body'.[34] As dancers lose themselves to the music, possibly enhanced by intoxicating body technologies, a possibility is opened for a temporary levelling out of social distinction within the overpoweringly sonically dominated and often carefully curated dance space, arguably creating a sense of oneness and a reported feeling of equity amongst participants.[35] Especially on dance floors that cater for marginalised social groups, such as gay clubs and the dance cultures that stem from this, the idea is embraced that regardless of social standing or material wealth all are included in the equalising throbbing mass of bodies on the dance floor. As the mass of bodies moves together to one unifying beat, a process of entrainment is triggered, producing a shared collective identity.[36] In the drawing together of a temporary sense of community for just one night or weekend, the dance floor intrinsically seems to evade formal structures of control, creating environments that are worlds within worlds: distinct from everyday social interactions, yet still embedded within broader society.[37] As such, dance floors may offer potential for cultural resistance, as expanded on by Ludewig in her contribution that addresses the dance party as space of protest. Some participants may even claim the dance floor helped them to review their living practices by finding alternatives close to countercultural claims that birthed alternative arts festivals such as Boom Festival in Portugal or Burning Man in the USA.[38] Yet, unless reinforced by longitudinal everyday contexts, such ideals can be short lived and even exploited by entrepreneurial party organisers as evidenced by many hugely successful EDM festivals and holiday destinations. Importantly, as Spencer, Gadir, Parsley, and O'Grady and Greasley point out in this collection, during electronic dance music events social differences can also be reinforced as dancers group together, while excluding others.

This collection sets the scene with a consideration of the main elements of an electronic dance music event, including the developments of notions and practices of the rave concept by cultural sociologist Beate Peter, which underpins most of the associations that readers may have with electronic dance music culture. This is followed by a discussion from an architectural perspective by Catharine Rossi of how the dance club evolved from both the nightclub and the development of immersive audio-visual art spaces.

The notion of the sound system is developed by cultural studies expert Caspar Melville, with reference to the Black Atlantic cultural links between the UK and Jamaica. The opening section is concluded with a contribution by ethnomusicologist Kai Fikentscher on the importance of the DJ's archive to the development of electronic dance music.

The collection moves forward to examples of geographically diverse cultural contexts while emphasising dynamics between local contexts and a globalised electronic dance music culture. Cultural anthropologist Bianca Ludewig addresses the relationship between techno dance parties and the encroachment of, arguably neo-liberal, gentrification of urban spaces in Berlin. Musicologist Stefanie Alisch provides a detailed ethnographic account of Angolan Kuduro sound system culture within a warzone in relation to Black Atlantic cultural politics. Sociologist Matthew Ming-Tak Chew relates an overview of how global dance culture is locally translated in various ways within China. Finally, Bernardo Attias, Professor of Media and Communications, and media philosopher tobias van Veen provide an account of online DJ performances using broadcast software that during the Covid-19 lockdown period (2020–2022) reached global audiences; using their own experience as a starting point they elaborate on mediation of electronic dance music culture.

With an understanding of the diversity of cultural contexts in which electronic dance music cultures can be understood, the collection next moves its focus towards the contexts of the music itself, with a set of distinct case studies, each offering a different approach to the subject. Media and music expert Chris Christodoulou shows from a music cultural perspective how within a British urban context, an aesthetic of acceleration is applied to the production of drum and bass and related subgenres. Rupert Till, Professor of Music, delves into a counter-narrative to accelerated culture with a genealogy of chill out music, a genre that developed in parallel to the frenzied dance floor. The issue of genre aesthetics in electronic dance music styles is further addressed by cultural anthropologist Botond Vitos in a chapter that investigates genre definitions in online music provider Bandcamp.

Having mapped out issues of style, the chapters that follow delve deeper into the aesthetics of electronic dance music, with case studies that illustrate the production of a range of subjectivities. Music psychologist Maria Perevedentseva provides a theoretical framework for the analytical study of timbre in electronic dance music. From the perspective of music practice, music producer Nicolas Bougaïeff delves into his approach to techno production to illustrate decision-making in creating a sonic palette. Taking an

American perspective on racial politics, Robert Fink, Professor of Music, explores ways to understand serendipity in music making, with a case study on the influential squelching sound of the Roland TB-303 Bassline instrument. Musicologist Tami Gadir completes this section with a critical analysis of the idea of flow on the dance floor, which is not as apolitical as dancers may perceive.

Gadir's critical assessment of flow segues into the narrative of the final section, which returns to the realities of social difference, based on ethnographic evidence. Samantha Parsley, Professor of Organization Studies, tackles gender politics with a case study of the production environments of EDM. Sociologist Ed Katrak Spencer notes gendered interactions on a brostep dance floor at an American EDM festival. The volume closes with the important issue of the ageing dancer, addressed by applied performance experts Alice O'Grady and Alinka Greasley. Are you ever too old to dance? We think not – keep on dancing!

Notes

1. Rietveld, H. C. (2018) 'Machine Possession: Dancing to Repetitive Beats'. In C. Levaux & O. Julien (eds.) *Over and Over: Exploring Repetition in Popular Music*. New York: Bloomsbury Academic, pp. 75–88.
2. McLeod, K. (2001) 'Genres, Subgenres, Sub-Subgenres and More: Musical and Social Differentiation Within Electronic/Dance Music Communities'. *Journal of Popular Music Studies*, 13(1), 59–75, p. 73. doi: 10.1111/j.1533-1598.2001.tb00013.x.
3. Negus, K. (1999) *Music Genres and Corporate Cultures*. London and New York: Routledge.
4. Toynbee, J. (2000) *Making Popular Music*. New York: Oxford University Press.
5. Salkin, M. E. (2019) *Do You Remember House? Chicago's Queer of Color Undergrounds*. New York: Oxford University Press; Sicko, D. (2010) *Techno Rebels: The Renegades of Electronic Funk*. Detroit, MI: Wayne State University Press; Rietveld, H. C. (2020) *This is Our House: House Music, Technologies, and Cultural Spaces*. London and New York: Routledge; Bergen, M. (2018) *Dutch Dance 1988-2018: How the Netherlands Took the Lead in Electronic Music Culture*. Amsterdam: Mary Go Wild; Schäfer, S., Schäfers, J., & Waltmann, D. (1998) *Techno Lexicon*. Berlin: *Raveline Magazine* / Schwarzkopf & Schwarzkopf Verlag.
6. Wiltsher, N. (August 2016) 'The Aesthetics of Electronic Dance Music, Part I: History, Genre, Scenes, Identity, Blackness'. *Philosophy Compass*, 11(8), 415–25.

7. Straw, W. (1991) 'Systems of Articulation, Logics of Change: Communities and Scenes in Popular Music'.*Cultural Studies*, 5(3), 368–88. https://doi.org/10.1080/09502389100490311.
8. Hall, S., Evans, J., & Nixon, S. (eds.) (2013) *Representation: Cultural Representations and Signifying Practices*. London: Sage.
9. Small, C. (1989) *Musicking: the Meanings of Performing and Listening*. Hanover, NH: Wesleyan University Press.
10. Harvey, D. (2005) *A Brief History of Neo-Liberalism*. New York: Oxford University Press.
11. Rietveld, H.C. (2004) 'Ephemeral Spirit: Sacrificial Cyborg and Soulful Community'. In G. St John (ed.) *Rave and Religion*. London and New York: Routledge, pp. 46–61; Rietveld, 'Machine Possession'.
12. For further examples of possible genealogies of electronic dance music subgenres house, techno, garage, and hardcore, illustrated with music examples, see: Wiltsher, N. (13 July 2016) 'The Aesthetics of Electronic Dance Music – Philosophy Compass'. *YouTube*. https://youtu.be/YY-30jTl5qU?feature=shared (accessed 15 July 2024).
13. Harrison, H. (2022) *Dreaming in Yellow: The Story of the DiY Sound System*. London: Velocity Press.
14. St John, G. (2001) 'Doof! Australian Post-Rave Culture'. In G. St John (ed.) *FreeNRG: Notes from the Edge of the Dance Floor*. Altona (Australia): Common Ground Publishing.
15. Malbon, B. (1999) *Clubbing: Dancing, Ecstasy and Vitality*. London and New York: Routledge.
16. Rief, S. (2009) *Club Cultures: Boundaries, Identities, and Otherness*. London and New York: Routledge, p. 3.
17. Strachan R. (2017) *Sonic Technologies: Popular Music, Digital Culture and the Creative Process*. New York and London: Bloomsbury, p. 8.
18. Rietveld, Hillegonda C. (2007) 'The Residual Soul Sonic Force of the Vinyl 12-Inch Dance Single'. In Charles R. Ackland (ed.) *Residual Media*. Minnesota: University of Minnesota Press, pp. 46–61.
19. As philosopher Jean Baudrillard observed prophetically around that time, 'The era of miniaturization [. . .] and of a microprocessing of time, bodies, and pleasure has come'. Baudrillard, J. (1988) *The Ecstasy of Communication*. Trans. Schütze, B., and Schütze, C. Los Angeles: Semiotext(e), p. 18.
20. On Frankie Knuckles, see: Frankie Forever (2024) *Faith*, 4(1). Rietveld's respondents claimed during her 1992 ethnographic in Chicago that the dance floor of The Warehouse used to be washed with amylnitrate (poppers) to excite dancers on arrival; as The Warehouse was already history at that time, it cannot be verified whether this was an exaggeration.
21. Butler, M. (2014) *Playing with Something that Runs: Technology, Improvisation and Composition in DJ and Laptop Performance*. Oxford and New York: Oxford University Press; Rietveld, H. C. (2016) 'Authenticity and Liveness in

Digital DJ Performance'. In I. Tsioulakis & E. Hytönen-Ng, (eds.) *Musicians and their Audiences*. New York, London: Routledge, pp. 123–33.
22. Porcello, T. (1991) 'The Ethics of Digital Audio-Sampling: Engineers' Discourse'. *Popular Music*, 10(1), January, 69–84.
23. Middleton, R. (2006) '"Last Night a DJ Saved my Life": Avians, Cyborgs and Siren Bodies in the Era of Phonographic Technology'. *Radical Musicology*, 1: 31 pars. www.radical-musicology.org.uk (15 July 2024).
24. Rietveld, 'Authenticity and Liveness in Digital DJ Performance'.
25. Harper, A. (2016) '"Dux Content: Life Style" and "The New Hi-Tech Underground"'. In T. Beyer & T. Burkhalter (eds.) *Seismographic Sounds – Visions of a New World*. Bern: Norient, pp. 478–83.
26. Pedro Peixoto, F. (2008) 'When Sound Meets Movement: Performance in Electronic Dance Music'. *Leonardo Music Journal*, 18, 17–20.
27. Ott, B. L., & Herman, B. D. (2003) 'Mixed Messages: Resistance and Reappropriation in Rave Culture'. *Western Journal of Communication*, 67(3), 249–70. https://doi.org/10.1080/10570310309374771.
28. D'Errico, M. (2022) *Push: Software Design and the Cultural Politics of Music Production*. Oxford: Oxford University Press.
29. Wiltsher, N. (August 2016) 'The Aesthetics of Electronic Dance Music, Part II: Dancers, DJs, Ontology and Aesthetics'. *Philosophy Compass*, 11(8), 426–36.
30. Reynolds, S. (1999) *Generation Ecstasy: Into the World of Techno and Rave Culture*. New York: Routledge, p. 28.
31. Rietveld, 'Ephemeral Spirit'; Rietveld, ' Machine Possession'.
32. Young, T. (2022) 'The Radical Temporality of Drum and Bass'. In M. Doffman, E Payne, & T. Young (eds.) *The Oxford Handbook of Time in Music*. Oxford: Oxford University Press, p. 577.
33. Baudrillard, J. (2002) *Screened Out*. London: Verso, p. 99.
34. Melechi, A. (1993) 'The Ecstasy of Disappearance'. In S. Redhead (ed.) *Rave Off: Politics and Deviance in Contemporary Youth Culture*. Aldershot: Avebury, p. 32.
35. Rietveld, H.C. (2020 [1998]) *This Is Our House: House Music, Cultural Spaces and Technologies*. Aldershot: Ashgate.
36. Witek, M. (2019) 'Feeling at One: Socio-affective Distribution, Vibe, and Dance-Music Consciousness'. In R. Herbert, D. Clarke, & E. Clarke (eds.) *Music and Consciousness 2: Worlds, Practices, Modalities*. Oxford: Oxford University Press, pp. 93–112.
37. Thornton, S. (1995) *Club Cultures: Music, Media and Subcultural Capital*. Cambridge: Polity Press. See also Straw, W. (2004) 'Cultural Scenes'. *Society and Leisure*, 27(2), 411–22.
38. St John, G. (ed.) (2018) *Weekend Societies: Electronic Dance Music Festivals and Event-Cultures*. New York & London: Bloomsbury Academic.

PART I

Setting the Scene

1 | Raves as Aesthetic Experience

The Blackburn Parties

BEATE PETER

Introduction

The Blackburn parties were events that took place between 1989 and 1990 in the town of Blackburn, Lancashire. Within about eighteen months these parties grew to become mass events, feeding a seemingly insatiable appetite for electronic music, dancing, and dance drugs. Like many other places in northern England, Blackburn had been known for its cotton industry, which has declined, mill by mill, since the early 1950s. The parties made use of what were perceived to be empty and available spaces, including the remaining shells of old mills and warehouses, while DJs provided the predominant soundtrack to the parties, playing mostly electronic dance music using turntables. The events had the allure of a secret society, perhaps even more so than similar dance parties. This is because the locations of the Blackburn parties were only known to very few people, including those who led convoys of hundreds of cars to an event. Most people would not know where the party was until they arrived. So, to be able to get there, drivers would park their cars near the Sett End, a pub now legendary for its role in the history of the parties. Some people would know which car to follow, others would recognise the convoy leader, yet others would simply join the queue that was forming outside the pub and follow the crowd. As a result, the journey to the venue was not made in isolation but as part of an ever-growing queue of vehicles driving to local venues. For the parties it meant a high level of collective anticipation, not only because of the mode of travel but also because the venue was kept secret, even from some of the people helping to set up the party: the PA would usually arrive at the same time as the convoy, and the participants would wait on the dance floor until the PA was set up and connected to an energy source. Essentially, people would be standing in the dark with no sounds other than their conversations to be heard until the moment the lights came on and the music started to play.

Being able to party for twenty-four hours is common practice in many cities of the twenty-first century, but UK licensing laws at the time prohibited any commercial venue from staying open later than 2 a.m., and with pubs closing at 11 p.m., nightclubs were the only places where one could continue to consume alcohol. The Blackburn parties would start after 2 a.m., when UK nightclubs used to close, and people appreciated being able to continue dancing well into the day – a new experience for many young people. Perhaps unsurprisingly, over the eighteen-month period that the weekly parties took place, they grew from small private gatherings to events for thousands of people. However, for reasons that are discussed here in more detail, the unlegislated parties were stopped by the police. Many consider them to have ended with the *Love Decade* party in July 1990, when more than 800 participants were arrested and detained, making it one of the biggest mass arrests in British history.

Using an ethnographic approach, this chapter provides insights from interviews with members of the organising collective.[1] These interviews became possible because the anniversary of some of the major events in rave culture's trajectory evidenced a historical distance that, perhaps for the first time, led to a widespread acknowledgement of raves as part of popular music history. The Second Summer of Love in 1988, for example, is generally considered to be the period in which acid house parties exploded in London and north-west England, to morph into raves during 1989, their music becoming the soundtrack to many young people's lives. Marking the end of that period and considered to be a result of this development was the introduction of the Criminal Justice and Public Order Act 1994. In response to an impromptu four-day music festival on Castlemorton Common in 1992, this piece of UK legislation includes provisions that ban raves as defined through their music (a succession of repetitive beats), their location, duration, and size (although the latter keeps changing in the legislation and has ranged from a gathering of 100 people to the present figure of 20 people). The general historical interest in raves became evident not only through increased coverage by popular media but also through funding that was made available for related projects. Most important for the material in this chapter was the creation of the Acid House Flashback Archive[2] about the Blackburn parties, and the Lapsed Clubber Audio Map,[3] both made possible by the National Lottery Heritage Fund. The projects sought to position rave culture outside of hegemonic discourses by focusing on the plurality of ravers' experiences. This chapter seeks to employ the same approach by focusing on the perspectives of the party organisers and distilling some of their common practices, beliefs, and values but also their differences. By doing so this chapter contributes to the historiography of raves in the UK.

A brief discussion of the term 'rave' is necessary, as it is used to denote a number of events in a variety of locations, more or less commercially positioned, accessible to varying degrees, catering for dozens or tens of thousands, lasting between a few hours or days on end. It might, or might not, refer to a particular period in time. Rave's origins are contested. Depending on the music culture, raves exist in a continuum of reggae sound system cultures as much as they define the acid house culture of the late 1980s and early 1990s. For example, Reynolds traces the use of the word 'rave' through earlier popular music history, establishing connections between raves, raving, and reggae sound system culture.[4] Recently, the re-emergence of the term 'rave' in relation to lockdown parties also means that, depending on participants' age and corresponding lived experiences, raves describe different events, circumstances, and historical moments.[5] Additionally, a hegemonic cultural memory, hugely influenced by media narratives about dance drugs, sees raves through a particular lens, which ignores other constitutional aspects of a rave. Significantly, the term 'rave' has been used retrospectively by the media, historians, and scholars to describe the events that are being discussed here. This is relevant insofar as the organisers themselves refuse to label the Blackburn events as raves, even though they seem structured as such within an era in the UK during which rave culture evolved. In order to acknowledge and respect this position, I will refer to these dance events as 'the Blackburn parties'. That does not detract from the fact that the parties are included in rave histories – and rightly so, because the argument that is made here is that the labelling of the events indicates an attempt at positioning a cultural product within an emerging market. That the organisers refuse to see their parties in this light shows some early tensions, which will be addressed here.

How can one begin to discuss these musical dance events? I suggest that in this context the term 'rave' can be thought of as connoting an aesthetic experience that is inherently flexible. Similarly to Mrozek's discussion on pop,[6] raves cannot be described through the consumption processes of interchangeable goods and have to be seen in the context of wider societal processes and the experiences these events provide. As a result, the changing meaning of the term 'rave' is a sign of evolving discourses in society as a whole. At the same time, it becomes possible to locate raves as aesthetic experiences in particular moments in time. Reckwitz argues that an aesthetic experience is noticed as such through the stimulation of the senses and affect.[7] In other words, the aesthetic experience has both an inherent dynamism (*Selbstzweckhaftigkeit*) and a self-directedness (*Selbstbezüglichkeit*) that are independent of rational action. The purpose of the experience is the experience itself. Slaby's concept of affective arrangement helps us to understand which aspects contribute to a particular aesthetic experience.[8] He states that 'an affective arrangement comprises an array of persons, things, artefacts, spaces, discourses, behaviours, expressions, or other materials that coalesce into a coordinated formation of mutual *affecting* and *being-affected*. While its composite materials are heterogenous, an affective arrangement is characteristically social.'[9] Considering raves as affective arrangements, they can become detached from hegemonic discourses on raves and electronic dance music, enabling their analysis as events *in situ*. That by no means suggests that conditions external to the events can be ignored, as they might impact on people's perceptions, assumptions, and expectations. Indeed, raves are a complex combination of a particular political time, the use of specific historical spaces, new technologies, sound aesthetics, new recreational dance drugs, a type of people that would be open to obscure dance experiences, and an aura of being part of a secret society, with a resulting sense of belonging amongst strangers – in short, a set of practices, behaviours, and values that are created as well as released through the musicking body on the dance floor. Although aspects such as the arrival of the new dance drug ecstasy[10] or the development of digital instruments such as drum machines cannot be ignored when describing raves as affective arrangements, a lot of attention has been given to telling rave histories either as drug experiences[11] or through technological innovation.[12]

On the basis of insights from the qualitative research that underpins this chapter, I argue that the Blackburn parties can be seen as aesthetic practices that foreground affect and that are the result of an affect deficit in society. Seen through this particular lens, the practices can then be understood as events that can be recreated, exported, imported, and adapted to specific political, social, or cultural conditions. A focus on what I would like to call 'the rave *moment*' would stand in stark contrast to any notion of a rave *movement*: the former being a collective effort to create the moment itself, the latter the collective effort to produce political, cultural, or social change by means of the moment.[13] Yet the self-directedness of the rave moment is the reason why the parties as realised in Blackburn can be understood as an exportable dance music event concept: one that has subsequently been understood as 'rave'. From an organiser's perspective, such a concept could be contextualised in different ways. In her book on ethics and cultural policy, Owen-Vandersluis identifies two different approaches to culture: one based on 'an ideological commitment to the free market',[14] the other on 'the premise that cultural activity fulfils important social functions'.[15]

The rave moment presents a challenge in that its foundation is that of an aesthetic sociality, and yet that social experience can be treated as a cultural product, waiting to be commercialised to varying degrees. What is addressed in this chapter is not so much a de-historicisation of music events but a departure from a historiography based on an event chronology in order to argue for an inclusive approach to raves and related electronic dance music events: the acknowledgement of different markets and concordant variations of the cultural product that is a rave. If an understanding of history as events in linear succession is replaced by a model that focuses on the stimulation and regulation of affect, how do we identify and contextualise these events? Is it possible to write a history of aesthetic musical events and not get muddled up in discussions on taste? If so, what new methodologies would be needed to establish a genealogy within electronic music studies? What are the implications for the role of electronic dance music events as part of culture?

The Blackburn Parties

Blackburn is defined by its mills, production of textiles, and subsequent industrial decline. Like many post-industrial towns in the north of England during the second half of the twentieth century, Blackburn suffered from the impact of de-industrialisation: high unemployment rates, housing issues, and higher levels of social problems. In 1976, the extreme-right National Party gained two council seats in Blackburn, and the terrace culture of football hooliganism, as well as gang feuds, meant that the town experienced street violence; it was divided in more than one way.[16] Hemment describes towns such as Blackburn as places of 'cultural desolation and economic death'.[17] Against this backdrop, a reading of the parties as escapism could be seen as valid. Such a view, however, would prohibit an understanding of the parties as particular aesthetic experiences that are part of a whole range of affective encounters in a person's life and which are used to self-regulate. For example, the party organisers agree that, despite Blackburn's post-industrial fate, there were plenty of nightclubs operating in town at the time that the parties started. The problem with these nightclubs, however, was their control over the club experience: bouncers would follow a strict door policy in which the dress code included a shirt and tie for men, and absolutely no trainers. As John put it: 'They would tell you what to wear, how to dance, who'd come in and who wouldn't. You'd go home at 2 a.m., and your regular night would usually end with a fight and a fuck.' According to Phil, John, and George, this frustration about the exclusive nightclub practices and culture that prevented them from participating was the motivation to put on a different type of night, one that was originally intended to be for friends only. The parties grew quickly, and most of the organisers agree that they felt a sense of duty towards all those people who had started travelling to Blackburn for a different aesthetic experience. There is a sense, then, that the organisers switched from seeking to create their own events to facilitating those of others. This shift evidences the entrepreneurial spirit that made a group of people come together and work as a team – each according to their skills and knowledge and bringing their own networks. In hindsight, John and George call their entrepreneurial endeavours naïve. The market potential was recognised only as the parties had reached a certain momentum, and even then it was impossible for some of the organisers to imagine their weekly events becoming part of a culture industry. However, competition for the newly identified market developed not only between the organisers themselves but also between entrepreneurs from further afield. Before these aspects are discussed, however, it is important to establish why these dance events had become so popular in the first place.

The Blackburn parties offered a new aesthetic experience, one that had not existed previously. In his definition of virtual sound worlds, Ingham refers to three aspects that particularly contributed to the experience: repetitive music, dancing, and drugs.[18] They created 'the combined emotional behaviour of the participants' and 'a sense of communality and belonging to something'.[19] The organisers all agree that the new dance music that had started descending on them from places such as Chicago and Detroit presented a rupture with everything they had engaged with until that point. Being 'beatsy'[20] and digitally produced, old and new songs could be mixed and layered by DJs and make people dance for hours. George, part of the organising group and regular DJ at the parties, remembers how the new music brought together people from different musical scenes, and how exciting it felt to be part of something new. Mike, used to setting up the sound equipment for rock bands and punk gigs, was amazed how little was needed for a DJ to start their work. Compared to setting up the PA for bands, doing it for the DJ was much easier and, therefore, faster. It proved to be an advantage for the parties, as speed was essential for the setting up and the taking down of the equipment. John, Mike, Phil, and Susie confirm that the extended hours of the experience added to the perception of starting something new; so did the fact that, compared to conventional nightclubs, there were no bouncers at the beginning who would select the people that were allowed to join the event and send away those who looked like they did not fit. The latter aspect, of filtering participants at the entrance door, changed particularly with the identification of the Blackburn parties as a commercial market. Reckwitz argues that for people to be motivated to engage in aesthetic events, these must be perceived as different.[21] As outlined, there are numerous aspects that identify the Blackburn parties as fundamentally different from previous nights out 'in town'. The stimulus of the parties is for people to be in the moment and to enjoy it for what it is. Reckwitz describes modern society as suppressing affect, resulting in a social affect deficiency, to which the response is the anaesthetisation of society and its affective practices. When describing his concept of affective arrangement, Slaby refers to 'an active allure, drawing actors in by offering occasions for immersion within a sphere of affective resonance, thereby potentially giving rise to longer lasting attachment, or even, at times, to forms of behavioural addiction'.[22] Arguably, the Blackburn parties did not invent the rave moment, but they helped to establish what Reckwitz calls an 'aesthetic sociality' among a particular demographic, facilitated by a group of social entrepreneurs.[23]

The level of secrecy that initially surrounded the Blackburn locations was very high. At times, only two of the organisers would know where the party was taking place. Cars would follow any driver who was setting off from the Sett End, blindly trusting that their way was the one leading to the party. Susie, who regularly led the convoys, would sometimes only find out the destination minutes before setting off, or at other times lead a decoy convoy. Similarly, the people setting up the equipment would occasionally only find out about the location after having been driven there or following the convoy just like every other reveller. This led to the unique situation where the equipment and the people setting it up would arrive at the same time as those who had come to dance. Once inside the venue, it would be dark and quiet until the technology was connected to a power source. Only then would the party begin. At the height of the parties, when police attention and intervention had become part of the experience, the party would only go ahead if the PA and the participants were inside the venues first, shutting themselves in. In the early years of the parties, the local police had neither the resources nor the training to break up the parties. According to the organisers, this cat-and-mouse game would add tension and anticipation for everybody involved, and so the ecstatic release upon hearing the first few beats would be second to none. In the words of Hemment, the Blackburn warehouse experience was 'fuelled by amplified noise, repetitive beats, relentless rhythms, alien soundscapes, police chases, drugs and late nights, ... something never before seen'.[24]

If, for many participants, these experiences did not appear to change fundamentally, they did so for the organisers. The original motivation was to create not-for-profit aesthetic experiences, but with their growing popularity it was naïve to assume that this 'hippie-bubble' would not be subject to what John perceives to be the exploitation by more economically driven entrepreneurs from within the group of organisers as well as outsiders. Several groups of people would argue about control over the doors and the income, as well as the transaction of dance drugs. At the same time, the organisers adapted increasingly lawless practices in their desire to source the PA system and its transport, replace sound technology that might have been confiscated by the police the previous week (and not yet been released), or tap into electricity circuits near the event location. Concurrently, the police would begin to be better organised in their attempt to stop the parties. John says that the 'Bright Bill'[25] and subsequent legal changes that increased penalties for party organisers had no impact on them as organisers, but the changes in the licensing law did. By allowing nightclubs to stay open past 2 a.m. it became clear that even the UK government had recognised the market potential of extending nightclub licences for young people to continue dancing into the next day. It appears that for the eighteen months or so during which the parties existed, everything changed: the organisers' common goal, legislation of venues and one-off parties, and the police's response to the parties. The dancers at the Blackburn parties had started to be recognised by different local, regional, and even national entrepreneurial groups as consumers, resulting in some of the original organisers breaking away from the Blackburn scene and others forcing their way in. Unsurprisingly, most of the original organisers who were interviewed for this chapter confirmed that their lives had become too stressful; the fun had disappeared, anxieties set in, and stress levels 'went through the roof'. It is not clear what exactly ended the parties, most likely a combination of all the above factors. How, then, can these parties be put into historical context?

Amongst the Blackburn party organisers, there is disagreement over when the parties first began. Some see them starting the first time a new type of electronic dance music, acid house, was played in the Blackburn club C'est la Vie in September 1988. Others understand them to begin when the parties found a temporary home at a small club called Crackers in March 1989. Popular cultural memory will see them as warehouse parties and define them through their use of that particular space, starting in April 1989. Without a generally agreed upon origin, it seems that for the individual organisers the parties started either when they themselves became involved or when they began to facilitate the dancing experience of others.

The same disagreement exists regarding the end of the parties. Those organisers who wanted to keep the parties accessible to people from all socio-economic backgrounds see them ending when they became promoted events at which the entrance fee would go up from the usual £3–£5 to £20. The open-air dance event *Live the Dream*, held on a farm near Blackburn on 16 September 1989, is such an example. For others, the parties ended on 24 February 1990 when a better-organised police force raided a party at Lomeshaye in Nelson. Although this party did not take place in Blackburn, the organising team were still the same. That changed after that event though, and the most infamous party, *Love Decade* in Gildersome near Leeds on 21 July 1990, is seen by some as no longer being part of the Blackburn parties. However, this event took place after the Entertainments (Increased Penalties) Act 1990 had been introduced,[26] and more than 800 people were arrested and detained – giving the Blackburn parties the mythical status they have today.

In between the fraying ends of an uncertain beginning and an unclear ending, the parties could theoretically be listed with clear dates and locations. Absent is information about the size of the events, the organising principles behind them, or the financial success of the parties: event planning seems to be circumstantial, and event management was non-existent. Rather than identifying the lack of planning and management as an aspect of a DIY culture that for some historians of popular music is characteristic of 'early' raves, it should be seen as an attempt to shift the focus of the event from measurable outcomes to the experience itself. The experience itself might include facets that are difficult to recognise, articulate, and measure. Consequently, the choice of what and how to narrate is crucial and invites a multi-perspective, cross-disciplinary approach. Interviewing members of the original organising collective means accepting partly contradictory narratives as told through different perspectives and memories. A chronological narration of the parties, as is common in popular music history, would fail to describe the simultaneous and interrelated developments at the time: organisers having different ideas about where to take the parties; groups breaking away or forcing their way in; promoted raves having licences past 2 a.m.; or nightclubs starting to cater for those who want to continue the party. What all of these have in common is the facilitation of a particular experience – the rave moment. Just to be clear: the rave moment is not rigidly defined. It changes over time and is dependent on a multitude of known and unknown factors. Herein lies the challenge for the commercial use of the rave as a cultural product. Framing the creation of such an aesthetic sociality and its economic facilitation, one can recognise the creation of demand and the development of a market-driven relationship between supply and demand. Such an interpretation would chime with some of the organisers' statements that they felt a duty towards the people who would turn up to the parties; a duty to organise party after party and to satisfy demand by finding larger locations. One could even see the confrontation with the police as a way in which a newly created aesthetic sociality defends its space and its related experiences. Czirak et al. suggest the concept of '(p)reenactment' to describe the 'repetitions of past events',[27] while Slaby goes further by arguing that, over time, such repetitions lead to a deeper historicity because '(a)s temporally stabilized agglomerations of materials and expressions, affective arrangements function as repositories of the past, which points to their complex, multi-scale historicity'.[28] Both concepts chime with Peter's notion of experiential knowledge[29] and, in the case of clubbing and raving, with the role of the body as a device to store the memory of such experiences. By considering the rave moment as a cultural product that can be re-enacted, copied, and facilitated, its permutations can be traced through time. Regarding event management, it would be beneficial for the recognition of the rave moment in different settings to focus on event design and the facilitation of the aesthetic experience, rather than on event planning with its focus on measurable outcomes. In the case of the Blackburn parties, I argue that the aesthetic experience was foregrounded, especially since planning was chaotic and relied heavily on creative solutions to a scarcity of resources. Such chaos would ensure that the organisers continued to focus on the experience. Considering the parties a success is possible when paying attention not only to the organisers' original motivation but also to how the history of the parties is told. Although commercially unsuccessful, the number of attendees at the Blackburn parties is testament to the creation of a successful cultural product.

Conclusion

The Blackburn parties are the result of a combined effort to create inclusive aesthetic experiences that fundamentally differed from the local nights out up to that point. Because of a perceived lack of diverse night-time experiences in Blackburn, social entrepreneurs came together to combine their skills, knowledge, and networks to put on parties. The post-industrial landscape of Blackburn with its availability of large empty buildings enabled these entrepreneurs to develop the parties and satisfy the demand that they had initiated locally. A new sonic aesthetic of electronic dance music combined with historically loaded venues, the arrival of a new dance drug called ecstasy, the freedom to dress in whatever clothes one wanted to wear, and the suspension of time well into the morning – all these factors helped create the Blackburn version of the rave moment. Heightened levels of anticipation, caused by the experience of people driving jointly in convoys to secret locations only to then stand and wait for the music to come on, helped shape a deeply affective experience. To understand the parties as self-referential can also be seen in their organisation: from one week to another it would be uncertain whether they would go ahead or not. Long-term planning was absent, hinting at a non-existing goal or direction.

With the growing popularity of the parties came a growing interest from new groups of entrepreneurs. Resulting conflicts, centred on the market potential of the events' aesthetic sociality, were not resolved. Instead, they led to changes in the organisation and running of the parties, with the organising community changing with regard to both members and motives. In addition to new entrepreneurs, who identified the dancing audience as potential customers, the state became an important player through legal changes that increased the penalties for the organisation of parties such as those in Blackburn on the one hand, and the facilitation of the parties' commercialisation through a change in venue licensing as well as health and safety regulations on the other. These processes further encouraged the packaging of the rave moment as a product. Although the Blackburn parties did not provide the blueprint for such experiences, they revealed different positions as to what to do with a newly identified cultural product.

The Blackburn parties are a great example of how to test and potentially diversify the market for a party concept. The aesthetic experiences in Blackburn have been exported and adapted, feeding into a multitude of events, all potentially facilitating the rave moment: free parties, festivals, new nightclubs and club nights, travelling sound systems, or licenced outdoor raves. One could argue that these diverse adaptations demonstrate the different value systems and affordances of their organisers, as they foreground the various aspects that contributed to the Blackburn warehouse experience. The negotiation of positions would be interesting to trace and map. Using interview data with the original party organisers, this discussion has started to address this issue and allows for a foregrounding of the aesthetic function of a rave and the meaningful experience it provides for people. To facilitate and protect such experiences should, therefore, no longer be the exclusive task of cultural entrepreneurs but also the responsibility of the state.

Notes

1. In order to protect the identity of the organisers, they have been given pseudonyms: Susie, Peter, George, Mike, John, and Phil. Their socio-economic backgrounds are diverse, as are their levels of education and their current mode of employment. They are, however, all middle-aged, and all of them left their jobs to pursue the organisation of the parties for as long as they lasted. Currently, all of them are living (back) in the north of England.
2. Holman, J., and Zawadski, A. Acid House Flashback, www.acidhouseflashback.co.uk (accessed 6 July 2023).
3. Manchester Digital Music Archive, *The Lapsed Clubber Audio Map*, www.mdmarchive.co.uk/map/the-lapsed-clubber-audio-map (accessed 6 July 2023).
4. Reynolds, S. (2013) *Energy Flash: A Journey Through Rave Music and Dance Culture*. London: Faber and Faber.
5. A great example of lived experiences of the raving trans community is Wark, M. (2023) *Raving*. Durham, NC: Duke University Press.
6. Mrozek, B. (2021) *Jugend- Pop – Kultur: Eine transnationale Geschichte*. Bonn: Bundeszentrale für politische Bildung, p. 742.
7. Reckwitz, A. (2013) 'Die Erfindung der Kreativität'. *Kulturpolitische Mitteilungen*, 141, 23–34, p. 25.
8. Slaby, J. (2019) 'Affective Arrangement'. In J. Slaby and C. von Scheve (eds.) *Affective Societies: Key Concepts*. London: Routledge, pp. 109–18.
9. Slaby, 'Affective Arrangement', p. 109.
10. 'Ecstasy' is a term for the entactogenic recreational drug MDMA, which allegedly fuelled the early formation of acid house and rave dance parties.
11. The moral panics that were fuelled by popular media reporting on the use of ecstasy at raves led to raves being treated as public health issues and made it difficult for scholars to research and write about them without having to position themselves in relation to the drugs discourse. Redhead, S. (1993) 'The Politics of Ecstasy'. In S. Redhead (ed.) *Rave Off: Politics and Deviance in Contemporary Youth Culture*. Aldershot: Avebury, pp. 7–28.
12. For a work narrating the history of electronic music through the history of innovative musical instruments, see Stubbs, D. (2019) *Mars by 1980: The Story of Electronic Music*. London: Faber and Faber.
13. For a discussion of both positions see Van veen, t. (2010) 'Technics, Precarity and Exodus in Rave Culture'. *Dancecult*, 1(2), 29–49.
14. Owen-Vandersluis, S. (2003) *Ethics and Cultural Policy in a Global Economy*. Basingstoke: Palgrave Macmillan, p. 15.
15. Owen-Vandersluis, *Ethics and Cultural Policy*, p. 26.

16. Singh, B. (2021) 'Thesis Flashback: A Conversation Between Balraj Singh (Bob) and Jamie Holman'. In A. Stripe and A. Wood (eds.) *Flashback: Parties for the People by the People*. London: Rough Trade Books.
17. Hemment, D. (1998) 'Dangerous Dancing and Disco Riots: The Northern Warehouse Parties'. In G. McKay (ed.) *DiY Culture: Party and Protest in Nineties Britain*. London: Verso, pp. 208–27, p. 210.
18. Ingham, J. (1999) 'Listening Back from Blackburn: Virtual Sound Worlds and the Creation of Temporary Autonomy'. In A. Blake (ed.) *Living through Pop*. London: Routledge, pp. 112–28, p. 117.
19. Ingham, 'Listening Back', p. 118.
20. To perceive that song or track as being driven by the beat, and to perceive this as the predominant characteristic, focusing on rhythm rather than melody.
21. Reckwitz, 'Die Erfindung der Kreativität', pp. 23–34.
22. Slaby, 'Affective Arrangement', p. 110.
23. Reckwitz, 'Die Erfindung der Kreativität', p. 26.
24. Hemment, 'Dangerous Dancing', p. 210.
25. The bill, proposed by MP Graham Bright, eventually became incorporated into the Criminal Justice and Public Order Act (CJA) 1994.
26. UK Government. Entertainments (Increased Penalties) Act 1990, www.legislation.gov.uk/ukpga/1990/20/contents.
27. Czirak, A., Nikoleit, S., Oberkorme, F., Straub, V., Walter-Jochum, R., and Wetzels, M. (2019) '(P)reenactment'. In J. Slaby and C. von Scheve (eds.) *Affective Societies: Key Concepts*. London, Routledge, pp. 200-09.
28. Slaby, 'Affective Arrangement', p. 111.
29. Peter, B. (2019) 'Experiential Knowledge: Dance as Source for Popular Music Historiography'. *Popular Music History*, 12(3), 275–94.

Further Reading

Peter, B. (2019) 'Experiential Knowledge: Dance as Source for Popular Music Historiography'. *Popular Music History*, 12(3), 275–94.

Reckwitz, A. (2017) *The Invention of Creativity: Modern Society and the Culture of the New*. Cambridge: Polity.

Seibt, O. (2010) *Der Sinn des Augenblicks. Überlegungen zu einer Musikwissenschaft des Alltäglichen*. Bielefeld: transcript Verlag.

Slaby, J., and von Scheve, C. (eds.) (2019) *Affective Societies: Key Concepts*. London: Routledge.

Stripe, A., and Wood, A. (eds.) (2021) *Flashback: Parties for the People by the People*. London: Rough Trade Books.

2 | The 'Affective Charge' of the 'Inexistent' Dance Floor

Exploring Nightclub Architecture and Design

CATHARINE ROSSI

Introduction

This chapter is concerned with nightclub architecture and design and its role in the construction of club culture experience. Specifically, it explores the role of the nightclub in the creation of what Simon Reynolds called dance music's 'affective charge', wherein, according to the music journalist, the dancer 'is hurled into a vortex of heightened sensations, abstract emotions and artificial energies'.[1] As such, Reynolds argues that writing about rave music requires 'a shift of emphasis' in comparison to other music genres, 'so that you no longer ask what the music "means" but how it works'.[2] Amidst a lack of academic attention paid to nightclub architecture and design, this chapter borrows Reynolds' music-based argument and transports it into the realm of architecture and design history. It asks not just what such spaces look like but, crucially, how they work; how architects and designers have sought to create environments that facilitate the experience of dance music culture; environments that, according to the Italian architect and nightclub designer Carlo Caldini, have an 'inexistent' architecture.[3]

Exploiting the resonances between Reynolds' and Caldini's arguments and the growing currency of affect and atmosphere in architecture research in recent years, this chapter will explore a handful of celebrated and lesser-known design-led venues from the 1960s to 1980s that exemplify qualities of the nightclub as a designed environment. It does not seek to claim that architects' and designers' decisions are the main determinatives of club culture experiences; as voices such as the architectural theorist and philosopher Hélène Frichot and philosopher Gernot Böhme have recognised, attempts to control affect and atmosphere are always limited.[4] Rather, it seeks to contribute a spatial and material dimension to the history of electronic dance music culture so far largely overlooked.

Fig. 2.1 Inside the upper level of Space Electronic, designed by Gruppo 9999. Visible are furnishings including salvaged washing machine drums turned into seating, a parachute suspended from the ceiling, the stage and bridge for audio visual equipment. Space Electronic, Florence, 1969. 9999 Archive, Courtesy Elettra Fiumi.

Italy's Prototype Nightclubs

Given this chapter's emphasis on the role of architecture and design in nightclub experiences, it might seem counterintuitive to embrace a voice seemingly arguing for their unimportance. This is Caldini in 1972, trying to capture the architectural qualities of Space Electronic (Figure 2.1), the experimental venue he co-designed and which opened in Florence in 1969:

The architecture of Space Electronic is inexistent; that flash in your eyes that beats like our hearts bothers us to the point of crying. Those reflexes on the silver walls have by now become a myriad of red stars like rotting strawberries in a wall of reinforced concrete impressioned with wooden planks. The filmy white, orange and green parachute from San Bernardino, California, floats like the foamy waves of the sea with the wind which blows from the yellow air conditioning vents vaporizing a light woody pine perfume. What is a space limit? An impossible space? And why do we think that space is not made by sounds and perfumes or by the dark like light is?[5]

Caldini's description of Space Electronic's architecture as 'inexistent' remains one of the first and few attempts to conceptualise nightclub space. As the venue's architect, Caldini was more than anyone aware that Space Electronic existed as a real, physical space. His advocation of its 'inexistent' qualities shows how he saw Space Electronic's existence as secondary to other, more intangible, elements in its design of nightlife experience. Caldini co-designed Space Electronic with Fabrizio Fiumi and other members of the architectural collective Gruppo 9999, and ran it with local friend Mario Bolognesi.[6] Spread over two floors of an old engine repair workshop, Space Electronic offered a multidisciplinary and multi-sensory experience: its opening night included live music, an architecture exhibition, theatre, and classical dance. Its programme in the late 1960s and early 1970s included live and recorded music, poetry, festivals, an architecture school, and even a vegetable garden installed on its dance floor. Each night performers and visitors were bathed in projections of colour, patterns, and film clips, and by the early 1970s could watch video recordings of performances by the likes of Donna Summer and the Rolling Stones screened around the venue's interior.[7]

Added in the 1970s, a pink neon sign outside the venue proclaimed that Space Electronic was technically a *discoteca* (discotheque) rather than a nightclub. While these two terms have since largely become synonymous, an approach this chapter adopts, it is useful to distinguish between them here given the latter's earlier twentieth-century roots in smoky cabaret venues and jazz bars such as Rome's Bal Tic Tac (1921) and the former's arrival in the post-WWII era, an innovation this chapter will shortly discuss.[8] Rome is also home to Italy's first discotheque, Piper, which opened in 1965 and which, like Space Electronic, is still going today. Piper was designed by the architects Manilo Cavalli, Francesco Capolei, and Giancarlo Capolei, who transformed an unused cinema into a multi-functional space facilitated by a movable stage for music performances, movable furniture, and advanced audio-visual equipment.[9] As with the history of discos and nightclubs more generally, Piper came out of an earlier history of spaces for dancing and listening to live music. These included the restaurants and live music venues La Capannina (1939) and La Bussola (1955), both on Italy's Tuscan coast and both designed by

Maurizio Tempestini, the Stork club in Milan (1961) by Gianfranco Frattini and Franco Bettonica, and the spectacular redesign of the Lutrario Le-Roi dancehall in Turin (1959–60) by Carlo Mollino with Carlo Alberto Bordogna.[10] With its flexible interior, use of sound and lighting technology, and youth orientation, Piper stood out as an architectural and cultural innovation, a new type of environment for Italy's emergent post-WWII youth culture and their largely imported musical tastes. The club was welcomed in Italy's architectural press as exemplifying what French art critic Pierre Restany called 'yé-yé architecture', a phrase that echoed the sound made by teenage fans of beat, pop, and rock 'n' roll music. Restany identified Piper as pioneering a new spatial typology that offered 'physical and auditory saturation' and 'collective trance' for Italy's youth.[11]

So popular was the Piper that it became the eponym for discos in Italy more generally, which were growing in number in the 1960s. They included several venues designed by architects associated with Italy's Radical Design avant-garde, to which 9999 belonged. As part of a broader mutiny against a then-dominant Modernist architectural ideology, Radical Design architects embraced the Piper as a new spatial typology unburdened by convention or commerce and which advocated participatory and flexible environments. This included another club, also called Piper, which opened in Turin in 1966 designed by locally trained architects Pietro Derossi, Giorgio Ceretti, and Riccardo Rosso. Like Space Electronic the Turin Piper was an industrial container: it featured aluminium walls, movable plastic furniture, and suspended rails fitted with lights, microphones, and speakers. Its programming was also inclusive; its calendar of music, arts, and performance was so diverse that Derossi described the Turin venue as a 'pluriclub' or 'pluri-discoteca'.[12]

Addressing an Absence: Researching Nightclub Architecture and Design

These 1960s Italian venues are largely absent from histories of electronic dance music. In many ways this is understandable. These rather niche spaces were more influential on architecture and visual design cultures than on music scenes – although Space Electronic is credited for its influence on Florence's rock scene, until it switched to playing recorded music exclusively in the mid-1970s.[13] Yet, until recently these venues and nightclubs were generally also near-missing from architecture and design research too, seemingly too frivolous or marginal for serious academic consideration. The last few years have seen a shift, with the advent of several exhibitions and publications on nightclub architecture and design history.[14] These initiatives assert the validity of nightclubs as an area of academic enquiry, yet research is often hampered by a lack of primary research material. Flyers and posters offer rich resources on clubbing's graphic design culture, but little remains in terms of architectural drawings, interior-focused photographs, or other records of nightclub architecture and design.

The paucity of evidence is partly due to a lack of club heritage culture, as well as the often-short time span and underground character of clubs. This is compounded by an interior design approach that advocated regular and often undocumented change. One of the ways in which Space Electronic worked (to evoke Reynolds' approach) was by repeatedly changing its interior over the years, with the addition of funfair design elements, a karaoke console, and fish tanks in the 1970s and 1980s. It altered its lighting from incandescent to LED, and moved its speakers from a bridge stretched over the dance floor to being suspended directly from the ceiling.[15] This iterative and often ad hoc design approach was not exclusive to Italy's Radical Design venues but also more well-known establishments: New York club AREA (1983–87) introduced new artist-led installations every six weeks for its four-year run and nearby Danceteria (1980–86) changed its location, and so its interior, six times.[16] Writing in her 1995 seminal study of teenagers in British clubs during the early 1990s, the sociologist Sarah Thornton attributed this tendency for design change to the demands of 'an ever-shifting market of youth'.[17] Given that AREA and Danceteria were targeted at a slightly older crowd, this need for design change could be said to be associated with club clientele more generally. As these examples suggest, changes were also tied up with technological innovations, the creative freedom of the nightclub interior, and the more pragmatic issues of a precarious industry. In all cases, the lack of detailed design documentation further compromises in-depth study, an absence this chapter aims to address.

Despite their marginality in academic research, venues such as Space Electronic and the Rome and Turin Pipers were influential, prototypical spaces in the histories of both architecture and design and electronic dance music. They typify Thornton's identification of 1960s venues for happenings defined by 'psychedelic and strobe lighting, slide projectors and hanging beads'.[18] They also exemplify architect Ippolito Pestellini Laparelli's 2016 description of venues in this period as 'a home for everything' and as being 'more similar to experimental theaters than actual discotheques'.[19]

Attempts to synthesise the architecture and design history of nightclubs are challenged by the heterogeneity of club culture, and the influence of local music cultures, social-cultural customs, and built environments on their design.[20] Nevertheless, there are striking similarities between Thornton's and Pestellini Laparelli's overviews of European and North American nightclub architecture and design history in the late twentieth century. This includes the emergence of what the former calls 'chrome party palaces' and the latter 'disco temples' in the late 1970s, a definition which encompasses New York's Studio 54 (1977–80), owned by Ian Schrager and Steve Rubell, the interior of which will be discussed in the last part of this chapter, and their subsequent New York venue Palladium (1985–87). Designed by Japanese architect Arata Isozaki, its spectacular transformation of a former music theatre included suspended banks of TV screens, walls covered in light-up squares, and a floor-to-ceiling Keith Haring mural.

Pestellini Laparelli and Thornton also describe the widespread occupation of industrial venues in the 1980s. One of its more formalised or long-lasting manifestations included Manchester's Haçienda (1982–97) with its Peter Saville-designed graphic identity and postmodern interior designed by Ben Kelly with Sandra Douglas, which mobilised industrial aesthetics and materials to create a space as significant to the culture of architecture and design as to dance music.[21] This appropriation of existing found spaces anticipated what Pestellini Laparelli calls the increasingly 'nomadic and ubiquitous rave culture' in the late 1980s and 1990s, one exemplified by event-based dance architecture such as the Spiral Tribe sound system (1990–), which had its roots in the sound system culture of 1960s Jamaica, and the raves and temporary clubs at Glastonbury festival, which first embraced dance culture in the late 1980s.[22] More recent examples include Belgian arts and music festival Horst, which included a temporary club structure by the British architectural practice Assemble in 2017.

Nightclub architecture in the 2000s is multiple and richly diverse, reflecting the globally distributed and locally rooted nature of music cultures as well as the continued existence of earlier architectural approaches through design-based sampling and copying. If anything, the last two decades have been defined by the eradication of nightclub architecture, with an industry weakened by lifestyle changes, ageing populations, and changing technologies, and subsequently pummelled by the Covid-19 pandemic.[23] More positively, the widespread closure of physical venues has been countered by the rise of virtual clubs such as Boiler Room since 2010, and Club Quarantine and Queer House Party, which announced their presence during the 2020 Covid-19 lockdowns.[24] While the screen-based offerings seem far removed from immersive physical interiors, their existence points to the persistent need of spaces for dance culture even in virtual realms, and it will be interesting to see how architects and designers respond to the possibilities of such rapidly evolving technologies to create environments which afford the 'affective charge' that Reynolds puts at the centre of dance culture.

Conceptualising Nightclub Architecture and Design

Attempts to summarise the history of nightclub architecture and design return this chapter to the question of how nightclub architecture works. As the venue's architect, Caldini was more than anyone aware that Space Electronic existed as a real, physical space. His invocation of its 'inexistent' qualities shows how he saw Space Electronic's existence as secondary to other, more intangible, elements in its design of nightlife experience.

The idea to set up Space Electronic was inspired by a visit by Caldini, Fiumi, and fellow 9999 member Mario Preti to Electric Circus (1967–71) in New York, an influential psychedelic and countercultural venue. The former ballroom interior was occupied by a tensile structure designed by architect Charles Forberg, onto which was projected light and sound orchestrated by individuals including synthesiser pioneer Don Buchla and electronic music composer Morton Subotnick.[25] The architectural historian and theorist Sylvia Lavin describes how their work, as well as Andy Warhol's multidisciplinary Exploding Plastic Inevitable (EPI) programme (1996–67), which was held at the venue, used 'light and sound ... to squeeze out the empty space of the existing room and refill it with a semisolid environment'. In the process it undid 'the legibility of the architectural frame' and made the physical fabric of 'building, both its structure and space' 'irrelevant, a mere prop'.[26]

More recently architectural theorists such as Ivan López Munera and Pol Esteve have similarly stressed the importance of the intangible and ephemeral in understanding nightclubs. López Munera uses the term 'discotecture' to describe 'the relationship between sound and lighting systems in the creation of a new kind of architecture'.[27] Writing specifically about Palladium, López Munera traces 'discotecture' back to Electric Circus.[28] Esteve, writing about Spanish clubs such as Barcelona's Maddox

(1967–2005), identifies three micro-technologies 'crucial to the production of ... spatial experience': light, sound, and 'psychotropic technologies' (recreational drugs).[29] All three are notable as ingredients which do not belong to the permanent, built fabric of a space, but pertain instead to dynamic and temporary interventions which involve the body as much as the surrounding environment.

The emphasis on the ephemeral and intangible in nightclub architecture makes sense. Nightlife folklore traces it back to the venue held up as the first discotheque, Paris's Whisky à Gogo, where in 1953 Régine Zylberberg transformed an existing venue by installing a lino floor and coloured lights and replacing the jukebox with two turntables, to ensure the uninterrupted play of music. Zylberberg was also known to stand on a stool waving her arms around to make rudimentary strobe lighting.[30]

The emphasis on nightclub's intangible qualities also aligns with more recent interests in questions of atmosphere and affect in the built environment, as noted in the Introduction to this volume. Writing about atmospheres, 'affective experience', and the Blackpool Illuminations, social and cultural geographer Tim Edensor considers 'how different configurations of objects, technologies, and (human and nonhuman) bodies come together to form different capacities and experiences of relationality'.[31] Such relational interplay is also found in Deleuze's conceptualisation of affect as a dynamic encounter between human and non-human beings, and Böhme's interest in atmosphere. Böhme positions atmosphere as an 'intermediate phenomenon, something between subject and object'. Crucially, atmosphere cannot be created. Rather it is the conditions for atmosphere, what Böhme calls a 'tuned space', which can be facilitated through architectural and design choices such as materials, furnishings, spatial arrangements, and lighting.[32] Drawing on Deleuze, Frichot similarly notes that affect is 'not something that can be stage designed' and is therefore outside of the architect's control, in comparison to more material components of built space.

Böhme also draws on the stage set, which he conceives as a defined space which sets the conditions for a performance. Böhme describes how the twentieth century saw 'the art of the stage ... expand into the general art of staging' and applied 'for example, in the decor of discotheques and the design of large-scale events such as open-air festivals'.[33] This chapter returns to the concept of the nightclub as stage in the discussion of Studio 54 below.

Collectively, these authors show the need to focus on both the material and intangible, or the existent and 'inexistent', in the creation of club spaces. As a constructed experience, Space Electronic only worked due to its existence as a physical space with specific material and structural dimensions, including its existence as an underground and windowless venue with large spaces for collective gathering, and technological devices. The lighting projections that are identified as so vital to nightclub space are dependent on physical equipment – at Space Electronic these included an overhead projector, Kodak slide carousel, and Super-8 film projector. The 'light woody pine perfume' that Caldini describes at the beginning of this chapter was wafted by air conditioning vents and rippled through a parachute (as well as projectors) purchased on the US trip the year earlier, following the visit to Electric Circus.[34]

The dance floor is arguably most paradigmatic of the dual tangible and intangible existence of nightclub architecture. Often used as shorthand for a nightclub space more generally, the dance floor is a sited three-dimensional entity whose materiality, placement, shape, and size contribute to the nightclub's atmosphere. The dance floor is often demarcated as a separate area through the use of distinct materials and lighting. In late nineteenth-and early twentieth-century ballrooms and dancehalls this was often a sprung floor, a then-new invention designed to lightly bounce underfoot and so make dancing less wearing on the body.[35] While the physical specificity of the dance floor is often overlooked in accounts of dance culture, this was not necessarily the case for those who experienced it at the time; Northern Soul dancers in the north of England during the 1970s as well as dancers at New York's The Fun House in the early 1980s would sprinkle talcum powder on the floor to stop it from becoming slippery, and clubs would have to regularly polish (and even replace) dance floors to ensure they stayed in good condition.[36]

In turn, the dance floor's physical distinctiveness informs its liberatory condition. Following Hakim Bey, the anthropologist Bryan Rill calls the dance floor a 'Temporary Autonomous Zone (TAZ)' for creative self-transformation, while in his research on queer dance cultures, José Esteban Muñoz argues that the proximity of bodies on a dance floor offers a 'kinaesthetic experience' that encourages tolerance for others.[37] Understanding the dance floor as a contemporaneously symbolic and material space shows the importance of understanding nightclub architecture and design as an environment that combines the tangible with the intangible.

The final section of this chapter mobilises this conceptualisation to explore how the conditions for dancing to electronic dance music and experiencing Reynolds' 'affective charge' were in part constructed by spatial arrangements, as well as materials and objects such as flooring, walls, furniture, lighting, and sound devices. It focuses on New York's short-lived but influential club Studio 54, as well as two clubs that it inspired: Paris' Le Palace (1978–84) and Hong Kong's lesser known Canton Disco (1985–92). These venues introduced key aspects of late twentieth-century nightclub design and architecture and are useful examples to consider the interplay between the intangible and tangible in their design.

Studio 54: Nightclub as a 'Total Environment'

Architecture critic Aaron Betsky used to frequent Studio 54 as a student in the late 1970s until its closure in 1980, where he observed that,

Instead of walls, floors and ceilings, here was a space that appeared and disappeared continually. Instead of places of privacy, where design was unwanted, and public places where architecture had to appear in a correct guise, here was a place where the most intimate acts, whether real or acted out in dance, occurred in full view through a structure of lights, sounds, and arrangements that made it all seem natural. Instead of references to buildings or paintings, instead of a grammar of ornament and a syntax of facades, here was only rhythm and light.[38]

Betsky's description of the venue as a challenge to conventional ideas of architecture resonates with the multiple conceptualisations of nightclub architecture's intangible qualities laid out in this chapter. It also adds a social dimension, describing how Studio 54 upended conventional divisions of private and public space and brought bodily intimacy to the fore. For Betsky, this was part of Studio 54's status as a 'queer space': that is, 'a space of spectacle, consumption, dance and obscenity' that embraced and validated the city's queer culture.[39]

Queer culture was key to the development of Studio 54, and New York's dance culture more generally. The club's managers, Ian Schrager and Steve Rubell, used to visit gay-friendly clubs while running Studio 54's predecessor, the Enchanted Garden in Queens, which opened its doors in 1975. Schrager later described how he preferred the sexually charged 'sensory overload' of clubs like Paradise Garage (1977–87) over the 'too fancy, over decorated, contrived, and pretentious' atmosphere of more entertainment-focussed or lounge-like venues such as jazz club Arthur's or Regine's (owned by Zylberberg, whose Parisian beginnings developed into a global empire).[40] Schrager states he was more interested in 'plain boxes with the carpets rolled up to make a dance floor'.[41] Arguably, Studio 54 combined qualities of both venue types, opulent yet functional, its extravagant venue designed for socialising, dancing, and licentious behaviour.

Responsible for the design of Studio 54 was Experience Space, a local firm composed of architect Scott Bromley, interior designer Ron Doud, 'furnishings expert' Robin Jacobsen, lighting designer Brian Thompson, and floral designer Renny Reynolds.[42] They worked with party promoter Carmen D'Alessio, sound designer Richard Long, and lighting designers including Jules Fisher and Paul Marantz, as well as electricians, who Schrager claimed 'were by far and away the most important people' as they had 'the most complicated job of making all of the lighting and stage effects work'.[43] Together, they would create what the club's press release described as 'New York's most original total environment'.[44]

Key to understanding Studio 54 is the spatial typology that Böhme identifies as the model for atmosphere creation: the theatre. The venue was originally built in 1927 as the Gallo Opera House, before becoming a CBS TV studio. While the stage and orchestra pit were removed to make space for a dance floor, the proscenium and theatrical rigging were retained, as were the balconies, furnished with informal 'lounging platforms' that enabled the watching of the dancers on the floor below. This was part of the seeing and being seen character of Studio 54's celebrity-driven club culture, analogous to a theatre that offered both the opportunity to participate in the spectacle, and watch it from a distance.[45] Influential nightclub lighting designer Tony Gottelier described Studio 54 as the club which 'first focussed the [nightclub] industry's attention on the relevance of theatre', and he attributes Studio 54's success partially down to the ambition to have 'theatrical flexibility'.

The Dance Floor as Stage

The theatre analogy extends to how Studio 54 created an embodied narrative experience. The journey to the dance floor was key to this. First you had to get through the famously selective door policy. Next was an ornate narrow foyer with a banana-leaf-patterned carpet. Schrager describes this 'transitional' space as

> a kind of a decompression zone between the pandemonium and crowds outside the door and the lights, music and energy of the dance floor, which got louder and brighter as you got closer. This was a real build-up of excitement that culminated

when you entered and saw the explosive, heart-stopping energy of the dance floor and felt the music.[46]

The 11,000-square-foot parquet dance floor was Studio 54's heart.[47] Its size meant it had to be managed throughout the night to ensure that the club always felt lively: at the beginning of the evening cut drops of different designs by set designers Aerographics (Richie Williamson and Dean Janoff) were lowered over the dance floor from the theatrical rigging above to divide it into smaller areas.[48] As the dance floor filled up the curtain was raised, prompting a flow of dancers across the floor; a physical change that facilitated an atmospheric shift. Aerographics created a variety of scenery for the club, such as a universe featuring planets, a moon, and a spoon (infamously loaded with cocaine).[49] Throughout the night, dancers would hear and feel music mixed by DJs, including Kenny Carpenter and resident DJ Richie Kaczor. Studio 54's sound system was designed by the pioneering figure of Richard Long, who, with his company, also created sound systems for other influential dance clubs including The Loft, AREA, Paradise Garage, the Enchanted Garden, and Palladium in New York, as well as New Jersey's Zanzibar, and the birthplace of house music, Chicago's The Warehouse. Like many of New York's nightclub clientele during the 1980s, Long lost his life to AIDS, an illness that later also took Rubell and Doud.[50]

The dance floor's physical and performative separateness was enforced by the club's lighting. Around the dance floor Schrager commissioned 'soft and stylish' architectural lighting 'where less is more'.[51] For the dance floor (Figure 2.2) they hired Jules Fisher and Paul Marantz, Broadway lighting designers who had also worked for Electric Circus and Arthur's.[52] They rejected the then-convention of the dark dance floor and instead staged it as a bright space to, as Marantz puts it, 'make all the patrons the stars and put them onstage', exemplifying Studio 54's attempt to construct an experience of immersive, embodied spectacle.[53] Lighting included chase poles suspended from the ceiling and lined with pulsating red and yellow lightbulbs, and a red police beacon at the base. The poles would slowly lower and rise over the dancers' heads during the evening. These vertical lights were accompanied by a 'flying ceiling' of rotating horizontal mirrored panels with pink neon lights that provided their own form of spectacle.[54]

Studio 54's performative light equipment contributed to its global influence, an area that merits further research. Visitors included Parisian club owner Fabrice Emaer. Both aghast at and enamoured by the venue he described as 'completely sterilised, a ghetto for model agencies', Emaer decided to create an even more glamorous venue in his own city.[55] He

Fig. 2.2 The main dance floor at Studio 54, showing the theatrical lighting designed by Paul Marantz and Jules Fisher, including the vertical chase poles and horizontal 'flying ceilings' suspended from ceiling rigging. Studio 54, New York, 1977. Photographer: Jaime Ardiles-Arce. Photograph courtesy of Scott Bromley.

discovered an old 1920s music hall and appointed young architects Patrick Berger and Vincent Barré to transform it into Le Palace (1978–84). Asked to review Le Palace in *Vogue Hommes*, cultural critic Roland Barthes admired how certain elements had been retained in the venue's transformation, including the stage, curtain, balcony, and orchestra pit, which had been turned into 'a splendid dance floor'. He was struck by one feature in particular; a huge sphere-like installation of coloured neon tubes, cables, and metallic elements suspended over the dance floor, which would rise and fall during the evening, just like in Studio 54.[56] It prompted him to ask:

Is not the great raw material of modern art, of our daily art – is it not, in this era, light? In ordinary theatres, light is remote, fastened to the stage. At Le Palace, it is the whole theatre that is the stage; here light occupies a deep space, within which it comes alive and performs like an actor; an intelligent laser, with a complicated and refined mind, like an exhibitor of abstract sculptures, produces enigmatic traces, with sudden mutations: circles, rectangles, ellipses, tracks, cables, galaxies, fringes.[57]

Barthes affirms the theatre-like character of Le Palace, and nightclubs more generally, and how its lighting equipment played a key role in this transformation of the space. It exemplifies the expanded 'art of staging' that Böhme describes and how this informed the club's affective atmosphere and the performative behaviour it encouraged.

The influence of Studio 54's innovative lighting and sound design reached beyond the US and Europe. Andrew Bull, a British expatriate living in Hong Kong who had worked as a DJ at seminal venues in the city including The Scene (1966) and Disco Disco (1978) (a venue key for the city's LGBTQ+ community), was another figure inspired by his visit to Studio 54.[58] In the mid-1980s Bull paired up with investor Tony Law to create Canton Disco, and employed New York-based firm O. J. Productions to produce 'a direct crib from Studio 54'. Bull even brought in Richard Long to create its sound system. Other borrowings included the moving chase poles found in Studio 54. As Bull describes, 'you'd be dancing and this gantry thing came down, this truss came down on a chain ... with police lights on the bottom'. Bull didn't just borrow from Studio 54, as the club also had 'an 80s style video wall', which he confesses he 'probably stole' from Palladium.[59]

Studio 54 did not just use its lighting and sound equipment, but a whole suite of effects to ensure the venue's atmosphere and affective experience were different every night, and different over the course of a night. Fog, confetti, and glitter would be emitted over the dance floor during the regular parties held at the club. The furniture on the ground floor was on wheels so that it could be easily moved around.[60]

Studio 54's design process was neither happenstance nor static. The original design was a considered and costly exercise, and it required regular upkeep to keep it functioning. As Matthew Yokobosky describes,

during the daytime, the parquet floor would be polished. On Thursdays, the lights were dusted and gels replaced, and on Fridays the speakers were vacuumed. There were light, sound, and theatrical drop pre-sets. DJs had set 'mood' music to begin the evenings. By 10 p.m. everything was inspected and had to be perfect before the doors would open.[61]

This maintenance was part of Studio 54's material and spatial transformations. Typifying the regular design change identified earlier in this chapter, Studio 54's interior was not a static, fixed entity, but one that changed regularly. As early as 1978, for example, they renovated the club, adding a new bar on the balcony, making the DJ booth round and raising it above the dance floor.[62] Such changes were not in place for long. Notoriously, the club closed in 1980 following Rubell and

Schrager's conviction for fraud – although the fickleness of New York's club scene meant that some saw the club as already 'over' by 1979.[63] This was not the end, however: five years later they opened Palladium in New York's Downtown, and Schrager has gone on to have a hugely successful hotel career.[64] Schrager talks about running nightclubs as having been 'a great training ground' for his hotel empire: 'it's all about the magic you can create, the elevated experience, stimulating the senses.'[65] It seems Schrager found a way to make space work in his running of nightclubs, a knowledge he then took into the design of other environments.

Conclusion

This chapter has sought to present a short overview of nightclub design and architecture through a focus on the 'home for everything' Space Electronic, and on 'total environment' 'disco temple' Studio 54. While geographically and chronologically separate, these clubs demonstrate how nightclub architects and designers can transform pre-existing spaces through spatial arrangements, furnishings, and lighting and sound technologies. While these two clubs weren't directly connected, this chapter shows how nightclub architecture and design often evolved through a transnational culture of design inspiration and copying: New York's Electric Circus inspired Florence's Space Electronic, while Le Palace in Paris and Canton Disco in Hong Kong were some of many clubs inspired by New York's Studio 54. They existed as part of a global nightlife ecology that is all the more fascinating for occurring in a pre-internet age with a very different network to that of today.

Overall, the discussion shows how nightclub environments work through the intertwining of existent and 'inexistent' architecture and design. It has mobilised concepts, including atmosphere and affect, to propose an approach for studying nightclubs as spaces that can be understood, following Böhme, as 'tuned' by tangible and intangible elements. These elements include lighting and sound equipment, furnishings, and floors, as well as spatial divisions and circulation, and of course people. Ultimately, all these elements are needed to make a nightclub: when the lights are off, the music has stopped, and the dance floor is emptied, the nightclub really is 'inexistent'.

Notes

1. Simon Reynolds, *Energy Flash: A Journey Through Rave Music and Dance Culture*, London and Basingstoke: Picador, 1998, p. xix.
2. Ibid.
3. Carlo Caldini in Gruppo 9999, *Ricordi di architettura / Architectural Memoirs*, Florence: Tipolitografia G. Capponi, 1972, page unknown.
4. Hélène Frichot, 'Infrastructural Affects: Challenging the Autonomy of Architecture' in Marko Jobst and Hélène Frichot (eds), *Architectural Affects after Deleuze and Guattari*, London and New York: Routledge, 2021, p. 10; and Gernot Böhme, 'The Art of the Stage Set as a Paradigm for an Aesthetics of Atmospheres', *Ambiences: The International Journal of Sensory Environment, Architecture and Urban Space*, (February 2013), p. 2.
5. Caldini, *Ricordi di architettura*, page unknown.
6. The club was conceived by Carlo Caldini and Fabrizio Fiumi. Other members of the group, initially known as Gruppo 1999, were also involved at the start: Paolo Coggiola, Paolo Galli, Andrea Gigli, Mario Preti, and Giovanni Sani. Emmanuele Piccardo, *Radical Pipers*, Busalla: Plug_In, 2016, p. 126.
7. For a fuller account of Space Electronic see Catharine Rossi, 'Architecture Goes Disco', *AA Files*, 69 (2014), 138–45.
8. For the earlier history of cabaret see Florence Ostende and Lotte Johnson (eds), *Into the Night: Cabarets and Clubs in Modern Art*, Munich: Prestel, 2019; Hillegonda Rietveld, 'The Nightclub' in Geoff Stahl and J. Mark Percival (eds), *The Bloomsbury Handbook of Popular Music, Space and Place*, New York: Bloomsbury Academic, 2022, 139–52.
9. Renato Pedio, 'Piper Club a Roma', *L'architettura: cronache e storia*, 138 (1967), 789–91.
10. Francesco Guzzetti, 'YéYé Style: artisti, architetti e cultura giovanile negli anni Sessanta', *In Situ Revue des patrimoines*, 32 (2017), 2–3.
11. Pierre Restany, 'Short History of the Yé-Yé Style', *Domus*, 446 (1967), 34–42.
12. Piccardo, *Radical Pipers*, 103. This publication also offers a useful overview of the Radicals' disco experiments.
13. Bruno Casini, *Rebelli nello spazio*, Arezzo: Zona, 2013, p. 31.
14. Exhibitions (all with accompanying catalogues) include *Energy Flash: The Rave Movement*, curated by Nav Haq, M HKA, Antwerp, June 17 to September 25, 2016; *Electro* curated by Laurent Garnier, Philharmonie de Paris, Paris, April 9 to August 11 2019; *Night Fever: Designing Club Culture 1960 to Today*, co-curated by Jochen Eisenbrand, Rossi and Nina Serulus, 2018– 2022; *La Boîte de Nuit*, co-curated by Benjamin Lafore, Sébastien Martinez-Barat and Audrey Teichmann, Villa Noialles, February 19–March 19, 2017 and *Into the Night: Cabarets and Clubs in Modern Art*, curated by Florence Ostende, Barbican Art Gallery, Oct 2019—19 Jan 2020.

15. Rossi, 'Architecture Goes Disco', 144; Interview with Carlo Caldini, 14 March 2014.
16. Dave Haslam, *We the Youth: Keith Haring's New York Nightlife*, Manchester: Cōnfigō Publishing, 2019, p. 12.
17. Sarah Thornton, *Club Cultures: Music, Media and Subcultural Capital*, Cambridge: Polity, 1995, p. 55.
18. Ibid., p. 55.
19. Ippolito Pestellini Laparelli, 'Club Amo', *Flash Art*, 311:49 (2016), p. 48.
20. Rietveld, 'The Nightclub' in Stahl and Percival (eds) *The Bloomsbury Handbook of Popular Music, Space and Place*, pp. 139–52.
21. Sally Stone, 'The Haçienda: The Manufactured Image of a Post-industrial City', *Interiors*, 5:1 (2014), 37–53.
22. Pestellini Laparelli, 'Club Amo', 48; Tim Guest, 'Fight for the Right to Party', *The Guardian*, 12 July 2009, www.theguardian.com/music/2009/jul/12/90s-spiral-tribe-free-parties (accessed 20 July 2022); Paul Sullivan, *Remixology: Tracing the Dub Diaspora*, London: Reverb, 2014, p. 7.
23. Anon., 'Don't Stand So Close To Me; The Future of Nightclubs', *The Economist*, 6 February 2021, https://go-gale-com.ucreative.idm.oclc.org/ps/i.do?p=AONE&u=ucca&id=GALE|A650703921&v=2.1&it=r&sid=summon (accessed 26 April 2023).
24. Esta Maffrett, 'Extending The Club Night Through Virtual Realities', *Museum of Youth Culture*, 2 March 2022, https://museumofyouthculture.com/digital-spaces-and-queer-clubbing/ (accessed 19 July 2022).
25. Anon, 'The Electric Circus, New York 1967' in Mateo Kries, Jochen Eisenbrand, and Catharine Rossi (eds), *Night Fever: Designing Club Culture 1960 to Today*, Weil am Rhein: Vitra Design Museum, 2018, p. 75.
26. Sylvia Lavin, 'Andy Architect™ – Or, a Funny Thing Happened on the Way to the Disco', *Log*, 15 (2009), p. 100.
27. López Munera, 'Discotecture: The Bodily Regime of Archi-Social Exploration' in Kries, Einsenbrand, and Rossi (eds). *Night Fever*, p. 127.
28. Ibid., pp. 119, 127.
29. Pol Esteve, 'Total Space' in Kries, Einsenbrand, and Rossi (eds), *Night Fever*, p. 140.
30. Anon., 'Régine Zylberberg Obituary', *The Times*, 5 May 2022, www.thetimes.co.uk/article/regine-zylberberg-obituary-2jfzs6dn8 (accessed 19 July 2022).
31. Tim Edensor, 'Illuminated Atmospheres: Anticipating and Reproducing the Flow of Affective Experience in Blackpool', *Environment and Planning D: Society and Space*, 30 (2012), p. 1105.
32. Gernot Böhme, 'The Art of the Stage Set as a Paradigm for an Aesthetics of Atmospheres', *Ambiences: The International journal of Sensory Environment, Architecture and Urban Space*, (February 2013), p. 2.
33. Ibid., p. 5.

34. Rossi, 'Architecture Goes Disco', p. 143.
35. James Nott, 'Dance Halls: Towards an Architectural and Spatial History, c. 1918–65', *Architectural History*, 61 (2018), p. 208.
36. Hillegonda Rietveld, *This is Our House: House Music, Cultural Spaces and Technologies*, Aldershot: Ashgate, 1998, p. 117; Nott, 'Dance Halls', p. 208.
37. Bryan Rill, 'Identity Discourses on the Dancefloor', *Anthropology of Consciousness*, 21:2 (2010), p. 140; José Esteban Muñoz, *Cruising Utopia, 10th Anniversary Edition: The Then and There of Queer Futurity*, New York: New York University Press, p. 66.
38. Aaron Betsky, *Queer Space: Architecture and Same-Sex Desire*, New York: William Morrow & Co., 1997, p. 5.
39. Ibid.
40. Ian Schrager, *Studio 54*, New York: Rizzoli, 2017, p. 31.
41. Ibid., p. 32
42. Tim Rohan, 'Bringing the Disco Home: Manhattan's Disco-Influenced Residences of the 1970s' in Kries, Einsenbrand, and Rossi (eds), *Night Fever*, p. 107.
43. Schrager, *Studio 54*, p. 18.
44. Ibid., pp. 28, 29.
45. Rohan, 'Bringing the Disco Home' in Kries, Einsenbrand, and Rossi (eds), *Night Fever*, p. 111.
46. Schrager, *Studio 54*, p. 41.
47. Bob Colacello, 'Introduction' in Schrager, *Studio 54*, p. 46.
48. Matthew Yokobosky, *Studio 54 Night Magic*, New York: Rizzoli Electa, 2020, p. 6.
49. Schrager, 'Interview with Ian Schrager' in Kries, Einsenbrand, and Rossi (eds), *Night Fever*, p. 101.
50. Tim Lawrence, *Love Saves the Day: A History of American Dance Music, 1970–1979*, Durham, NC:Duke University Press, 2004, p. 345; Andy Beta, 'Magic Touch: Richard Long's Life-Changing Soundsystems', *Red Bull Music Academy*, 20 May 2016, https://daily.redbullmusicacademy.com/2016/05/richard-long-feature (accessed 17 July 2022); Oliver Bradbury, *An Alternative Seventies: The Last Age of Radicalism – A Decade's Design and Styling, 1970–79*, London: Nantz Press, 2020, p. 83, www.academia.edu/43986524/An_Alternative_Seventies_Part_2 (accessed 20 April 2023).
51. Schrager, 'Interview with Ian Schrager' in Kries, Einsenbrand, and Rossi (eds), *Night Fever*, p. 101.
52. Schrager, *Studio 54*, pp. 33, 388.
53. Ibid., p. 388.
54. Rohan, 'Bringing the Disco Home' in Kries, Einsenbrand, and Rossi (eds), *Night Fever*, p. 111.
55. Andy Thomas, 'Nightclubbing: Guy Cuevas and the Paris Disco Scene: A Forgotten DJ and Two of the French Capital's Most Hedonistic

Nightclubs' *Red Bull Music Academy* 28 January 2016, https://daily.redbullmusicacademy.com/2016/01/nightclubbing-guy-cuevas-feature (accessed 20 July 2022).

56. Benjamin Lafore, Sébastien Martinez-Barat, and Audrey Teichmann, *La Boîte de Nuit*, Hyères: l'Association Villa Noailles, 2017, p. 34.
57. Roland Barthes, 'At Le Palace Tonight', *Vogue Hommes*, May (1978), page unknown.
58. Anon., 'Disco Disco: The Club that Launched Lan Kwai Fong's Nightlife', *South China Post*, 19 September 2021, www.pressreader.com/china/south-china-morning-post-6150/20210919/282351158606292 (accessed 22 June 2023).
59. Interview with Andrew Bull, 12 April 2022.
60. Rohan, 'Bringing the Disco Home' in Kries, Einsenbrand, and Rossi (eds), *Night Fever*, 111; Schrager, *Studio 54*, p. 24.
61. Yokobosky, *Studio 54 Night Magic*, p. 15.
62. Schrager, *Studio 54*, p. 202.
63. Brad Gooch, 'Club Culture', *Vanity Fair*, May 1987, no page, https://archive.vanityfair.com/article/1987/5/club-culture (accessed 22 June 2023).
64. Rubell died from AIDS in 1989, a disease that would take Ron Doud, Richard Long, and many others associated with New York's nightlife scene.
65. Schrager, 'Interview with Ian Schrager' in Kries, Einsenbrand, and Rossi (eds), *Night Fever*, p. 103.

Further Reading

Eisenbrand, J., Kries, M. and Rossi. C (eds) *Night Fever: Designing Club Culture 1960 to Today*. Weil am Rhein: Vitra Design Museum, 2018.

Fernández Contreras, J., Zancan, R. and Sacchetti, V. (eds) *A Nocturnal History of Architecture*. Leipzig: Spector, 2024.

Gillan, J. L, *Temporary Pleasure: Nightclub Architecture, Design and Culture from the 1960s to Today*. New York: Prestel, 2023.

Haslam, D, *Life After Dark: A history of British Nightclubs and Venues*. London: Simon & Schuster, 2015.

Lavin, S. 'Andy Architect™ – Or, a Funny Thing Happened on the Way to the Disco', *Log*, 15 (2009), 99–110.

Piccardo, E. *Radical Pipers*, Busalla: Plug_In, 2016.

Rietveld, H. C, 'The Nightclub,' Geoff Stahl and Mark Percival (eds) *The Bloomsbury Handbook of Popular Music, Space and Place*. London: Bloomsbury Academic, 2022.

Rossi, C. 'Architecture Goes Disco', *AA Files*, 69 (2014), 138–45.
Schrager, I. *Studio 54*, New York: Rizzoli, 2017.
Stone, S. 'The Haçienda: The Manufactured Image of a Post-Industrial City', *Interiors*, 5:1 (2004), 37–53.
Yokobosky, M. *Studio 54 Night Magic*. New York: Rizzoli Electa, 2020.

3 | Sound System Legacies

CASPAR MELVILLE

'Sound system culture has had a massive effect over every single sub-genre of music since the early 90s.'[1]

If you have ever been in a nightclub and had your ribcage rattled by the weight of the bass; if you've ever greeted the intro of a beloved tune with a call for the DJ to rewind the record; if you've ever seen someone grab a mic and freestyle over recorded rhythms; if you've ever seen a DJ twiddle the knobs to drop out the bass to build anticipation, before whacking it back in with a drop; if you've ever heard a dub version or a remix – then you have first-hand knowledge of the influence of sound system culture on contemporary electronic dance music.

Whilst bass-heavy sound systems are prevalent across a wide range of dance events and raves, they are originally associated with Jamaica's post-war Kingston. In the context of a tightly controlled Jamaican radio monopoly, and the lack of access for Kingston's poor to formal 'uptown' venues or media, sound systems have operated since the early 1960s as outlets for new music which was not heard on the radio. As temporary and mobile dance venues, they provided access to affordable entertainment and sociality, as well as training and apprenticeship for aspiring music producers.[2] As such, they functioned as the prime socio-sonic institutions through which Jamaican music was broadcast and shared, offering community hubs to share messages of resistance, counter-history, and inspiration. Through these functions, sound system culture functioned as labs for musical innovation, vital in developing a range of musical genres and scenes including ska in the 1960s and reggae in the 1970s, ragga and dancehall in the 1980s and 1990s, and associated genres like reggaetón and bashment thereafter.[3] As such, the sound system dance party that developed from Jamaica is an important starting point for the warehouse and open-air rave parties from the mid- to late 1980s onwards in the UK. In many ways sound system culture offers an important link to current electronic dance music spaces, including warehouse parties, raves, and teknivals as well as bass-heavy break-beat genres such as jungle/drum and bass.[4]

This chapter seeks to address the sound system beyond Jamaica, focusing on the influence of sound system culture on electronic dance music and its practices in the late twentieth and early twenty-first centuries. Although Jamaican music and sound systems (or sounds) are tightly linked, many kinds of music other than reggae have been played on and by sound systems, from the bebop, R&B, and jump blues that the early Jamaican sounds played before the development of domestic ska and reggae, to the funk and soul that sound system operators would intersperse with their reggae selections in the dance, to the electro, hip-hop, house, UK garage, and grime played by UK sound systems like Mastermind, Touch of Class, Shut Up and Dance, Shock, Rampage, and Rapattack since the 1980s. In this context, the discussion will address the legacy of sound system aesthetics, technology, and practice in musical genres other than reggae and dancehall, and argue that Jamaican-styled dance sound systems provide a vital model, outlet, and laboratory for electronic dance music and global dance club culture more generally.

Stringing Up

Jamaican dance sound systems emerged as a key social and sonic technology in the immediate post-war period in Kingston, as a response to economic crisis and a reorganisation of the musical economy of what was then the largest of the British colonies of the Caribbean. The pre-war Jamaican music economy had revolved around music played live by the many dance bands and orchestras that supplied music for the hotels and nightclubs hosting wealthy American and British tourists. But this live economy was severely damaged by WWII as musicians joined up and tourism dried up.[5] As the pioneering audio engineer Hedley Jones told journalist David Katz (in an interview conducted when Jones was ninety-nine years old), Jamaica's live music culture was one of the 'casualties of war'.[6] To fill the sonic gap and provide entertainment for Kingston's poor who had never had access to the tourist hotels and uptown nightclubs in the first place, Kingston's audio entrepreneurs of the late 1940s and 1950s experimented with 'the public re-performance of recorded music'.[7]

Jamaican migrants working in the American South, like Clement 'Coxsone' Dodd, who had worked as a farm labourer, were inspired by the outdoor block parties of Southern Afro-American culture and the money that could be made from them. Kingston had the right weather and available public space for outdoor parties,[8] and a generation of skilled and entrepreneurial engineers who started to adapt the available Public Address (PA) technology, used on the island for political rallies and outdoor religious services, for relaying recorded music. Soon they were building their own components. Hedley Jones, born in 1923, who had served as a radar engineer during the war and had already built the first electric guitar produced in Jamaica, took the lead in designing and building amplifiers which were adequate to the task of reproducing the sound of American R&B and jump blues at sufficient volume and clarity to project outdoors, compete for attention with rivals, and accrue prestige for the operator (owner and custodian of the sound system). Roy Johnson, another pioneering audio engineer, designed new speakers with the additional power to project the all-important bass frequencies, which he christened the 'house of joy'. Meanwhile Hedley Jones ordered up a pair of British Celestion speakers to go with the amps he was designing, the first 18-inch bass bins on the island and the start of sound systems culture's long and enduring relationship with bass.

More than just a way to play amplified music, the sound system is a 'multiple body' where assemblages of technology and human meet,[9] they are 'techno-social collectives'.[10] The 'set' (the term for the electronic hardware) comprises an assortment of technologies: records, turntable, needle, amplifiers, and pre-amps (which function as a kind of mixer), equalisers, crossovers, mixers, microphones, speakers (usually divided into three: the tops, or tweeters, the mids, and the all-conquering bass, each with their own amps, controlled through the pre-amp), and, as the technology became available and was adapted to the needs of the individual sounds, effects boxes, echo and reverb, and manifold other effects. A sound system is also an organic assemblage of people, involving the operator (who runs the sound); the selector who chooses the music, similar to the role of the DJ elsewhere; the engineers who build and maintain the equipment and ensure the quality of the sound after each set up; the box-boys who lug the equipment and records; the deejay (a term distinct from the later 'DJ') who 'toasts' (MCs or speaks) over the mic; and even the dancing crowd who support, criticise, and propel the reputation of the sound forward. Kingston's sound system became a way to big up the neighbourhood, to gain employment and reputation, a place to strut your stuff, and, for the operators, a way to advertise and sell your wares – Tom Wong promoted his hardware store, Reid his liquor store; by the mid-1960s, operators like Dodd and Reid were able to showcase on their sound system music they were themselves producing through their record labels, Studio One and

Treasure Isle respectively. Beyond that, sound systems were a way to voice new forms of identity. As cultural theorist Louis Chude-Sokei argues, sound systems played a crucial role in articulating and defining post-colonial Jamaican identity:

[Sound systems function] as an aesthetic space within which the members of the national or transnational Jamaican community imagine themselves. This is an imagined community which, unlike the one mapped out by Benedict Anderson's influential *Imagined Communities*, operates not by the technologies of literacy, but through the cultural economy of sound and its technological apparatus which is distinctly oral.[11]

The fact that the early sound systems used British-made components to play American-made music to a Jamaican audience makes clear that although sound systems were a Jamaican innovation, they emerge not from within one national environment but within the web of colonial relations established by the Atlantic slave trade, British imperialism, American post-war economic hegemony, and the counter-currents of intellectual and political resistance, often voiced most effectively in sound, which Paul Gilroy (1993) has named the Black Atlantic. The origins of sound system, just as of hip-hop and global dance music more widely, are, in Paul Gilroy's words, not 'ethnically pure ... [but] ... the mutant result of fusion and intermixture', a way in which Black music is circulated and mutated, as it comes into contact with other musical forms and with technology.[12]

While sound system culture has a distinct history in Jamaica, intimately linked to the burgeoning Jamaican recording industry, it also spread: by the mid-1970s sound system culture had gone 'outernational'.[13] The influence of sound system practices and aesthetics on the development of hip-hop during 1970s New York (a city that was by some estimates one quarter Caribbean, with migrants from Jamaica, other parts of the Anglo Caribbean, and from Puerto Rico, the Dominican Republic, and Haiti[14]) and, especially, the foundational role played by the Jamaican-born sound system operator Kool DJ Herc (Clive Campbell),[15] who helped develop the Bronx twist on reggae toasting which became US rap, provides one pathway of influence that links sound systems to contemporary electronic dance music through the hip-hop influences coming initially from North America and then spreading to become 'global noise'.[16] But another pathway is routed through the UK sound systems and it is this pathway I want to concentrate on in what follows.

Sound System UK

> 'Bass culture is folk culture, and the experiences of children around their parents' or even grandparents' sound systems are a vital part of how this is transmitted.'[17]

Mass migration from the British colonies of the Caribbean to Britain began in 1948, with the arrival of the now canonical SS *Windrush*, inaugurating a process that would bring in the region of 200,000 West Indians to Britain over the coming decades, which transformed the racial (and sonic) geography of the British city.[18] Just as the sound systems of Duke Reid and Clement 'Coxsone' Dodd were establishing themselves in Kingston in the mid-1950s, sound system pioneers Wilbert Campbell (Count Suckle) and Vincent Forbes (Duke Vin), who arrived together in 1952 having stowed away aboard a banana boat from Jamaica, were setting up the first sound systems in the UK. Both had served apprenticeships with Tom Wong's Tom the Great Sebastian sound system (Duke Vin had been a selector for Wong and was one of the early pioneers of reggae toasting), the champion Kingston sound until Wong was (literally) muscled out by Duke Reid and his posse. Duke Vin established the very first UK-based sound system in Notting Hill in 1954 – Duke Vin the Ticklers – swiftly followed by Count Suckle.[19] But these two were just the first of a generation of Jamaican migrants to the UK who passed on the knowledge they had accrued at home – combining the skills of audio engineering and carpentry, musical selection, and the logistical knowledge and hosting capabilities needed to, in Jamaican parlance, 'keep' the dance.

The character of British racism of the mid-late twentieth century broke cover in the light of the arrival of Black migrants from the British Caribbean from 1948 onwards – the period during which, according to historian Bill Schwarz, Britain 'discovered itself as white', just as Caribbean migrants to Britain, no matter their place on the Caribbean racial and class hierarchy, were, in Stuart Hall's words, 'discovering themselves as Black'.[20] Britain's Black urban communities, put under daily pressure from racist street thugs and violent forms of over-policing, were forced into 'self-defensive black colonies'. Largely excluded by racism from accessing Britain's leisure spaces such as football matches, the pub, and nightclubs, Black communities were obliged to develop their own cultural institutions, the most important of which became the networks of sound systems that emerged rapidly from the mid-1950s. Because the unreliable British weather, as well as the ever-present threat of unwanted police attention, prevented sounds from accessing the kinds of outdoor lawns and gardens where Kingston sounds set up,[21] UK sounds had to be inventive in finding spaces to play: private houses, squats, and shebeens (unlicensed drinking and social clubs), municipal buildings like church halls and town halls, where they could offer Black communities a 'relatively autonomous' space of security, enjoyment, and employment, a space within which counter-history could be shared and a Black British identity could be forged.[22]

During the 1960s and 1970s sound systems in the UK built a powerful integrated network of blues parties, dances, sessions, and sound clashes. Frequent sound clashes and cup dances,[23] where sound systems would compete with each other on the basis of the biggest, and sweetest bass and the freshest tunes, took place between sound systems from different areas of the city, and between different cities, creating an autonomous interconnected musical ecosystem operating outside the purview of the state (except when raided by police, which was a common occurrence in the 1970s and 1980s) and also outside the circuits of the commercial music industry, which largely ignored sound systems since they could not find a way to commodify them. These were spaces in which 'inter-family and peer group links were created and solidified', and where community was formed.[24] Here Blackness, treated with disdain if not outright hostility and violence in the country at large, could be reclaimed, loudly celebrated, and adapted to new circumstances, especially once the religio-political worldview of Rastafari, which offered the urban poor an alternative philosophy of resistance and liberation, and an explanation of the deep connection between racism and capitalist exploitation, began to predominate in 'roots' reggae from the early 1970s, voiced by militant dreadlocked figures like Bob Marley and Burning Spear.[25] Here 'alternative notions of being Black, both positive and negative, [were] discursively debated and disseminated across the urban landscape'.[26] By the mid-1970s there were hundreds of such sound systems in British cities, from the small and hyper-local to the mighty and celebrated, like Saxon from south-east London, Quaker City from Birmingham, and the Sir Coxsone Outernational from Brixton, which grew so big by the late 1970s that it split into two so it could play in different venues, even different cities, on the same night.

Alongside pioneers like Suckle and Vin and their heirs like Lloyd Coxsone and Jah Shaka, who operated the big, established sounds, were the generations of Caribbean families who played music at home, and built a sound system legacy from the ground up by gradually enhancing their domestic hi-fis – often the famed Blaupunkt (Blue Spot) radiogram – with bigger speakers and more amplifier power that enabled them to both steep their own families in the music of Afro-America, Jamaica, and West Africa, and to provide entertainment and inspiration information for the community at large. Thus, an appreciation of Afro-diasporic music, as well as an understanding of sound system practice and technology, was passed on through the Afro-Caribbean household, one of the most important – and overlooked – sites of pedagogy and the transmission of sonic knowledge. Reggae musician, producer, and dub innovator Dennis Bovell, for example, who came to the UK from Barbados in 1965 to join his mother, a nurse, and father who worked on London Underground in Battersea, south London, describes the sonic environment he grew up in like this:

> My dad was a record collector. He got records from America, from the Caribbean, because he had a sound system and whenever they had time off they'd have a party at someone else's house because they weren't into going to clubs and stuff. Then all the bus drivers and conductors and that would converge on the house and all the nurses from the nursing home and some doctors and medical people and then they would mix whilst my dad played his sound system.[27]

These parties were not entirely racially exclusive – his parents had white as well as Black co-workers and friends – but they were primarily a way in which the urban Black community were able to socialise, decompress, and innovate away from the harsh racial regime and surveillance that characterised life outside on the 'frontline'.[28]

Future Generations

A similar story can be told about subsequent generations of Black British musical innovators. Take a DJ like Norman Jay, from west London. A fixture on the London scene and, since the 1990s, international circuits of club culture, Jay's trajectory can tell us something about how the Jamaican sound system model was adapted to new circumstances in the UK. His father collected records – jazz, soul, R&B, ska – owned a Bush radiogram record player and music was ever-present at home especially on Sundays and at family parties. Norman's record collecting career started early, as he recounts in his autobiography *Mister Good Times*: aged ten he was sent with a fiver down to Webster's record stall ('a black record store where all the big boys went') in Shepherds Bush market to buy a batch of the latest 45s, to be played at family parties.[29] It was here that young Norman got the first hints of a social world around Black music, beyond the domestic space of his father's parlour sound system: 'to me the record shop, the black ones anyway, were a social place, a hub'.[30]

As a teenager Norman set up a reggae sound system, Great Tribulation, with his younger brother Joey (who had learnt engineering, as so many before him, from dismantling and rebuilding his parent's radiogram). But soon Norman was using the set to play not reggae but the soul, disco, funk, and hip-hop, which made up the mix in London club culture of the mid-1980s. He renamed the sound system Good Times and began a three-decade-long association with Notting Hill Carnival, where Good Times was one of the only systems not playing a strictly Jamaican repertoire. Jay became the leading figure of the 'rare groove' moment of the mid-1980s, when American funk of the late 1960s and 1970s was redeployed to a new audience in a sound system context, often at parties in disused industrial buildings, known as warehouse parties, which were based on the peripatetic model established by reggae sound systems.[31] Jay, who was also a DJ on the prominent pirate radio station KISS FM, describes the attitude that framed the warehouse parties as 'very sound system, very punk'.[32] As a DJ, Jay traced the evolution of Black dance music as successive waves broke, incorporating electro, hip-hop, and then the newer strains of New York, New Jersey, and Chicago house as import records began arriving in the UK from the mid-1980s (he also bought his fair share on his frequent trips to New York). But throughout his five-decade-long career Jay never deviated far from the sound system model in which he had been raised – big speakers, carefully balanced bass tones, and a concern with the dancing crowd, based on a recognition that the relationship established in the antiphonal communication between DJ and crowd lies at the heart of the nightclub experience.

Another example, this time from the mid-1990s, shows how the process of sound system culture feeding new innovations in electronic music continued. Paul Chambers, the north London founder of London's jungle label Ibiza Records in the mid-1990s, drew on both his experience of rave culture at the end of the 1980s and the reggae sound system culture of north London within which he grew up to innovate the jungle genre, which blended reggae basslines and sound system aesthetics with the electronic music of the rave scene: house and acid house, techno, Italo-house, Belgian NuBeat, hardcore. What for the young Paul was an in-depth sonic education was, for his father, also a source of income: 'that's how my dad was actually making money', he stated in the film *Bass Culture* in 2017, 'holding blues parties in our own house'.

In that same film, produced as part of the AHRC-funded Bass Culture research project led by Mykaell Riley at the University of Westminster, we hear testimony from a range of British electronic dance music artists representing distinct, but interlocking, genres – house, jungle, drum and bass, UK garage, grime, UK funky, and drill – on their familial links to sound system culture: Fonti, the DJ from the UK garage outfit Heartless Crew, had an Uncle Dennis who ran the Enforcer Sound System; Megaman from the UK garage collective So Solid Crew grew up surrounded by the music and tech of his dad's west London Sound, Memphis ('we woke up with it, we slept with it, we bathed with it'); Rapper Nadia Rose's dad also ran a sound system, as did grime MC Ghstly XVIII's; producer Terry T also grew up in a house with a sound system; 'I've got so many memories of waking up inside the speaker box,' he recalls. 'I was hooked on bass.' Rapper Roots Manuva, jungle producer and DJ Jumping Jack Frost, jungle producer Shy FX, grime MCs Ratty, Wiley, and Kano, the Drill Crew 67, all had close family who ran sound systems and their obsession with bass, 'crisp' tops (i.e. well-defined sound in the higher frequencies), and appropriate music selection, as well exposure to the antiphonic arts of the rewind and toasting, started young and informed their later musical innovations. The basement of grime producer Jammer's house in north London, a key site for the development of grime, was where Jammer's father, the reggae musician Jerry Power, kept his sound system and encouraged aspirant teenage rappers like Dizzee Rascal, Kano, and Wiley to trade bars in a competitive spirit informed by the practice of reggae toasting and the competitive sound system ethos.[33]

The multi-generational relationship between sound system culture and innovation in electronic dance music repeats in any UK city with a sizable Black population where sound systems had taken hold: Birmingham, Wolverhampton, Liverpool, Huddersfield, Sheffield, Bristol, Leeds, Manchester. Gerald Simpson, for example, an electronic music producer who records under the name Guy called Gerald, known best for the hugely influential recording 'Voodoo Ray' (one of the first UK techno releases to betray the influence of acid house and which spent eighteen weeks on the UK chart in 1989), grew up in the Moss Side area of Manchester, amongst his father's copious record collection and the sound system events which saturated the neighbourhood. His musical style draws on sound system sonics, the jazz-funk and electro-funk he danced to as a teenager, and the influence of house, which reached him via the younger Black 'soul' sound systems of the neighbourhood.[34] Bristol, in the south-west, provides another example of a family-related apprenticeship which provided the musical and technical background for a generation of Bristol musicians to innovate new forms: Roni Size cut his teeth selecting on his brother Carl's sounds system Digitech, through which he met his future collaborator DJ Krust;[35] the graffiti and music production crew The Wild Bunch adopted a sound system form of organisation and aesthetics, and blended hip-hop and soul with the fundamentals of sound system bass in the music made by their later incarnation Massive Attack and that of the idiosyncratic vocalist Tricky (Adrian Thaws), whose father Ray Thaws operated the Studio 17 sound system, one of the biggest in Bristol at the time.

Beyond Race

Although sound systems and the intricate networks around them played a profound role in the life of Britain's Black communities, their influence was not confined within racial borders. The nature of British racial geography, which has never seen the kinds of segregation typical of, say, American cities, meant that reggae music and sound system practices spilled over beyond the confines of the Black 'colony', and white Britons who shared housing estates, schools, and social space with Black people could easily fall under their spell, even far from the urban centre.

One such is the producer Adrian Sherwood, who has been a key figure on the UK dub scene, blending reggae with elements of post-punk and electronic music, with his Bristol-based sound system and label On-U Sound as well as the bands Tackhead and African Head Charge. Sherwood grew up in High Wycombe in Buckinghamshire, far from the urban sound system strongholds. However, he did have Black friends at school, many from the small island of St Vincent, who inducted him into the local circuits of sound system. He would hang around at his mate Gilbert Barker's house, whose parents had a big valve system, his sister had a collection of 45s, and his parents would cook up West Indian food as they listened. Sherwood was struck by the fact that whereas his own parents would have shouted for the music to be turned down, Gilbert's parents embraced and encouraged it. Then he was invited to a party: 'They brought in a sound system and I was like "Bloody Hell, this is Great". Really good bass end, and everybody dancing, a proper family thing, lots of friends and little kids, right through to the old folks.'[36] This exposure led Sherwood on a path that would see him become one of the UK's most influential dub and dance music innovators.

A generation later, Mark Quinn, aka the electronic producer and DJ Optical, grew up in a family of Irish migrants amongst the West Indian community of Shepherds Bush in London:

My next-door neighbours were in a reggae band. I can remember my mum holding her plates in the side cabinet when they were practising and going 'I love this music' but all the plates are going [shaking] on the wall . . . The effect that had on me was, you know, I've just got to be part of this . . . The Irish like to party . . . so our community was always drawn towards the reggae community I think in that way, we had something in common . . . dancing and drinking and having fun and loud music.[37]

The model of the sound system, not merely – or even – in terms of a physical sound system but as an integrated crew able to host and manage a dance and compete with other crews, just as the sound systems did at cup dances and sound clashes, was carried over into the structure of new electronic scenes like UK garage and grime. Whether or not in possession of an actual physical system, collectives like Top Buzz, So Solid, Heartless Crew, Pay As U Go Cartel, Boy Better Know, and the Dreem Team organised themselves like sound systems, and competed with other crews in staged battles that replicated the sound clash model.

Through the 'afro-technology'[38] of sound system culture ska and reggae began eventually to fuse with other genres – soul, jazzfunk, punk, synth-pop, electro, hip-hop, acid house – to integrate new technology and to nurture the emergence of what the Bristol drum and bass producer Roni Size named as 'new forms'. As the music writer Joe Muggs argues, sound systems and the 'bass culture' they inaugurated[39] have had a particularly important influence on music in the UK, where reggae met 'disco, electronic experimentation, and psychedelic bohemianism',[40] and given the prominence of the UK as an incubator of global club culture, it is partly through this route that sound system practice has acquired a truly global reach:

[This] low-end experimentation that took its cues from the music that came over with the Windrush generation of Caribbean immigrants and their children, injected its influence into the cultural circulatory system of the nation, and from there sent genre after new genre out into the world.[41]

Sound Science

Electronic dance music has benefited directly from the sonic innovations and attentiveness to audio-acoustics of the reggae sound systems, which using Robert Farris Thompson's terminology could be described as 'alternate academies, sites where people with no recognised status in societies as artists or performers hone their craft'.[42] As sound system researcher Julian Henriques has argued, sound systems bred and disseminated a particular kind of listening, and 'such listening ... has been developed through an apprenticeship system between the generations of Jamaican Sound System Engineers'.[43]

Since the early days of Hedley Jones, through the 'big men' sounds and on to the later work of engineers in the UK, like Harold Pettigrew (who designed Coxsone's famous pre-amp, Magnum), Barracuda, Metro (the Jamaican-born engineer behind Jah Shaka's monster 1,000-watt valve amp), the speaker-box maker Shortman (whose father was a carpenter), Jah Tubby, and, in the 2000s, Mark 'Mostec' Skeete (the pre-amp designer who has provided equipment for systems such as Jah Lokko, Roots Injection, and Bass-I), and many others (Carayol, ND), sound system engineers had a huge influence not only on the sound of the reggae systems they built, but also on the expectations of audiences.

Exposure to the superior audio quality of sound systems helped train the ears of a generation of producers and dancing crowds, spurring nightclubs on to up their sonic game. When Count Suckle started his residency at The Roaring Twenties club in Carnaby Street, Soho, in 1961, becoming the first sound system operator to be resident in a London nightclub, most West End nightclubs had underpowered systems with a distinctly thin bottom end. But the influence of Suckle's sound, and that of Sir Coxsone, who started a similar residency at The Flamingo in the early 1970s, demonstrated the depth and texture of sound that could be produced using a carefully calibrated assemblage of amps and speakers, painstakingly tested and balanced in real time. The specifications of the in-house sound systems at later purpose-built nightclubs like The Ministry of Sound, The End, and Plastic People, where house, jungle, dubstep, and other electronic genres were developed, betray the influence of sound system design especially in the depth and range of the bass.

In his analysis of the dancehall sound system set, Julien Henriques describes the meticulous and quasi-mystical craft involved in stringing up and tuning such an assemblage:

Every electromagnetic power, control or transduction device can be the subject of compensation, from the needle on the record to the speaker cones. The engineer listens and then adjusts, monitors, and then manipulates the value of a component. He monitors, he substitutes, he listens again, and so on. Based upon the auditory feed-back of what he hears, the engineer gradually closes he gap between what he is hearing and that for which he is listening. Explaining this process of fine-tuning further, 'Musical sounds are notoriously difficult to describe, but "clarity," "bounce," and "sweetness" are some of the terms used for the desired sonic qualities of the set. Most import [sic] of these is "balance."'[44]

Sound systems are not the only influence on the sound of contemporary dance music and nightclubs. In the 1970s and 1980s these sound system innovations were running parallel to the sonic engineering of sound designers in New York, like Alex Rosner and Richard Long, who specialised in kitting out the nightclubs that were popping up to serve the explosion of disco. Rosner specialised in clarity, achieving a crystalline sound, and designing a bespoke tweeter arrangement for David Mancuso's legendary Loft nights, which are frequently cited as the model for all subsequent club culture. Long, who had worked for Rosner before striking out on his own, was the man behind the punchier big bass systems at Studio 54, Zanzibar, and Paradise Garage, where, respectively, DJs Nicky Siano, Tony Humphries, and Larry Levan were laying down the blueprint for electronic dance music culture of the twenty-first century.

Rosner and Long's contributions to club culture have long been acknowledged, whereas the engineers of mobile sound systems go largely unacknowledged outside the reggae community. This is particularly problematic when we consider the difference between the resources Rosner and Long had at their disposal, and those available to the sound systems. Rosner and Long were working on big budgets for wealthy night-time entrepreneurs; reggae sound systems were built on a tight budget, handmade often from scavenged components and carpenter castoffs, and often built and maintained by the very same people who were playing music on them. Rosner and Long would drop by the nightclubs to tweak the systems, and be on call to fix and replace parts, but reggae sound systems had their engineers on hand to string up and balance the sound for each location, to maintain the balance through the night, and optimise the experience in real time. The engineers were from the same community as the operators, selectors, and dancers, and shared a love for the culture of music and dance. They orchestrated a direct and intimate relationship between the set and the dancing crowd. While in-house sound systems could be set up once to suit the acoustics of the space, mobile dance sound systems needed to be set up again and again in different venues, from houses to warehouses, each venue a new acoustic challenge.

Dub Aesthetics

While the sound system is an integrated system, it is itself part of a larger integrated system that links music production – recording, labels, studios – with live performance (the dance), with the dancing crowd. Here the sound system can be imagined as a kind of mobile production studio, where music on record is 'live mixed' using effects, equalisers, amps, and the voice of the deejay. Simon Jones and Paul Pinnock underscore this point by transcribing a sound clash between the Birmingham system Scientist and the Sheffield Sound Syndicate from 1983. This reveals that any given dance is itself a unique live performance composed partly of prior performances – the records – but enhanced and manipulated, re-performed in real time. Here a rewind, vocal interjection, or the flanging sound effects created by Scientist's bespoke effects box – named geng-geng – and the audience responses to these, rather than mere interruptions or embellishments of the authentic moment of the record, become part of the unique performance itself.[45] It is this symbiotic relationship that had previously led to the development of dub.

The art of dropping out elements of a dub mix – usually the lead vocal and often many other instruments – to emphasise the psychedelic properties hidden in the tunes and the woozy bass frequencies, emerged in Jamaica at the end of the 1960s due, as so many innovations in Black music, to a happy accident. Around 1972 engineer King Tubby, who operated the Hometown Hi-Fi sound system, was experimenting by playing a dub-plate (a one-off acetate, access to which greatly enhanced the reputation of a sound system) of a recording where the vocal 'dropped out of the sound mix in a trail of echo'.[46] The crowd went ballistic and inspired Tubby and fellow engineers to create more 'dub' versions of familiar songs, demonstrating the feedback loop that links studio production with audience response via the sound system. Soon reggae singles began to be produced with a dub version on the B-side, ideal as a musical bed for the toasting deejay to improvise over.

Building on the practice of 'versioning', the distinctly Jamaican practice of creating bespoke rhythm tracks ('riddims') that could be severed from the original song and reused for new songs,[47] which was enabled by Jamaica's hands-off attitude to intellectual property law, visionary engineers in Jamaica like King Tubby, Lee 'Scratch' Perry, Scientist, Jack Ruby, and Augustus Pablo, and those in the UK like Dennis Bovell and Neal

Fraser aka Mad Professor developed a new music-technical language which served both an economic and artistic imperative.[48] Economically it was good business to recycle already-existing musical patterns into new commodities, but this does not exhaust the significance of dub. Through dub, producers would become artists,[49] anticipating the structure of electronic dance music where the producer, rather than a band or singer, predominates, just as modified versions of songs – remixes – have become a staple of dance music culture.

Dub engineers would bring their dub plates – acetates – to the dance to test them on the system and with the crowd. This was a democratic form of peer review, enabling engineers to isolate those effects and mixes that really worked, and to refine and remix those that failed to move the crowd. This practice had a significant and lasting impact on dance music culture. The practice of bringing unfinished and unreleased dubs into the club to test on the crowd became, for example, a significant part of the emergent drum and bass culture in the UK in the 1990s at clubs like Metalheadz, at The Blue Note in Hoxton Square, where DJ/producers like Goldie, Peshay, Fabio and Grooverider, and Dillinger would test run new tunes; at Plastic People in Shoreditch, whose bass-heavy sound system was modelled on a reggae sound; and at DMZ at Mass in Brixton, a crucible for dubstep, where producers like Mala, Benga, and Plastician would test run their new cuts.

The Voice

One final way in which sound system culture influenced electronic dance music culture is in the foregrounding of the MC's voice on the microphone. It was in the late 1960s in Jamaican sound system culture, through the emergence of the reggae toaster, the first of whom was Count Machuki, followed by U-Roy and King Stitt[50] and then a whole new generation, including I-Roy, Dillinger, Nicodemus and Brigadier Jerry, Eek-A-Mouse and Yellowman, that a new style of performance was developed, coinciding with versioning and dub. One of the great advantages of the dub version was that it cleared out space in the mix, especially in the vocal range, for performers to take up the microphone in the dance and embellish the rhythm with rhymes, insider chat, shout outs, and improvisations. Known in reggae culture as toasters or deejays (marking the connection to the jive-talking radio disc jockey which was a primary influence), these vocalists – each of whom developed their own idiosyncratic style, and delivered dense lyrical performances which would combine 'guidance', the 'championing' of the sound, and 'instruction' to the dancers[51] – gradually moved to the fore in sound system culture, eventually supplanting the golden-age reggae singers like Dennis Brown and Gregory Isaacs, and coming to dominate dancehall, where deejays like Chaka Demus, Beenie Man, Elephant Man, and Vybz Cartel became the genre's biggest stars.

Reggae deejays were an aspect of British sound systems too, although until the mid-1980s they were often little more than derivative copyists of the Jamaicans. But with a new generation of sound systems and toasters in the early 1980s, particularly those around the London-based Saxon Sound System such as Peter King, Papa Levi, Tippa Irie, Smiley Culture, and Asher Senator, a distinctly British style emerged, which instead of repeating Jamaican-derived lyrics about the Yard and Jamaican politics, developed themes more in keeping with the context of the British city, and evolved a more rapid form of delivery known as 'fast chat'. These developments did not go unnoticed back in Jamaica, where Philip Levi's 'Mi God Mi King', produced by Maxi Priest and Paul 'Barry Boom' Robinson from the Saxon stable, reached number one in the Jamaican chart in 1984. That same year Smiley Culture charted in the UK with 'Cockney Translation'. This UK take on sound system lyricism created ripples that would lap across many different genres – Saxon Studio International DJs were acknowledged as a big influence on the emergence of a distinctive British style of rap by Rodney P of the London Posse; the emergence of a generation of jungle MCs, most of whom had cut their teeth in sound systems like GQ. MC Dett, 5-0, Navigator, General Levy, Apache Indian, Shabba, and Stevie Hyper-D demonstrated the direct path from the reggae sound system to the digital dance floor. When the next generation took what the jungle and UK garage MCs had done in the dance and developed it as a recorded genre, mixing patois, cockney, street slang, and references to US hip-hop with a frosty stripped-down digital backdrop with heavy bass, grime was born.[52]

Outro: The Ethics of Antiphony

In this chapter, I have shown how the developments in reggae sound system culture – in terms of engineering and the ethics of listening, in terms of the primacy of the bass, in terms of dub deconstruction and its influences on remix culture, and in terms of the role of the MC – have fed into and profoundly influenced electronic dance music. I have demonstrated that there is a direct line between sound systems and specific electronic genres like jungle/drum and bass, dubstep, and grime. It might be objected that these electronic music genres only amount to a small corner of electronic dance music culture, and are arguably less important than, say, trance, 'big room' house, or techno in terms of reach or scale. But this is to misunderstand the racialised structure of the popular music industry, which feeds off the creativity of the marginalised while rewarding those who can successfully assimilate and translate Black music styles into white popularity, something the American music theorist Reebee Garafalo describes as 'black roots, white fruits'.[53] While genres like techno and trance eschew sonic and musical elements that are too obviously coded as Black – for example the dialectical MC vocals and reggae-inspired basslines that permeate jungle and other two-step genres – nonetheless these genres continue to rely on the rhythmic and audio aesthetic legacy of sound systems and bass culture. As the UK garage DJ Spoony suggests, many working within contemporary electronic dance music scenes, like trance and techno, might not have been directly influenced by sound system culture, but the people who influenced them were. Warehouse parties, outdoor raves and doofs, and teknivals still bear the traces of bass-heavy mobile sound systems.

Reggae sound systems have declined in number and influence in both Jamaica and the UK since their late-twentieth-century heyday. Gentrification-inspired noise abatement legislation, the installation of noise limiters into many venues, and spurious security concerns have led to the shrinking availability of places for sound systems to play, and new electronic dance music genres have reduced the size of the audience for roots reggae. Though there has been a roots revival in Jamaica, with the emergence of artists fusing conscious roots reggae with digital dancehall like Protoje and Chronixx, in the UK powerful roots systems like those of Jah Shaka, Channel One, and Aba-Shanti-I continue to uphold the roots reggae tradition, while producer/operators like Joe Awira (Mad Professor's son) and Young Warrior (Jah Shaka's son) perform twenty-first-century dub on their newly crafted system (having had their original one stolen during lockdown), reggae sound systems no longer occupy the central position in Black British or Jamaican social and cultural life they once did. However, reggae sound system culture is far from dead; it has spread again: according to Dennis Bovell, the real heartlands of the reggae sound system these days can be found in Germany, France, Italy, Israel, and Argentina.[54]

The explosion of the Jamaican music economy from a cottage industry into a global force from the mid-1960s onwards, and the development of reggae, dub, and much later derivations like the digitised rhythms of dancehall, were inextricably tied to the social and political qualities of community-building and pleasure afforded by sound systems' practices of transfiguring public spaces into dance parties. The legacy of sound system culture can still be heard in the performance practices of electronic dance music genres such as jungle, drum and bass, underground garage, grime, and dubstep.[55] In short, sound system practices live on in the everyday aspects of electronic dance music culture – in the care and patience given to the reproduction and re-performance of recorded sound, in the remixing and dubbing of new music recordings, in the sonic manipulations of the DJ and producer (such as the rewind and the use of reverb), and in the antiphonal ethics of the very best dance parties and clubs, where recorded music, reproduction equipment, and dancing crowd – that is technology and the human – work together and strive for the perfect balance.

Notes

1. 'Navigator: The Evolution of a London MC', *Beat Culture London*, www.youtube.com/watch?v=F1Hwuu0V9Ak (accessed 24 August 2023).
2. Keyes, C. L. (2004) *Rap Music and Street Consciousness*. Urbana and Chicago: University of Illinois Press, 50–60.
3. Bradley, L (2001) *Bass Culture: When Reggae Was King*. London: Penguin; Katz, D. (2024) *Solid Foundation: An Oral History of Reggae*. London: White Rabbit.
4. James, M. (2020) *State of Bass: Origins of Jungle/Drum & Bass*. London: Velocity Press; Belle-Fortune, B. (2004) *All Crews*. London: Vision Publishing.
5. Hutton, C. 'Forging Identity and Community Through Aestheticism and Entertainment: The Sound System and The Rise Of The DJ', *Caribbean Quarterly*, 53:4 (2007), 17–31.
6. David Katz and Saxon Baird, *Ring the Alarm: A History of Sound System Culture* (2022), https://afropop.org/audio-programs/ring-the-alarm-a-history-of-sound-system-culture?curator=MusicREDEF (accessed 24 August 2023).
7. Jones S., and Pinnock, P. (2017) *Scientists of Sound: Portraits of a UK Reggae Sound System*. London: Baseline Books, p. 3.
8. See Hutton, 'Forging Identity and Community'.

9. Henriques, J. (2011) *Sonic Bodies. Reggae Sound Systems, Performance Techniques and Ways of Knowing*. London and New York: Continuum, p. 9.
10. William (Lez) Henry. (2006) *What the Deejay Said: A Critique from the Street!* London: Nu-Beyond, p. 151.
11. Chude-Sokei, L. (2015) *The Sound of Culture: Diaspora and Black Technopoetics*. Middletown, CT: Wesleyan University Press, p. 49.
12. Gilroy, P. (1993) *The Black Atlantic: Modernity and Double-Consciousness*. Massachusetts: Harvard University Press, pp. 6–7.
13. Of relevance here is the 'outernational' research project. Brian D'Aquino, Julian Henriques, and Leo Vidigal, 'A Popular Culture Research Methodology: Sound System Outernational', *Volume!*, 13:2 (2017), 163–75.
14. Lipsitz, G. 'The Racialization of Space and the Spatialization of Race: Theorizing the Hidden Architecture of Landscape', *Landscape Journal*, 26:1 (2007), 10–23. http://www.jstor.org/stable/43323751.
15. Kool Herc's 1970s block parties in the Bronx, NYC, initially offered a welcome alternative to New York's discotheques (dance clubs), which felt unsafe and were inaccessible for young people. See, for example: https://rockthebells.com/articles/jamaican-soundsystem-culture-history/.
16. Mitchell, T. (2001) 'Introduction. Another Root: Hip-Hop outside the USA'. In T. Mitchell (ed.), *Global Noise: Rap and Hip-Hop Outside the USA*. Middletown CT: Wesleyan University Press, pp. 1–38.
17. Muggs, J., 'Introduction'. In J. Muggs and B. D. Stevens (2019) *Bass, Mids, Tops: An Oral History of Sound System Culture*. London: Strange Attractor Press, pp. 14–23, p. 17.
18. Melville, C. (2020) *It's a London Thing: How Rare Groove, Acid House and Jungle Remapped the City*. Manchester: Manchester University Press.
19. Melville, *It's a London Thing*, p. 53.
20. Hall, S. 'Cultural Identity and Cinematic Representation', *Framework: The Journal of Cinema and Media*, 36 (1989), 68–81.
21. Hutton, 'Forging Identity and Community', p. 18.
22. Gilroy, P. (2004) *After Empire: Melancholia or Convivial Culture?* Oxford: Routledge.
23. See, for example, Paul Bradshaw (2019) 'System Clash: Sir Coxson Outernational'. *Red Bull Music Academy*. https://daily.redbullmusicacademy.com/2013/05/system-clash-sir-coxson-outernational.
24. Jones and Pinnock, *Scientists of Sound*, p. 7.
25. Gilroy, P. (2010) *Darker Than Blue: On the Moral Economies of Black Atlantic Culture*. Massachusetts: Harvard University Press.
26. Henry, *What the Deejay Said*, p. 93.
27. 'Navigator: The Evolution of a London MC'.
28. See Hall, S., Cohen, P., and Schwarz, B. (1998) *Frontlines Backyards*. London: Lawrence and Wishart.
29. Jay, N. (2019) *Mister Good Times*. London: Dialogue, p. 87.

30. Jay, *Mister Good Times*, p. 89.
31. Melville, *It's a London Thing*.
32. Jay, *Mister Good Times*, p. 298.
33. D. J. Target (2018) *Grime Kids: The Inside Story of the Global Grime Takeover*. London: Orion.
34. Rietveld, H. C. (2014) 'Voodoo Rage: Blacktronica from the North'. In Jon Stratton and Nabeel Zuberi (eds.), *Black Popular Music in Britain Since 1945*. Burlington VT and Farnham: Ashgate, pp. 153–68.
35. Muggs and Stevens, *Bass, Mids, Tops*, p. 215.
36. Muggs and Stevens, *Bass, Mids, Tops*, p. 55.
37. 'Navigator: The Evolution of a London MC'.
38. Chude-Sokei, *The Sound of Culture*.
39. Riley, M. (2014) 'Bass Culture: An Alternative Soundtrack to Britishness'. In Jon Stratton and Nabeel Zuberi (eds.), *Black Popular Music in Britain Since 1945*. Burlington VT and Farnham: Ashgate, pp. 101–14.
40. Muggs and Stevens, *Bass, Mids, Tops*, p. 15.
41. Ibid.
42. Thompson, quoted in George Lipsitz, 'The Racialization of Space and the Spatialization of Race: Theorizing the Hidden Architecture of Landscape', *Landscape Journal*, 26 (2007), 109.
43. Henriques, J. 'Auditory and Technological Culture: The Fine-Tuning of the Dancehall Sound System "Set"', *Journal of Sonic Studies*, 1 (2012), www.researchcatalogue.net/view/223120/223121.
44. Henriques, 'Auditory and Technological Culture', np. Henriques notes 'Women play a crucial role on the dancehall scene in numerous important respects, but none, as far as I have found, have become sound system engineers. I therefore refer to engineers with the male pronoun.'
45. Jones and Pinnock, *Scientists of Sound*, p. 99.
46. Jones and Pinnock, *Scientists of Sound*, p. 5.
47. Manuel P., and Marshall, W. 'The Riddim Method: Aesthetics, Practice, and Ownership in Jamaican Dancehall', *Popular Music*, 25:3 (2006), 447–70.
48. Vendryes, T. 'Versions, Dubs and Riddims: Dub and the Transient Dynamics of Jamaican Music', *Dancecult: Journal of Electronic Dance Music Culture*, 7:2 (2015), 5–24.
49. Chude-Sokei, *The Sound of Culture*, p. 56.
50. Hutton, C. 'Forging Identity and Community Through Aestheticism and Entertainment: The Sound System and The Rise Of The DJ', *Caribbean Quarterly*, 53:4 (2007), 16–110 www.jstor.org/stable/40654996.
51. Zuberi, N. (2014) '"New Throat Fe Chat": The Voices and Media of MC Culture 1'. In Jon Stratton and Nabeel Zuberi (eds.), *Black Popular Music in Britain Since 1945*. Burlington VT and Farnham: Ashgate, p. 185.
52. DJ Target, *Grime Kids*.

53. Garofalo, R. (2002) *Rockin' Out: Popular Music in the U.S.A*. Michigan: Pearson Education.
54. Personal interview with Dennis Bovell.
55. James, M. (2021) *Sonic Intimacy: Reggae Sound Systems, Jungle Pirate Radio and Grime YouTube Music Videos*. New York and London: Bloomsbury Academic; Henriques, J. (2011) *Sonic Bodies*.

Further Reading

Belle-Fortune, B. (2024) *All Crews*. London: Velocity Press.

Bradley, L (2001) *Bass Culture: When Reggae Was King*. London: Penguin.

Henriques, J. (2011) *Sonic Bodies. Reggae Sound Systems, Performance Techniques and Ways of Knowing*. London and New York: Continuum.

James, M. (2020) *State of Bass: Origins of Jungle/Drum & Bass*. London: Velocity Press.

Melville, C. (2020) *It's a London Thing: How Rare Groove, Acid House and Jungle Remapped the City*. Manchester: Manchester University Press.

4 | Let the DJ Tell the Story

Thoughts on Archiving and Genre Formation in the Age of Electronic Dance Music

KAI FIKENTSCHER

'Don't Judge People By their Color, Religion or Orientation. Judge them by their Record Collection.' (online meme)[1]

'I'm living and breathing music, all day and often all night. It's as if I built a rare book library over the last 40 years, and I'm flipping through the pages of every single volume.'[2]

The following discussion focuses on the DJ as a decisive force in the development of electronic dance music through the collection and management of music recordings. In this context, it is useful to distinguish between, on the one hand, the acronym 'EDM' as a rebranding of electronic dance music as a largely pop-dance, festival-based phenomenon of the second decade of the new millennium[3] and, on the other hand, electronic dance music as an umbrella music genre that, while convenient, is less descriptive or specific[4] than the DJ-driven categories of post-disco dance music it summarily refers to, such as house, techno, or dubstep. In order to connect the processes of synthesised proto-electronic dance music, such as Italo-disco or the iconic production work by Giorgio Moroder for Donna Summer's recording 'I Feel Love',[5] to post-disco dance music such as house, techno, and associated subgenres, the discussion proposes an examination of the DJ's relevance to the development of electronic dance music through their curatorial activities in collecting and archiving music recording and presenting these as collages to their audiences. The main argument here is that the development of post-disco dance music, involving the innovation and adaptation of new technologies as genre-defining factors, is essentially DJ-driven.[6]

Since the second decade of the new millennium, the acronym EDM has been used to distinguish early twenty-first-century dance music from late twentieth-century rave, the music played at eponymous festivals, first in the UK, then in the USA, as well as from electronica, an older category of electronic music marketed for listening as much as for dancing purposes.[7] While this distinction doesn't always hold,[8] the following discussion is based on the premise that electronic dance music of the late twentieth and early twenty-first century includes EDM (as millennial and post-millennial pop dance), rave, techno, and electronica, but is not limited to these categories. Rather, the creation, performance, dissemination, innovation, and development of most types of electronic dance music may be best understood when the DJ or DJ-producer is understood as the driving force in the genre formation of electronic dance music.[9] Most recently, DJs and DJ-producers of electronic dance music have taken on the additional roles of archivist and historian, confirming their central role in telling the story of the dance music that by now is an inextricable part of global popular culture.

The two roles of pioneer and archivist are related, not least due to technological innovations, as both DJ musicianship and the practice of archiving have moved into the digital realm. While a digital archive of electronic dance music presents its own challenges,[10] preserving and curating analogue archives is now more urgent than ever.[11] DJ collections, consisting chiefly of vinyl recordings, have grown in their role as canon-shaping institutions, exemplified by the recent attention given to the record collection of influential house music DJ Frankie Knuckles, housed in Chicago as of 2015,[12] with parts of this archive going on tour through the United States in 2021.[13] An even more recent example is the opening, in April 2022, of MOMEM (Museum of Modern Electronic Music), the world's first museum dedicated to electronic music, situated in Frankfurt, Germany.[14] The museum houses DJ Sven Väth's collection of about 20,000 vinyl records, many of which travelled the world with him during the 1990s, a time when the demand for his programme of electronic dance music (including his own productions) was peaking. On 6 April 2022, both Väth and fellow DJ Franziska Brems were commissioned to deejay at the museum's opening party, and both chose to play vinyl records that day, perhaps as a tribute to Väth's collection and the influence he exerted as resident DJ of several Frankfurt dance venues during the 1980s and 1990s, when vinyl recordings were prevalent.[15]

As the example of Väth's and Brems' opening vinyl-only DJ set illustrates, much electronic dance music history is told through the sum of recordings collected, circulated, promoted, managed, and, in many cases, produced by DJs. The tangible results of the processes spanning several decades are the record collections (or archives) of semi-professional and professional DJs, both active collections owned by living DJs and inactive collections owned by the estates of retired or deceased DJs (e.g. Knuckles). Access to this wealth of music is possible due to the durability and affordability of vinyl as a sound-carrier medium, which originally came in three main formats, the 7-inch single, the 10- or 12-inch EP and LP (long player) to which, since the mid-1970s, the so-called disco single, or 12-inch dance single, was added. Instances of lost archives or collections of vinyl records can be and are, at least in part, remedied by the digitisation of DJ mixtapes, exemplified by work done by the San Francisco Disco Preservation Society.[16]

With the literature on DJ cultures having grown by leaps and bounds during the last three decades, the DJ's multiple roles as musician, performer, composer, cultural gatekeeper, and secular shaman are now better understood. A latecomer to popular music studies, the many and varied contributions of the DJ to popular culture and popular music have been studied, compared, and commented on with considerable scrutiny.[17] Still, as popular music studies cover an ever-expanding time window, the genre-shaping force as exerted by DJs has not yet received sufficient scrutiny. DJs acting as innovators that end up shaping new genres are part of this still largely untold story that preceded and shaped the age of electronic dance music.

Between 1954 and 1958, radio jock Alan Freed called the type of music broadcast during his radio shows, programmed in Cleveland and later New York, 'rock and roll', thereby renaming rhythm and blues, an already-established category of US dance music.[18] Freed was not a club DJ, but his music programme, while not based on electronic sounds, shares with later DJ-driven dance music genres such as disco, house, techno, or jungle the ability of a newly minted type of music to attract followers across racial barriers, a socio-cultural innovation of considerable relevance, especially in the United States at the time. During the early 1970s, club DJs were to repeat this innovative process, creating 'disco music' from a heterogeneous soundtrack for equally heterogeneous segments of American society, which most noticeably resided in cities such as New York and San Francisco.[19] In the 1980s, local club DJs in Chicago and Detroit programmed music sets that attracted sexually and racially mixed crowds to regularly dance at underground venues such as The Warehouse (Chicago) and the Music Institute (Detroit). These two Midwest post-industrial cities are now considered the respective birthplaces of house music and techno music, two main genres of electronic dance music.[20] Parallel to the developments in Chicago and Detroit, European DJs, primarily in Germany and Belgium, began experimenting with electronic sounds in urban dance clubs.[21]

Even earlier, during the 1970s, disco-era DJs were also innovative in technological terms. Their work helped establish the 12-inch format as the main sound carrier from the mid-1970s on, well into the post-disco era.

The 12-inch format brought with it related changes in sound and compositional length, since this format provides more space for the groove than a 7-inch single, thereby widening the audio spectrum of the music – especially the bass frequencies, which are so important to moving the hips and dancing feet.[22] Following the example set by Tom Moulton, who produced extended mixes for disco labels such as Salsoul, disco producers doubled – even tripled – the length of the radio format of three to three and a half minutes for a song, responding to the priority of extended dancing in a dedicated space, in contrast to radio-listening habits that were conditioned by long-established radio and television conventions. When DJs began acting as music producers, bridging the technologies of the DJ booth and the recording studio, the electronic character of both environments came to define the sonic characteristics of the music itself.[23] In the process, analogue recording and playback equipment was gradually replaced by digital counterparts,[24] which in turn offer new affordances.

Most importantly for both genre formation and archival work regarding electronic dance music, professional DJs have an extensive working knowledge regarding repertoire. New York DJs such as the late David Mancuso or Larry Levan, for example, were known to have access to vast record collections that ranged widely in terms of musical style. Professional DJs act as living musical archives,[25] able to 'tell a story' by programming and mixing records. The way these stories are told becomes part of each DJ's individual style, which in turn forms the basis of their relationship with the dance floor, as well as of the definition of the dance music genre or subgenre.[26] This premise has not changed with the advent of digital audio, while the ways in which DJs access, organise, and present their repertoire have. The presence of metadata in dance music collections on vinyl, such as coloured cue marks and written annotations, gives valuable evidence of types of curation and categorisation that DJs engaged in before the switch to digital sound formats became the norm at the turn of the millennium.[27] The design of the normative Technics 1210 turntable, still in use by some DJs, although less frequently since the end of the twentieth century, has informed the design of various CDJ players, such as the Pioneer CDJ-1000 model that established Pioneer CD players as the new industry standard, especially after the MK2 model was introduced in 2003. Additionally, the rather quick development and easy availability of computer software for music recording and production purposes has made the laptop computer, combined with DJ software, another popular tool – especially for the travelling DJ.[28]

Both as a programme of music chosen for a night of dancing, and as a collection built up over years of playing music for dancing patrons, a DJ's record collection (or music archive) tells a story, the former on a micro, the latter on a macro level. Per night and per weekend, the story told through music differs, as comparable to performing jazz standards. Multiplied across places and years, even decades, these shared stories created and curated by DJs add up to histories of local dance cultures which in turn may amount to regional, even international, histories of dance music, thereby becoming essential components of DJ culture on a global scale. These histories may well be based on recordings of DJ sets dating back to the heyday of disco, though not necessarily.[29] Increasingly they can, and are, amplified and contextualised by first-hand accounts,[30] such as autobiographies and interviews,[31] and by practitioners of DJ scholarship,[32] even if work in the latter field has barely begun. In hindsight, my own ethnographic work on underground dance music in New York City would not have been possible without the gradual acquisition of DJ equipment and a sizable collection of 12-inch vinyl, both in LP and 12-inch single format, as well as the associated musicianship.[33] In 2013–14, I used these acquisitions as the basis for a monthly DJ set at Cafe am Hochhaus, Munich, Germany, calling the event 'The New York Experience'. Since the venue's closure 'The New York Experience' has returned to its static archival status,[34] the collection representing a historically and geographically framed chapter of (mostly) electronic dance music. This could also be said about what might very well be the largest dance music archive in New York City, veteran DJ Danny Krivit's record collection, over 80,000 strong, housed in his home and four additional storage locations while he continues to deejay regularly in the erstwhile capital of dance music, using primarily digital audio technology. What Knuckles archive means for Chicago, Krivit's collection means for New York City.[35]

The story of electronic dance music cannot be told without considering the total of music recordings as collected, circulated, promoted, archived, performed, and produced by DJs. A comprehensive history of electronic dance music will, however, not only depend on the stories DJs and their collections tell, but how these stories are received and made meaningful by those the DJ addresses, the dancers. These interpretations may depend less on audio technologies and more on the way music as sound relates to dance as movement in an interactive experience, as a collective dance experience.[36]

Notes

1. Whelan, Tim (21 January 2022). Meme shared on Facebook 'Don't Judge People by their Color, Religion or Orientation. Judge them by their Record Collection'. www.facebook.com/photo?fbid=10227707751698107&set=pb.1197173268.-2207520000 (accessed 6 June 2024).
2. Chan-Bevan, Julian (21 January 2022) – a personal Facebook statement on DJ Julian's activities. www.facebook.com/otm.shank.9/posts/4527213257402094 (accessed 6 June 2024).
3. For a detailed chronology, see Matos, Michaelangelo. 2015. *The Underground Is Massive: How Electronic Dance Music Conquered America*. New York: Dey Street Books.
4. The fuzzy character of 'electronic dance music' as a genre label is illustrated in the possibly first-ever instance of the use of 'EDM' as an acronym as early as 1980 for 'computer-programmed perfection for your listening pleasure' on the record cover of Landscape's 45 rpm single 'European Man' (RCA); the Spanish release of the same record, also on RCA, uses a cover featuring the repeated phrase 'dance music'. See also Kupfer, Rachel. 2022. 'Inside the Origins of Electronic Dance Music'. *EDM*. https://edm.com/features/inside-the-origins-of-electronic-dance-music (visited 1 June 2024).
5. Donna Summer (1977) 'I Feel Love'. Casablanca.
6. See, for example, Stanmore, Carl. 2021. 'The History of Electronic Dance Music: A Journey Through the Decades'. www.thedjrevolution.com/the-history-of-electronic-dance-music/ (accessed 10 May 2024).
7. Armada Music (2024); The Complete Guide to EDM (or Electronic Dance Music). www.armadamusic.com/news/edm-electronic-dance-music (last visited 6 June 2024); Collins, Nick. 2009. 'Electronica'. In Dean, Roger (ed.) *The Oxford Handbook of Computer Music*. Oxford: Oxford University Press, pp. 334–53.
8. See, for example, Osborne, Ben. 1999. *Twenty Years of Losing It: The A- Z of Club Culture*. London: Hodder & Stoughton, pp. 86–87.
9. This relevance is heightened even more by the fact that the early generation of original dance DJs is now passing away due to age or ill health.
10. As exemplified by DJ and scholar Lynnee Denise (www.djlynneedenise.com/bio), Andi Durant, co-founder of the Dance Music Archive (dancemusicarchive.com), or Brian Foo, Innovator in Residence at the Library of Congress and author of the project *Citizen DJ*, https://coffeehouse.dataone.org/2020/04/27/innovator-brian-foo-incorporates-citizen-djs-into-design-process/ (all accessed 5 May 2024).
11. Maloney, Liam, and Schofield, John (2 September 2022). 'Records on Records: Excavating the DJ's Sonic Archive'. *Archives & Records: The Journal of the*

Archives & Records Association, 43:3, 244–66. www.ingentaconnect.com/content/routledg/cjsa21/2022/00000043/00000003/art00002

12. Galil, Leon. 2015. 'Frankie Knuckles's Vinyl Gets a Permanent Public Home'. https://chicagoreader.com/music/frankie-knuckless-vinyl-gets-a-permanent-public-home/ (accessed 6 January 2024).
13. Townsend, Megan. 2021. 'Frankie Knuckles' Record Collection Is on Display in New York'. https://mixmag.net/read/frankie-knuckles-record-collection-display-new-york-news (accessed 1 August 2023).
14. Museum of Modern Electronic Music, Frankfurt, Germany. https://momem.org/ (accessed 1 August 2023).
15. Jägersberg, Wero, and Lief, Mariska (Directors). 2022. *Techno House Deutschland*. Documentary film, Frankfurt, Germany.
16. SF Disco Preservation Society. 2024. Preserving DJ & Nightclub History. www.sfdps.org (last visited 6 June 2024). Before the arrival of digital sound carriers, mixtapes were the main tool for DJs to document the artistic worth of their mix sets. Both reel-to-reel and cassette tape (and later DAT) were used in DJ booths in 1980s and 1990s US dance culture, such as in Chicago and New York. See also: Auerbach, Evan, and Isenberg, Daniel. 2023. *Do Remember! The Golden Era of NYC Hip-Hop Mixtapes*. New York: Rizzoli.
17. Bloustien, Geraldine, and Peters, Margaret. 2011. *Youth, Music, and Creative Cultures: Playing for Life*. London: Palgrave Macmillan, pp. 83–122; Poschardt, Ulf. 1998. *DJ Culture*. London: Quarter Books Ltd.; Fikentscher, Kai. 2000. *'You Better Work!' Underground Dance Music in New York City*. Middletown, CT: Wesleyan University Press; Fikentscher, Kai. 2013. "It's not the Mix, it's the Selection." Music Programming in Contemporary DJ Culture'. In Attias, B. A, Gavanas, A, and Rietveld, H. C. (eds.) *DJ Culture in the Mix: Power, Technology, and Social Change in Electronic Dance Music*. New York and London: Bloomsbury, pp. 123–49; Rietveld, H. C. 2013. 'Introduction'. In Attias, Gavanas, and Rietveld (eds.) *DJ Culture in the Mix*, pp. 1–14.
18. Peneny, D. K. 2023. *The History of Rock 'n' Roll, The Golden Decade 1954–1963*. www.history-of-rock.com/freed.htm (accessed 6 June 2024).
19. '"Steve Rubell [the founder of Studio 54] called it the mixed salad of cultures", says Eric Goode, a founder of Area, the famed '80s club in New York City … "That was something New York brought to nightlife: that mix of every gender, gay, straight, young, old, Black, white, Latin, whatever,"' in Trebay, Guy, 3 December 2020. 'New York City Was the Nightlife Capital of the World for Decades. Its History Will Be Its Future'. *Town & Country*. www.townandcountrymag.com/society/money-and-power/a34643600/new-york-city-global-capital-nightlife-history/ (accessed 22 August 2025).
20. Kolioulis, Alessio, and Rietveld, Hillegonda C. 2018. 'Detroit: Techno City'. In Lashua, B., Wagg, S., Spracklen, K., and Yavuz, M. S. (eds.) *Sounds and the City, Vol 2*. Cham: Palgrave Macmillan (Spinger), pp. 33–54; Sicko, Dan 2010. *Techno*

Rebels: Renegades of Electronic Funk. Detroit: Painted Turtle/Wayne State University Press; Rietveld, H. C. 2020. *This is Our House: House Music, Technologies, and Cultural Spaces*. London and New York: Routledge. See also: Abdelfatah, Rund et. al. 2023. 'From the Warehouse to the World: Chicago and the Birth of House Music'. www.npr.org/2023/03/02/1160484070/chicago-birth-of-house-music (visited 1 June 2023); Lee, Sammy, 'This Is the Story of a Techno Revolution'. *Red Bull Academy*. www.redbull.com/in-en/quickfire-history-of-detroit-techno (accessed 1 June 2024); Zlatopolsky, Ashley. 31 July 2014. 'The Roots of Techno: Detroit's Club Scene 1973–1985'. *Red Bull Academy*. https://daily.redbullmusicacademy.com/2014/07/roots-of-techno-feature (accessed 10 May 2024).

21. Examples are Sven Väth (Dorian Gray, Frankfurt, Germany) and Olivier Pieters (Boccaccio, Ghent, Belgium). See: Tomalia, Andreas. 2019. *Am Anfang war der Technoclub*. Frankfurt am Main: Henrich Editionen; Sextro, Maren, and Wick, Holger (Directors) (2008) *We Call It Techno*. Germany: Sense Music & Media, Media Atelier; Also: Reynolds, Simon. 1999. *Generation Ecstasy: Into the World of Techno and Rave Culture*. New York: Routledge.
22. Fikentscher, 'You Better Work', pp. 43–56.
23. Fikentscher, 'You Better Work', p. 48.
24. The emergence of dubstep in the early 2000s is a later example of this process, shown in the careers of UK-based DJ/producers such as DJ Hatcha, Skream, Mala, or Benga. See also Cook, Georgina. 2022. 'A Brief History of Early Dubstep'. *Museum of Youth Culture*. www.museumofyouthculture.com/a-brief-history-of-early-dubstep/ (visited 6 January 2024).
25. Fikentscher, 'It's not the Mix'; Rietveld, H. C. 2011. 'Disco's Revenge: House Music's Nomadic Memory'. *Dancecult: Journal of Electronic Dance Music Culture*, 2:1, 4–23. https://dj.dancecult.net/index.php/dancecult/article/view/298.
26. Sven Väth's close association with Frankfurt's techno scene is one example.
27. Maloney and Schofield, 'Records on Records'.
28. Butler, Mark. 2006. *Unlocking the Groove: Rhythm, Meter, and Musical Design in Electronic Dance Music*. Bloomington: Indiana University Press, p. 67.
29. For example, SF Disco Preservation Society (2024) https://sfdps.org/.
30. Popular music history includes second-hand accounts, including histories of dance music; for example: Aletti, Vince. 1973. 'Discotheque Rock '72: Paaaaarty!' *Rolling Stone Magazine*, 13 September 1973; Goldman, Albert. 1978. *Disco*. New York: Hawthorn; Haden-Guest, Anthony. 1997. *The Last Party: Studio 54, Disco, and the Culture of the Night*. New York: Morrow.
31. Examples include Brewster, Bill, and Broughton, Frank. 2022. *Last Night a DJ Saved My Life: The History of the Disc Jockey*. London: White Rabbit Books; Brewster and Broughton. 2018. 'Nicky Siano on the Gallery and the Dark Days of Disco'. Red Bull Music Academy. https://daily.redbullmusicacademy.com/2018/02/nicky-siano-interview-dj-history (visited 6 January 2024); DJ Disciple and Henry Kronk. 2023. *The Beat, the Scene, the Sound: A DJ's Journey through the*

Rise, Fall, and Rebirth of House Music in New York City. Washington, D.C.: Rowman & Littlefield Publishers; Haslam, Dave. 2018. *Sonic Youth Slept on My Floor: Music, Manchester, and More: A Memoir.* London: Constable; Saunders, Jesse. 2007. *House Music: The Real Story.* Baltimore: PublishAmerica.

32. For example: Denise, Lynee. 2014. 'The Afro Digital Migration: House Music in Post Apartheid South Africa'. www.djlynneedenise.com/menu (visited 1 August 2022); Compton, Wayde. 2015. 'DJ'. In Heble, Ajay, and Caines, Rebecca (eds.) *The Improvisation Studies Reader.* London: Routledge, pp. 443–46.

33. Fikentscher, Kai. 1991. 'Supremely Clubbed, Devastatingly Dubbed: Some Observations on the Nature of Mixes on 12-inch Dance Singles'. *Journal of Popular Music*, 1, https://onlinelibrary.wiley.com/doi/abs/10.1111/j.1533-1598.1991.tb00123.x (accessed June 1 2024); Fikentscher, 'You Better Work!'; Rietveld, Hillegonda C . 2007. 'The Residual Soul Sonic Force of the Vinyl 12" Dance Single'. In Ackland, C. (ed.) *Residual Media.* Minnesota: University of Minnesota Press, pp. 46–61.

34. Danny Krivit's vinyl archive is more or less solidified; he plays out using some of the same music, stored in digital formats.

35. THUMP (8 July 2016) 'Danny Krivit Reflects on 45 Years of DJing' www.youtube.com/watch?v=SpuzLGeAxb8 (visited 5 May 2024); Danny Krivit (n.k.) 'Danny Krivit. Biography' https://dannykrivit.net/biography (visited 5 May 2024).

36. Fikentscher, 'You Better Work!', pp. 79–92.

Further Reading

Attias, Bernardo Alexander, Gavanas, Anna, and Rietveld, Hillegonda C. (eds.) 2013. *DJ Culture in the Mix: Power, Technology, and Social Change in Electronic Dance Music.* New York and London: Bloomsbury.

Brewster, Bill, and Broughton, Frank. 2022. *Last Night a DJ Saved My Life: The History of the Disc Jockey.* London: White Rabbit Books.

Fikentscher, Kai. 2000. *'You Better Work!' Underground Dance Music in New York City.* Middletown, CT: Wesleyan University Press.

Matos, Michaelangelo. 2015. *The Underground is Massive: How Electronic Dance Music Conquered America.* New York: Dey Street Books.

Poschardt, Ulf. 1998. *DJ Culture.* London: Quarter Books Ltd.

PART II

Local and Global Contexts

5 | Party as Protest

Free Party, Teknivals, Early Rave Scenes, and Berlin's Hardcore Techno

BIANCA LUDEWIG

Introduction

This chapter addresses historic events related to the evolution of hardcore techno, and its intertwined genealogy with early rave and techno, in Europe during the late 1980s to the early 1990s. Illegal parties and a diverse sound system culture emerged in post-industrial Britain during this period, where acid house became the choice of a young party generation. Soon a harder and darker side of house music developed that was followed by London's Spiral Tribe, a party collective and sound system that later inspired the formation of 'teknivals' in mainland Europe. In Berlin, house music and techno arrived somewhat later, at a time that coincided with the fall of the Wall,[1] offering massive possibilities for partying due to empty buildings, vacant lots, and wastelands in East Berlin. Parallel to political transformations, a state of euphoria catalysed events such as the development of the free party movement in England, while Berlin saw the opening of various unusual dance venues and the introduction of the Love Parade. These events occurred while the computer and internet were evolving as a new means of communication and technology, and as the outcomes of a decade of neo-liberal, free market economies, such as those of Thatcherite Britain, were manifesting in many countries around Europe in political-economic cultures of privatisation, deregulation, commercialisation, and flexible labour.

The approach to the topic here is through a contemporary historical and ethnographic lens. I was not present at free parties in the UK nor was I in Berlin when the Wall came down, and I attended just a few teknivals or free tekno events. However, many of the people I have spoken with were there. During the past fifteen years I have lived on and off in Berlin and remain in contact with party people and continue attending events there. I am younger than most of the protagonists and musical activists under discussion here, but similarly exposed to German urban city life, politics, and underground music. Music has always been crucial for me: being a record collector since teenage times, writing about music as a journalist, and DJing helped me to keep going in an environment I largely rejected. New music genres – at least until the millennium – are usually linked to social and political developments. The following accounts of musical events can be interpreted in reaction to processes of economisation, gentrification of urban space, and the commercialisation of music and culture, in particular that of the techno party. The various ways in which it is perceived by its participants illustrate that the techno party has been a contested field from its inception.

The Early Rave Scene in Berlin

After the fall of the Berlin Wall, the West Berlin techno scene discovered the east of the city and nightlife shifted from posh clubs on Kurfürstendamm to the centre and east of the city, where empty, run-down cellars and halls were now available as venues. A semi-legal as well as an illegal party scene developed and East Berlin became the centre of this new techno scene, where countless spaces were occupied.[2] There were three reasons why Berlin became important to techno: the magic of the place, the energy of the sounds, and the freedom that promised everyone could make music. Plus, there was the disparate mix of people who attended the first techno parties: break-dancers from Alexanderplatz, the Schöneberg gay scene, the Kreuzberg squatter scene, British and US soldiers off duty.[3]

The early Berlin techno scene was also influential for the later emerging gabber and hardcore. As early as 1986, there were acid house parties at the Turbine Rosenheim in Schöneberg and the illegal UFO club (1988–89) in Berlin-Kreuzberg also presented new sounds: 'The UFO, a cellar underneath the DADA café Fischbüro, offered eighty to 100 enthusiastic dancers a futuristic ambience to create a new underground culture in Berlin.'[4] From 1989 onwards, the Love Parade became an annual meeting place for the local, and later the manifold national, scenes. Of special relevance for Berlin was the party series Tekknozid and a style of music that would become later known as techno started by Wolle XPD and others from East Berlin in 1990 with DJ Tanith as resident DJ. Johnnie Stieler, East Berliner and co-founder of Tresor, co-organiser of Tekknozid, and later operator of the Horst Krzbrg club, explains why:

Tanith filtered out electronic marginal fringes from EBM [Electronic Body Music] and noise, the smallest common multiple, which you can also confidently call techno; and that was something completely different from the Frankfurt sound, where this rather military-like four-to-the-floor sound was the order of the day. We were at record stores every day searching for something specific, but that wasn't acid house and neither was it EBM ... Tanith did exactly what we were looking for.[5]

The club Tresor – opened in 1991 by Dietmar Hegemann, alongside others – became famous for bringing Detroit techno to Berlin. Hegemann also produced the experimental Atonal Festival from 1989–91, where industrial, punk, and electronica came together. The club Bunker started in 1992,[6] showcasing the darker versions of electronic sounds. It was the first club in Berlin to play exclusively hardcore on one floor on some days of the week. From the beginning the evenings were under the apocalyptic motto 'Ready for the future? Prepare yourself for the worst' and the Bunker became popular as 'the hardest club on earth'.[7]

Another influence on the evolving Berlin hardcore scene was the British sound system Spiral Tribe, who were known for their fast and hard techno sounds: they reached Berlin by 1992, some in 1993, and joined the Mutoid Waste Company, who had collaborated with Spiral Tribe in London, a performance arts group founded by Joe Rush, Robin Cooke, and others. Techno was considered the 'hardest' music in the late 1980s to early 1990s, and even some DJs at the Berlin club Tresor believed at the time that the music was so hard that it could never be commercialised.[8] The new listening habits allowed for 'a radicality that even classified sounds that were hard on the edge of torture as pleasant dance music'.[9] Techno was hardcore, 'despite all the differences, the DJs in Belgium, England, Germany and the USA agreed on that'.[10] There was a desire at that time in Berlin among many DJs and producers to make techno or EBM harder: 'The DJs just played the records faster and faster, and then the producers just produced faster right away.'[11]

During the early 1990s, the Love Parade resembled a street protest that still represented an enthusiasm for technology and music as well as 'a reclaiming of space'.[12] This is also valid for the Berlin techno scene in general throughout the early 1990s as many of its members explored the city in a dérive manner;[13] some of them were squatters and new urban territories would be imaginatively transformed into locations for party, arts, and culture. The mottos of the first Love Parades such as 'The Future is Ours' could be interpreted in a utopian sense. However, within just a few years, the content and orientation of the parade changed. The subcultural entrepreneurs used their personal network effectively as subsidiaries, subcontractors, and companies were founded: 'The Love Parade was instrumentalised by the subcultural entrepreneurs, by the sponsors and by Berlin city politicians, each for their own economic interests.'[14] This is also underlined by Johnnie Stieler, who says that clubbing in Berlin deteriorated after a short while like in Frankfurt, where everything was always clearly regulated according to the bigwig principle: Jürgen Laarman, publisher of the *Frontpage* magazine, temporary shareholder and organiser of Love Parade and Mayday, 'was a strong advocate of bringing in this element, and many people ran after him because there were a lot of drugs in it and a lot of money to be made. Maybe it was fun at first, but the Love Parade surely had nothing to do with music or techno.'[15] Jürgen Laarman organised, alongside the Low Spirit label in 1991, the first major rave for the masses in Berlin – the Mayday; Laarman wanted to organise a kind of gigantic Love Parade afterparty. While initially the Love Parade became an apparent export hit, finding imitators in Zurich, Cologne, and Munich, which also initiated techno parades, the Mayday became the real export hit of Berlin.[16]

The image of hedonistic, innovative youth at techno parties and the Love Parade was soon used to position Berlin in the competition between regions and cities. Commercialisation was driven by the scenes and their entrepreneurial actors themselves.[17] Eventually the cultural gesture of the musical scenes was increasingly pushed into the background. A potent techno-economy developed here, whose operators networked with each other and were active in different techno-companies simultaneously. In the course of commercialisation, the music and appearance of the hardcore techno scene no longer fitted into the image of the Love Parade. The fees and costs for the participating groups increased to the point 'that only commercial music labels, sponsors, clubs and political parties could finance a truck at the parade'.[18] At the same time, the displacement of the diversifying techno subcultures from the inner-city spaces in Berlin's Mitte district was a crucial topic, but the 'displacement of subculture was not an issue for the Love Parade entrepreneurs'.[19] Many clubs had to close and gave way to a new economy; likewise the Bunker in 1997, where hardcore techno and gabber found a home and its guests felt safe from outgrowths such as flower- and Scooter-ravers after the nascent commercialisation of techno.[20]

The UK Free Party Movement

Meanwhile in the UK, the end of the 1980s also gave birth to new musical movements that had developed in the USA, such as Detroit techno or Chicago house. Transplanted to the other side of the Atlantic to London,

Manchester, and other cities in the UK, they would 'mutate beyond all recognition'.[21] House first reached holiday locations like Ibiza and was imported by British tourists and DJs to the UK, who brought also the new drug MDMA (ecstasy) from Ibiza to Britain along with a desire for house music, and that 'coincided with the first house imports in some kind of weird synchronicity'. MDMA enhanced immersive dance experiences;[22] it was even claimed that it enabled the breakdown of cultural barriers and that it subverted social preconceptions.[23] While the first wave of house aficionados sensed they had changed, conservative Britain hadn't. They wanted to dance to house music, but there was hardly any place that played this kind of music back then. It is not certain who promoted house music in Britain first, as none of the DJs at that time were playing house alone.[24] Harry Harrison of DiY experienced Graeme Park as one of the first DJs to publicly play house music in the UK in 1986. The first Detroit House compilation was launched in the UK in 1988 by 10 Records (Virgin) called *Techno! The New Dance Sound of Detroit*.[25]

It only took a couple of years and the bright and bouncy sounds of Balearic house[26] would be joined by the more machinic and up-tempo acid house sounds alongside darker versions of pre-techno that would become popular in Britain alongside MDMA – the new party drug of choice. Slowly scenes and genres would start to fragment. Despite the many mutations in sounds, feelings, and environments of the new party movement, acid house continued to grow. Empty warehouses were squatted or rented for raves and new clubs opened in various British cities. Meanwhile another movement in Britain had reached a critical mass – one that evolved around British-Jamaican sound system culture and free festivals, events of the remaining hippie movement. In the late 1980s, many members lived as travellers in vans around the cities and in the countryside. Christoph Fringeli of Praxis Records, who moved to London in 1990, said it was a huge movement, 'according to estimates, around 60,000 people', says Fringeli,[27] and Simon Reynolds suggests 40,000 people,[28] while Harry Harrison even estimates it involved 75,000 to 100,000.[29] This is important as it is a special context under which a phenomenon like the free party movement in the UK could emerge and flourish. Part of the travellers' subculture was the free festival, and those were happening all over England. The free festivals followed a certain ideology of, among others, anti-war protests and embodied utopian ideas of an alternative society and promoted a system of mutual support. The cooperative festivals of squatters and hippie travellers in the UK developed as a response to the more commercial events;[30] here environmental activists, squatters, and other autonomous-minded people would gather by the end of the 1980s.

Those travellers and alternatives were 'joined by the new electronic party culture, and the first sound systems brought the new music to the events'.[31] As Matthew Collin puts it in the foreword to *The Story of the DiY Sound System*:

> the cultural synergy of travelers and ravers was crucial to some of the most important developments that followed. The travelers had the sites and the outlaw wisdom; the ravers had the new sounds of house and techno, and, of course, the vital chemical accelerator ... – MDMA.[32]

Those scenes had met at free festivals, and one of them was the Glastonbury festival. This had grown slowly since its inception in 1970, and in 1985 there was a huge free festival adjoining the official one, 'including most of the travelling community and their vehicles', as Harrison of DiY explains.[33] Back then it was very much a minority interest in comparison to its current form. Also, there was very little else on the pay festival circuit back then except for Reading, and the police were not allowed on site.[34] As Harry Harrison explains, for him, his friends and artistic collaborators that was a revelation – to see that the travellers followed a completely different way of living:

> I had seen some sights in the free area that had been burned into my retina; ... beautiful dreadlocked women in big boots, Mutoid Waste Company's giant welded sculptures from the post-apocalyptic future, wild all night bars filled with amplified noise, open and unabashed drug-taking, frenzied hedonism.[35]

This inspired those who were not into the shiny new world Britain had on offer for young people: 'Live Aid and MTV, ... a growing obsession with material wealth, the seeming triumph of Thatcherite economics and a fascination with yuppie lifestyles.'[36]

As a precursor to free tekno and the evolution of hardcore techno, the free party movement and free festivals are here of relevance. And they reached a peak in England in 1992 at Castlemorton, when an estimated 20,000 to 30,000 participants[37] partied and even camped out there for nearly a week. As a result, the British government included provisions in the Criminal Justice Act 1994 which challenged the continuation of raves and free techno festivals in the UK.[38] Christina Breinl argues in her book on the history of free tekno that the economic premise of the free festival diametrically opposed the neo-liberal ideology of the British government and entertainment entrepreneurs.[39] Like the Jamaican sound systems – who built the massive stereo systems by themselves – the large, mobile electronic dance music sound systems were either built by the crews or purchased as a starting point.[40] With their music and lifestyle, sound systems like DiY and Spiral Tribe pursued the goal of opposing the commercial marketing of techno. To Harrison of DiY, 1990 revealed that 'the whole underground, illicit excitement of acid house had been commercialised and rebranded into a soulless and anodyne imitation': 'We could at least create transitory spaces for a night or a weekend where the standard rules of society would be suspended and replaced by a new radical set of rules based on equality or hedonism.'[41] Or as Mark Harrison of Spiral Tribe phrases it: 'Seeing society as a construct – manipulated and maintained for the enrichment of the few – is a double edged sword. This vision not only shaped Spiral Tribe but also mapped its position in relation to the mainstream. We weren't just counter-culture, we were experimenting with an entirely new culture; . . . enjoying our experiments in an open and sharing community.'[42]

Reynolds describes Spiral Tribe as a crossover 'between the rave scene and the "crusty" subculture – crusties being squat-dwelling anarcho-hippie-punk types named after their matted dreadlocks and postapocalyptic garb', which includes ripped clothes with patches and studs, tattoos, boots, and often dogs. The style of Spiral Tribe was made up of shaved heads and dark ex-military clothes and trucks.[43] Their provocative and loud attitude combined with their catchy artwork made Spiral Tribe and similar sound system crews like Bedlam particularly exposed to the authorities. Despite the differences, the free parties created a bond through drugs and dance between 'the travellers', 'the fashion-conscious middle-class ravers', and the 'ardcore proles' which formed an affective alliance.[44]

Spiral Tribe Sound System: Forward the Revolution

The Spiral Tribe crew consisted of many people drifting in and out, but the core team of the beginning was a group of four – Debbie Griffith, Simone Trevelyan, and Zander and Mark Harrison, but the evolving collective was fluid and open. 'As a collective we were able to channel ideas and bring them into being – quickly. We could be spontaneous. We could be inventive and experimental. I think that was only possible because we were squatters and had no shortage of space,' as Mark Harrison explains.[45] He relates that Zander and himself had visited many of the free festivals in their teenage years.⁴⁶ Harrison had just moved to London from Manchester, where he had spent a lot of time in the Haçienda night club and had become familiar with the acid house scene. They settled in an area in London where 'there was another cultural current that enlivened the streets – Notting Hill Carnival. We were living in the very heart of sound system central ... It is the biggest free party outside of Rio.'⁴⁷ By the summer of 1991, London was no longer large enough to contain the Spiral Tribe parties, 'so we went west. It was there, out in the wilds, that we discovered the scattered remains of the free festival movement,' argues Mark Harrison.⁴⁸ At the Castlemorton Common free festival, several members of the Spiral Tribe were arrested but later acquitted after a long and expensive trial that lasted almost two years.⁴⁹ This arrest was preceded by a warehouse party in London that was stormed by riot police forces.

Mark Harrison remembers: 'The brutality of this attack left many people injured and most of our equipment smashed ... Clearly this operation's purpose was to intimidate people – scare them away from unlicensed events.' As soon as the trial was over the Criminal Justice and Public Order Bill was debated in the House of Commons and implemented in late 1994 – 'and this drove much of the dance music scene back into the hands of the industry', believes Mark Harrison.⁵⁰ Simon Reynolds, who witnessed everything happening in London, remembers that though the scene didn't die, five months after Castlemorton 'the consensus is that this is the end of an era'.⁵¹ This is also stated by Harry Harrison of DiY: 'Although we didn't know it, that was the beginning of an end, both for the free festival movement and for DiY attending the dwindling number of festivals occurring after this point ... Eventually, Spiral Tribe and most of their associated systems, tired of the restrictive and culturally blinkered island on which we lived, loaded up their wagons and headed to the wide-open spaces of Europe.'⁵²

Spiral Tribe brought their ideas of free party and free music to Europe, where they were mixed with local influences. The ideas spread and the European free tekno movement was starting. The terms 'free party' and 'free festival' were used in the UK, but the events evolving in Europe after the exodus came to be known as teknivals. But, as Anne Petiau's article⁵³ on free party and gift exchange suggests, just like the free parties, free tekno was never completely free of charge. Organisers have expectations of reciprocity regarding their supply with music and infrastructure; it is based 'on the obligation to contribute to the event ... This participation can take the financial form of a donation but can also be made by helping to set up or clean the event,'⁵⁴ or to maintain it – and contribute arts, music, technical know-how, or enthusiastic dancing. This way the participants shared the responsibility for a successful teknival or free party. As mentioned above one, of the first stops of Spiral Tribe was Berlin in 1992. After the trial ended in 1993, more Tribe members followed. But the stop in Berlin was not for long; members of Spiral Tribe went on to various places including France, Italy, Holland, Austria, and the Czech Republic.

In the course of these events, the sound of Spiral Tribe contributed to the early development of hardcore techno. They wanted to counter the colourful commercial techno with a darker atmosphere that served as a reference again and again, especially for the experimental and darker styles that emerged later. 'In Holland and Germany, they [Spiral Tribe] get acquainted with a harder techno style and quickly switch to hardcore.'[55] Mark Harrison remembers:

The music energised every molecule it collided with, which set off an unstoppable chain reaction ... We still played a hugely diverse range of dance music and any DJs determined enough to drag their records around police road blocks ... were always welcome. Despite this diversity, there was a common undercurrent in the music. Deep, brooding bass lines and an ambiguous darkness, a darkness that could be both threatening and seductive.[56]

Harry Harrison of DiY viewed the musical developments with mixed feelings:

By the end of 1990 the scene was beginning to split into two. A musical form known as hardcore was emerging, the beats per minute were rising and harsh metallic or demonic noises were becoming widespread ..., this scene would explode during 1991 and would see young producers worldwide, seemingly unaware of the origins of house music, push sonic boundaries to breaking point.[57]

Teknivals and Free Tekno

It was in France where the free party attitude and hands-on do-it-yourself practices found a fertile soil for growth. It was there in July 1993 that the first free festival in Europe was organised, later coming to be known as 'teknival'. According to Breinl, from this point on the free festival movement transformed into the free tek(no) movement: 'The hippie element ... and the traveller way of life, which was still very widespread in England, was not present here in this form.'[58] Instead, the autonomous squatter scene was a point of reference. During these changes, the musical spectrum was also narrowed down to techno. Breinl states that the autonomous scene in France 'combined perfectly with the views of the English sound systems',[59] so that part of Spiral Tribe founded their Network 23 in Paris, and through a record deal with Killing Joke's Youth they financed their studio: 'We were now in a position to make all our own music and set up our own labels and distribution networks,'[60] recalls Harrison. Alternative and decentralised networks were key sites of identity formation for alternative music scenes. 'Those early Teknivals were fantastic collaborative events,' states Mark Harrison. 'Everyone sharing their equipment, their skills, their music. Although nothing quite like the free-party sound systems had existed in France before we arrived, they did at least have an outdoor culture of music and camping.'[61]

Teknivals spread throughout Europe. For example, the first teknival was organised in the Czech Republic in 1994, marking the beginning of CzechTek. However, repression and police violence followed, just as before in the UK, and the dissolution of CzechTek in 2005 was particularly notorious.[62] The criminalisation of free tekno has been repeated elsewhere, because in times of commercialisation, where experience becomes a commodity, large free events are still not appealing for local governments. 'In my opinion, it was purely to benefit commercial interests. The same-old: enclose the land, control the resources and the gatekeepers grow rich,' believes Harrison.[63] Meanwhile the pressure on inner-city organisers and the struggle for space under conditions of gentrification intensified in London, Paris, Berlin, and many other places to a previously unknown level.

Another important influence for independent music and free tekno is the understanding of rave as a Temporary Autonomous Zone (TAZ). This is also emphasised by Hekate Sound System, which in 1996 formed 'the most notoriously unlistenable sound system on the UK / European free party scene',[64] according to the uploader of a recording on the history of the Sound System. There, Hekate member Dan Moss explains that his motivation for participation in the sound system culture was the sound system as TAZ:[65] 'TAZ is a reaction against a capitalist system that makes space private and it's basically about reclaiming that space.'[66] But TAZ is more than that. Hekate consciously tried to avoid mass appeal through the breaking up of musical structures and repetition.[67] This also influenced other producers, such as Riccardo Balli from Italy, who also emphasises the importance of rave as TAZ. DJ Balli contributes on many levels to an international DIY music scene. He lived in London for a while in the early 1990s:

> I had the experience of rave from Bologna starting in 1993 ... For me coming also from punk, new wave and hardcore the Italian club music was too fluffy and not subversive. I was interested in the whole set up of the rave experience: Rave as TAZ. Music was just one part of it.[68]

Nonetheless the French free party scene continued, as Harrison explains: 'out in the wilds, in squatted venues, and sometimes it's even been embraced by supportive town councils ... and a part of French society ... still has a deep respect for resistance'.[69] Christoph Fringeli writes that the illegal parties and teknivals were something he and others 'had hoped could or would become the nucleus of a new counter culture'; instead they were attacked and destroyed in most of Europe and North America, 'a fact that has had little exposure, let alone critical reflection, in the media'.[70] Gilbert and Pearson argue that the free party movement, alongside early club culture, had made a crucial contribution to changing democratic and social values, such as anti-sexism, right to public space, right to freedom of expression, or new forms of community.[71]

The Berlin Fuckparade: 'Bad Conscience of Techno-Pop'

Hardcore techno, in contrast to hard techno, eventually moved away from its techno roots and developed its own style and sound, with its roots in metal, early techno, industrial, or noisy hip-hop: 'From 1996 onwards, you could see how the scenes split up, and then hardcore didn't really belong to techno anymore, neither scene-wise nor sound-wise.'[72] The feeling of techno being one family dissipated and not everyone in Berlin agreed with the open contradictions of the Love Parade and their techno-entrepreneurs. In 1996, ID&T, one of the largest Dutch organisers of hardcore parties, was prohibited from joining the parade with their truck, despite the motto being 'We Are One Family'. Due to this exclusion, the hardcore community started their own event. Their first anti-Love-Parade was called the Hate Parade and took place in 1997, back then as an explicit 'counter-demo' and 'against the commercialisation of techno'.[73] Martin Kliehm, a hardcore DJ called Trauma XP from Frankfurt, had joined the Love Parade in 1993 feeling the urge to demonstrate against public misconceptions of clubbing and drug use causing a hysteria around the new subculture. Kliehm and the Berlin producer XOL DOG 400 from the Bunker community were officially in charge of the organisation of the first parades. Prevalent issues of the Hate Parade were the evictions of clubs and bars due to increasing economisation, or the exposure of the finances of dubious entrepreneurs, one of them the Love Parade GmbH.[74] Jadranka Kursar believes that 'through the economisation of the Love Parade, a large part of Berlin's techno subculture found its way back to its actual roots and protest character'.[75]

The protest parade in 1997 consisted of six trucks with about 1,000 participants.[76] The Hate Parade activists were concerned that clubs were closed in order to put attractive properties like the Bunker on the open market. Thus, gentrification was a central theme from the very beginning. The Hate Parade was renamed as 'Fuckparade' in the following year because it caused misconceptions about the motivations behind the demonstration in the press and public. Its organisers used the harshness inscribed in hardcore music and its aesthetics as an expression against neo-liberal politics: 'Shock harmless ravers, girlies and bystanders with your music, but please don't riot. Peace!'[77] Moog_t, another main organiser, remembers: 'Everything was fogged in, every truck, every bridge ... All really hardcore.'[78]

The following year, in 1998, the demonstration had already doubled in size with eleven trucks and about 2,000 demonstrators.[79] Thematically, the Love Parade was no longer in the foreground, but the criminalisation of illegal parties and teknivals, or the increasing gentrification with the pressure of rising rents. They proclaimed: 'Show that subculture is alive, that techno can be political, demonstrate peacefully with us for your right to party!'[80]

Musically, the Fuckparade was dominated by the sound of EDM genres such as gabber, speedcore, breakcore, and drum and bass, as well as industrial and punk during its first years.[81] It is precisely the irony, ambiguity, and double coding of hardcore that is crucial in this context, which cannot only be understood logically-rationally, but also physically. For Kliehm, 'hardcore techno is also the punk of techno music'.[82] Later, the Fuckparade also integrated techno, house, or trance as 'the difference is more the attitude of the people who take part in the Fuckparade. They usually organise non-commercial parties all year round ... They don't care whether it's legal or illegal.'[83]

In 1999, there were again eleven trucks at the parade. In July 2000, the last Fuckparade with unrestricted demonstration status took place. The participants protested against the closing of pirate radio stations or the criminalisation of illegal parties. With twenty-seven trucks and an estimated 5,000 police to 10,000 participants (organisers), it was the biggest Fuckparade ever held, with sound systems from various European countries.[84] However, the Fuckparade in 2000 was also a moment of fear, as it became harder to secure the control of the masses. Also, the organisers did not want to produce a mass event like the Love Parade. Kliehm and XOL DOG 400 decided then to stop it with a final demonstration in the following year. And then everything changed 'because the head of authorities decided that he would no longer approve the Fuckparade as a demonstration. That actually ensured that it continued to exist',[85] as the organisers were ready to fight back.

From 2001 to 2006, the Fuckparade could only take place under harsh legal restrictions – amongst other things: a ban on music (2001), restrictions on volume, and a requirement of political-orientated speeches (2002), authorisation of demonstration at very short notice (2003), restrictions in size (2004).[86] As a consequence, Kliehm and the Fuckparade took legal action against the police and the city – all the way to the Federal Constitutional Court. The routes of the Fuckparade continued to pass endangered projects, places threatened with eviction. For example, the famous club Eimer was closed and the eviction of the legendary autonomous Art House Tacheles was prepared,[87] which Spiral Tribe and Mutoid had been a part of in the 1990s. The 2002 flyer comments: 'Thorn in the flesh of the Love Parade. Sand in the gears of the million-dollar corporation, bad conscience of techno-pop.'[88]

In 2005, due to police brutality at the CzechTek Festival the weekend before, the route was changed and led past the Czech embassy.[89] As a result of the CzechTek incidents the Fuckparade organised two more demonstrations in 2005 and raised money through solidarity parties. Due to the imposed restrictions every truck continued to have political banners, and flyers with route descriptions and political demands were handed to the residents explaining what it was all about. Later in 2005 the courts finally decided that the Fuckparade was allowed to protest with music. Moog_t stresses: 'The Fuckparade won back the fundamental right to music as a means of protest.'[90] In 2006, the tenth anniversary, the criminalisation of free parties and teknivals was continuing as well as evictions of cultural places.[91] Though the Fuckparade stated on its flyer that nothing had changed, it has to be noted that 2006 was an extraordinarily active and productive year for the Fuckparade, with various demonstrations taking place in Berlin and elsewhere in cooperation with it.

Berlin's Scorned Electronic Underground

After several court hearings that dragged on for a total of six years, the Federal Administrative Court ruled in 2007 that the police chief in Berlin should have treated the Fuckparade 2001 as an assembly in the sense of the Assembly Act. The ban in 2001 had been unlawful. Even without speeches and banners, only with music, the Fuckparade was a demonstration.[92] Unfortunately, the problems of the Fuckparade only really began there.

What is perceived by some as increased political commitment can be perceived by others as a blunt depoliticisation. At this point, much of the criticism came from within the scene itself, from the left spectrum. In 2001 internal debates started: what was seen as dark humour by many gabbers was unacceptable for other politically engaged participants. Some artists from the more radical left started to withdraw from engaging with the Fuckparade. One of them was Christoph Fringeli, who explains that he and his label Praxis participated in the first years but he stopped due to political differences.[93]

The following disputes were mainly about the proximity to right-wing ideology of some participants and marshals. Two handouts had been published by previously engaged leftist groups against the Fuckparade in 2003 and 2006.[94] This was an open sore for the Fuckparade, especially for the gabbers. Because for people like Curt Cocain, who played many times as a DJ at the Fuckparade, the political aspect was an important reason why he involved himself in the first place. He demonstrated likewise against the fact that gabber was seen as the 'black sheep of the techno scene and was hung with prejudices, such as all gabbers are Nazis'.[95] It is well known that, in some regions, there are people with an affinity to right-wing ideology attracted to hardcore techno – and East Germany is one such stronghold of neo-Nazis. Berlin is a city that is located in the east of Germany. That's why the Fuckparade always had 'Against Nazis' logos on the flyers and on the trucks, and why Berlin gabber had always been a more lefty scene, which was also marked by a special DJ-style, dress code, and attitude known as 'gabba'[96] as DJ Mad of Gabba Front Berlin explains:

> Pretty early on, people declared Gabba to be a harder style and Gabber to be a commercial 'Dutch thing'. Certainly, also to distinguish themselves from the gabber of the Dutch or in North Rhine-Westphalia, near the border. The scene there was more commercially oriented, often with politically questionable attitudes ... In Berlin we did not like Nazis, but instead preferred to listen to the records played a bit faster and favored the 'dress code black' with dark pants and black hoodies. Gabba with the 'a' had emerged as a bastardized, somewhat cooler and less commercial variant.[97]

There were also accusations that the Fuckparade organisers were only making pseudo-political demands, that the criticism did not go far enough. XOL DOG 400 and Trauma XP had always been united in their strategy and approach to seek dialogue – be it with police, or gabbers with an affinity for right-wing positions. But this attitude is largely neglected by leftist activists. The Fuckparade answered with press releases in response to the criticism, but there was no willingness to talk and the open hostility continued.

Over time, long-running conflicts between self-organised groups about inclusion and exclusion sapped the motivation of both organisers and the team. From 2010 a lot of changes happened and the organisation of the Fuckparade became chaotic at times; moog_t complains:

For me, the Fuckparade has actually been dead since 2014, that's when I decided to make a cut. Then the younger generation took over – all the Free Tek(no) systems from the area, and there was no more gabber. They just wanted to go on the streets with music. But as a political thing it died for me at that time.[98]

This statement seems ironic when regarding the common goals and ideas that sound system culture, teknivals, and the Fuckparade share, like the right to space, fewer commercially oriented parties, or the right to protest with and through music – outlined in this chapter. But how collectives execute them of course differs, as gentrification and commercialisation continue to be pressing topics in Berlin.

The Remains of the Berlin Clubbing Utopia

At the 'Death of Rave Berlin' panel at CTM festival 2013, the journalist Ulrich Gutmair outlined that when he came to West Berlin in 1989, the rent was expensive due to limited space; if you needed a flat you had to get up at 5 a.m. and check the newspapers only to find ugly overpriced flats outside the centre. After 1990, up until about 2010, he and most of the people he knew paid very little for their flats, as there were so many empty ones. He recalls that after twenty plus years a full circle is made, as such, that in 2013 the situation was the same again.[99] One can easily contend that this cycle was too fast, something must have gone wrong. In the following decade the situation became even worse. Johnnie Stieler emphasised during the same panel that alternative economies were built within nightlife after the fall of the Wall, and that clubbing was cheap and affordable for everyone: 'This allowed people to move freely in the urban environment. If there hadn't been this alternative economy, none of this would have happened.' He added that this was what he misses most in 2013: 'that Berlin as a city has never managed to establish a fair balance. Billions are thrown down the throats of corporations as subsidies, and alternative culture is gagged. This spirit, which is used to market the city, is actually being starved.'[100] In a 2018 *Tagesspiegel* report on Berlin clubbing, journalists note that techno became a million-dollar enterprise in Berlin and that 'the business is slowly but steadily eating up the passion'.[101]

The time when clubbing was cheap in Berlin is long over. Where you paid fifteen euros five years ago admission is now twenty to twenty-five euros, with the cost of drinks, wardrobe, and other necessary items on top. Without question this is not to rip off ravers in most cases, but the point is that a freedom to experience the city and its nightlife, or a diverse audience, especially concerning class, is not possible in such a setting. This is why the leftist club Mensch Meier decided to close in 2024, as it didn't want to impose these prices on its audience. 'We have reached a point where we can't help but raise admission and drink prices to such an extent that it would hardly be possible for our employees, for example, to attend our own events,'[102] says its spokesperson to the *Berliner Zeitung*.

The experimentations with space, music, and art in the 1990s are one reason why Klaus Wowereit, the Governing Mayor of Berlin from 2001 to 2014, and one of the defining politicians of post-reunification Berlin, claimed in a 2003 interview that Berlin was 'poor but sexy' as back then Berlin was one of the poorest regions in Germany, but for those interested in culture and music, one of the most exciting ones. The sentence became the city's leitmotif, and was quoted frequently. It was changed to 'Be Berlin' in its last big image campaign 2008, being promoted later in fifty different countries with the slogan 'the place to be'.[103] Geoff Stahl believes that through Berlin's club culture and festivals, the cultural and symbolic dimensions of Berlin are charged with intensities that are used to market Berlin's urban identity: 'Berlin . . . is packaged as a phantasmagoric site of cultural consumption embedded in a European as well as global tourism industry.'[104] Berlin's handling of its own image also as the place where techno culture was supposedly invented shows for Stahl a neglect of its past and its diversity, hiding its historical and social ruptures.[105]

The economisation of music culture and the branding of Berlin through techno works for its government and its techno entrepreneurs, as it continues to bring in a constant influx of techno-tourists. Berlin has become a world media city. 'In the 1990s,' write Ingo Bader and Albert Scharenberg, 'the club and music scene thrived, in particular in the deindustrialising inner-city areas, thereby paving the way for large media and music corporations to move to Berlin. The rise of the Berlin techno and electronic music scene, . . . is therefore closely connected to the urban transformation since the fall of the Berlin Wall.'[106] They argue that the development of creative milieus and the attraction of creative people is a matter of a transitory phase, which is open to experiments.

What is transforming is also the social and political, the values and views about the world we would like to live in. These are anticipated and articulated in music and subculture.

The relative prosperity and the welfare state of the post-war period allowed young people in Germany or the UK to live off welfare and housing benefits and/or what were back then still well-paid temporary jobs, while investing most of their time into music and/or activism, and there are various accounts of actors from both places for this. As Harry Harrison puts it, claiming those benefits himself: 'It has been said many times that the system of free higher education, which existed until the late eighties, was responsible for nurturing a generation of creative talent.'[107] He also explains that by the mid-1990s the stark effects of mass unemployment and neo-liberal economics 'split the UK into those who benefited and those who fell by the wayside'.[108] And this is equally true for Berlin though it happened with some delay due to an unclear legal situation after the fall of the Wall. But by the late 2000s only the Londoners and Berliners with financial strength looked optimistically into the future, and a fatalism started to spread amongst many.

This also applies to the journalist and former chief editor of the *Exberliner* D. Strauss. Globalisation, the internet, and gentrification make Berlin's decline inevitable for Strauss. As an example, he takes the popular Bar 25 (2003–10) with its endless and excessive parties, which he sees in retrospect as a playground of aristocratic children rebelling against their families. He, too, had enjoyed Bar 25, but for him it was a sign of the beginning of the end. Shortly after its closure, the people who ran it built a luxury hotel in the same place. He wonders how one should respond to that, arguing further that money laundering investments have created the breeding ground for Berlin as a lifestyle city: 'The economy of Berlin does not actually expand but resides on a series of bubbles: real estate, tech, restaurants. The only consistency is European crime money and clubs.'[109] The city's government now promotes its nightlife, while selling off iconic symbols of the city such as the East Side Gallery to investors. He calls Berlin a 'moneyed world without money', where aristocratic manners would edge into self-satire, and attain their mature form with bars such as KingSize, Trust, or Tausend, 'bars that feel like Munich . . . Class is the unspoken root of all German nightlife activity.'[110] Though Berlin, and also West Berlin, used to be a city that was specifically targeted by artists, punks, and activists.

In London as well as in Berlin gentrification is especially invasive, where culture itself has become a commodity and service needed for the so-called creative cities. Hardcore techno tried to ease the contradictions of consumerism and commercialisation with energy generated through fast, loud, and hard music that functioned as a temporary painkiller. Due to the ongoing eviction of countless contested projects in Berlin and elsewhere, festive protest seems like Sisyphus' work: however one pushes, the metaphorical stone keeps rolling back from the mountain. Despite that, 'cities have always been spaces in which difference can become productive as political emancipation – as socio-political resistance in the form of urban-social movements', as the professor for gender and cultural studies Yvonne Doderer argues. Though this ability is in danger in an era when social and democratic standards are increasingly eroding and where the massive loss of democratic participation and influence on the part of city residents 'is threatening a successful continuation of a heterogeneous urban society'.[111] She also stresses that diverse marginal groups, counter-movements, and protests have always been part of urban environments and that those will continue. One of the strengths of the early Fuckparade, and equally of the free party and festival movement of the late 1980s and early 1990s, has been grounded in its diversity – of scenes and sounds, of cultural and social backgrounds, something that many protagonists emphasise.

Producer and philosopher Steve Goodman stressed at the 'Death of Rave UK' panel at CTM 2013 that there was a confusion about hedonism and rave.[112] Part of the problem, of its decline, he believes is the over-exaggeration of hedonism in the most interesting moments of rave. This spills over into depressive or forced hedonism – that you must have a good time. To him what was most exciting about 90s rave was that it was not always pleasurable:

> There was a moment of submission to and domination by the DJ and the sound system, allowing yourself to be victimised by the intensity ... These collective instances were not about trying to enforce hedonism on people, and to be happy. It was about going through the dark side, through the paranoia, through the tension and channelling it rhythmically and vibrationally.[113]

These tensions come from social contexts, from political and economic transformation processes, but also from diversity and emerging collectivity, which is never just an easy pleasure, but also a struggle. Though something that can be fun, seriously fun. Alexandra Dröner of the Sick Girls, also co-founder of Tresor, who worked for clubs like Planet (1991–93) and E-Werk (1993–97), feels there was a decline in the 1990s, and that rave did not die, but rather is being rebuilt and sold over and over again, which also led to depression and disillusionment in me ... My approach was always the music and this was pushed more and more into the background ... This final death of rave does not exist. We still rave and the whole world comes to Berlin to rave ... This capitalised hippie-rave. We all put glitter on our faces and then we all go to these clubs that look like a ranch made out of wood ... Actually, rave is reproduced again and again like in an experience museum.[114]

Ulrich Gutmair insists in the same Berlin panel that there was always a diversity in what Berlin had and has to offer; if you did not like the big glossy clubs you could go to small ones, and listen to almost any electronic style: 'That was a completely different thing, not much money came in or was reinvested immediately. I agree with you about the theme park rave, but the music will not disappear.'[115] Ten years later, Berliners have to admit that these places are constantly becoming scarcer. Williams adds that intense musical experiences like in the 1990s are maybe not political but can be transformational: 'To me all this stands for the politics we are not allowed to have.' The question of rave being now dead or undead already goes back to failed revolutions like in 1968, he believes; 'which couldn't happen. So that impulse still reverberates throughout culture, and pops up every now and then – and early rave was one of these things,' he believes.[116]

Conclusion

The historical accounts detailed here relate to early techno music and to largely non-political groups and individuals who became politicised through economisation and criminalisation. They are crucial, as they serve as a reminder of a history of protest and counterculture linked to electronic music, when rave was still seriously fun – a sonic struggle, and a collective struggle through rhythms and vibrations. And not, as is often the case, forced hedonism and emptied lifestyle symbols to be sold to consumers. Currently, it might be difficult for younger ravers to imagine that things have not always been like this, that there are alternative ideas about rave reverberating in often clandestine niches of society. Though the conflicts continue, within the Fuckparade and elsewhere, more important is the fact that the Fuckparade continues to happen, teknivals continue to happen, and sound systems are still being built.

Notes

1. The fall of the Berlin Wall is a historic event on 9 November 1989, during the Peaceful Revolution, which marked the destruction of the Berlin Wall as part of a series of events that started the fall of communism in Central and Eastern Europe and the end of the Cold War a few weeks later. The fall of the inner German border took place shortly afterwards. and the German reunification took place in October the following year (see www.bbc.com/news/world-europe-50013048, www.bpb.de/themen/deutsche-einheit/mauerfall/, retrieved 10 February 2020).
2. See Schwanhäusser, A (2010) *Kosmonauten des Underground. Ethnografie einer Berliner Szene*. Frankfurt Main/ New York: Campus; Scharenberg, A., and Bader, I. (eds.) (2005) *Der Sound der Stadt – Musikindustrie und Subkultur in Berlin*. Dampfboot: Münster.
3. Denk F, at Death of Rave Berlin panel, CTM festival 2013. Available at https://soundcloud.com/ctm-festival/ctm13-the-death-of-rave-ii (retrieved 1 November 2014). Translation by author.
4. The UFO operators (including Dimitri Hegemann and Carola Stoiber) also ran the Interfish Records label and in 1991 the team subsequently founded the Tresor and the Tresor-Label as an alternative to Low Spirit, the oldest Berlin Techno label (1986).
Cousto H. (2001) 'Die Berliner Techno-Szene. Ein historischer Rückblick' (The Berlin Techno Scene. A retrospective, translated by the author), Eve & Rave Workshop, Berlin. fuckparade.org/ fuckparade2009.blogsport.de, 27 February 2012. See Henkel, O., & Wolff, K. (1996) *Berlin Underground. Techno und Hip Hop zwischen Mythos und Ausverkauf*. Berlin: FAB Verlag.
5. Stieler at the Death of Rave Berlin panel, CTM 2013.
6. In a former bomb shelter in Berlin Mitte near Friedrichstraße, artist Werner Vollert, who had rented the bunker, opened the Hardcore Techno Club as well as the Red Cross Club (Rot-Kreuz-Club). The techno club on several floors was the framing for the Rot-Kreuz-Club, later named the Ex-Kreuz-Club, a kind of S&M club that was Vollert's personal passion. The Ex-Kreuz-Club formed a symbiotic unit with the Bunker, which he conceived as an art project (cf. Interview XOL DOG 2018, Cousto 2001: fuckparade.org).
7. Bunker poster, see Ludewig, B. (2019) *Utopie und Apokalypse in der Popmusik. Gabber und Breakcore in Berlin*. Wien: Institut für Europäische Ethnologie.
8. Künzel, T. (dir) (2012) *SubBerlin – The Story of Tresor*. Berlin: Tresor Records.
9. Poschardt, U. (2001) *DJ Culture. Diskjockeys und Popkultur*. Hamburg: Tropen, p. 325. Translation by author.
10. Ibid, p. 328.
11. Interview with DJ Stailen (today DJ Spirial) 2012. In Ludewig, *Utopie und Apokalypse in der Popmusik*.

12. Kursar, J. (2007) 'Ökonomisierung einer Subkultur am Beispiel des Phänomens Love Parade: Eine kulturanalytische Annäherung'. Master's thesis, Department of European Ethnology, Humboldt University Berlin, p. 48.
13. Dérive is a practice promoted by the Situationists International, an avantgarde art group most prominent in the 1960s in Europe. A practice of exploring the city by strolling around it, and temporarily changing it through interventions into urban space. See Schwanhäusser, *Kosmonauten des Underground*.
14. Ibid., p. 65.
15. Stieler at the Death of Rave Berlin panel, translation by author.
16. See Henkel & Wolff (1996) p.106ff; see also press release Fuckparade (2001) join the cash republic, https://fuckparade.org/presse/2001-07-10/join-the-cash-republic/.
17. See Hitzler, R. (2001) 'Pioniere einer anderen Moderne? Existenzbasteln als Innovationsmanagement', *Sozialwissenschaften und Berufspraxis* 24, 177–91; Hitzler, R. & Pfadenhauer, M. (1998) 'Existenzielle Strategien. Zur Spaß-Politik der Technoiden', *Sociologia Internationalis* 36 (2), 219–39.
18. Kursar, *Ökonomisierung einer Subkultur*, p. 67. Cf. fuckparade.org: Join the cash republic, 2001.
19. Ibid., p. 25.
20. Glamorama (2009) Thema der Woche: Bunker. 16 June 2018. Available at Tanith.org.
21. Reynolds, S. (1999) *Generation Ecstasy*. New York: Routledge, p. 57.
22. Collin, M. (1998) *Altered State: The Story of Ecstasy Culture and Acid House*. London/ New York: Serpent's Tail, pp.50, 52.
23. 'This moment [of collectively taking MDMA] would provide a deep abiding bond between people and cultures separated by geography, class, and tribal loyalty. . . . This moment would cause hundreds of thousands of city dwellers to head for the fields and mingle with travellers to challenge centuries-old land rights.' In: Harrison, H. (2022) *Dreaming in Yellow. The Story of the DiY Sound System*. Bristol: Velocity Press, p. 60.
24. Collin, *Altered State*, p. 58; Harrison, *Dreaming in Yellow*, p. 2.
25. Sicko, D. (2010) *Techno Rebels. The Renegades of Electronic Funk*. Detroit: Turtle.
26. Balearic beats are influenced by Italo disco, early house, soul, funk, Latin music, African rhythms, or dub affectations and consist usually of beats under 120 BPM, often programmed in a laid-back manner; today most Balearic house would be heard as deep house. See also Gilbert, J., & Pearson, E. (1999) *Discographies: Dance Music, Culture, and the Politics of Sound*. London: Routledge; Bogdanov, V et al (eds.) (2001) *All Music Guide to Electronica: The Definitive Guide to Electronic Music*. San Francisco: Backbeat Books.
27. Interview with Christoph Fringeli, Berlin 2022. Translation by author.
28. Reynolds, *Generation Ecstasy*, p. 164.

29. 'In the spring of 1991 there was a large contingent of people living in buses, wagons, caravans, benders and even taxis on sites big and small . . . In terms of numbers, it's impossible to know but I'm guessing that seventy-five to one hundred thousand people were living nomadically, outside the traditional boundaries of society' (Harrison, *Dreaming in Yellow*, p. 144).
30. Breinl, C. (2012) *Free Tekno. Geschichte einer Gegenkultur*. Vienna: LIT Verlag, p. 10. All quotes translated by author.
31. Ibid.
32. Collin in Harrison, *Dreaming in Yellow*, p. xv.
33. Harry is a nickname and was used by Harrison of DiY to avoid confusion as his given name was Mark Harrison, the same name as one of the founding members of Spiral Tribe.
34. Harrison, *Dreaming in Yellow*, p. 29.
35. Ibid. pp. 31–32.
36. Ibid., p. 39.
37. Harry Harrison states he had read the West Mercia Police report, Harrison writes about 'tens of thousands'. Some press clippings with estimated numbers from 20, 000 up to 25,000 are listed on https://freepartypeople.wordpress.com/category/castlemorton/, e.g. *Western Daily Press*, 25 May 1992, where Giles Rees writes, 'Police powerless as 20,000 attend rave' (accessed 20 June 2023). See Breinl, p.82; she names around 20,000 in her book, referencing Collins' book *Stone's Fierce Dancing* (1996) and Lowe & Shaw's account on travellers (1993). Wikipedia's article on Castlemorton offers 20,000 to 40,000 but its data is based on accounts of press articles that came out much later and look back on the event, and likewise do not give references for the estimated numbers, e.g. the BBC and the *Guardian* state that 20,000 people attended but do not give any references. Without doubt the numbers varied throughout the days as the numbers increased due to intensified police and media reports which revealed the location.
38. In 1993 Dreadzone protest in their liner notes of the record 'Fight the Power' against the Criminal Justice Bill, and state that according to Shelter up to 'two million people are homeless in Britain'. And 'tucked away in 171 clauses are measures to tackle squatters, travellers and Gypsies. Traveller and Gypsy vehicles will be impounded and destroyed, the costs for the destruction of their homes will be met by the owners themselves.'
39. Breinl, *Free Tekno*, p. 141.
40. The term 'sound system' refers to the technical equipment, including speakers, but also to the people and crew who make use of it. The DiY Soundsystem purchased their sound system from ESS, a sound engineering company from which they had rented their equipment before. See Harrison, *Dreaming in Yellow*, pp. 127–28.
41. Harrison, *Dreaming in Yellow*, pp. 80, 92.

42. Transpontine N., and Harrison M. (2013) 'Spiral Tribe Interview', *Datacide* 13, 22–55. Here p. 24.
43. Reynolds, *Generation Ecstasy*, p.163.
44. Ibid, p. 164.
45. Transpontine & Harrison, Spiral Tribe Interview, p. 22.
46. Ibid.
47. Ibid.
48. Ibid., p.23. Harry Harrison states: 'The heart of this [movement] were post-industrial wastelands of former mill-towns dotted around the north-west of England … This whole region had long suffered economic decline, and this had greatly accelerated under the London-centric and ruthless market economies of Margret Thatcher'; *Dreaming in Yellow,* p. 64.
49. See Reynolds, *Generation Ecstasy;* Breinl, *Free Tekno*; Collin, *Altered State*.
50. Transpontine & Harrison, Spiral Tribe Interview, p. 24.
51. Reynolds, *Generation Ecstasy*, p. 172.
52. Harrison, *Dreaming in Yellow*, pp. 194, 198.
53. Petiau A. (2015) 'Free Parties and Teknivals: Gift-Exchange and Participation on the Margins of the Market and the State', *Dancecult* 7 (1) 116–28. Here: 116.
54. Ibid.
55. Arte TRACKS (2014) Spiral Tribe. France/ Germany. Available at YouTube Channel Tracks (accessed 10 November 2018).
56. Transpontine & Harrison, Spiral Tribe Interview, p. 23.
57. Harrison, *Dreaming in Yellow*, p.120.
58. Breinl, *Free Tekno*, p. 84.
59. Ibid.
60. Transpontine & Harrison, Spiral Tribe Interview, p. 24.
61. Ibid., p. 25.
62. Breinl, *Free Tekno*, p. 88.
63. Transpontine & Harrison, Spiral Tribe Interview, p. 25.
64. The Clear Spot Show (2006) History of Hekate Sound System, Resonance FM. Available at www.youtube.com/watch?v=KvLLtMOLY8I (accessed 15 March 2017).
65. See Bey, H (2003 [1985]) *The Temporary Autonomous Zone, Ontological Anarchy, Poetic Terrorism*. New York: Autonomedia.
66. The Clear Spot Show, History of Hekate Sound System.
67. Ibid.
68. Interview with DJ Balli, Vienna 2018.
69. Harrison, M., Datacite – Magazin for Noise and Politics, Berlin 2013, p. 25.
70. Fringeli, C8 forum (now obsolete) 2005.
71. Gilbert & Pearson, *Discographies,* pp.179–84.
72. Interview with DJ Lamagra Berlin 2012, In Ludewig, *Utopie und Apokalypse in der Popmusik*, p. 92. Translation by author.
73. Text on flyer, Hateparade 1997.

74. Kliehm in *Subculture – Public*, DE 2013.
75. Kursar, *Ökonomisierung einer Subkultur*, p.68.
76. Fuckparade.org, archive of flyers and press releases; press release Hate Parade, retrieved 7 February 2012.
77. Text on flyer, Hateparade 1997.
78. Interview with moog_t, Berlin 2018.
79. Fuckparade 1998: fuckparade.org, retrieved 10 February 2012. Cf. Interviews XOL Dog 400 & moog_t.
80. Text on Fuckparade flyer 1998.
81. For more details on the music and production see Ludewig, *Utopie und Apokalypse in der Popmusik*.
82. Kliehm, taz.de, 30 June 2003. Retrieved 10 September 2011. Quotes translated by author.
83. Ibid.
84. Interview with moog_t, Berlin 2018; interview XOL Dog 400, Berlin 2018.
85. Interview XOL DOG 400, Berlin 2018.
86. Cf. Cousto, H. 'Berliner Paradenstreit', fuckparade2009.blogsport.de/2011/08/01/der-berliner-paradenstreit/, 28 November 2011; www.tagesspiegel.de/berlin/fuckparade-mit-musik-lauft-hier-nichts-814120.html, www.tagesspiegel.de/berlin/fuckparade-marschiert-durch-alle-instanzen-1019812.html 3 December 2011.
87. With a sense of disappointment the tageszeitung describes what the newly opened Tacheles conveys:
    'In the months between the fall of the Wall and reunification, it was thanks to an artist's initiative that anything at all remains of the ruin of a huge shopping arcade built in the early 1900s. Only slightly damaged during World War II, the magnificent building fell into disrepair during GDR times and was partially demolished. In 1998, Berlin sold the site to an investor for an incredibly low 2.8 million marks. On an area of around 24,000 square meters, 180 apartments were built on the site, exclusively in the luxury segment.' https://taz.de/Zukunft-des-Berliner-Tacheles/!5956889/, 14 September 2023, translation by author.
88. Text on Fuckparade flyer 2002.
89. Cf. press release Fuckparade 4 August 2005, via fuckparade.org.
90. Interview with moog_t, Berlin 2018, translated by author.
91. Listed in the text on Fuckparade flyer 2006.
92. See press release Fuckparade: Cousto, 'Berliner Paradenstreit', fuckparade2009.blogsport.de/2011/08/01/der-berliner-paradenstreit/, 28 November 2011; Wick P (dir) (2013) documentary Subculture-Public, Berlin.
93. Interview with Christoph Fringeli, Berlin 2012, translated by author.

94. indymedia.org. Mogelpackung Fuckparade. Upload 26 March 2003, accessed 23 February 2012, Zugriff 23 February 2012; indymedia.org, Aufruf gegen die Fuckparade, Zugriff published 22 February 2005, accessed 18 October 2011.
95. Interview with Curt Cocain, Berlin 2012, translated by author.
96. Gabba with 'a' denotes a local Berlin variant of Gabber. This refers to a certain style of DJ-ing. DJ Cut-X pioneered a new style of DJing in Berlin. Coming from a hip-hop background, he applied the techniques of cutting and scratching to gabber, literally 'chopping' the records. This shaped the taste of the gabba audience in Berlin early on and influenced other Bunker DJs around Cut-X, such as the then-forming Gabba Nation, of which he was a co-founder, as well as younger DJs such as the Flash Fingarz crew, who were also influenced by hip-hop.
97. Interview with DJ Mad, Berlin 2012, translated by author.
98. Interview with moog_t, Berlin 2018, translated by author.
99. U Gutmair at Death of Rave Berlin panel, CTM 2013; translation by author. See also Gutmair, U. (2014) *Die ersten Tage von Berlin. Der Sound der Wende.* Stuttgart: Tropen Verlag. See also Holm, A (ed.) (2010) *Reclaim Berlin. Soziale Kämpfe in der neoliberalen Stadt.* Berlin: Assoziation A.
100. Stieler, J at Death of Rave Berlin panel; translation by author.
101. Erk, D. et al. (2018) 'Die Nachtschicht. Techno in Berlin – ein Millionengeschäft, Tagesspiegel', enclosure Berliner 6 (April), 14–21. Translation by author.
102. Plett, C (2023) Billig und viel feiern war einmal! Available at Berliner Zeitung online: www.berliner-zeitung.de/kultur-vergnuegen/musik/billig-und-viel-feiern-das-war-einmal-warum-sind-die-berliner-clubs-jetzt-so-teuer-li.367946 (published and retrieved 11 July 2023).
103. Oktay, E. (2014) 'The Unbearable Hipness of Being Light: Welcome to Europe's New Nightlife Capital'. In Stahl, G. (ed.), *Poor, But Sexy: Reflections on Berlin Scenes.* Bern: Peter Lang, 211–25; Here p. 224. See also Neate, R (2014). Available at www.theguardian.com/business/2014/jan/03/berlin-poor-sexy-silicon-valley-microsoft-google; https://taz.de/15-Jahre-Arm-aber-sexy-Spruch/!5546816/ (accessed 7 May 2020).
104. Stahl, *Poor, But Sexy*, p. 12.
105. See Ludewig, B. (2020) 'The Berlin Techno Myth and Issues of Diversity'. In Jóri, A. and Lücke M. (eds.), *The New Age of Electronic Dance Music and Club Culture.* Cham: Springer, pp. 29–54.
106. Bader, I, & Scharenberg, A (2010) 'The Sound of Berlin: Subculture and the Global Music Industry', *International Journal of Urban and Regional Research* 34:1, 76–91. The article summarises their book publication on the same topic.
107. Harrison, *Dreaming in Yellow*, p. 71.
108. Ibid., p. 80.
109. Strauss, D. (2013) 'Berlin Falling'. In Farkas, W. et al. (eds.), *Nachtleben Berlin 1974 bis heute.* Berlin: Metrolit, pp. 207–15. Here: 207.

110. Ibid., p. 208.
111. Doderer, Y. (2013) *Räume des Politischen. Dimensionen des Städtischen.* Münster: Monsenstein & Vannerdat, p.54. Translation by author.
112. Goodman, S at Death of Rave UK panel, CTM festival 2013. Available at https://soundcloud.com/ctm-festival/ctm13-death-of-rave-1-uk (accessed 9 April 2015).
113. Ibid.
114. Dröhner, A. at Death of Rave Berlin, translation by author.
115. Gutmair, U. at Death of Rave Berlin, translation by author.
116. Williams, A. at Death of Rave UK panel.

Further Reading

Collin, M. *Altered State. The Story of Ecstasy Culture and Acid House.* London: Serpent's Tail, 1998.

Harrison, H. *Dreaming in Yellow: The Story of the DiY Sound System.* London: Velocity Press, 2022.

Ludewig, B. *Utopie und Apokalypse in der Popmusik. Gabber and Breakcore in Berlin, Vienna.* Veröffentlichungen des Instituts für Europäische Ethnologie, vol. 47: University of Vienna, 2019.

Reynolds, S. *Energy Flash: A Journey Through Rave Music and Dance Culture.* London: Faber & Faber, 1998.

Stahl, G. (ed.) *Poor, But Sexy: Reflections on Berlin Scenes.* Bern: Peter Lang Verlag, 2014.

6 | Angolan Kuduro in the Context of Sound System Cultures of the Black Atlantic

STEFANIE ALISCH

Introduction

Kuduro is an electronic dance music from Angola, where it originated in the capital city of Luanda around 1990; it offers valuable insights for understanding EDM's socio-cultural role within transnational dynamics. With kuduro being tied to the timelines of EDM in the USA and Europe, kuduro is not an 'other' to techno and house, but an instantiation of how people around the globe embrace electronic dance music, making it their own through local practice. Besides the techno-house affiliation, kuduro is connected to South-to-South dynamics (such as zouk influence and relationships with African popular musics) as well as sharing characteristics with dancehall from Jamaica and axé music from Brazil.

Based on extensive ethnographic research, this chapter shows that we can usefully construe kuduro within the theoretical framework of sound system cultures of the Black Atlantic to illuminate its performative strategies within the larger configuration of global electronic dance music practices. After delineating the research approach, I lay out kuduro's history – both locally in the capital of Angola, Luanda, and in dynamic exchange with the Angolan diaspora – followed by an introduction to kuduro's sonic and bodily-performative practices, before focusing on the largely undervalued practice of animação to pinpoint the scholarly value of situating kuduro within the context of sound system cultures of the Black Atlantic.[1]

Research Approach

During research in Luanda (2011, 2012), London (2011), Maputo (2012), Lisbon (2012, 2013), Paris (2011, 2012), Amsterdam (2012), Salvador da Bahia (2023), and Berlin (since 2010) I employed a range of ethnographic methods including filming of and training in kuduro dance, DJing kuduro, and interviewing artists, producers, and fans. I spent hundreds of hours participating in kuduro activities in studios, backyards, and backstages, and occasionally performing on stage, in a mixture of practice and conversation that ethnologist Gerd Spittler calls 'thick participation'.[2] Kuduristas were mostly happy to participate in interviews or to receive me at kuduro-related activities, which I understand to be partly due to the vital importance of exposure to a kudurista's career. I honour this need in using their artist names when quoting kuduristas. Another explanation for participation may be kuduristas' desire to add to, and balance, the lopsided press coverage of kuduro.[3]

Kuduro's percussive electronic dance music is accompanied by dancing that can be competitive, ludic, acrobatic, comic, sensual, or theatrical. Computer-produced instrumentals called 'bits' are coupled with lyrics and free-flowing, or call-and-response animation delivered on the verge of shouting. When we listen to songs such as the classic 'Dança da Mãe Jú'[4] we notice certain characteristics that are typical of kuduro. The instrumental of this track has a tempo of approximately 140 beats per minute. Its pronounced four-to-the-floor bass drum is accompanied by corresponding rhythmic figures and beeping sounds reminiscent of 1990s techno. An interplay of isochronous and non-isochronous rhythmic figures, acoustic elements, and synthesised sounds points to musical genres like Euro dance, techno, and house, scraper sounds of Angolan traditional and earlier popular musics, puita friction drums of the Angolan carnival, and skipping rhythms of Caribbean carnival genres like soca or Brazilian axé music. These elements give the 'Dança da Mãe Jú' instrumental its forward-driving character that invites listeners to move. In the chorus, DJ Znobia refers over and over again to the dance of the dance salon Mãe Jú ('Mother Jú'). He invites his imaginary club guests: 'Dance any step, then we call it dance of the Mãe Jú.'[5] With this statement he points to two fundamental aspects of kuduro: firstly, the close link between dance and music, and secondly, the ease of a collective creativity that allows new lyrics, beats, and dance-moves to emerge playfully.[6] The act of verbally addressing the audience or dancers with the aim of engaging them dialogically is called animação ('animation'), and this antiphonic vocal style is closely linked with dance moves called toques. People who are active in singing, dancing, producing, or consuming kuduro typically display colourful, highly individual dress styles as well as innovative language use; they call themselves kuduristas.

For kuduristas, good kuduro is marked by carga ('charge'), an intensely competitive performance in dance, vocals, dress and styling, or musical production. Kuduristas create intense energy during their performances through artistic competition, hyperbolic speech, gestures, as well as interaction with co-performers and audience. In its competitiveness, carga distinguishes select individuals (who strive 'to be better than the other'). In addition, however, carga emerges by connecting with powerful music, fellow performers, opponents. As such, carga is a social phenomenon that is socio-affectively distributed, similar to 'vibe' in a rave setting.[7] Kuduro does not just happen in schoolyards, backyards, discotheques, street corners, and minibus taxis; it also appears on television and radio and on big stages. People access it via mobile phones, social media, and shared-hosting platforms. As such, kuduro is digitally produced and connected, yet is simultaneously experienced as an intensely corporeal music and dance genre. Kuduro dancing, production, and singing are organised through social groups and networks called staffs, turmas, or crews. The frequent and lengthy lists of shoutouts to vocalists, DJs, producers, distributors, discotheques, sponsors, and production companies reveal the importance of kuduro's social networks.

Pursuing an ethnographic approach, I adhere to kudurista-specific terminology such as bailarino ('trained dancer') or cantor ('singer') rather than using terms like MC, which kuduristas regard as a hip-hop term. Distinct roles on the kuduro circuit include producer ('producer'), cantora/cantor ('female/male singer'), artista ('artist'), músico ('musician'), DJ, animador ('animator'), empresário ('entrepreneur'), patrocinador ('sponsor'), compositor ('lyrics writer'), bailarina/bailarino ('female/male dancer'). These terms may be used with different or overlapping meanings: for example, a productor can be a music producer, but also someone holding the reins as artistic director, someone caring for organisational tasks, or someone who looks after marketing, booking, or artist management. Cantora/cantor, artista, músico all describe a kuduro vocalist who performs songs, but these terms serve as a distinction from animador by underlining the musical aspect of the vocal performance, placing kuduro vocalists closer to singers of other musical styles. An animador does not sing, but commands a crowd or stage dancers like an MC, usually over a microphone.

In kuduro, músico (in standard Portuguese 'musician') does not necessarily indicate that someone plays an instrument. Artista highlights that a vocalist is established with an image, a look, a following, and knows how to navigate different public and media situations – examples of revered artistas include Sebem, Noite Dia, and Os Namayer. An empresário is someone who sponsors an artist, provides for the production of a song, album, or video, or invests in music shows or other means to promote kuduro. Their money may come from businesses entirely unrelated to music. The term patrocinador ('sponsor') works similarly. Kuduristas often appeal to empresários or lament a lack of initiative from their side. A compositor in kuduro – different from standard Portuguese – is not a music composer but the person who writes lyrics. To call a kuduro dancer bailarina/bailarino ('female or male dancer') is a way to convey that they train and have the skills of a professional dancer, rather than an amateur ('dançarino/dançarina').[8] One and the same person may fulfil several of these capacities or transition between them, aspiring to higher prestige, better pay, and diversified musical practice.

The Angolan Context

The workings of Angola, a south-west African country by the Atlantic Ocean, are marked by several key historical processes: the internal and transatlantic trade in enslaved people, five centuries of Portuguese colonial interference, thirty-nine years of colonial and civil wars in the twentieth century, a socialist post-independence phase when the Movimento Popular de Libertação de Angola (Popular Movement for the Liberation of Angola, MPLA) was the only political party, an economic shift from a highly centralised economy towards more market orientation combined with transition to a nominal multi-party system during the 1990s, and finally peace from 2002 followed by an oil and construction boom. With the 2022 elections pronouncing the MPLA winner yet again, the country looks at fifty years of rule by the same party and this continuation of power is embedded within a larger historical arc. The urban power elites (also called creole elites for their thoroughly transnational history) have held onto power since they emerged through the transatlantic trade in the nineteenth century. Corruption helped them accrue unimaginable riches, siphoned off the profits of the petrol and diamond industry, but the majority of the population struggles from hand to mouth with less than two dollars a day income.

The seaport city Luanda is the capital city and national focal point of Angola in several ways. Portuguese colonisers, Cuban supporters, and Chinese contractors erected the buildings in the paved and high-rise city centre. Angolans and African immigrants built self-organised peripheral urban areas called musseques. In these densely populated informal neighbourhoods, public health, access to electricity, potable water, basic sanitation, and education remain problematic. At the same time, the musseques have, since the 1930s, been hotbeds of popular music.[9] The post-independence civil war – which raged intermittently between 1975 and 2002 – produced 4.1 million internally displaced people, and during the 1990s many of them settled in Luanda's musseques. Since the 1990s, the dynamic diasporic exchanges between Luanda and Lisbon (as well as Paris, London, and locations in the Netherlands or the USA) were vital to shaping kuduro. Many Angolans spent time abroad during the early 1990s because of the intensified civil war. They brought cassette tapes, VHS tapes, and CDs back to Luanda and started promoting Angolan music abroad; for example, DJ Carlos Pedro continued his DJ practice in Lisbon, became a radio host there, and spread kuduro to audiences in Portuguese-speaking African countries like Mozambique or Cape Verde via radio RTP Africa. Angolan musicians often contract services including mastering or CD manufacturing abroad, such as in Portugal and South Africa. Musical exchanges with other African countries continue to shape kuduro, as kuduristas appropriate sounds and dance moves from Congolese rumba or South African kwaito and gqom.

To understand the time window in the 1990s when several music, dance, and vocal practices coalesced to form the complex we now call kuduro, we need to go further back in time. In 1974, Angola gained independence from Portugal. Civil war ensued between former liberation movements MPLA, UNITA, and FNLA. Many Portuguese studio and record company owners left independent Angola and as a result the thriving music industry of the late colonial period crumbled. During the late 1970s, times of food rations and bread lines in the young war-torn nation, the expression cú duro ('hard ass') started to circulate in colloquial Portuguese in Luanda to denote 'toughing it out during times of hardship'.[10] The government supported culture in the service of socialist nation-building and Angolan popular music releases were consequently dominated by música de intervenção (interventional music). But young people could not party to these agitprop ballads and turned to Cape Verdean and Antillean dance tunes. At public events, called dancings, Luanda's musseque revellers accompanied these tunes with popular dance moves like bruxo e bruxa, brotuto, bungula, kabetula, kapreko, or vaiola. Angolan DJs observe international trends acutely. During the mid-to-late 1980s Angolan ears made contact with the sound of electronic dance music via the mainstream version of Italo disco in the synth-pop hits of Baltimora or Sabrina.[11] During the early 1990s, DJs played imported Chicago house or Latin house, techno, and Eurodance under the catch-all terms batida, techno, or underground at central Luanda's discotheques like Pandemônio, Bamuluka, Universo Parallelo 2000, Mathieu, Chiwawa, Saint-Tropez, UNIASES, or Bingo.[12]

Kuduro Genre Formation

In and around city centre discotheques, dancers rehearsed moves and numbers to battle each other individually or as troupes to the sound of imported EDM. Angolan musicians like Beto Max, M.G.M Zangado, Eduardo Paim, Bruno de Castro, Ângelo Boss, or Camillo Travasso have taken up the influences of house, techno, Eurodance, and Latin freestyle; they made these sounds their own as they started to produce electronic dance music that can retrospectively be understood as proto-kuduro. To these Angolan-produced EDM tracks, urban audiences continued the established practice of combining local dance moves like Gato Preto ('Black Cat'), Açúcar ('Sugar') or Ti Nogueira ('Uncle Nogueira') with selected tracks. From 1992–94 DJs Cláudio Silva, Ruca Fançony, and Zé Maria played house and techno three times a week at their programme Top Laser at Radio Luanda Antena Comercial (Radio LAC) where they invited guest animadores, such as Sebem. From 1993, they held raves outside the radio station at Praça Luther King in central Luanda. During the mid-1990s, the recreational centre Banca in the centre of Luanda served as party space where kuduro dancers showed their numbers and honed their skills at early Sunday night raves. Here Sebem picked the dancers to enter the dance circle and expertly animated them at the microphone.

Around 1995–96, dancer and former Michael Jackson impersonator Tony Amado circulated through Angolan discos to show off his animação-toques routines such as 'Dance que, dance que, dá Van Damme' ('Dance, dance, do Van Damme') and 'Amba cú-duro' ('Dance hard ass'). During this marketing spree he even danced on the show 'Conversas no Quintal' ('Conversations in the Backyard') on national TV. For the following decades Amado has continued to invoke in media interviews this first TV appearance as a foundational moment of kuduro. In 1995, Luanda-based label RMS released Angolan Bruno de Castro's album *No Fear*.[13] The CD's name and cover design resembled a US extreme sports clothing brand that was popular during the 1990s for promoting slogans of persevering to overcome obstacles. As such, the album title alludes to several facets of meaning at once: to a cosmopolitan connectivity in youth culture, to the sense of heightened excitement and transgression that marked 1990s rave and popular culture around the globe, and to an affective state when Luanda was simultaneously infused with the pressures of war-torn Angola and accompanying pleasure-seeking escapism. As such, *No Fear* gestures at the adrenaline that kuduristas often positively refer to when discussing carga. Label head Marcus Castro e Silva produced the CD with live musicians in Madrid as Luanda lacked functioning studios.[14] He promoted the album using kuduro as a genre name he had picked up from Tony Amado. As a DJ and owner of the discotheque Pandemônio, Silva enthused about DJs like David Morales or Junior Vasquez and expressly pursued a sound aesthetic from acid and Latin house with digitally emulated instruments and rave signals. But live musicians played digital drumsets, guitar, and keyboard on the album's tracks including 'Pra kata' and 'Chama Policia'. 'These were not loops', Castro affirms.[15] In 1997 Amado went to Boston to record his first album *Sexy Muza* ('Sexy Muse'), which contains a song called 'Kuduro'.

Up to this point, electronic dance music was a connoisseur affair of a small group of well-connected music industry folks who moved in a circuit that connected the discos, record shops, radio shows, and record labels of Lisbon and central Luanda. But in 1999 EDM became a wider phenomenon in Angola when Sebem's hit song 'A Felicidade' ('Happiness')[16] popularised kuduro with mass audiences in the sprawling musseques. The MPLA government quickly learned to leverage this popularity for its purposes. Between 2000 and 2002, the MPLA's army sent Sebem's and Tony Amado's troupes – comprising dancers like Salsicha, Manda Chuva, and Fogo de Deus – to provinces such as Benguela, Lubango, Bié, and Namibe. At the frontlines of war parties, MPLA and UNITA kuduristas danced and sang to entertain MPLA soldiers. In 2001, on the brink of peace, Virgilio Fire landed the smash hit 'Kazukuta Dance'. Its refrain 'Estamos sempre a subir' ('We're always on the up-and-up') alludes to Angolans' resilience during times of struggle and perceived exceptionalism that the Angolan government likes to invoke.[17] In 2002, the MPLA airlifted kuduro dancers of Sebem's crew from Luanda to the Moxico province to entertain UNITA troops and followers as UNITA leader Jonas Savimbi had just been killed. Even after the war, the MPLA government under President José Eduardo dos Santos used kuduro's mass impact by regularly booking kuduristas for day-long beer festivals called maratonas ('marathons') for election campaigns, or to round off speeches by the dictatorial president.

During the period 2003–5 DJ Walter Laton's recording space, JUPSON, in Luanda's Rangel neighbourhood brought together young kuduristas DJ Killamu, Mestre Ara, Fofando, Noite Dia, Gata Agressiva, Puto Prata, Bobany King, Puto Agressivo, Maquina do Inferno, Pai Diesel, Kome Todas, and others. They recorded vocals over pre-existing bits, developed their vocal style and producer skills, and developed networks there that shaped the future of kuduro and established the neighbourhood Rangel as a hub for the style.[18] In 2008, video maker Hochi-Fu released the video clip 'Sobe' ('Go up!', slang for 'Run from the police!')[19] of kuduro group Os Lambas, which established a new visual language that is sleek and ghetto at once. In 2009 the weekly kuduro TV show *Sempre a Subir* started broadcasting on TPA 2 and TPA Internacional. This widely remediated show was exclusively dedicated to kuduro and produced many interviews, recordings, and bifes (from 'beef', verbal duelling or banter) and made them accessible to the whole nation, the Angolan diaspora, and foreigners. In 2010, Cabo Snoop won an MTV Africa award for Best Lusophone Act with his kuduro hit 'Windeck',[20] which garnered special attention for kuduro from the African continent.

Previously, international attention for the genre had often resulted from initiatives outside of kuduro hotbed Luanda. For example, in Portugal, Angolan Rei Helder had re-released several songs by Sebem and Tony Amado as his own original music under the name 'Helder Rei do kuduro' ('Helder King of kuduro'), at first unbeknownst to the original performers. Back home, this fake act stirred up fierce controversy amongst kuduristas. And yet, Rei Helder spread kuduro in Portugal via the tangible archive of the CD and by touring discotheques and TV shows with his troupe that even included Tony Amado's former dancer Vaca Louca ('Crazy Cow') and Maninho da Vassoura ('Little brother of the broom'), who had previously danced with the artist Sebem.

The Lisbon-based group Buraka Som Sistema were inspired by kuduro artists and worked with some of them, such as DJ Znobia, to popularise the style amidst the international rise of commercial EDM. However, while enjoying the increased spotlight, many Angolans felt their toes stepped on by Buraka calling their music 'kuduro progressive' ('progressive kuduro'). Unsurprisingly, the implication that kuduro required some sort of enhancement from Portugal sparked anti-colonial resentment amongst Angolans. Around 2008 kuduro briefly caught the attention of European and American aficionados after the first funk carioca hype in those territories had waned. Funk carioca historically stems from electro/freestyle/Miami Bass and kuduro draws on house, techno, Eurodance, and Caribbean time signatures like soca. Despite these different trajectories, if the hyper-local references and wordplay in the Portuguese lyrics elude listeners, the skipping rhythmic feel of both genres is foregrounded in listening, which can accentuate their similarities for listeners from the Global North. The 2011 tresillo-based dance pop tune 'Danza Kuduro'[21] garnered international attention for the term kuduro. In Angolan discotheques DJs play this tune during the reggaeton section and people get down to it, while also lamenting how 'foreigners are making millions' using the genre name incorrectly and arguing that it is 'surely not kuduro'.

Kuduro's Musical and Embodied Practices

Since around the year 2000, kuduro has become the dominant sound and dance style in the youth culture of Angola and the Angolan diaspora. Despite its popularity, classist and culturally conservative voices in Angola resonate with colonial sentiments when they complain that 'kuduro is not real music', that it lacks history, and that 'all the ghetto youth jump and shout like that'. For kuduristas, quite the opposite is true: for them, producing kuduro with carga requires sharp skills and complex knowledge. Here I address two important elements, kuduro dance and animação,

Kuduro Dance

Comparable to Jamaican dancehall, kuduro songs are usually launched together with a signature dance move, the 'toque'. Toques form the basis of kuduro dancing and are one of the main promotional instruments for creating mass reception for a kuduro song, as fans appropriate the song via dancing. As star kudurista Noite Dia points out in an interview with me, kuduristas design their toques with the distinct intention that they can be copied easily by the general public.[22] Toques often gesture at the song's lyrics through a typical movement or by kinetically transmitting an energetic state. Noite Dia's nervous zombie-like staggering and head-shaking dance of 'Tá maluca' ('She's mad')[23] for example goes together with a paranoid bit by DJ Killamu and the lyrics 'Are you mad? She's mad, she's mad, she's mad, she's mad', all delivered in a tongue-in-cheek manner.

Kuduristas often discursively root their song-toques in the day-to-day conviviality of their neighbourhoods, drawing on everyday occurrences, images, and movements. In 'Dança Engraxador' ('Shoeshiner Dance')[24] the duo Os Namayer incorporate the typical rubbing circular hand movement of Luanda's many shoe shiners. In the 'Dance of the Generator', they embody the pulling of a generator's cord. With the frequent power cuts in the capital, this movement is ingrained in Luandans' collective kinetic repertoire. Puto Lilas' song-toque 'Enchimento' ('The filling')[25] celebrates the ample derrière or bosom of an imaginary female interlocutor. The toque entails cupped hands that gesture at the latter body part, going along with the lyrical line 'All of this is yours?!?' The backhanded compliment – conveyed through the conjunction of lyrics and toque – alludes to the fact that many Luandan women like to flaunt their curves, enhancing them through fashion and sometimes even plastic surgery. In 2014 Mauro Alemão launched the song-toque 'Catolotolo' ('Catolotolo').[26] With its disjointed dance moves of cramped joints at the shoulders, wrists, and ankles, it references an outbreak of catolotolo fever (caused by the chikungunya virus) in Angola in 2014. These few examples alert us to the close connection of kuduro dance to lifeworld movements and underline the fact that nonverbal elements are crucial in Angolan day-to-day interpersonal communication. If a toque catches on, it circulates not only on dance floors but also through several artists' performances and videos. Because they are so accessible, toques are one of the kuduro practices that most easily mobilise joy and collectivity.

Animação

Key to producing carga, charge, and thus to producing successful kuduro, is animação ('animation'). Animação is the hyping up of an audience with call and response phrases, jokes, references to the ongoing celebration, current affairs, bifes, and other established tropes. It is distinct from more structured and melodic singing, and outsiders often scoff at animação or deride it as 'mere shouting'. In a typical scenario a kuduro vocalist – between performing their songs – hypes up an audience over a microphone. When dancers share the stage with the vocalist, a more specific meaning of animação can be that of dance calling; shouting out names of dance-moves and dancers. When music is lacking, the animador can produce percussive noises vocally or through clapping hands or beating on thighs to emulate a bit – called adoçar ('to sweeten') – so the singer or dancer has a metrical reference to respond to. Another staple tool of animadores for creating carga, in the sense of connecting with others, is call and response, where the animador intones the first phrase, the audience chants the second. Mostly, these phrases are known as kuduro hits or popular dictums, but some are invented and learned during the ongoing performance. Some prominent examples are as follows:

Call: Olha ela!   Look at her!
Response: Amiga da gatuna.   The girlfriend of the female thief.
[From Madruga Yoyo's Vamú lá.][27]

Call: É por isso That is why
Response: Não nos gostam They don't like us
[By Queima Bilhas]²⁸

Animadores interact with both DJs and the audience, and most importantly with the dancers. Their verbal cues are crucial to creating carga through kuduro dance. Underground dancer Mangunay explains the dynamics between dancer and animators:

The animador gives the dancer inspiration. Likewise the dancer gives inspiration to the singer [i.e. animador]. ... A [good] animador is the one who is on top of the bit and he creates his thing in that moment. Maybe he is [with rhythmic intonation] animating, animating, animating, animating and maybe there is someone with a suit [in the audience]. And he sees this guy and goes 'Look, daddy is seeing you. Look daddy is seeing you'. Or you create a trick [i.e. dance-move] and that gives him inspiration, he catches the toque. Like you [Stefanie Alisch] when I was testing bungula and you asked, 'This dance-move, is it catch-the-mosquito?' An animador that is already animating, he could go [with rhythmic intonation] 'Kill ah, kill the mosquito'.²⁹

Skilled animadores incite and integrate different streams of performance. As they guide the proceedings, dancers hand over decision-making power and act within the framework maintained by the animador. Distributing labour in this way allows kuduro dancers to focus narrowly, and as such to experience and perform with intense carga, creating enthusiastic audience response and sometimes even mass euphoria. In kuduro, animação is pivotal to producing carga by spurring DJs, dancers, audiences, and camera operators into action, drawing attention to particular acts on stage and maintaining a performative framework.

With instructions like 'É pra sentir no osso' ('It's to be felt in the bone[s]') (Sebem in 'Felicidade'),³⁰ 'Se aguentam' ('Bear [this]'), or simply *Sentem*! ('Feel [this]'), animadores direct attention to the desired affective intensity of music and dance and thus co-produce these affective states together with sound and humans. Animadores can demand louder music from the DJ, commanding 'Sobe' ('Bring it up!'). Expressions like 'Estraga!' ('Ruin it!') or 'Avacalha!' ('Screw it up!') goad dancers on to do ever more drastic stunts. Shouting 'É mesmo assim' ('It's really like this'), they affirm and intensify the performance situation. These verbal practices are crucial aesthetic strategies to produce carga. Examining kuduro animação at this fine-grained level, while valuing the quality standards the kuduristas share amongst themselves, can reveal how they require expert knowledge, stamina, and technique.

The Black Atlantic: 'An Explicitly Transnational and Intercultural Perspective'

When translating the call-and-response lines above from Portuguese into English it becomes apparent how similar they are to lyrical practices of MCs in sound system cultures like hip-hop, house, grime, or jungle. Sociologist and cultural scholar Paul Gilroy describes this as 'playful diasporic intimacy that has been a marked feature of transnational Black Atlantic creativity'.[31] Gilroy observes that Black music and dance forms from different regions in Africa, the Americas, and Europe are consistently shaped by similar principles but also rife with contradictions and constantly evolving. To capture these dynamics, he forged the theoretical concept of the Black Atlantic, proposing to 'take the Atlantic as one single, complex unit of analysis to produce an explicitly transnational and intercultural perspective'.[32] This approach accounts for the complexities of kuduro's history and continuous interconnections by seeing the dynamic transnational movements of people, music, dance, and intellectual work around and across the Atlantic not as dangerous to culture and identity, but as constitutive to them.

The theoretical concept of the Black Atlantic provides a frame of thought to investigate kuduro as a style that emerged from a performative convergence of different sonic and kinetic practices: house and techno, themselves music genres born out of the emulation of West African principles of rhythm construction with beat machines;[33] American hip-hop music and dance that incorporated Jamaican sound system culture (for example, with tap, lindy hop, funk, and Afro-Latin dancing);[34] animation and dance practices that matured in Angolan semba-rebita, which in turn drew on Brazilian and Portuguese music;[35] but also, kwaito, picó, coupé decale, or reggeatón from the lusophone, francophone, or Hispanic Atlantic realms. Considering these connections, Gilroy asks:

> How are we to think critically about artistic products and aesthetic codes which, though they may be traceable back to one distinct location, have been changed either by the passage of time or by their displacement, relocation, or dissemination through networks of communication and cultural exchange?[36]

Linking Gilroy's question concretely with the 'playful diasporic intimacy' between kuduro and sound system cultures such as jungle, dubstep, UK garage, broken beat, or grime leads to the conclusion that in order to illuminate how kuduro works as an intricate practice, we must better understand it as a sound system culture within the Black Atlantic. The DJs who play percussive tracks, people doing antiphonic microphone work, all loudly amplified through massive speaker systems, stage dancers and an actively participating crowd clearly position kuduro within this larger realm of sound system culture.

Sound System as Performance Configuration in Electronic Dance Music

The sound system here stands as an abstract concept of an international music performance configuration. Highly pronounced and developed forms of this configuration are Jamaican dub/reggae/dancehall sound systems. Leading dancehall scholar Sonjah Stanley Niaah even regards the sound system as the Jamaican national instrument and has called for the design to be protected by copyright.[37]

That sound system culture travelled from Jamaica to the UK and formed the basis of popular music genres such as jungle, dubstep, UK garage, broken beat, or grime is widely accepted.[38] But hip-hop in the USA is based on Jamaican sound system practices, too.[39] Practitioners and researchers agree that the sound system goes beyond the 'giant community record player', as Les Back explains with reference to 1980s Jamaican reggae sound systems in the UK: the assembly of audio equipment that amplifies recorded music for a community of listeners. As a concept, a sound system not only consists of the speakers, amplifiers, and music replay equipment and microphone(s), it importantly includes the crew that runs it, comprising an engineer (called an 'operator' in Jamaica), an MC (deejay in the Jamaican context, or animador and commentator in Angola), and a DJ (also known as the selector in the context of Jamaican reggae sound systems).

But a sound system also depends on its audience, called 'the massive' in a Jamaica/UK context or 'o povo' ('the people') in the kuduro context. A sound system is a business model and also embodies a particular repertoire[40] that entails a specific 'way of knowing'.[41] The sound system affords highly interactive performances which often entail musical duelling and other forms of call and response. What unites sound systems, broadly speaking, is the use of amplified pre-recorded sound with hype strategies to make people dance, and the visual foregrounding of large speaker boxes further enhances the agency of the technical apparatus alongside the human performers.

Kuduro Construed as a Sound System Culture of the Black Atlantic

In the larger conversation around globalised popular musics, journalistic or scholarly concepts like world music and global beat,[42] world music 2.0,[43] global bass,[44] or global ghettotech[45] focus on sonic qualities, globalised distribution, or the effects of digitisation. They elaborate questions around power – who gains money and exposure and who doesn't? – or around the legitimacy of appropriating other people's cultural practices. However, observers from the Global North rather than cultural insiders coined these concepts with academic or commercial motivations. Their concepts seem mostly informed by listening to sonic artefacts like MP3s, CDs, or vinyl records and conducting interviews rather than active immersion into the intricate multi-modal processes of local musical practices. As such, these meta-concepts omit how the sound system as a socio-spatial, techno-sonic configuration – through which people perform and amplify recorded music, sound, vocals, dance, and gestures – shapes interactive processes across musical genres.

Construing kuduro as a sound system culture of the Black Atlantic affords several benefits. Examining the interactive dynamics that build between DJs, animadores, bailarinos, and o povo during a successful kuduro performance reveals the ways in which animação exceeds 'mere shouting', and thus illuminates blindspots created by classist ignorance at home in Angola. As a result of this conceptualisation, we understand the sound of kuduro with more nuance.

For example, when we hear on a CD or MP3 that a kuduro animadora repeats the same line over and over, we appreciate that she is creating a feedback loop with a responsive audience on a dance floor when the DJ plays this track. We further understand that the spaces between her vocal lines are not aesthetic, but strategic pauses, as they mark the moment when audience members chant the response line to her animating call or dance the corresponding toque. Posing sound system cultures of the Black Atlantic as a comparative model, we can comprehend how a kuduro animadora's microphone work is similar to that of a grime MC or house ballroom commentator, throwing the specificity of kuduro into sharper relief while also situating it within the larger context of similar practices.

Conclusion

The concept of sound system cultures of the Black Atlantic provides a way of comparing music and dance practice from disparate locations without running the risk of erasing local specificity with meta-concepts. Following Gilroy's entangled history, Sound System Cultures of the Black Atlantic as a concept further emphasises Black origins of European-based practices, including micro EDM genres such as freetekno, acid house, or breakcore. In popular opinion, these practices are often perceived as European-based but looking more closely it becomes clear that they explicitly or implicitly draw on the ethics and aesthetics of sound system cultures of the Black Atlantic. Investigating kuduro as a sound system culture of the Black Atlantic helps us to understand how cultural exchanges in the creolised Black Atlantic, especially South–South dynamics, shaped the genre. Kuduro is part of globally connected EDM, while it is simultaneously tied in with musical and day-to-day practices of Angola and popular music of the African continent.

Notes

1. Gilroy, P. (1993). *The Black Atlantic. Modernity and Double Consciousness.* Cambridge, MA:Harvard University Press.
2. Spittler, G. (2001). 'Teilnehmende Beobachtung als Dichte Teilnahme'. *Zeitschrift für Ethnologie*, 126, 1–25.
3. For my own guidelines on research ethics, see Alisch, Stefanie (2017). 'Angolan Kuduro: Carga, Aesthetic Duelling, and Pleasure Politics Performed Through Music and Dance' (Doctoral dissertation, Bayreuth International Graduate School of African Studies, Universität Bayreuth), 99.
4. DJ Znobia (2006). 'Dança da Mãe Jú'. DJ Znobia (Interpr.). Luanda. Available online at www.youtube.com/watch?v=jpYDSG9DBIE (accessed 28 March 2024).
5. Ibid.
6. Alisch, S. (2020). '"I opened the door to develop kuduro at JUPSON": Music Studios as Spaces of Collective Creativity in the Context of Electronic Dance Music in Angola'. *Contemporary Music Review*, 39:6, 663–83. https://doi.org/10.1080/07494467.2020.1863004.

7. See Witek, M. A. G. (2019). 'Feeling at One: Socio-affective Distribution, Vibe, and Dance-Music Consciousness'. In Ruth Herbert, Eric F. Clarke, and David Clarke (eds.), *Music and Consciousness 2*. Oxford: Oxford University Press, 93–112.
8. Nguizani, D. (2003). *Como dirigir um grupo e montar uma obra de dança*. Luanda: Editorial Nzila, 15.
9. Moorman, M. J. (2008). *Intonations. A Social History of Music and Nation in Luanda, Angola, from 1945 to Recent Times*. Athens, Ohio: Ohio University Press.
10. Moorman, M. J. (2014). 'Anatomy of Kuduro: Articulating the Angolan Body Politic after the War'. *African Studies Review*, 57:03, 21–40. https://doi.org/10.1017/asr.2014.90.
11. Pedro, Carlos (2012). Interviewed by Stefanie Alisch. Radio RTP Africa. Lisbon. 18 December 2012.
12. In interview, one of my interlocutors, Marcus Castro e Silva, underlines the presence of 'a lot of influence from Latin American DJs from Miami, David Morales, Junior Vasquez'. Castro e Silva, Marcus (aka Falcão) (2012). Interviewed by Stefanie Alisch. Café Mensagem. Luanda, August 2012.
13. Bruno de Castro (1995). *No Fear*. Luanda, RMS.
14. Castro e Silva, Marcus (aka Falcão) (2012). Interviewed by Stefanie Alisch. Café Mensagem. Luanda, August 2012.
15. Ibid.
16. Sebem (c. 1999). 'Felicidade. Sebem'. Available online at https://youtu.be/yAA3dfHlmwU (accessed 28 March 2024).
17. Kindanje, J. (2011). *Kuduro, um reinado sem rei nem coroa. Verdades históricas sobre a origem de um produto cultural genuinamente angolano*. Luanda: Jornal de Negócios, 140. See also Alisch, S. (2018). 'Ästhetisch übergriffig und politisch zahm? Kalkulierte Transgression und subtile Dimensionen des Politischen im angolanischen Kuduro'. In Stefanie Alisch, Susanne Binas-Preisendörfer, and Werner Jauk (eds.), *Darüber hinaus ... Populäre Musik und Überschreitung(en). Proceedings 2. IASPM D-A-CH-Konferenz Graz 2016*. Oldenburg: BIS-Verlag der Carl von Ossietzky Universität Oldenburg, 27–39.
18. Alisch, 'I opened the door'.
19. Os Lambas (2008). 'Sobe'. Hochi Fu (producer). Luanda, Powerhouse. Available online at www.youtube.com/watch?v=RQW1sSppdGM (accessed 15 March 2024).
20. Cabo Snoop (2010). 'Windeck'. Hochi Fu (producer). *Bluetooth*. Luanda.
21. Don Omar feat. Lucenzo (2011). 'Danza Kuduro'. From *The Soundtrack Fast & Furious 5*. Available online at www.youtube.com/watch?v=71sqkgaUncI (accessed 30 March 2024).
22. Noite Dia (2011). Interviewed by Stefanie Alisch. Club Showcase. Paris 6 October 2011.

23. Noite Dia/DJ Killamu (2009). 'Ta maluca'. Hochi Fu (producer). Luanda. Available online at https://youtu.be/bkf9IXwPMKI (accessed 22 March 2024).
24. Os Namayer (2011). 'Engraxador'. Luanda. Available online at www.youtube.com/watch?v=28oT0S3wjJ4 (accessed 22 March 2024).
25. Puto Lilas (2011). 'Enchimento'. Available online at www.youtube.com/watch?v=6gQdOeDMms8 (accessed 22 March 2024).
26. Mauro Alemão (2014). Catolotolo. DJ Padux (producer). Luanda.
27. Madruga Yoyo (2012). 'Vamos lá'. Available online at www.youtube.com/watch?v=000E0JSjSfs (accessed 11 April 2024).
28. Kindanje, 'Kuduro', 66.
29. Mangunay (2012). Interactive dance interview kuduro. On video shooting location Luanda Sul, Luanda. Interviewed by Stefanie Alisch 8 May 2012.
30. Se Bem (2006) 'Felicidade'. *Kuduro – África*. Europe: Newcolors. (Cat #ZM00135).
31. Gilroy, *Black Atlantic*, 16.
32. Gilroy, *Black Atlantic*, 15.
33. Butler, M. (2006). *Unlocking the Groove. Rhythm, Meter, and Musical Design in Electronic Dance Music*. Bloomington: Indiana University Press.
34. Pabon, Jorge Popmaster Fabel (2011). 'Physical Graffiti. The History of Hip Hop Dance'. In Murray Forman and Mark Anthony Neal (eds.), *That's the Joint! The Hip-Hop Studies Reader*. 2nd ed. New York: Routledge, 56–62.
35. Kubik, G. (1991). 'Muxima Ngola – Veränderungen und Strömungen in den Musikkulturen Angolas im 20.Jahrhundert'. In Veit Erlmann (ed.), *Populäre Musik in Afrika*. Berlin: Staatliche Museen Preussischer Kulturbesitz, 201–71.
36. Gilroy, *Black Atlantic*, 80.
37. Stanley Niaah, Sonjah (2021). Festivals at the Crossroads. Response and Resilience in the Reggae Transnation. SSO#7 *Sound Systems at the Crossroads*. Goldsmith College, University of London, https://sites.gold.ac.uk/sound-system-outernational/sso7/.
38. Henry, W. 'Lez', and Worley, M. (eds.) (2021). *Narratives from Beyond the UK Reggae Bassline*. Cham: Springer International Publishing. See also Singh Brar, D. (2021). *Teklife/Ghettoville/Eski. The Sonic Ecologies of Black Music in the Early Twenty-First Century*. London: Goldsmith Press.
39. Gilroy, *Black Atlantic*, 33.
40. Alisch, Stefanie (2009). '"Tell Me, Tell Me, Can You Feel the Vibe?" – Broken Beat in London. Ein kleines Szene-Porträt'. Magisterarbeit. Berlin, Humboldt Universität zu Berlin, 51.
41. Henriques, J. (2011). *Sonic Bodies. Reggae Sound Systems, Performance Techniques, and Ways of Knowing*. New York: Continuum.
42. Feld, S. (2005). 'Notes on World Beat'. In Charles Keil and Steven Feld (eds.), *Music Grooves. Essays and Dialogues*. 2nd ed. Tucson: Fenestra, 238–46. '

43. Burkhalter, T. (2012). 'Weltmusik 2.0. Musikalische Positionen zwischen Spass- und Protestkultur'. In Theresa Beyer and Thomas Burkhalter (eds.), *Out of the Absurdity of Life. Globale Musik*'. [Deitingen]: Traversion, 28–47.
44. Font-Navarette, D. (2015). 'Bass 101: Miami, Rio, and the Global Music South 1'. *Journal of Popular Music Studies*, 27:4, 488–517. https://doi.org/10.1111/jpms.12152.
45. Rocha, C. (2024). Global Ghettotech. The Brazilian journalist Camilo Rocha interviews the ethnomusicologist, DJ, and Norient writer Wayne Marshall about the latest musical trends around the globe: reggaeton, kwaito, kuduro, and grime. Available online at https://norient.com/stories/rochaglobalghettotech (accessed 10 April 2024).

Further Reading

Alisch, S. (2017). 'Angolan Kuduro: Carga, Aesthetic Duelling, and Pleasure Politics Performed Through Music and Dance' (Doctoral dissertation, Bayreuth International Graduate School of African Studies, Universität Bayreuth).

Alisch, S. (2020). '"I opened the door to develop kuduro at JUPSON": Music Studios as Spaces of Collective Creativity in the Context of Electronic Dance Music in Angola'. *Contemporary Music Review*, 39(6), 663–83. https://doi.org/10.1080/07494467.2020.1863004.

Gilroy, P. (1993). *The Black Atlantic. Modernity and Double Consciousness*. Cambridge, MA: Harvard University Press.

Henriques, J. (2011). *Sonic Bodies. Reggae Sound Systems, Performance Techniques, and Ways of Knowing*. New York and London: Continuum (Bloomsbury).

Moorman, M. J. (2008). *Intonations. A Social History of Music and Nation in Luanda, Angola, from 1945 to Recent Times*. Athens, Ohio: Ohio University Press.

Discography

Cabo Snoop (2010). 'Windeck'. Hochi Fu (producer). *Bluetooth*. Luanda.
Bruno de Castro (1995). *No Fear*. Luanda, RMS.
DJ Du Marcel (c. 2007). *Tribal Sound*. Luanda.
DJ Znobia (2006). 'Dança da Mãe Jú'. DJ Znobia (Interpr.). Luanda. Available online at https://youtu.be/jpYDSG9DBIE (accessed 28 March /2024).
Don Omar feat. Lucenzo (2011). 'Danza Kuduro'. From *The Soundtrack Fast & Furious 5*. Available online at www.youtube.com/watch?v=71sqkgaUncI (accessed 30 March 2024).
Madruga Yoyo (2012). 'Vamos lá'. Available online at www.youtube.com/watch?v=000E0JSjSfs (accessed 4 November 2024).

Mauro Alemão (2014). *Catolotolo*. DJ Padux (producer). Luanda.

Noite Dia (2011). 'Fogareiro. Apaga Fogo. Gueto Producoes'. Available online at www.youtube.com/watch?v=b_YIvg8Ly7U (accessed 27 March 2024).

Noite Dia/DJ Killamu (2009). 'Ta maluca'. Hochi Fu (producer). Luanda. Available online at https://youtu.be/bkf9IXwPMKI (accessed 22 March 2024).

Os Lambas (2008). 'Sobe'. Hochi Fu (producer). Luanda, Powerhouse. Available online at www.youtube.com/watch?v=RQW1sSppdGM (accessed 15 March 2024).

Os Namayer (2011). 'Engraxador'. Luanda. Available online at www.youtube.com/watch?v=28oT0S3wjJ4 (accessed 22 March 2024).

Puto Lilas (2011). 'Enchimento'. Available online at www.youtube.com/watch?v=6gQdOeDMms8 (accessed 22 March 2024).

Sebem (c. 1999). 'Felicidade. Sebem'. Available online at https://youtu.be/yAA3dfHlmwU (accessed 28 March 2024).

Titica (2012). 'Ablua'. Available online at https://youtu.be/iverlIH__h8 (accessed 28 March /2024).

7 | Chinese Electronic Dance Music Cultures

An Analysis of Their Local Cultural and Social Characteristics

MATTHEW MING-TAK CHEW

The globalisation of electronic dance music (EDM) has been ongoing for four decades, a process that has been rapid and far-reaching. Similarly, dance club and rave party formats have been distributed, from the USA and the UK respectively, across the world. Despite some degrees of localisation and reinterpretation, EDM cultures seem relatively similar across borders. Yet, if one considers localised EDM cultures, the globalisation of EDM is varied and complex. Globalisation has not merely helped popularise major EDM styles and cultures across the world; it directly triggered the development of numerous local EDM styles and cultures in various societies on the margins of globalising hegemonic processes and became domestically influential. Local forms of EDM and EDM cultures in mainland China exemplify this phenomenon. This chapter identifies and analyses five major EDM cultures of mainland China: mainstream clubs-based EDM culture; local clubs-based EDM culture; klubbing-based EDM culture; provincial dancing-based EDM culture; and mic-shouting-based EDM culture. The first two EDM cultures take place in the dance club, the third is based on karaoke venues, and the final two have developed on social media. The discussion that follows will focus on clarifying their local cultural characteristics and social implications.

Local Responses to Global Cultures

The concept of 'cultural localisation' was developed within the interdisciplinary field of globalisation studies to understand the local reaction against cultural globalisation. Studies of localisation find that when a locality imports any cultural items or ideas from foreign societies, it always alters them. The term 'localisation' describes such processes of alteration; the term 'localised culture' describes the outcome of such alteration processes. Localisation and localised culture can be very different across different cases. Localisation may be created by misunderstanding and subconscious distortion, or it may be intentionally and carefully crafted. In most cases, localisation helps resist global homogenisation. In a minority of cases, localisation yields innovative local cultural items that rival the original imported items in aesthetic value and global legitimacy. Terms such as 'hybridity' and 'glocalisation' are coined to describe these successful cases. I argue that local EDM styles remain globally unrecognised though, even though they may be domestically and regionally popular.

What may be called 'core EDM style' developed within the cultural histories of the Black Atlantic, as well as in the post-industrial contexts of North American and European urban regions, and the introduction of affordable electronic music technologies from Japan. Its global development seems rather insular, neglecting styles that develop outside of that cultural circuit. Such EDM cultures which developed outside of the global popular realm are, to date, insufficiently explored, which this discussion of local EDM styles in China aims to rectify. The local EDM cultures and styles of China have not gained global circulation; they only attain a small degree of translocal regional circulation. However, they were given ample opportunity to develop due to a very large domestic night-time economy. Consequently, several large-scale local EDM cultures and a few local EDM styles have been developing in China during the past few decades. They are locally distinctive and millions of clubbers and audiences in China participate. The local EDM styles have already been identified and analysed in several studies,[1] but the corresponding local EDM cultures have not yet been explored.

Despite a perception in international scholarship that the Chinese night-time economy is small, the night-time economy of post-reform China is well developed, rich, and diversified.[2] The recent coining of the term 'Eastern night-time economies' by urban studies scholars is in part a reaction against such misunderstanding.[3] The Chinese night-time economy is one of the largest national night-time economies in the world. It is composed of disparate commercial and non-commercial sectors, in addition to the EDM-based clubland and rave party events. In terms of the scale of participation, the largest commercialised sectors are EDM-based dance clubs and karaoke clubs (which are largely based on pop-rock). In terms of revenue and profits, commercial sexual-service-based night-time institutions, such as the hostess karaoke club, are arguably leading the way.[4] The non-commercial sector is also very large. For example, the most well-researched sector is 'square dancing' (*guangchangwu*), which involves local residents' grassroots organisation of social dance, traditional Chinese dance, and various contemporary dances (including EDM-associated dancing) in parks, street corners, and other public spaces.[5]

Only a tiny sector of the night-time economy in China, the Chinese underground dance club circuit, is almost completely based on non-local, transnational EDM styles and cultural practices. It is composed of around two dozen underground dance clubs in Chinese metropolises such as Beijing, Shanghai, Guangzhou, and Hong Kong; a dozen underground clubs in other Chinese cities; and occasional rave parties set up by international organisers.[6] In addition to such a cosmopolitan, yet underground, dance club circuit, several localised EDM cultures have emerged in China. These local EDM cultures are based on China's mainstream dance clubs, local dance clubs, karaoke clubs, hostess clubs, square dancing, street dancing, online games, and local social media. These EDM cultures are much more popular with many Chinese clubbers and audiences than the Chinese underground club circuit.

Methods and Data

This chapter's objective is to address the local and social characteristics of three major electronic dance music (EDM) cultures of mainland China. The analysis is based on two datasets. The first dataset was collected by the author between 1996 and 2018 as part of a long-term research project on the 'nocturnal sociology' (the study of night-time society) of China. I adopted various qualitative methods including participant observation, in-depth interviewing, and primary documentary search to investigate local club culture, EDM, service work in dance clubs, and the neoliberalisation of the night-time economy.[7] The participant observation was conducted in dance clubs and other nightlife venues in over a dozen cities in China. The informants included a wide variety of clubbers, service workers, DJs, other creative workers, managers, and owners in the Chinese night-time economy. Between 2001 and 2016 a wide variety of primary online documentary data were collected, such as clubbers' evaluation of music, DJs, and dance clubs, online forum discussions concerning local nightlife, and videos of DJ sessions of various dance clubs. Additionally, some quantitative data were collected through a questionnaire survey conducted with clubbers in Beijing in 2016.

The second dataset, which relates to social media-assisted local EDM cultures, mainly consists of online primary materials on mic-shouting and provincial EDM-based dancing (hereafter abbreviated as 'provincial dancing'). This dataset was collected between 2018 and 2022. The materials include performances found on video platforms such as Bilibili and

TikTok, debates on these two cultures on platforms such as Zhihu, fan discourses found on platforms such as Tieba, journalistic reports from news portals, and intellectual commentaries found in various Chinese portals.

China's Dance Club-Based EDM Cultures

The local club-based EDM culture and mainstream clubs-based EDM culture of China have been moderately transforming between the late 1990s and the present. Instead of examining the complex details of their transformation, I focus on some ideal-typical features of these EDM cultures, based on my first dataset of 1998–2018, and on engagement with these EDM cultures at numerous Chinese clubs in different Chinese cities over the past twenty-five years.[8] Based on this research, the discussion that follows offers a review of two distinct EDM scenes in China, the local-based EDM culture and its clubbing practices, and the mainstream club-based EDM, after which follows a reflection on the social characteristics of these two Chinese EDM cultures.

Musical Styles of the Local Clubs-Based EDM Culture

China's local club-based EDM culture features both non-local and local EDM styles, in various combinations. Even in clubs that predominantly play globally familiar EDM (most of which originated in North America, the UK, and Western Europe), local EDM tracks often assume an important role by occupying the climactic hour, or peak, of the Chinese club night.[9] Since the mid-1990s, a range of global EDM styles have been played in China's local club circuit. There are some long-standing preferences, such as techno and happy hardcore. In the early 2000s, for example, popular techno tracks played in local clubs included 'Knights of the Jaguar' by DJ Rolando, 'Better off Alone' by Alice Deejay, and 'Sandstorm' by Darude.[10]

There are three major Chinese EDM styles: Mandopop EDM, mic-shouting (*hanmai*), and provincial EDM (*tuhai*). Different local clubs devote their sessions to these three styles to different extents. Most commonly, local clubs play provincial EDM more than the other two styles in a club night. Research on the historical development and musical characteristics of Mandopop EDM and provincial EDM is very underdeveloped. A few studies examine mic-shouting.[11] Several studies investigate

Cantopop EDM, which is similar to Mandopop EDM but developed slightly earlier.[12]

The development of the three Chinese EDM styles can be traced to the mid-1990s. Mic-shouting is a style of local MC-ing and rapping accompanied by EDM tracks (instead of hip-hop music). Its historical roots include the Manchurian traditional folk singing and dancing from the north-east of China, known as 'two-people rotation' (*errenzhuan*); the Chinese traditional folk vocal art of *shulaibao*, which features the rhythmic recital of comical content; twentieth-century Hong Kong style mic-shouting; and global styles of EDM.

By contrast, provincial EDM does not precisely designate a musical style, but refers to domestically made EDM that is (perceived by numerous commentators in China to be) distorted, poor-quality, and/or commercialised in provincial ways. The negative evaluation of this EDM style as provincial is evident in the only, and broadly used, Chinese name of this style: *tuhai*. '*Tu*' means provincial and '*hai*' refers to EDM tracks.[13] I observed that from the late 1990s to the 2000s, techno was the most popular global EDM style chosen by Chinese DJs to create provincial EDM. From the early 2010s, other global styles including, for example, Melbourne bounce were added to the repertoire from which Chinese DJs created provincial EDM. Melbourne bounce is a subgenre of electro house that became globally popular in the mid-2010s.

Finally, Mandopop EDM refers to domestically made EDM tracks that emphasise pop-rock influence, vocals, and Chinese lyrics. These tracks are forms of Mandopop because they are sung in the official Chinese language, Mandarin. A significant portion of these tracks can be classified as electropop. Others vary in their composition of pop and EDM elements, because they are produced by DJs who perform EDM remixes of already published local pop-rock songs. When a DJ heavily minimises the vocal, lyrical, and pop-rock dimensions in remixing a track, the track sounds less like electropop. The remixing is drawn from various global EDM genres, most commonly house and techno.

Clubbing Practices of the Local Clubs-Based EDM Culture

China's local clubs-based EDM culture differs from global EDM cultures in clubbing practices as well as musical styles. This section discusses several such practices, namely entertainment, dating and sex, drinking games, and physical space. Although some clubs across the world also accommodate EDM-irrelevant entertainment elements, China's local clubs more heavily rely on them to attract customers. The first example of EDM-irrelevant entertainment elements is non-dance music styles such as ballads and pop-rock tracks from Chinese pop charts. In a significant minority of local clubs, one or two of these tracks are played within an hour or between EDM sessions. They are sometimes performed live by singers and staged with a karaoke music background. Another example is the lucky draw. It usually takes place around midnight and lasts for over ten minutes. The DJ acts as an MC by hosting this event, often performing mic-shouting at the same time. Yet another example is eating food in the club; the most widespread foods are fresh fruit plates and finger snacks such as chicken wings. Larger clubs additionally offer full menus that include regular restaurant dishes. The final example is live dance performances featuring sexily dressed female dancers with dance crews, to which significant time and support are devoted to the extent that EDM sessions are sometimes interrupted to let clubbers focus on these performances.

The management and service workers in local Chinese clubs developed informal work routines that shaped the local club culture. An example is a dating service that supports previously unacquainted clubbers to start dating. Another example is the offer of female escorts (or 'hostesses', as can be found in East Asian hostess bars and clubs) for male clubbers. In some cases, this service is nominally free; clubbers pay by buying drinks for the hostess. Some of these practices are highly institutionalised. For instance, in clubs in Shenzhen during the late 1990s, the spatial setup of the 'ring-shaped bar table' (*huanxingbatai*) was introduced to facilitate interaction between dance club hostesses and male clubbers.

Customers of China's local clubs tend to spend much time and effort during their club nights playing drinking games. The most prevalent games are the 'liar's dice', which is a Chinese dice game, and finger-guessing games. For these clubbers, dancing, EDM listening, and other conventional clubbing practices such as recreational drug-taking become secondary. Furthermore, this emphasis on drinking games alters the subcultural capital repertoire – drinking games skills become one of the most coveted subcultural capital in the local clubs-based EDM culture.

The final practice to discuss concerns space. Most local clubs adopt a spatial arrangement that devotes a moderate fraction of the club space to enclosed 'VIP rooms'.[14] This arrangement limits open space, sociality, and collective effervescence. It encourages clubbers to engage in non-EDM-based practices such as singing karaoke and playing cards. It also reinforces socioeconomic hierarchy among clubbers due to the higher charges for VIP rooms.

The Mainstream Club-Based EDM Culture

China's mainstream clubs avoid Chinese EDM styles and feature fewer local clubbing practices than China's local clubs. Mainstream clubs prefer global EDM styles and rising global music genres. They occasionally invite leading globally popular DJs to do live performances. Local EDM tracks are not played, but in general, they play global EDM tracks that are more commercialised and less progressive than those played in branded mainstream clubs elsewhere in global cultural culture, such as London's Ministry of Sound.

China's mainstream club practices and management are best described as subtly localised. I illustrate this with two examples. The first concerns what sociologists call 'ethnoracial performance' in the dance club.[15] This ethnoracial performance aims to make the clubbing experience more authentically global or Western for customers, who are mostly ethnically Han Chinese. Mainstream club managers pay wages or offer free drinks to ethnoracially non-Chinese youths to have them hang out in their clubs. White youths are preferred; they can be found in many clubs in Beijing and Shanghai. High-end mainstream clubs hire good-looking white (male and female) models from modelling agencies instead of regular white youths. The practice of hiring female models to enhance the buzz is found in mainstream clubs in the USA and Europe, but it does not involve ethnoracial performance. In Chinese cities such as Guangzhou, in which few white people can be hired, mainstream clubs instead hire people of colour to undertaken this ethnoracial performance.

The second example concerns the creation and use of status markers. China's mainstream clubs invent numerous ways to encourage wealthy customers to spend. For instance, the status-marking ritual of 'Chinese champagne towers' was developed. A spectacular several-feet-high tower consisting of champagne bottles is placed near the table of big spenders, serving to publicly glorify the big spenders and help them flaunt their wealth to others during the club night. Such rituals are widespread in China's clubland.

Social Characteristics of the Two Chinese EDM Cultures

Global EDM-based clubbing cultures are found to offer important sociocultural experiences. These experiences include what Ben Malbon calls 'oceanic feeling', what Graham St John calls 'religiosity', and what Dick Hobbs and collaborators call 'liminality'.[16] I understand them as the collective effervescence that derives from EDM culture. Like these cited scholars, I interpret these experiences as a valuable socio-cultural impact of EDM-based clubbing.

From the mid-1990s to the late 2000s, I observed that both local and mainstream clubs in China were quite capable of sustaining these experiences for clubbers despite various obstacles such as local spatial arrangements. But as commercialisation became rampant in the late 2000s, they became less capable of sustaining such experiences. The mainstream club circuit increasingly caters to wealthy occasional clubbers. Such rampant commercialisation has heavily undermined the socio-cultural experience of clubbing. I observed that the local club circuit drastically contracted during the 2010s; many local clubs went out of business or transformed into mainstream clubs. Nevertheless, what is left of the local club circuit is still moderately sustaining these socio-cultural experiences.

The commercialisation of dance clubs seriously undermines socioeconomic equality in two Chinese EDM cultures. The exclusion of non-wealthy clubbers is unrelentingly institutionalised in China's mainstream clubs. The minimum charges of having a table at mainstream clubs in Shanghai and Beijing became exorbitant in the 2010s, with an average table costing a few thousand US dollars for a single evening. Clubbers without a table are either forbidden entrance or pressured to leave by frontline workers in Chinese mainstream clubs.

Neither local or mainstream clubs are socially exclusionary in the sense that they do not discern between clubbers with different amounts of subcultural capital. Yet, mainstream clubs rigorously exclude clubbers based on socioeconomic criteria. Based on my participant observation and interviews with clubbers, I learn that even upper-middle-class urban Chinese regard the consumption expenditure for a mainstream club night as prohibitive. The overall Chinese night-time economy is found to have moderately contracted in the 2010s.[17] Socioeconomic exclusion is likely an important contributing factor. As an unintended secondary effect, this exclusion also pressures Chinese audiences to cultivate new local EDM cultures that are not based on dance clubs.

The Chinese state interferes with all aspects of civil society including popular culture, and clubland is no exception.[18] The state suppresses unruly dance clubs and banned some local EDM practices, such as dancing with head-shake moves and clubbers' mic-shouting on the dance floor.[19] The authorities effectively compelled dance clubs to enforce the ban. Through interviews with managers, I have found in my research that this cooperation between the club management and the authorities is common in both local and mainstream clubs.

China's Klubbing-Based EDM Culture

Due to EDM's popularity in China, it has overflowed outside the dance club sector of the Chinese night-time economy. A seriously affected part is the karaoke club sector. I coined the term 'klubbing' to refer to the resultant EDM-based nightlife practice in karaoke venues.[20] A klubbing-based EDM culture arose from klubbing practices. Klubbing emerged in 1999, grew in the 2000s, and slightly declined in the 2010s due to the modest contraction of the karaoke entertainment sector. Klubbing integrates karaoke-singing activities with dance-clubbing practices inside the spatial setting of the karaoke room. Most karaoke venues in current China do not have any open and shared party spaces. Instead, they are composed of numerous separate rooms that cater to individual groups of customers. Customers do not normally socialise or party with strangers in other karaoke rooms. Klubbers tend to spend the majority of their club night singing karaoke. Occasionally, they turn their small karaoke room into a mini dance club by playing EDM, turning off the lights, and dancing in the limited open space in their room. The EDM most usually comes from Mandopop EDM tracks and provincial EDM sessions supplied by the karaoke machine. Alternatively, it comes from specialised compact discs brought by the klubbers or even klubbers' makeshift DJ booths. Klubbing in karaoke clubs displays more DIY elements than clubbing in China's mainstream and local clubs. During my participant observation of klubbing, I felt that the original socio-cultural experiences of global EDM culture were minimised, yet still present. In regular karaoke venues, the collective effervescence of klubbing facilitates bonding between the members of a group of klubbers, and collective karaoke-singing facilitates bonding, but the embodied practice of dancing in klubbing further helps to achieve it.

In regular karaoke venues, klubbing does not generate any special social implications for gender. However, this is the case in the setting of hostess karaoke clubs, where the klubber is a sex client. The gender power relations in hostess karaoke clubs are originally hierarchical. The hostess club encourages highly ritualistic and patriarchal gender relations for the social and entertainment needs of its male clients,[21] but when klubbing occurs, the EDM-based dancing, sociality, and socio-cultural experience may, temporarily, alter gender relations. EDM-based dancing and sociality in hostess clubs permit hostesses a leadership role in the interactive microsituation because hostesses usually have more clubbing-relevant subcultural capital than their middle-aged clients. They also temporarily relieve hostesses from the ritualistic labour of reproducing patriarchy and the emotional labour of supplying romance to clients. I observed that in cases where klubbing occurred, most hostesses truly enjoyed the klubbing moments during their work night. Their clients either participate in EDM-based dancing as a klubber, or they sit back and enjoy the energetic vibe and ritually relaxed atmosphere. Meanwhile, I also observed that such club clients – perhaps the majority —would not let klubbing occur, as it interrupts the conventional hostess service and the clients' patriarchal power.

Based on my long-term observation between the mid-1990s and the late 2010s, I found that the hostess club culture in China has been modestly reshaped by the local EDM culture of klubbing. In the late 1990s, composite clubs that integrated a hostess club and a dance club under one roof emerged in Shenzhen. Composite clubs still exist, such as MGM Club in Beijing's Sanlituan district. Many mainstream clubs in Shanghai in the 2010s also offered 'hostesses on demand'. Although these dance clubs do not formally employ or manage hostesses, they invite hostesses to the club when a clubber demands such service. Namely, these clubs covertly function as hostess clubs. At the same time, composite clubs remain a niche market. A minority of clients of hostess clubs, especially the younger ones, have switched from conventional hostess clubs to composite clubs or mainstream dance clubs with hostesses on demand. As one of my informants explained, he increasingly felt that 'conventional hostess clubs are boring while dance clubs are vibrant and lively'. Additional research is needed to explore whether the patriarchal institution of hostess clubs is negatively transforming mainstream dance clubs and whether the egalitarianism of EDM culture is positively transforming hostess labour.

China's Social Media-Assisted EDM Cultures

Two local EDM cultures, involving mic-shouting and dancing to provincial EDM respectively, emerged in China between the late 2000s and the 2010s. Even though it is unsurprising that EDM can diffuse through social media, these two Chinese EDM cultures largely rely on social media in terms of emergence, financial support, and development. I call them 'social media-assisted EDM cultures'. Chinese social media – especially short video platforms and live-streaming platforms – constitute the current infrastructure of these two EDM cultures. China's social media is significantly separated from the global market by state censorship and protectionist policies, and so these platforms mainly feature domestically made content. Moreover, many Chinese social media users prefer domestically made content. Other factors that facilitate the two EDM cultures include the contraction of the local club circuit, the highly commercialised nature of local social media platforms, and China's strict lockdown policy in response to Covid-19.

DJs, emcees, and dancers – including many amateur ones – create online performances of mic-shouting and provincial dancing. Local social media platforms supply the distribution channel, capital investment, technical help for production, and economic revenue that drive these performers to produce more and better performances. Audiences watch these performances and discuss them online. Their reception is not passive; they train themselves to do memetic and derivative performances of mic-shouting and provincial dancing. They mostly do this offline – in their homes, street corners, parks, and local clubs. A minority of them upload their performances online or subsequently become performers. Mainstream media, including official television and journalism, help mainstream the two local EDM cultures by drawing general citizens' attention to them. Since the late 2010s, music critics, pop music artists, intellectuals, and educated netizens have increasingly commented on these two EDM cultures and their associated EDM styles.

The Mic-Shouting-Based EDM Culture

A social media-assisted EDM culture based on mic-shouting began in the late 2000s. Hong Kong-style mic-shouting was created during the second half of the 1990s. Chinese DJs and MCs immediately adopted it and introduced modest changes. For example, the lyrics were written in Mandarin instead of Cantonese. Political satire became a major theme until state suppression. In the late 2000s, Chinese DJs started to perform mic-shouting to social media audiences instead of clubbers in local clubs. A fandom grew around prominent mic-shouters. But the lyrics, music, and rapping style did not differ much from early Chinese mic-shouting in the late 1990s. Reliance on social media instead of dance clubs indirectly facilitates two new stylistic developments of mic-shouting. In the early 2010s, a new literary source of lyrics was found: Chinese fantasy webnovels. During the second half of the 2010s, the rapping style underwent modest development – the tone and timbre of the mic-shouting voice increasingly became an artistic focus. These new developments strengthened the mic-shouting EDM culture by enabling new and meaningful audience practices.

The earliest mic-shouting during the late 1990s in Hong Kong and China came in three forms: live DJ performances of mic-shouting in dance clubs; recorded mic-shout tracks; and clubbers' mic-shouting on the dance floor with clubber-generated lyrics. Clubbers' mic-shouting was forcefully banned in 1999 and 2000 because of its critical political content. The introduction of Chinese fantasy vocabulary and narratives helps revive the practice of clubber (or audience in the case of social media) mic-shouting. Such vocabulary and narratives express socio-political discontent in apparently apolitical ways. Besides listening to mic-shout performances, audiences also emotionally and artistically express themselves through their own mic-shouting. In such cultural reproduction, audiences experiment with different mic-shouting voices and tones. Some imitate famous mic-shouters' tones. Others play with different tones and timbres to generate their unique mic-shouting versions of hit tracks such as MC Liudao's version of 'Clap of Thunder' (*Jinglei*).[22] The resultant EDM culture may not be as intimate as dance club-based EDM cultures, but it is as interactive and convivial.

The Provincial Dancing-Based EDM Culture

Although EDM culture associated with mic-shouting is fully based on mic-shouting, the social media-assisted EDM culture associated with provincial EDM is not exclusively based on provincial EDM. The latter involves dancing in front of the camera while provincial EDM is heard in the background. The audience's primary focus is dancing, rather than listening to provincial EDM. Furthermore, although mic-shouting is stylistically shaped by its associated EDM culture, provincial EDM is not stylistically shaped or transformed by its associated EDM culture. At the same time, provincial EDM has benefited from social media in terms of broadening its audience base and increasing income and fame for provincial EDM DJs such as Sister Seven (Qimei).

The most definitive dance meme of the provincial dancing-based culture is the 'social shake' (*shehuiyao*).[23] This dance meme involves relatively minimal repetitive steps and bodily movements, containing a mixture of hip-hop, contemporary, and rave party dance elements. The dance moves of the social shake can be partly traced to those of China's local clubs in the late 1990s, in which head-shaking movements were emphasised. As mentioned, the state banned such head-shaking movements in clubs in 2000, which was partly due to its association with an ecstasy-related dance drug culture.[24]

In 2014, provincial dancing became a very popular short video entertainment genre on Chinese social media platforms such as Kuaishou and TikTok. Provincial dancing was popularised with some viral videos of the social shake, which were choreographed and performed by Mengqi Li and his dance team.[25] Before 2014, provincial dancing was uncommon on Chinese social media. After going viral in 2014, the social shake has remained popular online up to the present. At the time of writing, it is still seen as the representative of this local EDM culture. Li was the most prominent dancer until being banned in 2018.[26] At the same time, various less-known dancers and less-known dance memes such as the 'shoulder shake' (*doujianwu*) and 'seaweed dance' (*haicaowu*) emerged. Some of these less-known dances were performed with Mandopop EDM instead of provincial EDM. Audiences and fans learn the social shake, practise it at home, and perform it online and offline. In turn, internet celebrities have adopted this dance style and added provincial EDM dancing to their online performance repertoire.

The provincial dancing-based EDM culture differs from the mic-shouting-based culture in a few aspects. Social shake dancing diffuses to public and semi-public spaces; it is not limited to mediated and online contexts. The social shake is danced by some in physical spatial settings such as neighbourhood street corners, parks, and dance clubs. Additionally, while mic-shouting is performed individually, the social shake is quite often collectively performed. Both performers and fans prefer to dance the social shake with a team in synchronised moves. Although such dancing has not evolved into a very widespread urban phenomenon, it has created what may be called 'poor persons' club spaces' that resist socio-economic exclusion from China's current club circuit.

The provincial dancing-based EDM culture is less obviously socially relevant and politically critical than the mic-shouting-based one. Because it is based on embodied movements and devoid of vocal text, it is inherently less capable of conveying critical social messages than mic-shouting. Consequently, it was occasionally endorsed and reproduced by the hegemonic media including the New Year Gala television show, which is the state's major propaganda programme. Nevertheless, provincial dancing is increasingly regarded by audiences, commentators, and the state as deviant culture, because Mengqi Li and other performers dress and act like deviant youths. To some extent, this association is also turning provincial dancing into a symbol that represents the social underdog.

Social Implications of the Two Social Media-Assisted EDM Cultures

Several insights can be gathered regarding the social implications of the two social media-assisted EDM cultures. Firstly, the two cultures have helped develop a local EDM style – mic-shouting – and have economically sustained two local EDM styles, mic-shouting and provincial EDM. In this way, social media have enabled the promotion of diversity that can resist global cultural homogenisation. Secondly, due to mediation by information technology, these two EDM cultures do not fully maintain the original socio-cultural experience of global EDM cultures. Namely, their EDM-derived collective effervescence is less intensive and intimate.

A third social implication is that the two social media EDM cultures greatly contribute to the social inclusion of rural working-class audiences of EDM.[27] Both the underground and mainstream club circuits in China cater to urban middle-class audiences. This is a notable difference between the field of EDM culture in economically developed societies and that in developing ones. In wealthy societies, non-wealthy clubbers can still afford underground clubs and non-commercialised rave parties. In developing societies such as China, a large portion of the population consists of rural residents, poor rural migrants in cities, and residents of provincial towns. Around 100 million rural migrants and rural residents are under thirty years old in China; this figure goes up to 300 million if one counts those between thirty-one and fifty years old.[28]

Social media-assisted EDM cultures and their associated local EDM styles enable members of the rural migrant working class to participate in, and enjoy, EDM. For example, on the Kuaishou short video platform, which is known to be the platform preferred by rural residents and migrants, the number of followers of Mengqi Li was 35 million in 2018, and for MC Tianyou this was 40 million in 2017.[29]

Finally, the two EDM cultures help resuscitate local Chinese EDM's political critique against the authoritarian state. The Chinese fantasy lyrics of mic-shouting and the deviant culture of provincial dancing are driving this critique. The authoritarian state is aware of this threat and banned MC Tianyou in 2017 and Mengqi Li in 2018 from all performances.[30] The ban scared other mic-shouters and dance performers, who in turn self-censor their performances. Nevertheless, the two cultural forms are still surviving by switching to new material that is less directly critical in the political sense, and the images are now less associated with gangster culture.

Conclusion

The research identified five major EDM cultures of China and the discussion further elaborates on their local cultural and social characteristics. Describing the basic practices of each EDM culture, their difference from global EDM cultures and one another, and the history of their development, it offers a brief evaluation of how they implicate socio-cultural experiences, gender relations, authoritarian political control, and social inclusion. As an empirical base and with the contextual knowledge required for its interpretation, the findings contribute to a now developing field of Chinese EDM studies. Additionally, the discussion yields two sets of findings that involve general theoretical issues. The first set of findings concerns studies of Chinese pop music and EDM. My analyses of the five EDM cultures collectively illustrate that globally neglected local EDM cultures, such as those in China, deserve scholarly investigation and are of both cultural and social interest. Some versions may not translate beyond their local context, but others could eventually gain a degree of global recognition due to their cultural novelty and local distinctiveness.

The second set of findings concerns two positive social outcomes from Chinese EDM cultures. A first implication directly generates progressive social and political consequences, such as the impact of klubbing practices on gender relations and the presence of political critique in mic-shouting; this is of conceptual interest because these phenomena are not operating, or even observable, within global EDM cultures. A second type of implication resides within socio-political struggles, such as the rise of two social media-assisted EDM cultures, which enabled Chinese EDM participants to fight Chinese clubland's socio-economic exclusion practices. Moreover, the prospering of multiple localised EDM cultures in China demonstrates successful efforts by Chinese audiences to resist the cultural hegemony of global EDM styles and cultures.

Notes

1. Zhang, Ge and Jian Xu. 'A Brief Genealogy of Hanmai'. *China Perspectives*, 3 (2019), 63–68; Chew, Matthew M. 'Hybridity, Empowerment and

Subversiveness in Cantopop Electronic Dance Music'. *Visual Anthropology*, 24:1–2 (2011), 139–51; Chew, Matthew M. 'Cultural Localization and its Local Discontents: Contested Evaluations of Cantopop Electronic Dance Music'. *Social Stratification in Chinese Societies*, 5 (2010), 165–90; Chew, Matthew M. 'Mic-Shouting in China and Hong Kong, 1996–2020: Toward Histories of non-Western Local Electronic Dance Music'. In Luis-Manuel Garcia and Robin James (eds.) *The Oxford Handbook of Electronic Dance Music*. Oxford University Press (2023).

2. Chew, Matthew M. 'Research on Chinese Nightlife Cultures and Night-Time Economies'. *Chinese Sociology and Anthropology*, 42:2 (2009), 3–21; Farrer, James. 'Nightlife and Night-Time Economy in Urban China'. In Weiping Wu and Mark Frazier (eds.) *The Sage Handbook of Contemporary China*, pp. 1112–1130. London: Sage (2018).
3. Hadfield, Phil. 'The Night-Time City. Four Modes Of Exclusion: Reflections on the *Urban Studies* Special Collection'. *Urban Studies*, 52:3 (2015), 606–16.
4. Zheng, Tiantian. *Red Lights: The Lives of Sex Workers in Postsocialist China*. Minnesota: University of Minnesota Press (2009).
5. Martin, Rose, and Ruohan Chen. *The People's Dance: The Power and Politics of Guangchang Wu*. Singapore: Springer Nature (2020).
6. Yiu, Alex and Damien Charrieras. 'On the Fence: Electronic Dance Music Cultures in Hong Kong and Shenzhen'. In Sébastien Darchen, Damien Charrieras, and John Willsteed (eds.) *Electronic Cities*, pp. 223–41. Palgrave Macmillan: Singapore (2021); Chew, Matthew M. 'Assessing Localization with its Local Sociocultural Dynamics: How Hong Kong's Localized Clubculture Was Undermined By Wealth And Power Disparities'. *Globalizations*, 17:4 (2020), 730–45.
7. Chew, Matthew M. 'New Boundary Work of Rural Migrants: How it Opens up New Potential ways of Remaking Rural-Urban Symbolic Boundaries in China'. *Chinese Sociological Review*, 5:4 (2020), 421–47.
8. Being a first attempt to analyse these EDM cultures, future studies may surely challenge or revise my findings.
9. For most clubs in China excluding those in Hong Kong, the climactic hour is between eleven o'clock and midnight.
10. Alice Deejay, 'Better off Alone', Violent (Studio 4045), Hilversum, Netherlands, 1999; Darude, 'Sandstorm' JS16, Finland, 1999; DJ Rolando, 'Knights of the Jaguar', Underground Resistance, United States, 1999.
11. Chew, Matthew. 'Mic-Shouting' offers an in-depth musical analysis of mic-shouting. A historical account of the development of mic-shouting is provided by Zhang, Ge and Jian Xu, 'A Brief Genealogy'.
12. For an in-depth analysis of Cantopop EDM, see Chew, Matthew, 'Hybridity, Empowerment'.

13. This chapter sets to one side the question of whether provincial EDM is truly provincial and inferior. Only dedicated studies of provincial EDM can resolve this question.
14. Chew, Matthew. 'Assessing Localization'.
15. Chew, Matthew. 'How the "Commercialized Performance of Affiliative Race and Ethnicity" Disrupts Ethnoracial Hierarchy'. *Sociology*, 56:2 (2022), 333–50.
16. Malbon, Ben. *Clubbing: Dancing, Ecstasy, Vitality*. Oxford: Routledge (2002); St John, Graham, (ed.) *Rave Culture and Religion*. London: Routledge (2004); Hobbs, Dick, Stuart Lister, Philip Hadfield, Simon Winlow, and Steve Hall. 'Receiving Shadows: Governance and Liminality in the Night-Time Economy'. *The British Journal of Sociology*, 51:4 (2000), 701–17.
17. Farrer, James. 'Nightlife'.
18. Chew, Matthew M. 'Non-Digital Fan Networking: How Japanese Animation and Comics Were Disseminated in China Despite Authoritarian Deterrence'. *International Journal of Cultural Studies*. 26:1(2023), 34–51.
19. Chew, Matthew M. 'Decline of the Rave Inspired Clubculture in China: State Suppression, Clubber Adaptations and Socio-Cultural Transformations'. *Dancecult: Journal of Electronic Dance Music Culture*, 1:1 (2009); Chew, 'Mic-Shouting'.
20. Chew, Matthew M. 'Hybridization of Karaoke and Dance Clubbing Practices in Chinese Nightlife'. In Yiu Wai Chu and Eva Kit Wah Man (eds.) *Contemporary Asian Modernities*, pp. 287–307. Bern: Peter Lang (2010).
21. Allison, Anne. *Nightwork: Sexuality, Pleasure, and Corporate Masculinity in a Tokyo Hostess Club*. Chicago: University of Chicago Press (1994); Hoang, Kimberly Kay. *Dealing in Desire*. Oakland: University of California Press (2015); Zheng, *Red Lights*.
22. The MC Liudao version of 'Clap of Thunder', first performed in 2020 on Chinese TikTok, is accessible with English subtitles on YouTube at www.youtube.com/watch?v=HdPc46oUEsY. Tracks such as this do not have formal discography and copyright. They are informally produced and distributed on Chinese social media.
23. I interpret the social shake as a 'dance meme' because it is a dance routine that has gone viral on the internet. It is not exactly a style of dance. For example, a globally well-known dance meme is the galloping dance featured in the music video of 'Gangnam Style', performed and popularised by PSY in 2012.
24. Chew, Matthew 'Decline of the Rave'.
25. Studies on the social shake or provincial EDM are lacking, with the exception of a few publications that tangentially discuss the media background of the social shake. See Zhou, Min, and Shih-Diing Liu. 'Becoming Precarious Playbour: Chinese Migrant Youth on the Kuaishou Video-Sharing Platform'. *The Economic and Labour Relations Review*, 2:3 (2021), 322–40.
26. Xu, Jian and Ge Zhang. 'The Rise and Fall of the "King of Hanmai"—MC Tianyou'. *Celebrity Studies*, 12:2 (2021), 333–38.

27. Hou, Jiaxi 'A Platform for Underclass Youth: Hanmai Rap Videos, Social Class, and Surveillance on Chinese Social Media'. *First Monday* (2021). n.p.
28. National Bureau of Statistics of the PRC, 'National survey report on rural migrant workers 2020' (in Chinese), 30 April 2021. Available at: www.stats.gov.cn/tjsj/zxfb/202104/t20210430_1816933.html.
29. Wanghongjiaofu 'The MC Tianyou fandom has reached 40 million', 11 Jan 2018. Available at https://kknews.cc/entertainment/p6nz66z.html; Shenqishijieqimiaowuyu. 'The success story of social shaker Mengqi Li, who has 35 million fans on Kuaishou', 7 May 2018. Available at https://kknews.cc/entertainment/pnknam2.html.
30. Xu, Jian and Ge Zhang. 'The Rise'.

Further Reading

Chew, Matthew Ming-tak. 'Mic-Shouting in China and Hong Kong, 1996-2020: Toward Histories of non-Western Local Electronic Dance Music'. In Luis Manuel Garcia-Mispireta, and Robin James (eds.) *The Oxford Handbook of Electronic Dance Music*. Oxford University Press: Oxford, UK (2024).

Chew, Matthew Ming-tak. 'Assessing Localization with its Local Sociocultural Dynamics: How Hong Kong's Localized Clubculture was Undermined by Wealth and Power Disparities'. *Globalizations*, 17:4 (2020), 730–45.

Hou, Jiaxi. 'A Platform for Underclass Youth: Hanmai Rap Videos, Social Class, and Surveillance on Chinese Social Media'. *First Monday* (2021).

Yiu, Alex, and Damien Charrieras. 'On the Fence: Electronic Dance Music Cultures in Hong Kong and Shenzhen'. In Sébastien Darchen, Damien Charrieras, and John Willsteed (eds.) *Electronic Cities*, pp. 223–41. Palgrave Macmillan: Singapore (2021).

Zhang, Ge, and Jian Xu. 'A Brief Genealogy of Hanmai'. *China Perspectives*, 3 (2019), 63–68.

8 | Taking the Mix to Twitch

Streaming DJ Culture during and after the Pandemic

TOBIAS C. VAN VEEN AND BERNARDO ALEXANDER ATTIAS

DJ culture has long been associated with the collective experience of the dance floor in electronic dance music cultures (EDMCs), yet it has also spread through various forms of broadcast technology, from radio to television and the internet. In this chapter, we seek to explore the ways that DJ culture adapted to the conditions of social isolation that defined the Covid-19 pandemic. On the one hand, we are interested in the adoption of internet technologies, particularly the live-streaming platform Twitch, to facilitate various aspects of virtual belonging and online community that emerged to redress the absence of the shared physical dance floor. On the other hand, we are interested in how 'online DJing' constructs the conditions for virtual engagement by *remediating* forms of broadcast media, often reframing and transforming the kinds of social interaction and audience participation that have historically been a part of DJ and dance music shows on television and live mix shows on radio.

The internet itself is arguably a remediation machine,[1] and, with the widespread adoption of broadband internet over the past decade, has proven itself capable of devouring prior media forms – particularly bandwidth-heavy forms of 'moving pictures' – that preceded it. It is precisely because of these technological conditions that its infrastructure has been capitalised upon by commercialised platforms such as Twitch, providing the hard materiel for all manner of streaming culture during the pandemic. When Bolter and Grusin coined the term 'remediation' in the 1990s as 'a *defining* characteristic' of what was then called 'the new digital media', they were also reiterating a central point made by McLuhan: that 'the representation of one medium in another' is arguably a necessary condition of all media.[2] What interests us here is less the formal argument over media forms, and more how the 'content' of an online DJ broadcast 'remediates' not just other forms of media (such as television or radio) but its history of cultural expression in DJ culture, such as in the mix show, live dance show, or dance floor itself, particularly its affective aspects. Key to this inquiry is understanding how Twitch became a focal point for DJ culture to embrace feeling-together, as a site of collective belonging, vibe,

Fig. 8.1 DJ tobias (left) and DJ Professor Ben (right) DJing vinyl back-to-back on PANDEMiX! using Streamyard, 20 November 2020.

and *communitas* during a period of protracted interpersonal isolation during the pandemic, as well as after (Figure 8.1).

A Brief History of Online DJ Culture – and a Thesis

In the early days of the pandemic, most in-person electronic dance music events were cancelled or postponed, and many DJs, both professional and hobbyist, took their activities to the internet.[3] DJ culture has its own history of online DJ performance, mostly beginning with the release of the proprietary Real Audio codec in 1995 by Seattle's RealNetworks. However, it was with the 1999 release of Icecast, an open source audio streaming server and codec, that DJs were able to host their own internet radio stations without having to pay for commercial software.[4] Indeed, Icecast was developed for the radio station at Southern Methodist University (SMU) by then-students Jack Moffitt and Barath Raghava. These developments led to 'dot com'-era websites that focused on online DJ performances, utilising Real Audio or Icecast streaming technology to host guest DJs in live spaces, such as Seattle's Groovetech.com and San Francisco's Betalounge.com, the latter of which to this day maintains an archive of over 700 artists and 900 shows from 1996–2019.[5] What was innovative about these streaming websites is that the audio (and sometimes visual) broadcast was accompanied by a chat room, allowing for a degree of online interaction with viewers.

It is Club Equinox, however, that takes credit for being 'the world's first virtual nightclub', having opened in 1999 and offering streaming music events in an LGBTQ-friendly virtual space.[6] Collective streaming events also experienced something of a heyday in the mid-2000s with online virtual reality platforms Second Life and Kaneva.[7] These online events were treated seriously by many of their participants, in many cases with promoters selling tickets, booking well-known DJs, etc. It's important to add that rave culture's global dissemination has gone hand-in-hand with the advent of cyberculture since the 1980s, making use of BBS (Bulletin Board Systems), email listservs (such as the Hyperreal.org regional discussion lists), websites and forums on the World Wide Web (WWW), Internet Relay Chat (IRC) services, early peer-to-peer (P2P) file sharing such as Napster, and especially since the build-out of broadband infrastructure, audio and full-video streaming through various platforms.[8]

The pandemic, however, signalled a broader shift in global EDMCs, wherein many of their activities were transitioned to computerised or 'virtual' experiences, including the affective aspects of raving and clubbing that encompass hearing, seeing, and dancing to a DJ performance. We seek to better understand this transition by unpacking some aspects of one of the predominant platforms for DJ culture online in the 2020s: Twitch. Our concerns range from a thorough understanding of Twitch as a platform, embracing software and platform studies, to positioning that understanding within the development of online community in general during the pandemic. While the full scope of this study exceeds our limits here, in this chapter we want to address how DJ culture and performance, as key aspects of EDMCs, navigated the transition from in-person events to the screen, and how affective experiences of the dance floor, the 'vibe', and its *communitas* transformed during this process.

Seeking forms of collective belonging during a period of isolation marked the experience of the pandemic for many. This desire for belonging-and-bonding together marks what Victor Turner described as the desire for *communitas*, that 'flash of mutual understanding on the existential level, and a "gut" understanding of synchronicity'.[9] Graham St John remarks on how 'communitas assists explanation for the optimum social dance music experience regarded by participants as *the vibe*', which he further describes as 'a desire for a sacred sociality, a social warmth howsoever temporary, perceived to have been lost or forgotten in the contemporary world of separation, privatisation and isolation'.[10] In short, the desire for *communitas*, as the condition for communal relations, creates the experience of the vibe. What we observed from our study of Twitch DJ culture is how such affects of collectivity can be 'felt' in physical isolation, suggesting a complex relationship between viewer, screen (as the interface medium), and streaming 'content' that produces a collective imaginary of belonging together, a 'vibe' often expressed by users in their messages and emotes in the chat.

These at times paradoxical yet affective elements of a 'collective-belonging-in-isolation' are at the heart of the pandemic experience; they are also the condition for all affective relations online. We also found that *parasocial* elements of belonging were observed in viewer behaviours. The parasocial signals an overidentification and idealisation of on-screen personalities, manifesting in a false sense of intimacy with an on-screen 'celebrity'. The 'parasocial performance' is arguably capitalised upon by particular kinds of DJs, just as an 'affect economy' is built into the platform's reward schemes that entice users for micropayments, in ways akin to the 'affective engagement' offered by adult streaming platforms such as OnlyFans or Chaturbate. The parasocial has been remarked elsewhere as defining the affective economy of social media (and its 'gambling' impulses) while amplifying stalker behaviour and narcissism.[11] We will return to the parasocial below.

A Twitchy Remediation of Radio and Television

The pandemic coincided with the increasing popularity of Twitch, which was first founded in 2007 as Justin.tv with the aim of encompassing a range of streaming content. Upon launch, the streaming platform was quickly adopted by video-gamers who wanted to share their gaming performances in live streams,[12] which led to the spin-off of video-gaming-focused Twitch.tv in 2011, and the shuttering of Justin.tv in 2014 after its acquisition by Amazon.com. The Twitch platform made it relatively easy for gamers to combine multiple audio and video sources (a computer screen on which a video game is played, for example, and a camera pointed at the face of the gamer), using open source broadcasting software known as OBS.[13] Twitch also offers users a 'chatroom', which uses the Internet Relay Chat (IRC) protocol to allow viewers and streamers to interact using text.[14] It is worth noting that Twitch is not reducible to 'social media', though it utilises its aspects. While Twitch provides an algorithmically curated feed of content on its primary webpage, along with the means to 'follow' accounts, its algorithmic feed is not the primary user experience (UX) of the platform.[15] Twitch is better framed as an audiovisual broadcasting platform combined with IRC, integrating several digital engagement, notification, and monetisation schemes. In this respect it creates the affective experience of 'community' by focusing on real-time user experiences with live broadcasters.

On screen, Twitch has the visual appearance of television, accompanied by a scrolling chat, and its interface relies upon a combination of technologies and media frameworks. The desktop version, accessible using a web browser, features a scrolling chat on the right, the video feed in the middle, and a list of 'Followed' and 'Recommended' channels on the left. One of the primary means of Twitch's social interaction, insofar as users feel affectively 'connected' to the streamer and each other, is through the scrolling chat. In the mobile version of Twitch, the scrolling chat is located beneath the video in vertical view, occupying a similar position of prominence.

The centre of the screen's real estate is occupied by streaming video, which is, most of the time, a live feed generated by the channel's producer (the 'streamer'). While non-live feeds are possible on Twitch, including replays and rebroadcasts, the overall Twitch community thrives upon live streams, which offer the most affective engagement. This aspect of real-time engagement is an important part of Twitch, and distinguishes it from other social media that, though they may proffer a 'feed' of video, does not focus on real-time streaming. Even social media platforms that allow for live-streaming (such as Instagram, and to an extent Facebook) are not focused on live interaction as their primary means of engagement (rather, it's 'the algorithm', the feed of content selections in an endless scroll). Twitch, by comparison, rewards *singular attention*. It rewards user engagement with a single channel, watched over time, by offering 'Channel Points' for engagement that can be redeemed for 'Viewer Rewards', the activity of which is determined by the streamer (the defaults include highlighting messages and special emotes, while streamers can add anything they desire: custom DJ sets, record rewinds, shout-outs, dance moves, 'hydrating', etc.). While Twitch utilises an algorithm to provide 'Recommended Channels', there is no scrolling 'feed' of channels as with social media. For this reason, it is important to recognise that in the way Twitch *remediates* existing broadcast and IRC technologies, it is not 'social media'. It is, rather, a hybrid form of interactive broadcasting, a 'platform' closer to live cable television with an appended chat room, coupled with a host of engagement-focused features, from 'Viewer Rewards' to notifications, emotes, and badges.

DJ Culture Crashes Twitch

Since its inception, DJs and other musical artists have found Twitch a useful tool to connect with fans and expand reach. Well-known artists like Steve Aoki and deadmau5 were using the platform as early as 2014 for live shows and to supplement their relationship with fans. With the pandemic shutting down typical dance venues, Twitch quickly became the most important platform for many DJs, and viewers began to witness the rise of the 'Twitch DJ', whose DJ careers began and mostly exist entirely on Twitch. Today some 'Twitch-only DJs' routinely command over 1,000 live viewers on their streams.

Twitch earns revenue from on-screen advertising, combining stream-stopping 'television ads' with on-screen banners. Purchasing a channel subscription grants ad-free viewing for the particular channel, while offering Affiliate- and Partner-level streamers a cut of the revenue (as of 2022, approximately 50 per cent for most streamers). While viewers can purchase 'Twitch Turbo', a platform-wide, ad-free subscription at higher cost, most opt to support individual channels. As the overall labour of performance is not compensated from the shared revenue of the platform, it is up to each Twitch DJ to entice subscriptions and tips to their channel. The individualisation of earnings reflects wider economic trends of (undercompensated) 'gig labour' in the 'attention economy' that marks neo-liberalism and 'late' capitalism.[16] Like social media such as Instagram, Facebook, and TikTok, Twitch's interactive cues utilise 'dopamine-driven feedback loops',[17] with visual prompts such as 'emote explosions', 'Hype Trains', on-screen 'shout-outs', animations and audio cues that encourage viewers to purchase micropayments, including channel subscriptions, 'cheers', and 'bits'.

For a small selection of top-tier 'Twitch DJs', this revenue is not an online supplement to an ongoing 'real-life' DJ career but rather constitutes their career (or at least a part-time job), speaking to broader trends in society around 'remote' work and performance, from online sex work to other forms of cognitive labour and 'screen jobs'. While top-earning Twitch DJs, such as Pyka and Jessu, reportedly earn 'at least $30,000 [USD] per month', many dedicated semi-professionals and hobbyists with viewers averaging under 70 per stream, though putting in similar hours performing online, earn anywhere from $0 to $200 a month.[18] The aesthetic and cultural engagement at the low end of the financial (and often viewer) spectrum speaks to what we call 'narrowcasting', whereby niche is privileged over reach.

Along with the financial success of top-earning streamers and the ongoing participation of their fans, the creative persistence of semi-pros and hobbyists in forming small-scale online communities – even long after most in-person dance venues have reopened – suggests that the platform is successful in offering viewers an ongoing appealing experience. This experience serves multiple purposes, offering viewers a sense of connection that for some might address personal conditions of isolation.

These connections are further enhanced by one of the most significant addenda to the Twitch platform, the 'raid'. When a performer is finishing their stream on a Twitch channel, they have the option of 'raiding' another active channel, prompting a countdown process with a timer that, once completed, refreshes the screen and transfers viewers to the target channel and its chat. Raids are generally announced by the finishing performer, along with suggestions to follow the next performer and show them support. The incoming raid is usually greeted excitedly by viewers in the new channel, with further prompts to follow the raiding performer. The raid boosts the audience in the new channel and adds to the level of 'hype', frequently leading to further donations or subscriptions. It also creates a means of ad hoc networking and exposure between channels and their communities.

Twitch raids facilitate the formation of networks and affiliations between channels and their communities as new and different viewers interact in the chat. Raids also keep users perpetually engaged; not only is there always a 'party' going on, but the user will be sent to the next stream without any activity on their part. In fact, the user must actively close their browser to exit the raid and its next channel. These ever-expanding networks have also become institutionalised through organised 'raid trains' – effectively online DJ festivals, with their own organising teams, aesthetics, flyers, promotions, on-screen banners, and titling – that allow DJs around the world to keep the beats flowing around the clock.[19]

As these communities form around Twitch DJ channels, there also arises the proliferation of online social roles, with some viewers granted 'Moderator' privileges that allow for creative and disciplinary engagement in the chat (with the creation of 'commands' that can trigger phrases, games, and metrics, or deploy bans against spammers and unfriendly viewers). Thus a complex social strata has evolved around various channels, with Moderators, VIPs, and subscribers of various tiers receiving visual icons and emotes that represent their role and status in the chat.

Parasociality in the Twitchverse

Since the advent of television, media theorists have addressed the ways in which consumers tend to form one-sided or 'parasocial' relationships with celebrities through television and other mass media.[20] Parasociality signals an overidealisation of a mediated persona. While DJ culture, at least on radio, has a connection to parasociality due to the intimate nature of the radio voice – a 'hot' medium in McLuhan's parlance – the rise of the 'superstar DJ', from the 1970s to the '90s, calls for the kind of analysis developed for television and film actors, rock stars, and other celebrities.[21] Twitch complicates parasocial theory in various ways, in part due to the ways in which the medium is structured as an unequally distributed, two-way interaction rather than a purely one-way transmission such as television. Quite simply, you can chat back. Of course, the clear distinction between performer and audience that is at the heart of the parasocial exists on Twitch, and Twitch performers, particularly women, can be subjected to unwanted adulation and 'oversharing' from users, to the point of abusive language and stalking. One could even argue that Twitch *accentuates* the visibility central to some DJs insofar as it remediates television, just as how some DJs who use the microphone (especially those who deploy 'ASMR' techniques) remediate radio. While it is beyond our scope here to elaborate, Twitch's visual-oriented culture correlates to an observable shift in DJ culture from rave culture's 'aesthetics of disappearance' to the rise of 'festival culture', with audience attention shifting from dancing with each other (often facing the speakers) to facing the DJ as central (and celebrity) figure. This trend corresponds to the increasing commercialisation and mediatisation of the 'DJ-as-celebrity' that also signals a shift in *sensory regimes* from *hearing* and *feeling* to *seeing*. This correlation goes hand-in-hand with a general shift from vinyl DJing to more visually-oriented (and automated) digital DJ setups.[22]

In this way, the chatroom and engagement features that reward two-way interaction help build a sense of intimacy that can just as equally produce parasocial interactions as they can produce the affective relationships of *communitas*. This bidirectional affective potential is not found in other streaming formats, such as BoilerRoom.tv, where the viewer is 'looking in' on the DJ rather than interacting with them, akin to one-way mass media.[23] While there are 'superstar' DJs on Twitch who make no effort to interact with viewers (indeed, there are a number of Twitch setups that feature just a camera inside a club, where the 'real' interaction is assumed to be taking place), many Twitch DJs at varying levels of success expend a significant amount of time and focus on the chatroom, interacting either by text or microphone. While Twitch has featured prominently in media studies on parasociality, the majority of the work has focused on gaming rather than DJing, which by way of its competitive nature and its visual culture, involves a different understanding of 'celebrity'.[24]

Streaming Vibes: Being-Scene on Twitch

Parasociality also seems to be an effect of scale and celebrity capital. We can in a way distinguish between the parasociality of large-following, 'celebrity' Twitch DJs, whose viewers often try to express adulation for the performer – and get their attention in chat – with substantial purchases of tips and subs, and the 'narrowcasting' vibe of *communitas*. The latter, in our experience, has led to collective efforts to organise online and in-real-life (IRL) events, forming friendships in the flesh. Although it is not possible to re-create an in-person dance online, the Twitch platform arguably facilitates the conditions for the *vibe*, or sense of affective connection among viewers and the DJ. Sally Strommer attempts to define the *vibe* in underground house music clubs as 'an active communal force … the vibe is an active, exhilarating feeling of "now-ness" that everything is coming together'.[25] While Sommer includes *dancing* as key to the vibe, here the vibe takes shape through *hearing* the music, *seeing* the on-screen elements (which may or may not focus upon the DJ), and *textuality* in the chat, which serves as the focal site of engagement. As Graham St John writes, summarising the history of the vibe, 'the "vibe" is inherently a subversive dance music experience, a virtual world enabling a measure of cultural autonomy and even integration within an oppressive, alien, world'.[26] However we must consider that even when listening to 'dance' music, the act of dancing together, or even dancing itself, is not inherently necessary to engender the affective conditions of the vibe. Indeed, from a perspective critical of what has been labelled 'the attention economy' and its triggering of dopamine responses for profit, the engagement-reward system of Twitch itself could be seen as (insidiously) constitutive of the vibe.[27]

The Twitch vibe is unavoidably entwined with the financial incentives of consumption. The purchase of what Twitch calls 'support events' (subscriptions, cheers, or 'bits'), within a certain amount of time and surpassing a set threshold, results in a 'Hype Train'. The Hype Train is a visual countdown that encourages viewers to purchase more support events, with the perk of receiving special 'hype emotes' for buying-in.[28] Since 2022, there has not been a maximum 'level' for Hype Trains, with videogamer Kai Cenat holding the current record at level 47, with some 90,000 concurrent subscriptions.[29] Insofar as the majority of club and rave events also demand paid attendance, along with the intersecting festival economies of dance fashion and drug consumption, a deeper investigation of how the consumer enticements of capitalism expropriate and monetise 'the vibe' needs to be considered.[30] However, even the 'vibe' of monetised Hype Trains relies upon the creativity, energy, and activity of the DJ to prompt a degree of interactivity. This engagement, which can take place regardless of monetisation, and not because of it, can culminate in an affective, shared sense of 'cultural autonomy', a *communitas* expressed in the chat's interactive messaging and emotes, whereby a Twitch channel can be experienced as a refuge in an 'oppressive, alien world'. From our experience in creating Twitch DJ shows such as *Darkvibe Therapy*, DJing on Twitch can create a therapeutic space for healing the effects of pandemic isolation, economic anxieties, and personal trauma.

The Twitch 'vibe' at its best exceeds the fandom of online spectatorship, arguably producing social conditions for 'scenes'. Will Straw defines a scene in all its ambiguity as 'a default label for cultural unities whose precise boundaries are invisible and elastic'.[31] As van Veen writes, scenes in general are 'always in-transit, both in-between its spaces and materialised by them', and whether in-person or via an online platform such as Twitch, a scene designates 'a nodal point in a globalised network and the localised spaces in which such interaction takes place'.[32] In this sense, a 'scene' is interoperable between offline as well as online space, and in the twenty-first century the latter is often a condition of the former. As we saw through our participation, such scenes can self-organise multiple-DJ events (or raid trains) on Twitch, while extending chat-based *communitas* into other online platforms such as Discord.

As pandemic restrictions lifted, some Twitch DJs began organising small-scale IRL events, featuring live dance floors and DJ line-ups that were simulcasted on the platform.[33] This has led to a new category of hybrid events, whereby in-person participants on the dance floor login to Twitch so that they may simultaneously 'be in the chat' while being on-camera, often dancing around or behind the DJ. Both modalities constitute forms of 'being-seen in the scene'.[34] Such events remediate the mass media models of broadcasting dance floors found in television shows such as *Soul Train* (1971–2006) and *Electric Circus* on Canada's MuchMusic (1988–2003). While the dance floor is mostly central to in-person events, as well as televised dance music shows, the same cannot be said for the remediation of televised DJ culture on Twitch. The persistent tie between online and offline vibe, even at hybrid events where there is streamed 'social' dancing, does not appear to privilege the in-person dance floor over the chat. Signalling the experience of *feeling*, one is collectively listening to music

Fig. 8.2 DJ tobias (left) and DJ Professor Ben (right) DJing vinyl back-to-back on PANDEMiX! using VDO.Ninja, 2 August 2023.

with others, both in person and in the chat, which in Twitch DJ culture can be *equally* 'authentic' means of 'being-scene' (Figure 8.2).

Timely Conclusion: Cutting it Close to the Mix

Kai Fikentscher, writing nearly a decade before the global pandemic spurred a renaissance of online DJ streaming, was already honing in on the diversity of temporal experiences between the DJ and the dance floor.[35] When considering an online DJ performance (particularly asynchronous broadcasts on YouTube channels like Boiler Room or Hör), DJs and listeners have a different temporal experience than that of a singular live performance.[36] Instead, 'both performer and audience are divorced from an instantaneously shared framework made up of time, space and culturally grounded conventions, a *schizophonic* split between sound and its associated event'.[37] For Fikentscher, this creates a problem for the curatorial art of the DJ, which is understood as a dynamic between the preparation of music and the performance that comes together throughout the mix.[38] Fikentscher emphasises the DJ's nonverbal interaction with the dance floor, leading to a *flow* wherein the DJ responds 'to the moods and variables of a given time and space, manipulating them in turn through choices in music programming that shape the experience of the event'.[39] For Fikentscher, this flow is disrupted by online performances, which alienate both DJ and audience from these nonverbal interactions. A similar observation can be made of radio DJs or televised DJ shows.

However, as Langlois argues, '[h]ouse music "works" in context because, whilst functioning in a communal ethos ... each individual is able to concentrate on (withdraw into) their own sensual "danceworld" – to "lose themselves in the music"'.[40] In other words, anxieties over 'schizophonia' exist in both spaces; temporal diversity is not exclusive to the 'virtual dance floor'. As we have shown above, the live-streaming DJ experience on Twitch creates its own sense of time and its own sensual 'danceworld' of affective relations, *communitas*, and vibe, with or without actual dancing. Indeed, the most disorienting yet entirely common aspect of live-streaming events is the mundane revelation that each participant is experiencing a different 'danceworld', as they use different technologies (laptop, mobile) in different settings (bedroom, toilet, car, cooking), with some chatting, others 'lurking'. While live-streaming fragments any fantasy of a unified ground of reception, the diversity of 'dance floor' reception itself is already a part of the DJ culture experience in many contexts. Even when there is a singular dance floor with a single soundsystem, the diversity of bodies, and their moves, times, positions, substances, and subjectivities all shape differing experiences of the 'same' temporality (and space). This temporal schizophonia is often amplified by the music itself. The role of the DJ is to construct a narrative from bits and pieces of pre-recorded material, to take recorded moments out of their historical contexts and weave them together to create new histories in real (and virtual) time. In this light Jeff Chang calls the DJ a 'historian of the future. Who knows better the possibilities of the past than the one who will plunge a needle into it blind?'[41]

These kinds of layered observations, intersecting technology, performance, music, and philosophy, further our understanding of the complexities of the Twitch DJ 'scene', of which there is not one, but many. While technological conditions for DJ streaming can be generalised across Twitch's vast range of channels, other factors vary considerably. Overall, the scene to be found in various Twitch DJ channels can be more, or less, focused on the music itself. There is a continuum between DJs who are visual and parasocial performers, where on-screen personality and superficiality of appearance can attract high numbers of viewers regardless of the music being played, and DJs who tend towards a visual 'aesthetics of disappearance' that emphasises the music by resisting the 'screen-scene' commodification of DJ culture. In our estimation, the most creatively 'interesting' Twitch DJs blend these approaches, balancing aspects of being-scene while selecting and mixing music, shifting between presentation and performance, keyboard and mixer. However, such observations are ethnographically niche, and entirely contextual to various scenes. Our reflections here, mostly though not all drawn from English-language DJs in relatively affluent geographies, scarcely scratch the surface of a global platform as large as Twitch.

Notes

1. See Jay David Bolter and Richard Grusin, *Remediation: Understanding New Media* (Cambridge, MA: MIT Press, 2000).
2. Bolter and Grusin, *Remediation*; Marshall McLuhan and Lewis H. Lapham, *Understanding Media: The Extensions of Man*, Reprint edition (Cambridge, MA: The MIT Press, 1994).
3. Joseph J. Palamar and Patricia Acosta, 'Virtual Raves and Happy Hours during COVID-19: New Drug Use Contexts for Electronic Dance Music Partygoers', *International Journal of Drug Policy* 93 (1 July 2021): 102904.
4. An early adopter was author tobias c. van Veen (aka dj_tobias), who hosted an online DJ show called 'Target Circuitry' from 1999–2001 using a self-hosted Icecast server and namesake website. The number of listeners was initially limited by coaxial bandwidth to 10 audio streams at 56kpbs. The show was relaunched as 'Control to Chaos' in Montréal with DJ Fishead, offering 128 kbps streams from 2005–2007. The streaming technology was still novel enough to DJ culture that the show was covered in local arts and culture papers the *Hour* and *Montréal Mirror*.
5. Including author tobias c. van Veen, who DJ'ed Betalounge on 11 May 2000; on the audio recording one can hear the response of the live audience with the start of the set at the 2-hour mark (see: https://betalounge.com/2000/05/11/inhuman-tobias/).
6. 'Club Equinox // The World's First Virtual Reality Danceclub', Club Equinox, www.clubequinox.com/home.html (accessed 13 July 2023).
7. Matthew Schifrin, 'Rocking the Virtual World', *Forbes* (Forbes Inc., 24 December 2007).
8. See Michaelangelo Matos, 'How the Internet Transformed the American Rave Scene', *NPR*, 11 July 2011, sec. The Record, www.npr.org/sections/therecord/2011/07/17/137680680/how-the-internet-transformed-the-american-rave-scene.
9. Victor Turner, *From Ritual to Theatre: The Human Seriousness of Play* (New York: PAJ Publications, 2001).
10. Graham St John, 'Neotrance and the Psychedelic Festival', *Dancecult: Journal of Electronic Dance Music Culture* 1:1 (2009): 38–39.
11. See Sherry Turkle, *Alone Together: Why We Expect More from Technology and Less from Each Other* (New York: Basic Books, 2011).

12. See Max Sjöblom et al., 'The Ingredients of Twitch Streaming: Affordances of Game Streams', *Computers in Human Behavior* 92 (1 March 2019): 20–28.
13. See 'Open Broadcaster Software | OBS', https://obsproject.com/ (accessed 13 July 2023).
14. The use of the IRC protocol hearkens back to at least 1989, offering users a text-based chat environment which, although rich in graphical chat 'emotes' on Twitch, retains the otherwise lo-fi aesthetic of 'original' IRC (see Jarkko Oikarinen and Darren Reed, 'Internet Relay Chat Protocol', Request for Comments (Internet Engineering Task Force, May 1993)). This aesthetic brings with it a certain nostalgia for older users while at the same time offering younger users a familiar interface not dissimilar to the Short Message Service protocol (SMS) used by mobile phone services; see Erik Wilde and Antti Vaha-Sipila, 'URI Scheme for Global System for Mobile Communications (GSM) Short Message Service (SMS)', Request for Comments (Internet Engineering Task Force, January 2010, see https://www.ietf.org/about/introduction/).
15. In 2023, Twitch announced a new 'Discovery Feed' for its mobile app that introduces an algorithmically curated, scrolling feed of channel content that will feature user-generated 'Clips'. We suspect this addition will alter Twitch engagement, shifting the (mobile) platform from narrowcasting to the kind of attention fragmentation common to social media. See Morgan Sung, 'Twitch Is Launching a Discovery Feed and Other Short-Form Video Features', *TechCrunch* (blog), 10 July 2023, https://techcrunch.com/2023/07/10/twitch-discovery-feed-stories-tiktok-youtube-twitchcon-paris-new-features/.
16. See Benjamin Alan Wiggins, 'The Culture Industry, New Media, and the Shift from Creation to Curation; or, Enlightenment as a Kick in the Nuts', *Television & New Media* 15:5 (July 2014): 395–412. Wiggins suggests that the rise of the social media celebrity corresponds with a decrease in financial compensation for labour in the entertainment industry. Also see tobias c. van Veen, 'Technics, Precarity and Exodus in Rave Culture', *Dancecult: Journal of Electronic Dance Music Culture* 1:2 (2010): 29–49.
17. Trevor Haynes, 'Dopamine, Smartphones & You: A Battle for Your Time', *Science in the News* (blog), 1 May 2018, https://sitn.hms.harvard.edu/flash/2018/dopamine-smartphones-battle-time/.
18. Based in Vancouver, BC, Pyka and Jessu began DJing on Twitch using digital media controllers in 2020, playing 'Dad house' mixed with newer EDM styles. As 'GenZ' performers, Pyka and Jessu embrace the 'e-girl' interactivity and attractive fashion common to social media 'influencers', and with Jessu's audience rapidly growing to 171,000+ followers by September 2023, she and her co-DJ Pyka (with 121,000 followers) have become two of the highest-earning DJs on Twitch. Hard data on Twitch DJ earnings are difficult to come by, though it appears that DJs among the top 100 streamers earn 'at least $30,000 per month' (see 'How to DJ on Twitch: A Step-by-Step Guide', *Zip DJ* (blog), 8 February 2023, www.zipdj.com/blog/how-to-dj-on-twitch). While

the figure is not sourced, it is consistent with payout information from a data breach of some 10,000 streamers (mostly videogamers; see Steven Asarch, 'Twitch Leak: 10 Biggest Revelations from the Unprecedented Data Breach', *Inverse*, 8 October 2021, www.inverse.com/gaming/twitch-leak-hack-data-breach-streamer-payout-earnings). One analysis focused on music streamers found that 'The top 10 music accounts on Twitch by direct earnings make between $50,000 and $400,000 a year from channel subscriptions, ads and Twitch Bit donations. The vast majority of these accounts belong to independent artists, and there is almost no correlation between an artist's Spotify followers and their Twitch earnings'; in Cherie Hu, 'How Much Are Artists Really Making on Twitch?', Water & Music, 18 October 2021, www.waterandmusic.com/how-much-are-artists-really-making-on-twitch/.

19. One such raid train, organised by the Twitch DJ collective Birdcage Radio in August 2023 (of which both authors are members), was scheduled to last around the clock for eight days straight; after the end of the scheduled train, associated DJs continued the raid for another two days (including the authors). Author tobias c. van Veen has also organised numerous 'raidfests', some of which raised funds for charity, including *Set For Love*, *Planet Techno*, *ViNYL VAULTs*, the 2021 conference raidfest for *Dancecult: Journal of Electronic Dance Music Culture*, and the *24H DJ Cypher* for the 2022 Black Speculative Arts Movement (BSAM) exhibition at Carnegie Hall (see raidfest.com).

20. See Donald Horton and R. Richard Wohl, 'Mass Communication and Para-Social Interaction', *Psychiatry* (1 August 1956); Klaus Bruhn Jensen, 'The Politics of Polysemy: Television News, Everyday Consciousness and Political Action', *Media, Culture & Society* 12:1 (1990): 57–77; Jason Zenor et al., *Parasocial Politics: Audiences, Pop Culture, and Politics* (Lanham, MD: Lexington Books/Fortress Academic, 2014).

21. Bill D. Herman, 'Scratching Out Authorship: Representations of the Electronic Music DJ at the Turn of the 21st Century', *Popular Communication* 4:1 (February 2006): 21–38.

22. See van Veen, 'Technics, Precarity and Exodus in Rave Culture'; tobias c. van Veen, 'Being-Scene at MUTEK: Remixing Spaces of Gender and Ethnicity in Electronic Music Performance', in *Weekend Societies*, ed. Graham St John (London: Bloomsbury Academic Press, 2016), 195–218; tobias c. van Veen and Bernardo Alexander Attias, 'Off the Record: Turntablism and Controllerism in the 21st Century (Part 1)', *Dancecult: Journal of Electronic Dance Music Culture* 3:1 (2011); tobias c. van Veen and Bernardo Alexander Attias, 'Off the Record: Turntablism and Controllerism in the 21st Century (Part 2)', *Dancecult: Journal of Electronic Dance Music Culture* 4:1 (2012).

23. Guillaume Heuguet, 'When Club Culture Goes Online: The Case of Boiler Room', *Dancecult* 8:1 (2016): 73–87. See also comments by Fikentscher cited below.

24. See, for example, Michael George Blight, 'Relationships to Video Game Streamers: Examining Gratifications, Parasocial Relationships, Fandom, and Community Affiliation Online', PhD thesis (University of Wisconsin, 2016); Alex P. Leith, 'Gameplay Livestreaming: Human Agents of Gamespace and Their Parasocial Relationships', PhD thesis (Michigan State University, 2019); Alex P. Leith, 'Parasocial Cues: The Ubiquity of Parasocial Relationships on Twitch', *Communication Monographs* 88:1 (2021): 111–29; Brett Sherrick et al., 'How Parasocial Phenomena Contribute to Sense of Community on Twitch', *Journal of Broadcasting & Electronic Media* 67:1 (1 January 2023): 47–67; Abbie Speed, Alycia Burnett, and Tom Robinson II, 'Beyond the Game: Understanding Why People Enjoy Viewing Twitch', *Entertainment Computing* 45 (1 March 2023): 100545.
25. Sally R. Sommer, '"C'mon to My House": Underground-House Dancing', *Dance Research Journal* 33:2 (2001): 73. See also Jason Del Gandio, '"Pulsating with Love and Light": A Case Study on Phish and the Vibe', *Public Philosophy Journal* 4:3 (June 2022).
26. Graham St John, 'The Vibe of the Exiles: Aliens, Afropsychedelia and Psyculture', *Dancecult: Journal of Electronic Dance Music Culture* 5:2 (2013): 59.
27. Arguably, Twitch engineers the commodification of 'community', whereby financial buy-in authenticates 'being-scene'. In 2023, Twitch introduced 'Monetization' as a category in its 'Creator Dashboard' in the streamer user interface, thereby emphasising this (profiteering) aspect of Twitch. The social effects of monetised belonging can be deleterious, amplifying issues of inequality. The question remains as to how to recognise curation, design, and channel moderation as 'in-kind' forms of 'support' on a platform that rewards a transactional economy by virtue of its design. Twitch, as a monetised platform, is at odds with the 'gift economy' ethos common to rave and festival culture.
28. See 'Hype Train Guide', Twitch, https://help.twitch.tv/s/article/hype-train-guide (accessed 1 March 2024).
29. See Blaine Polhamus, 'Kai Cenat Breaks Hype Train Record on His Journey to Become Twitch's Most-Subscribed-to Steamer', *Dot Esports* (blog), 27 September 2022, https://dotesports.com/streaming/news/kai-cenat-breaks-hype-train-record-on-his-journey-to-become-twitchs-most-subscribed-to-steamer.
30. See Jeremy Gilbert, 'Break/Flow/Escape/Capture: The Energy and Impotence of the Hardcore Continuum', in *Black Popular Music in Britain Since 1945*, ed. Jon Stratton and Nabeel Zuberi (Farnham: Ashgate, 2014), 169–84.
31. Will Straw, 'Communities and Scenes in Popular Music', in *The Subcultures Reader*, ed. Ken Gelder and Sarah Thornton (New York: Routledge, 1997), 248.
32. van Veen, 'Being-Scene at MUTEK', 198.

33. Twitch DJ communities have even organised larger 'meetup' events that included weekend-long DJ parties with live-streaming events. At least two such events took place in 2023, one in Las Vegas and one in Miami, bringing together DJs and Twitch regulars from various parts of the world to party together live and stream the party. Such live events allowed parasocial relationships to develop into 'actual' social relationships, many of which have lasted beyond such events as local Twitch communities have thrived in various places.
34. The term 'being-scene' speaks to 'who is being *seen* as being part of the *scene*'. Various (music) scenes have different means of authenticating – and policing – *who* is a 'legitimate cultural actor' in the 'scene', often by *what* technologies they use. See van Veen, 'Being-Scene at MUTEK'.
35. Kai Fikentscher, '"It's Not the Mix, It's the Selection": Music Programming in Contemporary DJ Culture', in *DJ Culture in the Mix: Power, Technology, and Social Change in Electronic Dance Music*, ed. Bernardo Alexander Attias, Anna Gavanas, and Hillegonda Rietveld (New York, London, Delhi, and Sydney: Bloomsbury Academic, 2013), 123–49.
36. For a detailed discussion of the way in which Boiler Room navigated some of the challenges of online performance see Heuguet, 'When Club Culture Goes Online'.
37. Fikentscher, 'It's Not the Mix', 131.
38. Fikentscher, 'It's Not the Mix'.
39. Fikentscher, 'It's Not the Mix'. 145.
40. Tony Langlois, 'Can You Feel It? DJs and House Music Culture in the UK', *Popular Music* 11:2 (1992): 236.
41. Jeff Chang, 'Needle into the Groove: Snippets from an Omnidirectional History', in *The Record: Contemporary Art and Vinyl*, ed. Trevor Schoonmaker, Illustrated edition (Durham, NC: Duke University Press Books, 2010), 119.

Further Reading

Fikentscher, Kai. '"It's Not the Mix, It's the Selection": Music Programming in Contemporary DJ Culture', in *DJ Culture in the Mix: Power, Technology, and Social Change in Electronic Dance Music*, ed. Bernardo Alexander Attias, Anna Gavanas, and Hillegonda C. Rietveld (New York, London, Delhi, and Sydney: Bloomsbury Academic, 2013), 123–49.

Sommer, Sally R. '"C'mon to My House": Underground-House Dancing', *Dance Research Journal* 33: 2 (2001): 73.

Taylor, T. L. *Watch Me Play: Twitch and the Rise of Game Live Streaming* (Princeton: Princeton University Press, 2018).

Turkle, Sherry. *Alone Together: Why We Expect More from Technology and Less from Each Other* (New York: Basic Books, 2011).

van Veen, tobias c. 'Being-Scene at MUTEK: Remixing Spaces of Gender and Ethnicity in Electronic Music Performance', in *Weekend Societies: Electronic Dance Music Festivals and Event-Cultures,* ed. Graham St John (London: Bloomsbury Academic, 2016), 195–218.

PART III

Genre Aesthetics

9 | Drum and Bass as Cultural Accelerator

Underground Resistance or Ecstatic Concession to Speed?

CHRIS CHRISTODOULOU

Drum and bass is one of the most recognisable electronic dance music (EDM) genres to emphasise speed as core experience. Initially referred to as 'jungle' or 'jungle techno', the genre developed during 1992 as the soundtrack to London's multiethnic inner-city rave scene and is based on breakbeats digitally recorded, or 'sampled', from existing sources, and powerful bass riffs and tones, typically inspired by Jamaican dub and reggae. Breakbeats (or 'breaks') are real-time drumming performances which, on drum and bass tracks, are repeated, or 'looped' – a technique drawn from 1980s US rap and hip-hop and accelerated to approximately 170 BPM (beats-per-minute); around twice the speed of the 1960s and 1970s African American soul and funk records from which these drum patterns are often sourced. While the genre hosts a wide range of coexisting styles and subgenres, other recurring sonic elements include abstract, futuristic soundscapes, and harsh, mid-frequency synthesiser stabs. Drum and bass has achieved some limited commercial success; for example, the radio-friendly track 'Hot Right Now',[1] by DJ Fresh featuring Rita Ora, which, in February 2012, was the first drum and bass single to reach Number 1 in the UK national pop chart, while the musician with whom the genre is most associated, Goldie (a pseudonym that refers to the artist's idiosyncratic gold-plated teeth and whose real name is Clifford Joseph Price), regularly appears in the mainstream media, such as performing at the closing ceremony of the 2022 Commonwealth Games in Birmingham. However, for non-drum and bass audiences, the music is often heard via soundtracks for screen media, such as on the racing simulation game series *Forza Horizon* (2012–present), by Microsoft, whereby speed is a requirement for progression within the game, and in science fiction feature films, such as *The Matrix*,[2] in which extraordinary movement is a constituent element of the film's thematic concern with omnipresent yet barely visible power structures in a high-tech culture of dehumanised simulation.

Sonic, visual, and lexical references to speed and acceleration throughout drum and bass attest to the destabilising conditions wrought by an accelerated culture, particularly for those living at the socio-economic margins of deindustrialisation. For such groups, the genre offers the fantasy of ecstatic suffering as a pre-condition for becoming inhuman, thereby assimilating the dehumanising effects of techno-capitalism. In the Afrofuturist manifesto *More Brilliant Than the Sun*, Kodwo Eshun examines drum and bass and other 'sonic fictions' as forms of 'Alien Music' that have been inflected by African and Caribbean diasporic experiences of industrial and post-industrial Othering.[3] Diverging from the transcendental humanism of rave culture's PLUR (Peace, Love, Unity, Respect) discourse, the alienation of the human subject articulated in drum and bass suggests the potential of acceleration to unleash future states of dehumanisation. This chapter will consider the dual positioning of drum and bass as, on the one hand, an accelerationist extrapolation, embracing post-humanisation via technologically induced experiences of ecstatic speed, while, on the other, conveying anxiety at the prospect of the human subject's dissolution through a prevalent 'dark' thematic. Drew Hemment refers to the dark sonic spaces of the EDM dance floor, where, he argues neither 'subject nor object exist in music ... acoustic space [is] itself "boundless, directionless, horizonless, the dark side of the mind"'.[4] In the specific context of drum and bass, 'dark' also evokes a dystopian discursive framework. formed out of lived experiences in the post-industrial inner city, and the embracing of an 'underground' marginality – comprised of the staging of legal and illegal dance events, unlicensed pirate radio broadcasting, and the black economy of recreational dance drugs – that structures its participants' feelings of unending powerlessness. Thereby, the accelerationist impulse of drum and bass reveals a form of late-capitalist hopelessness, and hence, the limits of accelerationism as a fast-track to the future.

'Accelerated Culture'; 'Faster'; 'Let It Roll'; 'Movement'; 'Rupture'; 'Speed'; 'Set Speed'; 'Soul in Motion'; 'Tempo'; 'Tempo Tantrum' are terms that connote speed and dynamic or forceful movement as well as being names of dance events from the past and present where drum and bass (often lengthened to 'jungle drum and bass' in recognition of its immediate predecessor, jungle, or shortened to 'D&B' or 'JDB') is the main EDM style. In Sukhdev Sandhu's introduction to the novel *Junglist* by Andrew Green and Eddie Otchere (aka Two Fingas and James T. Kirk), speed is recognised as intrinsic to the pleasures conferred by the genre:

> He [Green] found jungle intimate and immersive – a sometimes demonised music to which young kids, in darkened spaces the size of chill-out zones, were still figuring out how to dance. It was a music that was impossibly accelerationist. Its rhythms thrillingly alien. Its darkness radiant.[5]

In the summer of 2004, forty drum and bass DJs and musicians gathered in London to discuss the recent acceleration of the genre's already rapid tempos, the result of which was suspected to be a variety of unwelcome musical and behavioural effects. As journalist Brian Belle-Fortune recounted:

Somewhere between the crowds, DJs and producers, a force has driven D&B's beats per minute ever faster. Instead of rolling along between 160–170 BPM, some tunes are now racing at 178, threatening to exceed the 180 sound-barrier. Both Storm and Andy C feel that the BPMs have evolved with the music. But it's not to everyone's taste. So just like the mid-90s when JDB's movers and shakers held the Foundation meetings to define musical directions, 40 headz met in summer 2004 and called for order. The word on the streets was that this meeting was supposed to be a secret – wasn't it?[6]

Belle-Fortune highlighted two key issues raised at the meeting. The first involved the sense that the music's increasing speed was a threat to its break-beat-driven 'funkiness'. Anne Danielsen posits that funkiness appears 'when a layer of potential cross-rhythm is used to create small stretches in time that fall between a dominant basic pulse'.[7] While referring to this 'funky' sensibility, drum and bass tracks contain tempos of around 170 BPM, thereby subsuming funkiness within a post-human machine aesthetic. The second issue raised concerned the hostile and aggressive conduct of some of the music's audiences, perceived as a direct result of the music's increasing tempos. According to Joanna Hall, drum and bass audiences can appear 'confrontational and evoke images of anti-social youth, "lager louts" and the "vulgar" corporeality ... embodied by working-class football fans'.[8] The clandestine nature of the meeting attests to the divisiveness of debates among the genre's participants about the extent to which audience demands for ever-faster music should be met in light of media reports of anti-social behaviour at dance events. In an early article on the genre in *i-D* magazine, Eshun argued, 'jungle is the one music everyone agrees is no good', while 'the very fact that questions of race and class come up over and over indicates unease with the music's following, who they are and what (its participants are) up to'.[9]

The entwining of an accelerationist sensibility with discussions about the antisociality of drum and bass audiences points to the workings of speed as *jouissance*, a form of masochistic desire. Jouissance refers to a type of extraordinary bliss experienced by a child when still inside its mother's womb.[10] It is when the child enters the symbolic order of social relationships, sexual difference, and language that it falls from this state of grace, establishing the potential for subjective dissolution in adulthood. Jouissance has been examined in the context of EDM by Hillegonda Rietveld, who suggests that 'it is this desire which makes people dance all night and urges them to come back for more ... the (intoxicated) dancer may also want to "let go" of all desire to acquire a sense of totality. In that case the untying of the subject occurs in a state of complete jouissance, in a loss of its construction in language.'[11] Thereby, jouissance emerges when the materiality of the means of signification interrupts meaning, such as in speech. The range of sounds offered by EDM styles like house, techno, and jungle drum and bass can achieve this experience through the deliberate foregrounding of non-verbal material effects. In the early 1980s, Chicago-based DJ Frankie Knuckles and his colleague Larry Levan built on this practice by mixing disco, europop, and soul records with synthesised drum machine rhythms, thereby creating the genre now globally recognised as 'house'. As house music developed in Chicago, Detroit producers Juan Atkins, Derrick May, and Kevin Saunderson, who shared similar interests in science fiction, the European synthesiser music of artists like Kraftwerk and Depeche Mode, and the dramatic futurological predictions of Alvin Toffler, collaborated to develop a style of minimal, rhythmically-heavy EDM form they called 'techno'. Like house, techno was aimed at making people dance continuously, and DJs specialising in the genre employ the same seamless mixing style with which house music is associated. Emerging from the rapidly de-industrialising regions of UK cities like London, Birmingham, and Bristol in the early-1990s, jungle techno, and its successors, jungle and drum and bass, drew on the futuristic soundscapes of Detroit techno while emphasising heavy basslines and sped-up breakbeats that bordered on the unbearably fast – as suggested by the BPMs referenced in the title of the early jungle track by Mixrace, 'Too bad for Ya (Is 180 Too Fast for Ya?)' from 1992[12] – to establish a direct relationship with the body that subjectivity can find uncomfortable. In this regard, such sounds can be felt as both intense pain and pleasure.

Jouissance can be pivoted towards the widely used tag of 'dark' in jungle drum and bass (as in 'darkcore' or 'dark jungle') as a means to highlight a prevailing sense of uncertainty about the near future, framed as a dark age where human priorities, especially those of localised urban working-class populations, lag behind the shadowy interests of accelerating financialisation in techno-capitalism. In an interview with Peter Shapiro of *The Wire* magazine, producer A Guy Called Gerald emphasised the significance of the term 'jungle' in relation to overlapping connotations of pre-industrial naturalism and post-industrial imperilment:

There's so much colour in it. So much rhythm ... so much texture. You could go into a jungle and find these things. You could sit there in a pool in the middle of a jungle and there would be flowers, insects, dangerous animals ... dangerous plants. But there would be a lot of beautiful sounds. That's one concept of it. Another is that the whole of society is becoming like a jungle anyway.[13]

A duality of anxiety and desire permeates Gerald's description; the music is described as containing 'a lot of beautiful sounds', thereby signifying the fantasy of a return to the innocence of an idealised antediluvian coexistence with the natural world. On the other hand, 'jungle' signifies a state of nature in which survival requires violent competitiveness; 'dangerous animals' struggle in an amoral Darwinian scenario of 'the survival of the fittest'. Dialogue sampled from dystopian science fiction films, such as *Blade Runner*[14] and *The Terminator*,[15] enunciate suspicion and hypervigilance as necessary psychological conditions in a scenario where organic workers are replaced by the undead labour of technology. For example, 'Terminator'[16] by Rufige Kru features a line of dialogue uttered by the incredulous heroine of the eponymous film: 'We're talking about things I haven't done yet!' The track was one of the first jungle techno tracks to extensively apply time-stretching – a technique that changes a sound's tempo without altering its pitch, enabled by digital samplers, notably the Akai S-950, in 1992 – to increase a break's speed while retaining its original timbre. The follow-up track 'Terminator II'[17] includes several time-stretched versions of the same breakbeat – improvised by Clyde Stubblefield on the 1970 single 'Funky Drummer' by James Brown[18] – which seems to uncannily exist in different time periods simultaneously. The temporal dissonance that follows from the information overload predicted by Alvin Toffler back in 1970[19] is thereby transmuted into the thrill of being hunted and haunted by the future.

The notion of the urban jungle as a militarised space in which subjective survival can only be achieved in post-human form persists throughout drum and bass culture. For example, the dance event AWOL – subtitled 'A Way of Life' on promotional flyers, but whose title is also derived from the acronym 'Absent Without Leave', referring to a soldier's unexplained absence from the battlefield – furnishes its venues with militaristic décor and camouflage designs and where battlefield scenes are projected onto walls. Additionally, recording nomenclature like *Guerilla Warfare*,[20] a compilation album from the Renegade Hardware label, boasts the inclusion of '50 explosive drum & bass anthems including 15 unreleased bombs'. Focusing on the military origins of information and communications technologies (ICTs), Paul Virilio examines speed as a regime or milieu of accelerated culture; the 'battlefield is first a field of perception. Seeing them coming and knowing that they are going to attack are determining elements of survival. In war, you can't be surprised, for surprise is death.'[21] In this quasi-martial condition of instantaneous information and communication, a perpetual 'state of emergency' is created; 'The violence of speed has become both the violence and the law, the world's destiny and its destination.'[22] Virilio argues that the commensurability of progress with speed has led to a nihilistic politics of 'pure war' in which the human subject is in a permanently embattled state. The city is described as a 'concentration camp of speed'[23] where the 'colonisation of the human body by technology'[24] is most intensely felt, and the self becomes 'plural, multiform, fluidiform, coagulated here and there in social, animal or territorial bodies'.[25] Ultimately, the modern subject dissolves through fusion with accelerative technologies that effectively wage war on the human. Adopting Virilio's line of analysis, the experience of speed in jungle drum and bass from the perspective of the rigidly localised urban working class – where locality is experienced as destiny, and where social mobility stops at the boundaries of the urban jungle – can offer a sense of subjective interconnection with the violent mobility of the post-human.

In contrast to Virilio's moral opposition to accelerated culture as an inevitable outgrowth of modernisation, the Cybernetic Culture Research Unit (CCRU), led by Sadie Plant and then Nick Land between 1995 and 2003, adopted the language of science fiction and the 'schizoanalytic' methodology of Gilles Deleuze and Felix Guattari to argue for the accelerationism offered by deterritorialisation in techno-capitalism. Whereas Virilio lamented the loss of unity through the schizoid fusion with accelerative technologies, Deleuze and Guattari argued that subjective deterritorialisation in the form of schizophrenic breakdowns constitute failed attempts to break through capitalism's limits. Deterritorialisation as a generalised social condition was thereby needed to 'accelerate the process' towards post-capitalism.[26] For Land, 'accelerating the process' involves shedding the politics of the state and democracy, 'the last great sentimental indulgence of mankind',[27] where human labour disappears *into* capital. Labour has already significantly shifted in this direction in late-capitalist economies like the USA and UK, where economies once based on industrial manufacturing have transitioned into service-led consumer societies dominated by finance and information and communication technology. As Andy Beckett identifies, accelerationists 'argue that technology, particularly computer technology, and capitalism ... the most aggressive, global variety, should be massively sped up and intensified – either because this is the best way forward for humanity, or because there is no alternative'.[28] In light of the failure of political ideologies and movements to moderate or reverse the 'already hugely disruptive, seemingly runaway pace of change in the modern world', accelerationism is a direct response to post-industrial economic deceleration that embraces the speed offered by high-tech financialisation. For Land, such a response means embracing the market economy in its most deregulated, decentralised, and digitalised form, even though, as Land admits, unleashing a techno-capitalist offensive can 'seem a little inhuman, as it rips up political cultures, deletes traditions, dissolves subjectivities, and hacks through security apparatuses'.[29]

Accelerative aesthetics in EDM are significantly registered in increasing BPMs, making the tempos of drum and bass, located at the faster end of the EDM spectrum, an indicator of the urgency of hedonistic youth for unlocking the pleasures of the present moment. Rietveld and Alexei Monroe observe that the Dutch EDM genre of gabber – whose developmental trajectory in Rotterdam parallels the formation of jungle in London in the early 90s, albeit emphasising fast and heavy kick drums instead of jungle's time-stretched breakbeats – similarly emerged out of working-class frustration at having been excluded from the opportunities mobilised by neo-liberal capitalism during a period of economic recession.[30] As with gabber, the formation of jungle drum and bass was also intertwined with the digitalisation of music production, specifically in the form of computer-based digital audio workstations (DAWs), which enabled the exclusion of humanist residues in EDM, such as the voice, along with an intensification of the speeds made possible by musical automation. For a working-class demographic, bearing the harshest effects of techno-capitalist deterritorialisation, music that is closely linked to the continuous acceleration of the computational power promises what Noys describes as the 'upgrading of the integrated meat that can finally keep pace with capitalism'.[31] The sense of the technological 'upgrading' of human rhythms in drum and bass is particularly emphasised by the techstep subgenre; record label names like Computer Integrated Audio (CIA), Technique, and Virus; artist pseudonyms like Digital, Photek, and Total Science; and visual iconography, such as the prevalence of abstract recording artwork that rarely contains images of the music's human producers. The tendency for the working class to celebrate its own powerlessness was identified by Jean-François Lyotard, originally in 1974, who argued that workers experienced jouissance in the imposed 'mad destruction of their organic body', and who took pleasure in the 'hysterical, masochistic, whatever exhaustion it was of hanging on in the mines, in the foundries, in the factories, in hell, they enjoyed it'.[32] These examples attest to a fetishisation in drum and bass of the very accelerationism that undermines the life chances of many of its deindustrialised participants, offering a fantasy of integration with the destructive power of high-tech culture as the future for the traditional working class collapses into permanent underemployment.

For Dick Hebdige, dance subcultures constitute 'both a declaration of independence, of Otherness, of alien intent, a refusal of anonymity, or subordinate status', where underground activity 'is also a confirmation of the fact of powerlessness, a celebration of impotence'.[33] For example, the diffusion of powerlessness offered by dance subcultures was at least in part precipitated by usage of the hallucinogenic amphetamine or speed-based dance drug ecstasy (whose chemical name is 3, 4-methylenedioxymethamphetamine, or MDMA). While enhancing the sensations generated by rhythmically driven EDM, ecstasy could also facilitate feelings of empathy and communality among crowds, thereby obfuscating the presence of socially inscribed power structures. In the context of drum and bass, 'alien intent' can be understood to refer to the alienation of working-class labour power in late capitalism. Being 'underground' suggests a form of realism that acknowledges the primacy of material conditions in the urban jungle, while framing as inevitable the future disintegration of the human subject. As such, the genre's idiosyncratic 'street futurism' is evidenced,[34] comparable to the Afrofuturism of Detroit techno, but with a more fatalistic outlook than its predecessor. From a musical perspective, the 'celebration of impotence' can also be found in the traces of drumming's human performativity, which, after having been digitally sampled, time-stretched, and looped, is only just discernible. This demonstrates the tension required between the human subject and digital technology to grasp the genre's accelerative pleasures. As Noys astutely observes, the 'felt sense of aesthetic acceleration depends on the slowing down and increasing of speed, the differences between elements that generate a productive friction'.[35] This friction between digital speed and human performative flaws, such as minor deviations and mistakes in timing, troubles the assumption of smoothness implied by the CCRU's emphatic accelerationism, while distinguishing Virilio's notion of 'pure speed' from the variability needed to confer ecstatic speed in drum and bass. If, as Danielsen argues, the quality of funk is synonymous with human characteristics such as 'soul', bodily odour, and sexuality, the acceleration of human rhythms to speeds and degrees of syncopation impossible in real-time drumming internalises the painful inevitability of a deadly lag behind digitalisation.

Accelerative friction is a key feature of music that Simon Reynolds refers to as belonging to the 'hardcore continuum'; genres whose direct antecedents are 'Hardcore Techno or Hardcore Rave, or sometimes simply Ardkore',[36] the multiregional British colloquialism 'ardkore' indicating the aggressive EDM favoured by hedonistic working-class audiences in the UK. According to Reynolds:

From Jungle to 2-step to today's Grime and Bassline, the basic parameters of the music have stayed the same as they were in the early Hardcore, although the relative balance of various sources (reggae, rap, R&B, Eurotechno, etc) has shifted, and the beats-per-minute has fluctuated wildly. Those core elements are: beat-science seeking the intersection between 'fucked up' and 'groovy'; dark bass pressure; MCs chatting fast over live-mixed DJ sets; samples and arrangement ideas inspired by pulp soundtracks and orchestrated pop.[37]

It was the demands of inner-city rave audiences for faster BPMs in the early 1990s that led some hardcore DJs to modify their Technics turntables to override the manufacturer's imposition of a +8 per cent speed limit. By removing the upper casing of a Technics turntable, a blue variable transistor located on the main circuit board ('pot VR301') could be turned clockwise to its furthest point, enabling records to be played at speeds up to 15 per cent faster than their original tempos. As a result, a breakbeat recorded for playback at 33 rpm could play as much as 53 per cent faster at 45 rpm and at the modified +15 per cent pitch setting. Thereby, the creative friction that occurred between the musical characteristics identified by Reynolds and the practices of EDM DJs – requiring physical friction in the adjusting of tempos during the mixing process and in the hacking of turntables to play records faster – laid the foundations for the emergence of drum and bass. This repurposing of playback technology also identifies DJs as exponents of what Hebdige calls 'bricolage', where 'new meanings' can be generated by placing 'another range of commodities ... in a symbolic ensemble which serves to erase or subvert their original straight meanings'.[38] In contrast to the fetishisation of acceleration in drum and bass, slower BPM rates are a feature of drum and bass-influenced genres like 2-step garage – a subgenre of UK garage that lacks the regular kick drum more typical of its parent genre – and grime – a derivative of UK garage that foregrounds the performances of MCs ('Masters of Ceremonies', in the context of reggae-derived performance and sound system culture) – suggesting deceleration as an oppositional response to techno-capitalist speed.

In 'Swarm 1' of their 1996 *Abstract Culture* pamphlet series, Land and the CCRU claimed that jungle contained the potential to foment 'inhuman' consciousness based on its emphasis on 'dread' bass frequencies, alongside its speed and syncopation; 'Don't get into a false sense of security. It's not just music. Jungle is the abstract diagram of planetary inhuman becoming. Dread out of control. A post-spectacular immersive tactility that no humanist vision can put you in touch with.'[39] For Julian Henriques, 'dread' in reggae sound system culture refers to the deep sonority of bass, which is felt more than heard, and is thereby experienced as 'everywhere, hardly even making the dualistic division between here and there', thereby unsettling European humanist distinctions of inner and outer, surface and depth, subject and object.[40] In the ecstatic frictions that take place between human and technological temporal scales, and in the radical in-betweenness of 'dread bass', the CCRU identified a deterritorialised space from which machinic desire can emerge. In particular, the prevalence of subsonic bass frequencies – which, at 20 kHz or less, operate below the threshold of human hearing – link an emergent post-human consciousness to its pre-subjective intertwining with the maternal body.[41] As the child's first exposure to sound is through its physical proximity to the mother's internal organs and a hearing range that is limited to very low frequencies, bass can reawaken both the immanence felt from inside the womb and the subjective collapse threatened by its failure to fully enter into subjectivity outside it. For Julia Kristeva, the womb or 'chora' signifies either 'fullness' or 'emptiness' – it is 'unnameable' and 'improbable'[42] – but is always its own point of reference. This immanence reinforces the machinic immediacy without mediation promised by accelerationism, allowing jungle to articulate 'impending human extinction [as] accessible as a dance floor'.[43] For Rietveld, EDM facilitates a disappearance of subjectivity and a sense of merging with 'a matrix in terms of both the womb and grid system, making the experience of self-annihilation in the context of a machine aesthetic a deeply spiritual cyborgian suture. It is at the same time a sacrifice of the body as well as of a sense of the self.'[44] In jungle drum and bass, this suturing is felt as the ecstatic inevitability of merging within a digital technological matrix driven at uncanny speeds by 'dread' post-industrial market forces that are 'out of control'.

Alongside Land, fellow former CCRU members Kodwo Eshun and Mark Fisher also enthusiastically drew attention to the accelerationism of jungle drum and bass. Eshun evoked Alvin Toffler to challenge the 'future-shock absorbing' tendencies often found in music journalism and academic writing about African and Caribbean diasporic music.[45] Toffler coined the term 'future shock' in 1970 to convey 'the shattering stress and disorientation that we induce in individuals by subjecting them to too much change in a short time'.[46] Concurring with Toffler's view that '[c]hange is the process by which the future invades our lives',[47] Eshun positioned future shock against the reterritorialising humanist narratives of roots, redemption, and soulfulness through which African and Caribbean diasporic music is often evaluated. It is in this post-colonial sense that Afrofuturism extols identification with the future; if the foregrounding of Black cultural narratives in the future can be identified, the prospect of further white colonialisation can be short-circuited. Additionally, 'future shock' can imply the schizophrenic enfolding of the future into the present; the fast and frenzied character of drum and bass stresses immediate pleasure-seeking over future rewards that are achieved by deferring gratification in favour of the pursuit of long-term employment, financial security, and a stable family life. For mainly working-class and substantially Black 'junglist' audiences, the lack of control over personal, social, and environmental changes in the present makes the attainment of such a future difficult. Instead, the music articulates the allure of a 'future unknown', to borrow the title of a 1997 track by DJ Krust,[48] which, as McKenzie Wark identifies, is 'an idea, a feeling, an orientation that might make most sense among those for whom the past was not that great anyway'.[49]

For Mark Fisher, it is the inability to imagine the future as part of a neat continuum with the present that can lead to the masochistic desire to impel its manifestation, even in its darkest forms. In an interview with Andrew Brooks for *Crack* magazine, Fisher referred to future shock as a means to understand the radical temporality of jungle drum and bass; a radicality that has since failed to emerge in other forms of popular music, and, notably, the genre itself:

I think that sense of future shock is what has disappeared, which was in retrospect a very rapid turnover of styles one was accustomed to. I suppose coming to musical consciousness at the end of post-punk, when there was a more or less explicit intolerance towards the recent past, never mind the deep past of cultural time, that was what created my expectations. And when that (post-punk) played out, other areas of music took over, most notably jungle, which when you heard it you thought, 'I've never heard anything like this'. That's the simple sense of future shock.[50]

Instead of functioning as a permanent and universal condition, Fisher indicates that, since the mid-2000s, techno-capitalist deterritorialisation has produced a schizophrenic temporality in which culture seems to have both sped up – driven by an accelerated rate of technological change on the one hand – and decelerated, weighed down by the excessive plenitude of online content from varying points in recorded time, which, on the other hand, eliminates the possibility of erasing the past, and consequently, the potential for forging new futures. This paradox of accelerated culture has been reinforced by the declining wealth and social mobility of young people who have traditionally been the harbingers of modernity in pop culture. By preceding the mass adoption of the internet, jungle drum and bass was able to frame the accelerationist future as a disturbing yet thrilling certainty; despite being substantially formed out of fragments of soul and funk recordings from the past, the genre was able to produce jouissance by enfolding ecstatic experiences of speed with a sense of dread about techno-capitalism's implications for the future. In this context, the genre could produce feelings of shock *about* the future, because, to paraphrase Noys, the 'differences between elements' could still be discerned. While the nomenclature of recent tracks like 'Accelerator'[51] by Dan Structure and 'Turbocharged'[52] by Rohaan and The Caracal Project – two of the biggest drum and bass tracks at the time of writing (winter 2021) – shows that the genre continues to dramatically evoke the destabilisation of work, culture, human and social identity wrought by techno-capitalist acceleration, its ability to generate future shock has dissipated as speed has deeply penetrated into most people's everyday lives.

Rather than oppose or challenge the post-industrial conditions underpinning accelerationism, drum and bass celebrates the speed of techno-capitalism and its inhuman effects as a form of dark jouissance. Pervading the genre's time-stretched breaks and dread bass is the lagging of the post-industrial working class behind the uncanny and fast-changing conditions of their physical and cognitive environments, leading to the schizoid embracing of a dystopian high-tech fantasy that valorises the destructive speed of technology, propelled by the late-capitalist adjoining of desire and machinic hyper-efficiency. Additionally, direct referencing to the post-humanisation of the self, often drawn from dystopian science fiction and horror films in the form of sampled soundscapes, sound effects, and dialogue, conveys the relentless, emotionless character of uninhibited and technologically driven marketisation. By functioning as an accelerationist extrapolation, the genre conveys the fantasy of breaking through the limits of techno-capitalism; it is futile to oppose such forces from within the capitalist system, so better to develop a sensibility that Noys refers to as 'deterritorialization to the absolute end'.[53] In this respect, drum and bass alerts us to the future shocks to come, as well as to the adaptive alien subjectivities that may be needed to survive them at a time when the future itself is uncertain.

Notes

1. DJ Fresh and Rita Ora, 'Hot Right Now', Ministry of Sound, 2012.
2. *The Matrix*, directed by Andrew and Larry Wachowski (Warner Brothers, 1999).
3. Eshun, K. *More Brilliant Than the Sun: Adventures in Sonic Fiction*, London: Quartet, 1998, p. 00[-005].
4. Hemment, D. 'e for Ekstasis', *New Formations*, 31 (1997), p. 57, quoting Justin Barton.
5. Two Fingas and James T. Kirk. *Junglist*, London: Repeater Books, 2021, p. 2.
6. Belle-Fortune, B. *All Crews Muss Big Up: Journeys Through Jungle/Drum and Bass Culture*, London: Vision, 2005.
7. Danielsen, A. *Presence and Pleasure: The Funk Grooves of James Brown and Parliament*, Middletown: Wesleyan University Press, 2006, p. 71.
8. Hall, J. 'Rocking the Rhythm: Dancing Identities in Drum and Bass Club Culture', *Bodies of Sound: Studies Across Popular Music and Dance*, Cook, S. C. and Dodds, S. (eds.), London, New York: Routledge, 2013, pp. 108–09.
9. Eshun, K. 'Jungle! Jungle! The Last Dance Underground', *i-D*, 128 (1994), 43–44.
10. Barthes, R. 'The Grain of the Voice', *Image, Music, Text*, Heath, S. (trans.), London: Fontana, 1977, pp. 179–90.
11. Rietveld, H. C. *This is Our House: House Music, Cultural Spaces and Technologies*, Aldershot: Ashgate, 1998, p. 148.
12. Mixrace, 'Too Bad for Ya (Is 180 Too Fast for Ya?)', Moving Shadow, 1992, vinyl.
13. Shapiro, P. 'Nubian Sound Systems', *The Wire*, 159 (October 1996), p. 29.
14. *Blade Runner*, directed by Ridley Scott (Warner Brothers, 1982).
15. *The Terminator*, directed by James Cameron (Orion Pictures, 1984).
16. Rufige Kru, 'Terminator', Synthetic Hardcore Phonography, 1992.
17. Rufige Kru, 'Terminator II', Reinforced, 1993.
18. James Brown, 'Funky Drummer', King, 1970.
19. Toffler, A. *Future Shock*, London; Bantam, 1990.
20. Various, *Guerilla Warfare*, Renegade Hardware, 2005.
21. Virilio, P. *Negative Horizon*, London: Continuum, 1999, p. 26.
22. Virilio, P. *Speed and Politics*, New York: Semiotext(e), 1986, p. 151.
23. Virilio, *Negative Horizon*, p. 59.
24. Virilio, P., and Lotringer, S. *Pure War*, New York: Semiotext(e), 1997, p. 69.
25. Virilio, P. *Speed and Politics*, p. 75.
26. Deleuze, G., and Guattari, F. *A Thousand Plateaus: Capitalism and Schizophrenia*, London: Continuum, 2004, p. 260.
27. Land, N. *The Thirst for Annihilation: Georges Bataille and Virulent Nihilism*, London: Routledge, 1992, p. 197.

28. Beckett, A. 'Accelerationism: How a Fringe Philosophy Predicted the Future We Live In', *The Guardian*, 11 May 2017 (accessed 17 April 2022) www.theguardian.com/world/2017/may/11/accelerationism-how-a-fringe-philosophy-predicted-the-future-we-live-in.
29. Land, N. *Fanged Noumena: Collected Writings 1987–2007*, Falmouth: Urbanomic/Sequence Press, 2011, p. 338.
30. Rietveld, H. C. and Monroe, A. 'Gabber: Raising Hell in Technoculture', *Metal Music Studies*, 7:3 (2021), 399–42.
31. Noys, B. *Malign Velocities: Accelerationism and Capitalism*, Alresford: Zero Books, 2014, p. 61.
32. Lyotard, J-F. *Libidinal Economy*, London: Continuum, 2015, p. 124.
33. Hebdige, D. 'Posing ... Threats, Striking ... Poses', *The Subcultures Reader*, Gelder, K., and Thornton, S. (eds.), London: Routledge, p. 297.
34. Noys, B. 'Dance and Die: Obsolescence and Embedded Aesthetics of Acceleration', *Accelerated Youth*, 2014, p. 294.
35. Noys, 'Dance and Die', p. 305.
36. Reynolds, S. 'Simon Reynolds on the Hardcore Continuum: Introduction', *The Wire*, 300, February 2013 (accessed 17 April 2022) www.thewire.co.uk/in-writing/essays/the-wire-300_simon-reynolds-on-the-hardcore-continuum_introduction.
37. Ibid.
38. Hebdige, D. *Subculture: The Meaning of Style*, London: Methuen, 1979, p. 104.
39. CCRU, 'Swarmachines', *Abstract Culture, Swarm*, 1 1996 (accessed 17 April 2022) http://ccru.net/swarm1/1_swarm.htm.
40. Henriques, J. 'Sonic Dominance and the Reggae Sound System Session', *The Auditory Culture Reader*, Bull, M, and Back, L. (eds.), Oxford: Berg, 2003, p. 459.
41. Christodoulou, C. 'Rumble in the Jungle: City, Place, and Uncanny Bass', *Dancecult: Journal of Electronic Dance Music Culture, Special Issue on DJ Culture*, 3:1 (2011), 44–63.
42. Kristeva, J. *Desire in Language*, Gora, T., Jardine, A., and Roudiez, L. S. (trans.), New York: Columbia University Press, 1980, p. 133.
43. Land, *Fanged Noumena*, p. 398.
44. Rietveld, H. C. 'Ephemeral Spirit: Sacrificial Cyborg and Soulful Community', *Rave and Religion*, St. John, Graham (ed.), London and New York: Routledge, 2004, pp. 55–56.
45. Eshun, *More Brilliant Than the Sun*, p. 01[02].
46. Toffler, A. *Future Shock*, p. 2.
47. Toffler, A. *Future Shock*, p.1.
48. DJ Krust, 'Future Unknown', Talkin Loud, 1997.
49. Wark, M. 'Black Accelerationism', 2017 (accessed 17 April 2022) https://non.copyriot.com/black-accelerationism/.

50. Brooks, A. 'Do You Miss the Future? Mark Fisher Interviewed', *Crack*, 12 September 2014 (accessed 17 April 2022) https://crackmagazine.net/article/long-reads/mark-fisher-interviewed/.
51. Dan Structure, 'Accelerator', Echus Chasma EP, Delta9, 2021.
52. Rohaan and The Caracal Project, 'Turbocharged', Pilot, 2021.
53. Noys, 'Dance and Die'. p. i.

Further Reading

Belle-Fortune, B. *All Crews Muss Big Up: Journeys Through Jungle/Drum and Bass Culture*, London: Vision, 2005.

Cybernetic Culture Research Unit (CCRU), 'Swarmachines', *Abstract Culture, Swarm*, 1 1996, http://ccru.net/swarm1/1_swarm.htm.

Fisher, M. *Capitalist Realism: Is There No Alternative?*, Winchester: Zero Books, 2009.

Noys, B. *Malign Velocities: Accelerationism and Capitalism*, Alresford: Zero Books, 2014.

Virilio, P. *Speed and Politics*, New York: Semiotext(e), 1986.

10 | Chill Out

Seeking Ecstatic Trance in Low-Tempo EDM

RUPERT TILL

Studies of electronic dance music forms have often focused primarily on club cultures, the dance floor, and an upbeat range of music making. This chapter draws attention to downtempo music, and the development of chill out music. Major music-streaming platform Spotify breaks down the primary genre of electronic music into twenty-two subgenres, one of which is chill out.[1] Chill out and related downtempo electronic dance music culture (EDMC) genres were popularised from 1989 but have roots stretching back to the late 1960s and 1970s, much like more uptempo forms. Chill out mirrors dance floor club music and culture while focusing on stillness rather than movement. It features low-beats-per-minute tempos and relaxed moods, operating as a contemporary equivalent to easy-listening music. It is used by EDMC participants and others after dancing or clubbing, or in moments of stillness at home, in bars, in chill out rooms in clubs, in chill out venues, and on chill out stages at music festivals. There are chill out artists, websites, and record labels, and chill out is today a significant sector of the music industry. While the terms 'chillout' or 'chill out' are most common, leading streaming service Spotify has sometimes labelled the form 'chill-out' or even simply 'chill'. The two-word form 'chill out' will be used in this chapter.

It consists of low-tempo music that draws upon the same electronic soundworld, beats, and samples as dance floor music. It is listened to individually or in small groups rather than on communal dance floors. Like dance floor music it embraces contextual clubbing elements such as subcultural capital and drug taking, but is linked to substances that slow heartbeats such as cannabis, rather than those that increase them, such as ecstasy or amphetamines. It embraces the euphoric mindful meditivity associated with (comparative if not always absolute) stillness, rather than the dance floor's overloaded possession trance achieved through extended periods of dancing. It is strongly associated with electronic dance music cultures, and is the private inward-facing complement to the dance floor's outward-facing scene.

A number of emergent genres – including ambient, ambient dub, ambient techno, chill out, downtempo, ambient house, chillhop, and trip hop – connect with ecstatic forms of trance. Listeners use such music to induce states of relaxation, stillness, meditation, blissful somatic consciousness, euphoria, or to lower tension or stress levels, in various contexts. As will be described later, the term 'chill out' emerged in the context of club culture events, where people used chill out music and chill out rooms to provide participants a sonic space to either 'come up' and prepare for, or to rest and recover from, intense dancing. Perhaps because of these functions and uses of chill out music, it has sometimes become associated with spirituality.

Historically, spirituality has been defined in opposition to materiality and corporality, but it is difficult to securely define.[2] It has been described more recently as being able to include elements beyond organised religion or traditional religious practices and beliefs; it is today often closer to a philosophy than a set of practices and traditions. In suggesting chill out music engages with issues of spirituality, three definitions of spirituality give an impression of how that term is being used: 'the feelings, thoughts, experiences, and behaviours that arise from a search for the sacred';[3] 'the capacity and tendency present in all human beings to find and construct meaning about life and existence and to move toward personal growth, responsibility, and relationship with others';[4] and 'the way individuals seek and express meaning and purpose and the way they experience their connectedness to the moment, to self, to others, to nature, and to the significant or sacred'.[5] It is thus defined in terms of individual experiences and seeking, rather than shared tradition, faith, or belief.

This chapter begins by outlining the functions of chill out, its meanings, and the context of its listeners, exploring the phenomenology of its listening experiences. It then discusses the development of EDMC chill out music, by first tracing the various precursors that influenced its development, in order to understand why it has specific characteristics. This provides a foundation from where it is possible to trace the different influences and sources of inspiration that made chill out possible, which are not only taken from Eno's concept of ambient music and the European and Euro-American twentieth-century avant-garde, but also from Ibiza's laid-back Bhagwan-inspired club scene, Jamaican dub-reggae, and South Asian spiritual music. It explores the musical techniques used to address these contexts, and that help chill out to achieve a range of musical and cultural functions.

Phenomenology and Embodiment

Music manipulates the listener's experiential perception. From the first human culture, we can see that music, space, and place interact to provide an ambient sonic background to rituals and meaning making.[6] Music in religious contexts has much in common with the related electronic sub-genres of ambient and chill out music; Christian or Tibetan chant, Hindu mantras, and Sufi prayers all place music at the centre of religious and spiritual practices. Chill out draws from these traditions, as well as from examples that are influenced by spirituality rather than the overtly religious, such as in the case of Cage, Stockhausen, minimalism, 1960s popular music counterculture, and new age spiritualities. EDMC activities also often evidence religion-like elements,[7] involving ecstatic merger, *communitas*, connection, and collective effervescence, creating powerful emotional experiences.[8] Peter[9] describes the dissolution of the self on the dance floor as similar to a collective Jungian therapy, often enhanced by the social lubricant of recreational drug taking.[10] This kind of behaviour needs space before or after such liminality to prepare for or process the resultant psychologically intense experiences, something afforded by chilling out to downtempo music, whether in a club chill out room or elsewhere.

With chill out, popular music culture fulfils a need for a soundtrack that supports those seeking a range of ecstatic states, within a blissed out oceanic experience.[11] Chill out music focuses on a highly contextualised psychic relaxation, on engaging with nothingness, setting an atmosphere, and turning space into place. Yi-Fu Tuan[12] defines space and place, suggesting that whereas space affords movement, a contextualised place is defined by stillness: 'each pause in movement makes it possible for location to be transformed into place'. When humans stay in one space, they establish meaning and memory in that location, creating a place. Cresswell describes places as contextualised spaces:

> Place is also a way of seeing, knowing and understanding the world. When we look at the world as a world of places ... we see attachments and connections between people and place. We see worlds of meaning and experience.[13]

In a similar way, Demers relates ambient music to space that is situated, and to the listening context of the audience, 'not only the environments in which sound propagates but also those that listeners physically and metaphorically occupy'.[14] She describes listening to spaces within ambient music as 'a composite of the perceived spatial characteristics of a work'.[15] For Demers, 'ambient music excels at creating the impression of an acoustic cocoon that surrounds the listener'.[16] When listening to the time-based medium of music in a specific place, we pause within the soundscape of that place.[17] Listening to ambient or chill out music helps to turn a neutral, physical space into a contextualised, meaningful place, the music interacting with external sonic references by blanketing or absorbing them, disrupting a conventional sense of time by inserting its own free association with temporality.

A number of scholars have explored how music and sound are used in a passive context. Cage drew attention to and composed with background sounds, by exploring silences in music.[18] Influenced himself by Erik Satie and by Zen Buddhism, Cage in turn influenced Eno and British minimalist composer Gavin Bryars (who studied with Cage), who then influenced chill out pioneers the Orb and KLF. Tagg describes background music as invisible music,[19] Kassabian describes it as ubiquitous music;[20] both draw attention to unconscious rather than active listening. Various kinds of background music are used to change listeners' perception in a range of contexts, including in sales,[21] medical treatment,[22] and exercise.[23] This illustrates that chill out music is highly functional, interacting with a 'habitus' of individual listening and relevant to the 'field' of the genre.[24] It provides background atmospheres and affords the loss of self in ecstatic experience.

Music's use is similar in many spiritual traditions. Hindu's Carnatic Raags aim to inspire particular moods, Buddhists use music to enhance meditation, Sufis use music and movement to achieve ecstatic states. As with chill out music, all go beyond a use to mask background sounds: rather, music listening is focused upon an individual's 'refining of emotional essence, a distillation of his or her emotion that will lead to a transformation of consciousness to a higher level of spirituality ... closer to the divine'.[25] Just as in chill out music,

> silent, still, focused listening is also the habit in some other musical traditions, notably the north Indian Hindustani tradition, where one sits quietly, introspectively listening to the gradual developing filigree of the musical structure ... Thoughts and feelings are turned inward. The setting is intimate, conducive to introspection and a distancing from one's fellow listeners.[26]

This Hindu tradition is particularly relevant due to its influence in Ibiza via the followers of Bhagwan, as discussed in more detail later in this chapter.

Becker describes such participants as deep listeners, characterised by expressions of transcendence and gnosis, in which out-of-body sensations bring the person into an altered state of consciousness, a sacralised loss of boundaries between self and other, affording experiences of wholeness and unity. Having experienced the loss of self while immersed in the dance floor, post-clubbing chill out affords a reconnection with an internal world, as one returns from a liminal state.[27] Ambient music embraces such embodied phenomenological listening. This can provide

> a special blessing, a benediction ... a life-enhancing skill ... with the resulting intensely felt emotion and feelings of transcendent numinosity ... to temporarily abide in an eternity ... to feel more purposefully alive and in direct communication with the Holy ... in an enchanted world.[28]

With its effectiveness sometimes enhanced by the religious practices of alternative spiritualities, or the drug taking of EDMC,[29] chill out music, culture, and practices have for many become an important part of everyday spirituality, sacralising home life or routine secular contexts within a sacred popular,[30] and allowing for the blurring of the boundaries between alteration of mood and modification of consciousness. Whether encountered during an intense meditation session or while shopping in a supermarket, ambient and chill out music play a part in a re-enchantment of our daily lives.[31]

Physically, chill out music seeks entrainment, the synchronisation of bodily rhythms to the slow external rhythms of music, to relaxed breathing and a slow heartbeat: 'Music alters autonomic body functions, such as respiration and pulse rate, blood pressure, and heartbeat, and thereby synchronizes the external auditory rhythm with the internal body rhythm.'[32] Whereas some trance practices seek synchronisation between individuals on the dance floor and loss of and disconnection from self, perhaps through sustained frenetic dancing to loud repetitive sounds, ecstatic chill out trancing explores separation from conventional time in order to connect with the self, as a form of experiential phenomenology.[33]

Phenomenology focuses on activities that bring people and contacts together as a 'We',[34] examining embodied experiences. Entrainment can lead to trance, the key symptomatic evidence of which is loss of time or, at least, a disconnection with a sense of the usual passing of time. This has been discussed as flow,[35] deep-flow,[36] or total immersion.[37] Unlike the distanced-from-self zombie-like experience of loss of memory that can come with an intense drug-fuelled dance floor experience, in which the self is lost through dissolution in the music as well as the group, such individualised ecstatic trance experiences afford a more intense connection with the self. 'Music alters autonomic body functions, such as respiration and pulse rate, blood pressure, and heartbeat, and thereby synchronises the external auditory rhythm with the internal body rhythm.'[38] 'We enjoy the feeling of nothing but our own bodies in a space.'[39] Ecstatic experience results from entrainment and entrancement of the body and mind, perceptions and expectations coordinated by this entrainment to what is heard.[40] Listening to ambient music can play a part in an ontological experience, focusing on being and becoming, and relationships with others. We will now explore the various musical and other elements that come together to develop as chill out music.

History and Context

One of the earliest forms of chill out music was by French composer Erik Satie in what he called Furnishing Music (or Furniture Music). The music was intended to have the function of providing background music while audiences were in a theatre show's interval break, and was not intended to be distracting, having a similarly functional role to the furniture on which people sat.[41] Satie's work resonates with a number of elements of ambient and chill out music cultures. He was interested in repetition, suggesting that performances of his piano piece *Vexations* be repeated 840 times, and that if one did so one should prepare with a period of silence and immobility. Repetition is also culturally evidenced in his personal life, for example through owning seven identical velvet suits and hats, which were the only clothes he wore for ten years.[42] He was interested in mysticism and religion and founded his own cult: the *Église Métropolitaine d'Art de Jésus Conducteur*. He wrote dreamy, spacious music, such as his *Gymnopodies*, compositions which feature pattern repetition and a gentle mood and that often appear in contemporary ambient piano music Spotify playlists. It has been suggested that Satie had many of the traits associated with Asperger's syndrome.[43] Whatever the source of his musical idiosyncrasies, his interest in the use of music to still the mind, block out background noise, or dial in to a deep human desire for a ritualistic repetition to induce trance-like consciousness was evident; as such, he is an early pre-cursor both to classical minimalism and ambient and chill out music.

Music has often been used as a 'background' to other things. For example, research shows that classical and popular music have similar effects when used as background music for eating, whether in restaurants to set a mood and encourage higher spending or in the home to soothe guests at a dinner party.[44] Music has often been used to provide a sonic background to spiritual content, from Buddhist chant to Bach; the deep emotions stimulated by musical listening can lead to spiritual experiences, but the focus is on the mystical search for meaning, not the music. The power of music to inspire or enhance spiritual experience may be due to culturally driven expectation, the direct effect of the music on phenomenological experience, or a mixture of the two, but it has immense power even when not the conscious focus of attention.[45]

John Cage is another relevant composer in this context, who became interested in Zen Buddhism, including elements of a religiously inflected perspective in his musical exploration of silence or, rather, the role of the environmental sounds that are brought forward within consciousness when one is silent.[46] He famously composed a piece of music called 4'33",[47] which consists of a musical performer being silent, focusing attention on the soundscape surrounding the listener, on the environmental sounds present within a particular context of music performance. Similar themes pervade his work, such as in his composition *Apartment House 1776*,[48] where some of the musical content can be performed aloud or silently. Cage also discovered and published (for the first time) Satie's *Vexations*, performing it for the first time – as suggested, repeated 840 times – which takes eighteen to twenty-four hours depending on how fast you play. Musical cultures often attempt to encourage listeners to focus on musical pitches and the way they are played. In this performance, the musical pitches become static through repetition, placing emphasis on everything else present – that is, the ambient sounds present, the complete acoustic ecology of the listening environment. In *Vexations*, repetitive music provides a musical wallpaper that covers the acoustic landscape, and as a result drives the listener's attention inwards, into themselves, and into their own interpretation and perception. The latter seems to correspond to the focus on mindfulness in Buddhism.

Cage in turn inspired a number of classical minimalist composers from Britain and the United States, including La Monte Young, Terry Riley, Steve Reich, Philip Glass, Michael Nyman, and Gavin Bryars.[49] Like Cage, these composers were interested in non-Western spiritually infected traditional musical cultures, for example Indonesian and Balinese Gamelan temple music, as well as West African percussive trance rhythms, and Hindu Indian classical music. This embracing of related musical and spiritual content from global cultures would be adopted many years later in chill out music, at least in part transmitted by minimalism as an earlier rhythmic repetitive forerunner, minimalism preparing the ground for ambient music, and influencing early chill out artists. Repetition and patterns interested the minimalist composers, and like these global forms, minimalist music embraced repetition as a key identifier, creating an aesthetic again relevant to meditation practices. La Monte Young in particular was interested in time, exploring the

> relationship to universal structure and to time. Even in as simple a way as where do we come from, why are we here and where are we going? ... Time is really a very important aspect of universal structure. What I have learned is it goes very slowly.[50]

Influenced partly by Young, minimalist pioneer Terry Riley also composed in a spiritual context, using systemic approaches and reduced resources: 'staying on one note, there's different ways but that's definitely a way to ecstasy'.[51] His performances were influenced by peyote and shamanism, and he was involved in all-night musical events focused on improvisation. 'You developed a kind of feeling, like you were a sort of channel for the energy that was coming in from the space. You were all joining together, which was more of a ritual experience.'[52]

Riley was especially influenced by spiritual and psychological elements of Indian classical music. Both minimalism and its interest in South Asian musical forms are also set within the counter cultural context of an experimental 1960s search for new spiritual paths. Philip Glass and Steve Reich in the United States, and Michael Nyman and Gavin Bryars in the UK, all developed minimalist musical ideas further, and influenced later popular ambient and chill out music styles.

Additional relevant musical forms developed within popular music culture in Europe from the end of the 1960s through the 1970s. Electronic and minimalist popular music groups introduced innovative and influential material, such as the southern English band Pink Floyd with *Dark Side of the Moon* (1973),[53] German groups Tangerine Dream with *Phaedra*,[54] and also Neu! and Can, plus Vangelis from Greece, and English Mike Oldfield with *Tubular Bells*.[55] French electronic musician Jean-Michel Jarre published electronic album *Oxygène*,[56] influenced by his time as a member from 1969 of Groupe de Recherches Musicales (GRM), directed by electronic music composer and pioneer Pierre Schaeffer. Jarre also spent time at composer Karlheinz Stockhausen's studio shortly afterwards,[57] while Tangerine Dream and Kraftwerk were equally influenced by Stockhausen's pioneering experiments in electronic music. Stockhausen spoke often about time, metaphysics, and spirituality, and describes the importance of spirituality to his music:

contact between a particular moment of this life on this planet and the most important spiritual variations of the centre of the universe, which is the future and past and everything at once. It's no longer even the future, it's 'It', beyond time.[58]

There was frequent interaction between the work of art music composers such as Stockhausen and both the minimalist composers and popular music composers such as Kraftwerk or Aphex Twin.

Composer Brian Eno provides a good example of a mixed career. He was a member of Cornelius Cardew's Scratch Ensemble, performing art music within a framework of experimental free improvisation and text-based scores, and he also played synthesiser in an early line up of British pop group Roxy Music. In 1975 Eno released *Another Green World*,[59] an album that used random chance to structure its music, influenced by John Cage, while staying broadly within a popular music form. In the same year Eno launched a record label, Obscure Records, which released his album *Discreet Music*,[60] involving Robert Fripp's use of tape loops and Bryars conducting an acoustic ensemble. This piece was inspired by an experience in hospital, in which Eno listened to music that was playing very quietly, drawing his attention to ambient background sounds such as raindrops, and giving him the idea of writing music intended to interact with its ambient environment. This was the moment which first inspired within Eno the idea of ambient music.[61]

In 1978 Eno released the first of a series of four albums labelled Ambient 1 to Ambient 4. The first was *Ambient 1: Music for Airports*,[62] in which 'lyrics are not involved. Instead, each track organises clusters of sound that repeat at irregular intervals and without any backing rhythms. Not only is it impossible to sing along, none of the tracks sustain the attention they initially gather. And yet it remains too interesting to ignore.'[63] It contained extensive liner notes, in which Eno defined what he meant by ambient music:

I have become interested in the use of music as ambience ... using the term Ambient Music. My intention is to produce original pieces ostensibly (but not exclusively) for particular times and situations ... Ambient Music is intended to induce calm and a space to think. Ambient Music must be able to accommodate many levels of listening attention without enforcing one in particular; it must be as ignorable as it is interesting.[64]

Many predecessors, whether composers, musicians or music producers, had written music in a similar vein, but Eno coined the term 'ambient music', and composed within this genre overtly, setting out a manifesto to deliberately write ambient music, and in doing so establishing and naming this as a new genre. As Demers puts it, Eno:

provides the template for many later works: repetitive, tonal language, an absence of abrasive or abrupt attacks, long decays, and non-teleological writing, as if the melody could continue on indefinitely.[65]

Ambient music and Brian Eno would later directly influence chill out music's development, Eno's conceptualisation of ambient principles preparing the ground for chill out and related forms.

Ambient music was predated by light music, lounge, easy listening, and musak. Light music included the UK BBC Radio's Light Programme (begun in 1945), composers Mantovani and Henry Mancini, and the US Boston Pops Orchestra. Lounge music was played live or on recordings as background music in hotel lounges, restaurants, and bars. *Billboard* hosted an easy listening chart, which was rebranded as the Adult Contemporary music chart in 1979. Musak (with capitalised 'M'), a private company providing copyright-free background music for commercial use, is now a generic term for background music, library music, lift music, or elevator music. Notable examples include Bert Kaempfert and James Last (instrumental), Klaus Wunderlich (organ), and Richard Clayderman (piano). The various forms of easy listening music, including some popular classical music, were an important pre-cursor to ambient and chillout music.

In the early 1980s new age music emerged as a related form with a significant audience, mixing the electronic synthesiser popular music influences described above with ambient and background music; this was music aimed, for example, at providing a background for meditation, massage, or other 'new age' activities. Early examples include Paul Winter's 'Missa Gaia'/'Earth Mass';[66] George Winston's *December* (1983);[67] and R. Carlos Nakai's *Changes* (1983).[68] In 1987 a Grammy for Best New Age Album was established, and in 1988 *Billboard Magazine* instigated a weekly 'New Age' chart, recognising the large sales of the format. This provided an overtly spiritual form of ambient popular culture music and provides a prototype for the chill out music that would emerge in its wake.

Chill Out Emerges

Of importance to understanding the chill out concept is Ibiza, a Spanish Balearic island in the Mediterranean Sea, which was well known for its bohemian attitude as a part of the 1970s hippie trail, and had a reputedly lax law-enforcement attitude to drug taking.[69] The island's tourist and traveller audiences offered an inspiring nightclub culture, making it an attractive place for DJs or club promoters. About the club Amnesia, Johnny Walker reports that 'in the middle of the open air dance floor was a mirrored pyramid, then around the edges were bars and chill out areas with cushions, and Mediterranean and tropical plants. It was high walled, like being in a tropical garden.'[70] In the club the participants alternated periods of dancing and chilling, enhanced by the drug MDMA, colloquially known as 'ecstasy' or 'E', which had been introduced to the island by followers of Bhagwan Sri Rajneesh (later Osho).[71] Osho's sannyasin followers and other Ibiza residents had spent time in ashrams in India and Goa, and also brought back with them an interest in meditation, yoga, spirituality, and the achievement of ecstatic states. This interest in spirituality mixed into the proto-chill-out culture at Amnesia, which was particularly countercultural.

While chilling out at Amnesia, and other venues, periods of rest allowed participants to absorb and appreciate the intense ecstatic experiences of the serotonin and dopamine euphoric rushes induced by dancing and drug taking. Ibiza's warm climate, the hot cramped spaces of dance floors, the bodily heating created by dancing, and the recreational consumption of MDMA led people to seek space in which to cool down and rehydrate. MDMA also has an effect of enhancing empathy in users, and chill out spaces furthermore offered a space to talk and socialise. These chill out bar areas in the club were also reflected in the culture at other bars on the island, especially a beach bar in San Antonio (Saint Antoni de Portmany) called the Café Del Mar.

The Café Del Mar was unusual on Ibiza in being a large bar which faced west, and so provided a perfect vista for visitors to watch the sunset. This experience was usually accompanied by listening to music, making it a popular venue for chilling out before going out, or in the evening having earlier been in clubs like Amnesia or Space that closed at 12 noon or later. Alongside dancing in clubs like Amnesia (in the middle of the island) or Pacha (on the east side of Ibiza), chilling out at sunset in the Café Del Mar became a must-do activity for Ibiza clubbers. While most Ibiza clubs had large dance floors, Ibiza's chill out culture would over time become associated with Café Del Mar in particular, due to a range of branded chill out compilation albums that capitalised on this reputation, in turn helping to establish downtempo club music as chill out music. Ibiza's dance floor culture would play a significant part in the media popularisation of an existing and globally widespread electronic dance music culture in the late 1980s. Ibiza's chill out culture would similarly inspire the birth of chill out as a genre. Although chill out has many different influences and sources, the template seen in Ibiza in both Amnesia's chill out spaces and the Café Del Mar is a pattern that was to be echoed across club culture in the future, taken to Ibiza from India and Goa, and from there to London and worldwide.

Having visited Ibiza in the past, English DJ Paul Oakenfold went to Ibiza in 1987 to celebrate his birthday with Johnny Walker, Nicky Holloway, and Danny Rampling, all of whom went on to become well-known DJs and/or musicians. They took MDMA at Amnesia, a transformational experience for them all, and returned to Ibiza a number of times that summer, becoming increasingly influenced by what they experienced on the island. After the close of the Ibiza holiday season in 1987, back in London Oakenfold started club night Spectrum, Rampling started Shoom, and Holloway started the Trip. These clubs kickstarted a new MDMA-driven acid house scene in London.[72] Spectrum was held in the London nightclub Heaven, where Oakenfold also started a night called Land of Oz. In an upstairs VIP room at this latter event, Oakenfold and some friends set up a chill out room called the White Room,[73] where dancers could take a break from the intensity of the dance floor. Oakenfold instructed the DJs, 'don't get them to dance'.[74]

Jimmy Cauty and Alex Patterson were the White Room's DJs, mixing samples, tapes, records, and sound effects as sources, remixing these together as an extended ambient DJ set. These improvisations developed into a first single in 1989 by them as band The Orb, 'A Huge Ever Growing Pulsating Brain That Rules from the Centre of the Ultraworld'.[75] The rear of the single proclaimed it 'ambient house for the E generation',[76] underlining the idea of listening to EDMC ambient music under the influence of drugs. Cauty left The Orb, and released some of The Orb's material written with Patterson as a solo artist as *Space*,[77] and with Bill Drummond as the album *Chill Out* by The KLF.[78] The KLF coined the term chill out for this musical form, but with music developed as The Orb. The KLF referenced ambient music with 'file under ambient' written on a sticker on the cover of an early KLF record.[79] With a soundscape of bird and water noise alongside ambient synthesiser sounds, these releases provided a template for electronic ambient music, providing a new term for a new genre, chill out.

The Orb and The KLF have specific links to ambient music precursors. The Orb's Alex Patterson had heard Eno's album *Music for Films*[80] while tripping having taken LSD on tour as a roadie with Killing Joke, and was inspired to create similar music.[81] The Orb's producer Youth was a member of Killing Joke. Patterson had also worked for Eno's EG records, the label that released Eno's ambient series.[82] The KLF sampled Pink Floyd's 'On the Run'[83] on 'Madrugada Eterna' on *Chill Out*,[84] which featured synthesisers, global music samples, and found natural sounds. The Orb sampled 'Electric Counterpoint'[85] by Steve Reich on 'Little Fluffy Clouds', and on the same album [86] their single 'A Huge Ever Pulsating Brain That Rules From The Centre of the Ultraworld (Loving You)' samples Pink Floyd's 'Shine On You Crazy Diamond'.[87] Much as Eno names then releases ambient music, The Orb and KLF name and release chill out, each defining then establishing a related but distinct subgenre of electronic music. The Orb's sessions at the Land of Oz club acted as a launchpad and template for what was to become defined as the chill out scene.

This second birth of ambient music as chill out had a particular function. The music was particularly targeted at clubbers who were taking a break from the dance floor, but chill out music soon became popular with those who were recovering at home after a night out clubbing – still perhaps kept awake by the chemical stimulants taken during the night, but their ecstatic state coming down from the night before – or hanging out with friends or partners after a night dancing as the sun came up and the nightclubs closed. A range of EDM artists produced downtempo tracks for these audiences following The Orb and KLF's lead.

One example was two releases by label Warp Records, who released a range of experimental tracks on compilation albums *Pioneers of the Hypnotic Groove*[88] and *Artificial Intelligence*,[89] leading to the intelligent dance music (IDM) chill out sub genre. Aphex Twin released *Selected Ambient Works 85–92*.[90] Another compilation *Ambient Dub Volume 1 (The Big Chill)*[91] showed an influence of Jamaican dub music on EDMC in general, and chill out culture in particular, especially the reverb- and echo- laden productions of Lee Scratch Perry and King Tubby.[92] William Orbit produced a number of *Strange Cargo* albums; Massive Attack developed the Bristol-focused trip hop scene with *Blue Lines*.[93] Ambient house, ambient dub, IDM, psybient, Balearic, cinematic, and various other sub-genres emerged, as chill out developed the previous field of ambient music. Club chill out rooms proliferated alongside separate chill out club nights; chill out websites appeared, as did downtempo-focused festivals such as the Big Chill. As Sylvan puts it, 'There is a rhythmic temporal oscillation between the intensity of the dance floor and the relaxing break of the chill room.'[94] Chill out music provides a space to achieve balance, to socialise and talk with fellow dancers and trancers, and to explore the stillness of ecstatic trance rather than the upbeat music of dancing. Ambient music found a new home and function within club culture as part of the chill out phenomenon.

Techniques

Toop describes Ambient music as

drifting or simply existing in stasis rather than developing in any dramatic fashion ... encouraging states of reverie and receptivity in the listener ... engendered by techniques for disrupting a conventional relationship with time. ... often [using] multiple time signatures, a range of periodicities, or combinations of groups of prime numbers of beats ... disrupted by a lack of musical beat.[95]

A number of musical techniques are employed within chill out music to entrain audiences into trance-like ecstatic flow states. Although the listener can control whether such states can be achieved, music and thus the musician play a part in mediating and facilitating such a transformation. The musical style of ambient music affords a perception of *kairos*, or qualitative time, rather than *chronos*, quantitative time. Listeners understand 'musical experience as deep emotional states with a loss of feeling of space and time'.[96] A non-teleological musical approach allows pause, the creation of place, and the opportunity to slow the frantic pace of life for a moment. A Western world characterised by stress and fear, that is a fluid post- or liquid culture in which it is difficult to find one's place, has led many towards a sense of the homeless self,[97] creating a desire for reconnection and recontextualisation. Chill out sets a context, a sense of place that is calming and serene, re-establishing a sense of home. It draws the listener inwards, stilling time and moving the deep listener into a sense of *kairos*, to a greater or lesser extent. Even when ambient music is being largely ignored by the listener, the music is fulfilling this function, helping to set a scene, situating those who are listening to or ignoring the music, subconsciously penetrating the psyche and acting on the listener's state of mind. Becker suggests that

By enveloping the trancer in a soundscape that suggests, invokes, or represents other times and distant spaces, the transition out of quotidian time and space comes easier. ... One is moved from the mundane to the supra-normal: another realm, another time.[98]

Music listening modes have been discussed by a number of scholars.[99] All imply that unconscious or casual absorption of music is of lesser value to conscious musical listening engagement, using pejorative terms such as reduced or casual listening. In contrast, deep listening[100] describes positively the transcendence, gnosis, sacredness, self-loss, or wholeness typical of chill out and ambient music's embodied phenomenological listening.

Ambient music is often now differentiated from chill out, referring to music that aims at a sense of atemporality, avoiding chill out's pulse trains, rhythmic sequences of notes, or percussive beats, which are replaced by sustained sounds. Timbre becomes a key focus, the frequency spectrum or sonic texture of an individual sound. Synthesised sounds are dominant, components of which can be automated or have envelopes that change over time, in order to vary their amplitude or frequency content. Notes are sustained and long, often with slow attack and release, so their start and end may be disguised or softened. A small number of textures may be used. Sounds with fast attacks that could create rhythms are separated temporally, so that they are perceived as occurring in durations of seconds, rather than as rhythms, by simply not having them happen in quick succession. Otherwise they happen with musical rubato or at irregular intervals. These approaches avoid setting up a rhythmic grid, a repeating structure of durations that creates a sense of passing time. Ambient music seeks to take the listener out of time by providing no temporal reference, no clock-like ticking, so that the listener is distanced from their ability to track the passing of time.

Chill out music tends to have a greater sense of rhythm than ambient, and drum or percussion parts are common. Its tempo tends to be low. For example the Spotify official playlist 'Chillout Classics' features 100 tracks and as can be seen in Figure 10.1, they vary between 60 and 120 BPM.[101]

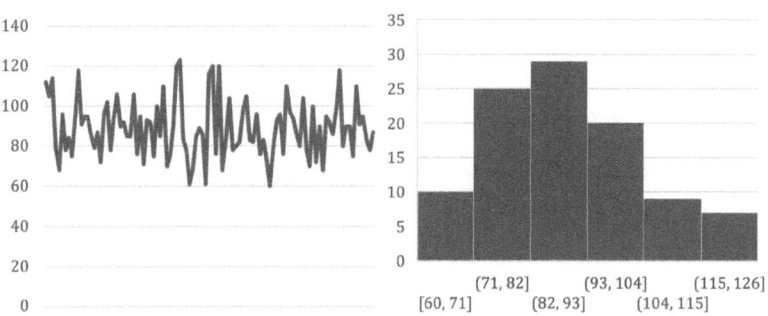

Fig. 10.1 Chillout Classics Spotify Playlist BPM, 2023

Figure 10.1 plots the BPM of each track, and a bar graph illustrates the number of tracks in a number of equal BPM ranges, with the largest number between 82 and 93. Soundscape elements are often present, including nature sounds, birdsong, wind, water, and vinyl record sounds such as scratches. World music sounds are also prevalent, for example the sitar or tabla of the Indian subcontinent, adding a non-Western if somewhat Orientalist perspective. Studio effects often feature prominently, such as: reverb; echoes (especially ones that sound like tape echoes); dub effects such as compressed feedback delays, manipulation of equalisation, or filtering; effects added to individual sounds or beats; effects that are chained to place a filter before (or after) a delay and/or reverb. Structurally the music often features long sections, with breakdowns where the music is stripped back to feature little or no percussion.

Another important musical element of chill out is the use of semiotic indicators of context, in particular with hints of mysticism or spirituality. As described above, The Orb and The KLF used recordings from non-Western traditions such as Tuvan throat singing samples in their music at the beginning of the chill out scene, and musical content related to spiritual traditions evokes an implicitly religious sensibility.[102] Bands such as Banco de Gaia and Transglobal Underground developed this theme. This approach helps draw the listener's expectation towards an altered state of consciousness, or creates a sense of mysticism. Some chill out music features a specific religious tradition, such as in Enigma's use of Gregorian chant,[103] the Beloved[104] and Orbital's[105] use of Gothic Voices' recording[106] of compositions by Abbess Hildegarde of Bingen, or Massive Attack's remixes of Nustrat Fateh Ali Khan's Qawwali music.[107]

Conclusions

An implication within intellectual studies of music that seems to be repeated in various contexts is that subconscious, culturally contextualised, or casual absorption of music is of different value or seriousness to critical engagement with a musical text, or to conscious attempts to identify or codify meaning. Listening to ambient music is therefore sometimes described using terms which imply a pejorative attitude, such as reduced or casual listening. Music has been used by humans to alter mood and atmosphere for tens of thousands of years,[108] in particular within spiritual or ritual contexts. It is my argument here that contemporary chill out music is a genre and style of music that has its roots in this context, and has a particular historical trajectory that has imbued it with qualities drawn from furniture music, minimalism, new age music, world music, dub reggae, as well as early electronic popular music pioneers. Chill out differs from contemporary ambient music in that ambient tends not to feature drum kit-like sounds and is not used in club culture settings, even though the two forms are closely interrelated.

Chill out is used to afford access to altered states of consciousness, ranging from a gentle sense of relaxation, though a mild daydream, to meditative ecstasy. Using entrainment and entrancement techniques, it takes the embodied self's phenomenological experience out of a day-to-day *chronos* perception of time, into a *kairos* temporal state, moving the listener into a state of flow by using a range of specific musical techniques to disrupt connection to the ordinary rhythms of life, and often navigating liminal states. Although chillout developed initially within chill out rooms of nightclubs during the EDMC and club culture boom of the 1990s, it has become a significant form in its own right, with its own culture and expanding context. In a twenty-first-century world where fast-paced technologically driven living has brought high-stress lifestyles and removed many traditional forms of spiritual ritual, chill out provides a significant place for listeners to connect inwardly and find a moment of calm.

Notes

1. The full list of electronic music subgenres is big room, breaks, chill out, deep house, drum and bass, dubstep, electro house, electronica/downtempo, funk/soul/disco, glitch hop, hard dance, hardcore/hard techno, hip-hop/r'n'b, house, indie dance/nu disco, minimal/deeptech, progressive house, psy-trance, reggae/dancehall/dub, tech house, techno, trance.
2. Oman, D. (2013). 'Defining Religion and Spirituality', *Handbook of the Psychology of Religion and Spirituality*, 2: 26.
3. Hill, P. C., Pargament, K. I., Hood, R. W., McCullough, J. M. E., Swyers, J. P., Larson, D. B., & Zinnbauer, B. J. (2000). 'Conceptualizing Religion and Spirituality: Points of Commonality, Points of Departure', *Journal for the Theory of Social Behaviour*, 30(1): 66.
4. Myers, J. E., & Williard, K. (2003). 'Integrating Spirituality into Counselor Preparation: A Developmental, Wellness Approach', *Counselling and Values*, 47(2): 149.
5. Puchalski, C., Ferrell, B., Virani, R., Otis-Green, S., Baird, P., Bull, J., ... & Sulmasy, D. (2009). 'Improving the Quality of Spiritual Care as a Dimension of

Palliative Care: The Report of the Consensus Conference', *Journal of Palliative Medicine*, 12(10): 887.

6. Mithen, S. (2005). 'A Creative Explosion?', in S. Mithen (ed.), *Creativity in Human Evolution and Prehistory*. London and New York: Routledge, pp. 132–52.
7. St John, G. (2004). *Rave Culture and Religion*. London: Routledge, pp. 131–66.
8. Till, R. (2010). *Pop Cult: Religion and Popular Music*. London: Continuum.
9. Peter, B. (2009). 'Jung on the Dance Floor: The Phenomenology of Dancing and Clubbing'. PhD Thesis, University of Salford (United Kingdom).
10. Till, R. (2009). 'Possession Trance Ritual in Electronic Dance Music Culture: A Popular Ritual Technology for Reenchantment, Addressing the Crisis of the Homeless Self, and Reinserting the Individual into the Community', in C. Deacy, & E. Arweck (eds.), *Exploring Religion and the Sacred in a Media Age*. London: Ashgate, pp. 169–87.
11. Malbon, B. (2002). *Clubbing: Dancing, Ecstasy, Vitality*. London: Routledge.
12. Tuan, Y. (1977). *Space and Place: The Perspective of Experience*. Minneapolis, MN: University of Minnesota Press, p. 6.
13. Cresswell, T. (2004). *Place: A Short Introduction*. Oxford: Blackwell, p. 11.
14. Demers, J. (2010). *Listening through the Noise: The Aesthetics of Experimental Electronic Music*. Oxford: Oxford University Press, p. 113.
15. Ibid., p. 116.
16. Ibid., p. 119.
17. Till, R. (2014). 'Sound Archaeology: Terminology, Palaeolithic Cave Art and the Soundscape', *World Archaeology*, 46(3): 292–304.
18. Shultis, C. (2013). *Silencing the Sounded Self: John Cage and the American Experimental Tradition*. Hanover and London: University Press of New England.
19. Tagg, P. (2011). 'Caught on the Back Foot: Epistemic Inertia and Visible Music', *IASPM Journal*, 2(1–2): 3–18. doi: 10.5429/2079-3871.
20. Kassabian, A. (2013). 'You Say Invisible, I Say Ubiquitous: A (Formally Former) Student's Response to Philip Tagg's "Caught on the Back Foot: Epistemic Inertia and Visible Music"', *IASPM Journal*, 3(2): 86–95.
21. Biswas, D., Lund, K., & Szocs, C. (2019). 'Sounds Like a Healthy Retail Atmospheric Strategy: Effects of Ambient Music and Background Noise on Food Sales', *Journal of the Academy of Marketing Science*, 47: 37–55; Kemp, E. A., Min, D. J. D., Williams, K. H., True, S. L., Borders, A. L., & Lester, D. H. (2019). Enhancing the Service Environment: The Effect of Music and Mood in Service-Based Business. Conference, Atlantic Marketing Association Proceedings, New Orleans, 2018. Published online at https://digitalcommons.kennesaw.edu/ama_proceedings/2018/ETHBIZ-MRKTCONS_T09/1/.
22. Hsieh, F. C., Miao, N. F., Tseng, I. J., Chiu, H. L., Kao, C. C., Liu, D., ... & Chou, K. R. (2019). 'Effect of Home-Based Music Intervention Versus

Ambient Music on Breast Cancer Survivors in the Community: A Feasibility Study in Taiwan', *European Journal of Cancer Care*, 28(4): e13064.
23. De Prisco, R., Guarino, A., Lettieri, N., Malandrino, D., & Zaccagnino, R. (2021). 'Providing Music Service in Ambient Intelligence: Experiments with Gym Users', *Expert Systems with Applications*, 177: 114951.
24. Bourdieu, P. (1977). 'The Economics of Linguistic Exchanges', *Social Science Information*, 16(6): 645–68.
25. Becker, J. (2004). *Deep Listeners: Music, Emotion, and Trancing* (Vol. 2). Bloomington: Indiana University Press, p. 76.
26. Ibid., p. 69.
27. St John, G. (2015). 'Liminal Being: Electronic Dance Music Cultures, Ritualization and the Case of Psytrance', in A. Bennett and S. Waksman (eds.), *The Sage Handbook of Popular Music*. London: Sage, pp. 243–60.
28. Becker, *Deep Listeners*, p. 195.
29. St John, G. (2012). *Global Tribe: Technology, Spirituality and Psytrance*. Sheffield: Equinox.
30. Till, *Pop Cult*.
31. Partridge, C. (2005). *The Re-Enchantment of the West: Volume 1: Alternative Spiritualities, Sacralization, Popular Culture and Occulture*. London: Bloomsbury.
32. Demmrich, S. (2020). 'Music as a Trigger of Religious Experience: What Role Does Culture Play?' *Psychology of Music*, 48(1): 35–49. doi: 10.1177/0305735618779681, 36.
33. Rouget, G. (1985). *Music and Trance: A Theory of the Relations Between Music and Possession*. Chicago: University of Chicago Press.
34. Kersten, F. (1976). 'Preface', in F. J. Smith (ed.), *Fragments on the Phenomenology of Music, In Search of Musical Method*. London: Gordon and Breach Science Publishers, pp. 6–22.
35. Csikszentmihalyi, M. (1990). *Flow: The Psychology of Optimal Experience*. San Francisco: Harper and Row.
36. Pujol-Tost, L. (2019). 'Did We Just Travel to the Past? Building and Evaluating with Cultural Presence Different Modes of VR-Mediated Experiences in Virtual Archaeology', *Journal on Computing and Cultural Heritage*, 12(1): 1–20.
37. Brown, E., and Cairns, P. (2004). 'A Grounded Investigation of Game Immersion', in *Proceedings of the CHI'04 Extended Abstracts on Human Factors in Computing Systems*. Vienna: ACM, pp. 1297–1300. Doi: 10.1145/985921.986048.
38. Demmrich, 'Music as a Trigger', p. 36.
39. Becker, *Deep Listeners*, p. 38.
40. Berger, J., & Turow, G. (2012). *Music, Science, and the Rhythmic Brain: Cultural and Clinical Implications* (Vol. 1). London: Routledge.

41. Remes, J. (2014). 'Serious Immobilities: Andy Warhol, Erik Satie and the Furniture Film', *Screen*, 55(4): 448–49.
42. Davis, M. E. (2007). *Erik Satie*. London: Reaktion Books, p. 59.
43. Fung, C. H. M. (2009). 'Asperger's and Musical Creativity: The Case of Erik Satie', *Personality and Individual Differences*, 46(8): 775–83.
44. Wilson, S. (2003). 'The Effect of Music on Perceived Atmosphere and Purchase Intentions in a Restaurant', *Psychology of Music*, 31(1): 93–112.
45. Demmrich, *Music as a Trigger*.
46. Shultis, *Silencing the Sounded Self*.
47. Cage, J. (1952). *4'33"*.
48. Cage, J. (1975>). *Apartment House 1776*.
49. Potter, K., and Gann, K. (2016). *The Ashgate Research Companion to Minimalist and Postminimalist Music*. Abingdon: Routledge.
50. La Monte Young quoted in Toop, D. (1995). *Ocean of Sound: Aether Talk, Ambient Sound and Imaginary Worlds*. London: Serpent's Tail, pp. 178–79.
51. Terry Riley quoted in Toop, *Ocean of Sound*, p. 185.
52. Ibid., p. 186.
53. Pink Floyd. (1973). *Dark Side of the Moon*. Harvest.
54. Tangerine Dream. (1974). *Phaedra*. Virgin.
55. Mike Oldfield. (1972). *Tubular Bells*. Virgin.
56. Jean-Michel Jarre. (1976). *Oxygène*. Disques Motors.
57. Sánchez Arsenal, M. (2010). 'Jean Michel Jarre y Pierre Schaeffer: un vinculo excepcional entre Oxygène (1976) y la musique concrète', *AATTAC: Acoustical, Art and Artifacts: Technology, Aesthetics. Communication*, 7: 135–42.
58. Felder, D. and Stockhausen, K. (1977). 'An Interview with Karlheinz Stockhausen', *Perspectives of New Music*, 16(1): 85. doi: 10.2307/832850, 98.
59. Brian Eno. (1975). *Another Green World*. Island.
60. Brian Eno. (1975). *Discreet Music*. Obscure Records.
61. Eno, B. (1996). *A Year with Swollen Appendices*. London: Faber and Faber, pp. 293–97.
62. Brian Eno. (1978). *Ambient 1: Music for Airports*. E.G. Polydor.
63. Lysaker, J. (2019). *Brian Eno's Ambient 1: Music for Airports*. Oxford: Oxford University Press, 1.
64. Eno. *Ambient 1: Music for Airports*. Liner Notes.
65. Demers, *Listening Through the Noise*, p. 117.
66. Paul Winter. (1982). *Missa Gaia/Earth Mass*. Living Music.
67. George Winston. (1983). *December*. Windham Hill.
68. R. Carlos Nakai. (1983). *Changes*. Canyon.
69. Moss, S. (2021) 'The Evolution of Electronic Dance Music Spaces in Leeds, UK', in E. Mazierska, T. Rigg, and L. Gillon, (eds.), *The Evolution of Electronic Dance Music*. New York: Bloomsbury Publishing USA, p. 184.

70. Warren, E. (2007). '"The Birth of Rave", the Guardian Online'. Available at: www.theguardian.com/music/2007/aug/12/electronicmusic. (Accessed 9 July 2023).
71. D'Andrea, A. (2006). 'The Spiritual Economy of Nightclubs and Raves: Osho Sannyasins As Party Promoters in Ibiza and Pune/Goa', in G. St John (ed.), *Culture and Religion: An Interdisciplinary Journal.* 7(1), pp. 61–75.
72. Other scenes already existed in, for example, New York and Chicago and in Manchester and Sheffield in the UK, and Belgium and Holland in Europe. However, this London scene gained mass media attention alongside a moral panic over drug taking at events.
73. Reynolds, S. (1999). *Generation Ecstasy: Into the World of Techno and Rave Culture.* London: Routledge, p. 189.
74. Norris, R. *Paul Oakenfold: The Authorised Biography.* London: Bantam, 2007, p. 135.
75. The Orb. (1991). *The Orb's Adventures Beyond the Ultraworld.* Big Life.
76. Reynolds, *Generation Ecstasy,* p. 190.
77. Space. (1990). *Space.* KLF Communications.
78. KLF. (1990). *Chill Out.* KLF Communications.
79. Toop, *Ocean of Sound,* pp. 58–63.
80. Brian Eno. (1978). *Music for Films.* EG.
81. Prendergast, M. (2003). *The Ambient Century: From Mahler to Moby – the Evolution of Sound in the Electronic Age.* London: Bloomsbury, pp. 407–12.
82. Reynolds, *Generation Ecstasy,* 191.
83. Pink Floyd. *Dark Side of the Moon.*
84. KLF, *Chill Out.*
85. Steve Reich (1989). Different Trains/Electric Counterpoint (Pat Metheny soloist). Nonesuch.
86. The Orb. *The Orb's Adventures Beyond the Ultraworld.*
87. Pink Floyd. (1975). *Wish You were Here.* Harvest. Prendergast, *The Ambient Century,* p. 408.
88. Various Artists. (1991). *Pioneers of the Hypnotic Groove.* Warp.
89. Various Artists. (1992). *Artificial Intelligence.* Warp.
90. Aphex Twin. (1992). *Selected Ambient Works 85–92.* Apollo – R&S.
91. Various Artists. (1992). *Ambient Dub Volume 1* (The Big Chill). Beyond.
92. Partridge, C. (2010). *Dub in Babylon: Understanding the Evolution and Significance of Dub Reggae in Jamaica and Britain from King Tubby to Post-punk.* London: Equinox.
93. Massive Attack. (1991). *Blue Lines.* Wild Bunch; Virgin.
94. Sylvan, R. (2002). *Traces of the Spirit: The Religious Dimensions of Popular Music.* New York: New York University Press, p. 138.
95. Toop, *Ocean of Sound,* p. ii.
96. Demmrich, 'Music as a Trigger', p. 37.

97. Heelas, P., & L. Woodhead. (2001). 'Homeless Minds Today?', in L. Woodhead, P. Heelas, & D. Martin (eds.), *Peter Berger and the Study of Religion*. London: Routledge, pp. 43–72
98. Becker, *Deep Listeners*, p. 27.
99. Schaeffer, P. (1966). *Traité des Objets Musicaux: Essai Interdisciplines*. Paris: Éditions des Seuil; Subotnik, R. R. (1996). *Deconstructive Variations: Music and Reason in Western Society*. Minneapolis: University of Minnesota Press; Dell'Antonio, A. (ed.) (2004). *Beyond Structural Listening?: Postmodern Modes of Hearing*. Oakland, CA: University of California Press; Tuuri, K. and Eerola, T. (2012). 'Formulating a Revised Taxonomy for Modes of Listening'. *Journal of New Music Research*, 41(2): 137–52 doi: 10.1080/09298215.2011.614951; Chion, M. (2019). *Audio-Vision: Sound on Screen*. New York: Columbia University Press. doi: https://doi.org/10.7312/chio18588-004.
100. Becker, *Deep Listeners*.
101. Spotify. (n.d.) *Chillout Classics*. Available at https://open.spotify.com/playlist/37i9dQZF1DXcG4kXwIFULb. (Accessed 9 July 2023).
102. Bailey, E. (2002). *The Secular Quest for Meaning in Life: Denton Papers in Implicit Religion*. New York: Edwin Mellen Press.
103. Enigma (1990). *MCMXC a.D*, A.R.T.
104. The Beloved, (1990). 'Sun Rising', *Happiness*, WEA.
105. Orbital, (1991). 'Belfast', *Orbital*. FFRR.
106. Gothic Voices, (1982). *A Feather on the Breath of God*. Hyperion.
107. Nusrat Fateh Ali Khan, (1990). *'Musst Musst (Massive Attack Remix)'*. Real World.
108. Morley, I. (2013). *The Prehistory of Music: Human Evolution, Archaeology, and the Origins of Musicality*. Oxford: Oxford University Press.

Further Reading

Becker, J. (2004). *Deep Listeners: Music, Emotion, and Trancing*. Bloomington: Indiana University Press.

D'Andrea, A. (2006). 'The Spiritual Economy of Nightclubs and Raves: Osho Sannyasins as Party Promoters in Ibiza and Pune/Goa', *Culture and Religion: An Interdisciplinary Journal*, 7(1): 61–75.

Demmrich, S. (2020). 'Music as a Trigger of Religious Experience: What Role does Culture Play?' *Psychology of Music*, 48(1): 35–49. doi: 10.1177/0305735618779681.

Malbon, B. (2002). *Clubbing: Dancing, Ecstasy, Vitality*. New York: Routledge.

Rouget, G. (1985). *Music and Trance: A Theory of the Relations Between Music and Possession*. Chicago: University of Chicago Press.

Till, R. (2010). *Pop Cult: Religion and Popular Music*. London: Continuum.

Toop, D. (1995). *Ocean of Sound: Aether Talk, Ambient Sound and Imaginary Worlds*. London: Serpent's Tail.

Discography

Aphex Twin. (1992). *Selected Ambient Works 85–92*. Apollo – R&S.
Brian Eno. (1975). *Another Green World*. Island.
Brian Eno. (1975). *Discreet Music*. Obscure Records.
Brian Eno. (1978). *Ambient 1: Music for Airports*. E.G. Polydor.
George Winston. (1983). *December*. Windham Hill.
KLF. (1990). *Chill Out*. KLF Communications.
Jean-Michel Jarre. (1976). *Oxygène*. Disques Motors.
Massive Attack. (1991). *Blue Lines*. Wild Bunch; Virgin.
Mike Oldfield. (1972). *Tubular Bells*. Virgin.
Paul Winter. (1982). *Missa Gaia/Earth Mass*. Living Music.
Pink Floyd. (1973). *Dark Side of the Moon*. Harvest.
R. Carlos Nakai. (1983). *Changes*. Canyon.
Space. (1990). *Space*. KLF Communications.
Tangerine Dream. (1974). *Phaedra*. Virgin.
The Orb. (1991). *The Orb's Adventures Beyond the Ultraworld*. Big Life.
Various Artists. (1991). *Pioneers of the Hypnotic Groove*. Warp.
Various Artists. (1992). *Artificial Intelligence*. Warp.
Various Artists. (1992). *Ambient Dub Volume 1 (The Big Chill)*. Beyond.

11 | Genre Classification in Electronic Dance Music Culture

From Localised Histories to the Bandcamp Underground

BOTOND VITOS

Introduction

This chapter addresses issues in genre classification of electronic dance music (EDM). The discussion will focus in particular on how the emergence and genre negotiation of techno, a genre of EDM, are shaped by socio-cultural contexts and processes as they developed from the specific localities and spaces to current online community building and tagging practices. The engagement with genre definitions of techno in the online world is addressed through a case study of an automatic genre classification and clustering algorithm that predicts stylistic repertoires of techno labels on the music platform Bandcamp. The discussion aims to understand how the diversity of what have been termed 'folksonomies' enables DJs and producers to destabilise industry-prescribed taxonomies while remaining distinct from dominant forms of techno.

As a cultural anthropologist, I have been involved in the study of electronic dance music scenes and event-based cultures; as is often the case, this interest has permeated into my personal life. Consequently, I have first-hand experience of grassroots artists resisting classification of their music on the grounds that such labels are narrow and limiting. At the same time, such categories provide basic orientation within a kaleidoscopic musical landscape, which can be particularly useful for newcomers to a music scene. Consumer-oriented music streaming services, such as Apple Music or Spotify, orchestrate music provision in partnership with major recording companies. On a smaller scale, producer-oriented platforms such as Soundcloud and Bandcamp aim to support independent musicians, who upload and promote content that can be made accessible to general audiences.[1] Bandcamp was founded in 2008 as a stripped-down online marketplace, imitating self-publishing websites and offering a 'riposte to the algorithmically determined monoculture' of so-called mainstream distributors.[2] As a digital content management platform, it caters predominantly for prosumers (DIY entrepreneurs), allowing direct distribution of music and related artefacts, narrowly targeted marketing, and interaction with fans.[3] Its revenue charge of 15 per cent can provide a financially viable alternative to the streaming platforms from which it sets itself apart. Bandcamp does not employ automatic classification and recommendation algorithms: the genre categories on the platform are assigned independently by the users (vendors) to their releases.

Bandcamp Librarian is a self-developed open-source python project aimed at the algorithmic genre classification of Bandcamp's techno labels.[4] The audio classifier is trained on the industry taxonomy of electronic dance music vendor Beatport. In other words, it predicts track genres based on Beatport's subgenre classification system. The algorithm is employed to detect stylistic clusters within Bandcamp label libraries by analysing their digital music files and distributing them into groups that are based on audio similarities. To investigate, the algorithm outputs links to three representative Bandcamp tracks in each cluster and their folksonomical tags. The latter free-form tags are predominantly genre descriptors attached, as mentioned earlier, by music labels and musicians to their Bandcamp releases. Thereby it is possible to compare the algorithmic classification results (based on Beatport's industry-based genre taxonomy) with the folksonomies prescribed by artists on Bandcamp.

After an initial foray into genre theory, this chapter engages with the formation of genre categories within the early decades of electronic dance music. The subject matter is delineated as music that is typically but not exclusively[5] characterised by, as Butler puts it, 'electronic sound production and performative consumption through dance',[6] directed by participatory dance-cultural traditions and modes of performance. The discussion then moves on to the negotiation of genre in the age of digital music distribution, with particular attention to classification systems, contrasting industry taxonomies with user-generated folksonomies or tagging systems prioritised by Bandcamp.

Research Context: Genres in Popular and Electronic Dance Music

Music is a social activity: one goes to an event and meets like-minded people or experiences a sense of togetherness triggered by a shared appreciation of the performance and, at electronic dance music events, the dance floor vibe.[7] The socio-cultural embedding of music events may prescribe forms of belonging, dress and behaviour codes, and common values and practices, and is prone to economic regulation.[8] Audiences rely on verbal genre labels that aid orientation within the musical landscape, act as marketing devices, make recommendations easier, and are linked to extra-musical practices. According to Fabbri's broad understanding of music genre, such categorisations help identify musical events 'whose course is governed by a definite set of socially accepted rules'.[9] Yet music is fluid, porous, and even a challenge to decipher, as Holt points out,[10] due to the complexity of experiences and meanings music can carry, emphasising the unspecificity of musical signification. Furthering this argument, remixing and DJ practices in the realm of electronic dance music enhance a sense of fluid genre-bending and redefinition.

Fabbri's notion of music genre considers the codification of rules regulating the relationship between musical expression and content, and the mutability of their social understanding with respect to the historical development of genres. The codification and subsequent decodification of genre rules by adept audience members (in electronic dance music, particularly by DJs and remixers, who are at once audience and producers) may trigger the transgression or re-evaluation of genre boundaries and facilitate new classification categories.[11] However, although acknowledging the mutability and plurality of subgenres, Negus considers Fabbri's work overly deterministic, claiming that his emphasis on rules results in a rather static idea of music, highlighting constraints rather than possibilities.[12]

Reflecting on Fabbri's discussion of music genre, McLeod argues that, particularly in electronic dance music scenes, genre rules are often contested, which may usefully generate creative criticism.[13] For Negus, even though one may be well aware of the rules, 'there always seems to be something more', contributing to a less rule-bound and more dynamic experience of music genres.[14] By providing an edited list of 97 EDM subgenre names that occurred in releases and publications over a two-year period between 1998 and 1999, McLeod[15] draws attention to a proliferation of subgenres in electronic dance music[16] that is not only related to rapid stylistic developments but also to other factors ranging from political-economic influences to cultural processes, such as group identity formations. The role of the specialist music and style press as gatekeeper in the development of such identities has been acknowledged, for example during the sudden public attention in the UK to EDM subgenre acid house in the late 1980s.[17] By means of music journalism, at the localised level of the record store, and later on internet-based community platforms, a multitude of subgenre categories have been generated and contested, which in turn denote varying production, participation, and consumption patterns. With respect to the dynamic between producer and the dance floor in the development of dance music, Rietveld underlines that 'new dance genres evolve as the music is adapted for the DJ', who in turn responds to the preferences of the dancing audience.[18] Lindop stresses the need for detailed categorisations for DJs who string together similar tracks in their performances and rely on refined stylistic variation when assembling a musical journey.[19] Classification categories of music genres also serve as indicators for partygoers, contributing to the creation and maintenance of what Thornton calls 'subcultural capital'.[20]

The orientation within the abundance of subgenres in electronic dance music may be facilitated by means of a hierarchical classification system, constructed along the categories of metagenre, genre, and subgenre (or even sub-subgenre). Shuker defines the metagenre – such as electronic dance music – as a loose amalgam of various styles, the more particular forms of which crystallise into genres, which can then be further divided into subgenres.[21] According to Pachet and Cazaly, similar categorisations are used by music industry and internet music retailers, resulting in somewhat arbitrary taxonomical systems which are not unified and suffer from numerous flaws.[22] For Lindop, the main characteristic of most metagenres is that, unlike 'actual' genres crystallised around specific musical features, they are primarily defined in terms of extra-musical elements such as attitudes, values, ideologies, or marketing strategies.[23] However, in his discussion of UK psytrance (psychedelic trance), Lindop establishes the coexistence of both actual and metagenres within the same category by showing how other electronic dance music (sub)genres are incorporated and 'psychedelicised' at psychedelic trance parties.[24] This may happen at dance events where a second dance floor is dedicated to non-psytrance styles which nevertheless shares the visual or sonic aesthetic of psytrance. A similar process can occur within music production practices where musical forms characteristic of psytrance are applied to other genres, leading to hybrid genres such as psybient, psybreaks, and progressive psytrance.[25]

Genre Histories and the Development of Techno

Negus highlights the interconnectedness of genre cultures and the music industry through a reciprocal process in which industry and culture are constantly shaping each other.[26] In the spider's web of major record companies, 'ongoing dynamic genre practices continually confront their translation into codified rules, conventions, and expectations'.[27] Electronic dance music is less affected by corporate strategies because it develops within sonic-cultural dance spaces directed by DJ-producers, and its production is often characterised by relatively accessible technologies and is often carried out entirely by the artists, who may even run their own recording labels. This relative distancing from major recording companies can be illustrated by looking at the development of techno, one of the foundational genres of electronic dance music.

The earlier development of electronic dance music during the 1980s and 1990s is extensively covered in music journalism.[28] Commonly acknowledged is the importance of the 1970s disco era preceding the early development of electronic dance music, with the appearance of New York's genre garage associated with the club Paradise Garage, and the formation of house music, initially linked with the Warehouse club in Chicago during the early 1980s, both developing from New York's underground disco culture.[29] While the origin of techno was tied to parallel developments in Germany, Belgium, the Netherlands, and the United States, Anglophone UK marketing gave dominance to the mid- to late 1980s output of young middle-class Black musicians in Detroit, in the United States. The musical influences of Detroit techno included Chicago house, but also Kraftwerk, funk, Italo-disco, and European synthpop.[30] Its development was embedded in the dystopian environment of the city of Detroit shattered by economic recession, a post-industrial cityscape marked by defunct factories and abandoned residential areas.[31] This ambivalent relationship with technology is aligned with the aesthetic tradition of Afrofuturism depicting imaginary worlds after the occurrence of the disaster. By creating 'alien music', Detroit artists 'reclaimed their outsider status to highlight the incongruities and injustices of [the] world as they saw them'.[32]

Detroit techno was pioneered by the Belleville Three, a suburban group of young Black producers influenced by science fiction and paying increasing attention to instrumentation details in their tracks. The first use of the term 'Detroit techno' was connected to a 1988 Detroit compilation album released by major record label Virgin Records in the UK. To emphasise the difference from Chicago house[33] for the UK market, the compilation was titled after the song 'Techno Music' by Juan Atkins, who in turn was inspired by Alvin Toffler's[34] portrayal of 'techno-rebels' appropriating 'the technologies . . . of a post-industrial era that is based on an information-economy'.[35] The music press played an important part in the early formation of techno, as the Detroit-based producers realised that the intellectualisation of the genre was also a way of promoting their music.[36] They consciously took part in the myth-making that contributed to the artistic integrity of the genre and its global expansion[37] – even though its production technologies and dance floor dynamic were not dissimilar to those of house music at the time of the release of the compilation.

In the early 1990s, during the second wave of Detroit techno, DJ-producer collectives such as the Underground Resistance and +8 developed a harsher sound inspired by electro, UK synth-pop, industrial music, and electronic body music, partly as a counter-reaction against the popularisation of the genre and its incorporation into the mainstream entertainment industry.[38] After the second wave, techno music disseminated across the globe, yet never really gained widespread popularity in its home country.[39] The onset of illegal dance parties in late-1980s Britain and the consequent popularisation of rave culture interlinked the genre with dance drug consumption and played an integral part in the dispersion of techno, along with the burgeoning German techno scene of the 1990s. With the proliferation of illegal parties in Berlin during the transitory period after the fall of the Berlin Wall,[40] and the consequent appearance of clubs and labels such as Tresor, as well as record shops such as Hard Wax, Berlin became the second bastion of global techno. Here techno was used as a soundtrack for the celebration of reunification, representing a promise of liberation. With the development of a Berlin–Detroit axis, a number of Detroit DJs were moving to Berlin, followed by other international producers. By the mid-1990s the institutionalisation of techno in Germany (and in Europe) triggered the protest of 'underground' crews such as Mille Plateaux and Spiral Tribe.[41] The latter was one of the founding crews of the 'teknival' movement promoting illegal and free techno parties all around Europe, downstream from the early UK raves and their clashes with British authorities (and their subsequent legislative prohibition in 1994).[42]

By the 2000s, Berlin arguably solidified its international status as the techno capital, exhibiting a mythic veneer of authenticity as well as professionalism, with many of its legal clubs and professional nightlife venues having their roots in the early illegal venues. This leading position was enabled by various factors including the city's post-1989 culture clash, its post-industrial readjustment toward a service-oriented entity, its unique socio-cultural dynamics, its ambience of tolerance, and the flexibility of its night-life economy.[43] Berlin's contemporary significance extends beyond a single electronic dance music genre as the city currently hosts over 200 professional clubs[44] as well as the headquarters of various global players in the music industry.[45] The mythical authenticity of Berlin techno is sanctioned and fetishised by the flocks of techno-tourists visiting the city, who dismiss conventional tourism as artificial and misleading.[46] In turn, the music scenes thriving in Berlin and elsewhere in the world have arguably inspired the organisation of the *Movement Electronic Music Festival* in Detroit (inaugurated in 2006), where techno is appropriated by the city authorities as a tool for cultural revitalisation.[47]

Prone to localised adaptations and interpretations, the development of genre in electronic dance music is inseparable from extra-musical factors, which in the case study of techno include the racial and economic turmoil of Detroit; its early branding as a genre distinct from Chicago house by a UK record label; the rave cultural movement in the UK, enabling its global dissemination; the unique social-political circumstances that led to the solidification of its stronghold in Berlin. These narratives are integral to the formation of what Holt would describe as the 'genre canon and its mythologies in center collectivities'.[48] In certain nodes of this network, a music genre may acquire symbolic meanings closely attached to such mythologies. For instance, Kolioulis and Rietveld point out that in techno scenes as far apart as Tbilisi and Athens, 'the techno sound of the post-Fordist era functions as a soundtrack of transformations brought about by the acceleration of electronic information technologies',[49] and the genre may offer sonic opportunities to internalise and challenge the alienating or controlling dimensions of mediatised societies.[50]

Yet, anchoring meaning to hegemonic narratives carries the risk of imposing prefabricated interpretations, which is resisted by (niche) artists in particular. Crucially, genre formation is influenced by the dynamic between record shops, DJ-producers, events, and dancers. This relationship is currently partly taking place in social media, and the global profusion and diversity of genre concepts can be traced in recent classification practices aided by digital technologies. With its emphasis on the sharing of user-generated content, the emergence of Web 2.0 in the 2000s increased the potential for musicians to define their positions in between genre canons and 'engage with multiple genre concepts, discursive strands and musical histories',[51] which the discussion will address next.

Classifying Music in the Digital Age: From Taxonomies to Folksonomies

Since the late-1990s technology boom, there has been an unprecedented proliferation of music facilitated by digital distribution tools and media channels: first peer-to-peer 'pirate' platforms such as Napster, then, increasingly, legal streaming services.[52] The music streaming platform Spotify, established in 2006, for example, makes over 100 million songs available.[53] From an avant-conservative perspective the hyper-exposure of music is not only exploitative to the artists but also degrading to the cultural experience.[54] Advocates of this view claim that while in the past the limited availability of obscure or fringe music was the token of underground authenticity, the more recent flooding of content and the sense of instant gratification enabled by digital downloads renders our engagement in underground culture superficial and passive. Conversely, supporters of a digital liberationist position celebrate the growth of free digital culture, where the production and accessibility of music is tied to less constraints, and musical experience is enriched by blogs, podcasts, and weblinks.[55]

When it comes to fringe genres, I argue that the proliferation of digital music does not erode engagement in niche content and associated concepts of subcultural credibility and capital.[56] The distinction from the mainstream has been a focal concern of popular music cultures at least since the commercialisation of rock music into 'rock/pop'.[57] Within the digital ecosystem, the means of achieving this are reproduced in novel ways: beyond the possession of underground music, other factors come into play such as being able to effectively search, select, and share it in the online context.[58] Instead of disappearing, physical media such as vinyl records and cassettes acquire renewed interest because their consumption offers symbolic resistance to the ubiquity of digital content as they 'code musical and cultural difference in material form'.[59] Such artefacts are commonplace in the offerings of Bandcamp labels (listed in the 'merch' section), as the platform seemingly conjures 'a messy online record store where you can stumble around and, in a roundabout way, find what you like'.[60] This is evinced through various aspects of its ecology, such as the situatedness of its artist pages that appear as discrete entities rather than nodes of a viral network interlinked via an autoplay function, its editorial (as opposed to algorithmic) recommendation system, or the pictorial representation of 'fans' supporting the releases that contrasts the 'facelessness' of conventional quantitative metrics.[61]

Keeping up with the abundance of new releases can be challenging for music professionals and audiences alike; therefore, digital music distribution platforms typically employ algorithms to make personalised recommendations or to automate the categorisation of music. Music tech companies attempt to cut through the turmoil of genre labels in electronic dance music by providing (and improving) relatively detailed taxonomies, or well-designed labels that help both humans and algorithms to find and connect to music. Leading in EDM, Beatport distributes its electronic dance music catalogue into thirty+ subgenres as of 2023, while its taxonomy encompassed twenty-three subgenres in 2016 and twenty-nine in 2018.[62] As part of a merchandising strategy, such top-down models reflect standardisation attempts within a music industry that is more preoccupied with market segments than genre cultures.[63]

Categories in popular music are fuzzy and fluid.[64] Genre descriptors, like 'house' or 'punk', may sound straightforward and less confusing, but they are also less useful for uncovering complexities and nuances. More specific categories, like 'future funk' or 'cold wave', are more practical in this regard, but may sound obscure or even esoteric to outsiders. When it comes to niche genres, bottom-up free tagging systems, or *folksonomies*, representing the 'wisdom of crowds' capture diversity and creativity better, although this may come at the cost of precision.[65] The term was coined in 2004 to account for the emergence of user-defined labels in categorising and sharing electronic information, and the subsequent development of a thesaurus that draws on individual meaning-makings and vocabularies.[66]

Indicating the formal and informal musical expertise of artists and audiences,[67] folksonomical tags may refer to affective qualities and localities or articulate free associations.[68] Supported by certain independent music promotion and marketing websites, they may provide swift reactions to stylistic inventions and aid the discovery of fringe music composing a statistical long tail.[69] As a platform oriented towards independent producers and labels, Bandcamp encourages the use of folksonomies by its users. In certain cases, such tags may offer a refreshing contrast to Beatport's genre categories.

Bandcamp Dance Librarian

The audio classifier of the Bandcamp Dance Librarian project is based on the methodology of Caparrini et al., which, in contrast to earlier attempts at algorithmic classification within the field of electronic dance music, detects a relatively high number of classes (the repeated experiment detects a relatively high number of classes, or Beatport subgenres).[70] Correspondingly, for the Bandcamp Librarian project, in January 2021 I trained a predictive model on a dataset of ninety-two audio features extracted from two-minute samples of audio tracks within Beatport's Top-100 lists in thirty-two subgenres. This ensured that the classification of the audio tracks would be based on the Beatport taxonomy.[71] Subsequently, I applied the algorithm to detect the class (subgenre) probabilities of Bandcamp techno tracks, through audio analysis of the full-length (low-bitrate) streams offered as track previews on the platform. I processed complete Bandcamp libraries, and in the next step I employed a clustering algorithm to distribute the tracks into groups or clusters based on their detected subgenre affiliations. The project output included the identified clusters (which were amalgams of Beatport genres), the most frequent tags (folksonomies) attached by the labels/artists to their tracks on Bandcamp,[72] and a more detailed report on three representative tracks from each cluster (if possible, from different artists).[73] The experiment confirmed my expectation that the genre categories detected by the algorithm would be aligned with the artist folksonomies. Further details and the datasets used are available in the project's GitHub repository.[74]

The first working example is the Bandcamp catalogue of Sonic Groove, a Berlin-based industrial techno label with strong EBM (Electronic Body Music) influences from a niche side of the electronic dance music spectrum. EBM developed in the early 1980s mainly from the industrial genre, integrating the use of drum machines and sequencers in the production of songs with a predominantly martial and dark character that was further articulated through vocals and spoken words with limited tonal range and occasional distortions. It was influenced by a more general shift towards danceable rhythms in the post-punk era.[75] Sonic Groove was founded in 1995 in New York and is currently managed by Adam X, who relocated to Berlin in 2007.[76] The processed Bandcamp library contains 488 tracks released between 1998 and 2020. The Beatport taxonomy does not include the industrial techno and EBM techno categories, so one can expect that the classifier detects stylistically similar subgenres. After running the Librarian a report is produced that proposes three genre clusters.

Cluster 1: Techno, Electro, and Indie Dance

The first group (Cluster 1) is tentatively associated with three Beatport genres: Raw / Deep / Hypnotic Techno (9 per cent probability); Indie Dance (7 per cent probability); Classic / Detroit / Modern Electro (7 per cent probability), to which 238 tracks are assigned, based on their similarity with the audio features of the cluster centre.[77] For each cluster, the algorithm provides three centrally located track examples, complete with links to their Bandcamp pages and their associated folksonomical tags. The examples from Cluster 1 are the following:

- Adam X – 'Catenary'[78] (2014; Bandcamp tags: Adam X; desolation; electronic; futurism; industrial; purism; Sonic Groove; techno; acid techno; EBM techno; electro techno; industrial techno; techno; Berlin)[79]
- Traversable Wormhole – 'Negative Energy Density'[80] (2013; Bandcamp tags: electronic; acid techno; deep techno; industrial techno; techno; Berlin)
- Orphx – 'Vanishing Point'[81] (2013; Bandcamp tags: electronic; dance; electro; industrial; noise; techno; Toronto)

The first two tracks are both produced by label boss Adam X. Traversable Wormhole is a project described by the producer as 'sci-fi music' inspired by his interest in astrophysical concepts and 'industrial-based, slower [music]'.[82] Both tracks are relatively slow-paced and spacious, with 'Catenary' incorporating looped vocal samples and clearer EBM influences. Orphx are a long-standing Canadian duo whose dance music output is influenced by EBM, rhythmic noise, and experimental music: accordingly, 'Vanishing Point' is described as 'dark industrialized techno body music' on the Bandcamp page.

The most frequently occurring Bandcamp tags of this cluster are (with number of occurrences in brackets): acid techno (ninety-one); industrial techno (eighty-eight); EBM techno (seventy-six); industrial (fifty-six); ambient (fifty-five); electro techno (fifty); EBM (thirty-seven). All of these tags denote music genres; it should be noted, however, that the acid techno, EBM techno, electro techno, and industrial techno tags are used as boilerplate for Sonic Groove releases when no other (more specific) tags are provided, referring to the general sound of the label. None of these subgenres are included among the more dominant genres of the Beatport taxonomy. Raw / Deep / Hypnotic Techno and Classic / Detroit / Modern electro can be considered as fitting categories detected by the classifier, while the emergence of Indie Dance could be attributed to the occasional vocal content and slower tempo of the EBM-influenced tracks. Not all tracks of the cluster are restricted to the identified styles, as the clustering is based on best approximation, and the accuracy can be improved by increasing the number of clusters.

Cluster 2: Techno to Hard Techno

With a total of 203 tracks, the second cluster detected by the classifier is crystallised around more pronounced techno influences: Techno

(Raw / Deep / Hypnotic) (28 per cent); Techno (Peak Time / Driving) (17 per cent); and Hard Techno (9 per cent). Track examples:

- Blush Response – 'Instrumentality'[83] (2017; Bandcamp tags: electronic; cyberpunk; EBM; IDM; industrial; rhythmic noise; techno; Berlin)
- Adam X – 'I Sit Alone'[84] (2005; Bandcamp tags: electronic; acid techno; EBM techno; electro techno; industrial techno; techno; Berlin)
- Ancient Methods VS Adam X – 'Mitral Regurgitation' (Ancient Methods Mix)[85] (2010; Bandcamp tags: electronic; acid techno; EBM techno; electro techno; industrial techno; techno; Berlin)

Compared to the examples of the first cluster, in these tracks the kick drum is more articulated, the sonic textures are less washed out and more abrasive, and the tempo is higher. In short, they are pronouncedly harder and positioned closer to the dominant stylistic tendencies within techno. The tracks are rich in metallic sounds and distortions, and the EBM influence is still present, most noticeably in the spoken word of 'I Sit Alone'. The most frequent Bandcamp tags in this cluster are industrial techno (seventy-eight), acid techno (sixty), industrial (fifty-four), EBM techno (forty-three), electro techno (thirty-seven), EBM (twenty-five), and electro (twenty-three).

Cluster 3: Ambient

The last cluster is composed of forty-seven tracks predominantly classified as ambient: Ambient (44 per cent), Melodic House & Techno (6 per cent), and Progressive House (6 per cent).

The example tracks are highly atmospheric, rich in reverbs, and their beats are less pronounced:

- ADMX-71 – 'Uncompleted Remnants'[86] (2012; Bandcamp tags: ambient; downtempo; electronic; experimental; industrial; techno; Berlin)
- Dino Sabatini – 'Step 4'[87] (2011; Bandcamp tags: Berlin)
- Orphx – 'Walk into the Broken Night'[88] (2016; Bandcamp tags: electronic; dance; electro; industrial; noise; techno; Toronto)

The three tracks sound dark and mysterious, with 'Walk into the Broken Night' featuring poignant female vocals and spoken words. Dedicated to experimental ambient/downtempo releases, ADMX-71 is just another side project of label boss Adam X. The 'ambient' classification result is confirmed by the list of frequent tags in this cluster: ambient (forty-three); industrial (twenty-nine); experimental (twenty-eight); downtempo (twenty-three); Adam X (ten); New York (nine); Sonic Groove experiments (nine).

Within the Sonic Groove catalogue, the folksonomy tags may refer to aesthetic modes (futurism; purism; cyberpunk), localities (Berlin; Toronto; New York), and most frequently music (sub)genres, such as: ambient; acid techno; EBM (techno); electro (techno); experimental; IDM; industrial (techno); noise; rhythmic noise. By clicking on the tag on Bandcamp and navigating further, the user can discover similar releases (based on the artist folksonomies stored on the platform). The majority of Sonic Groove's subgenres are excluded from the Beatport taxonomy; producers are required to submit their tracks to Beatport in one of the pre-defined genres, and the vendor may change the genre of the submission, based on editorial decisions.[89] The contrast between the two classification models resonates with the divergent ways in which the two vendors allow access to independent musicians: while Beatport accepts independent submissions only through distributors, on Bandcamp anyone can create an artist account.

Sonic Groove's folksonomical genre definitions are situated in the cracks between the categories prescribed by Beatport to its artists, illustrating the dynamic between genre cultures and the music industry. As Negus argues, if the industry acts as a gatekeeper and cultural intermediary by solidifying and sustaining genre conventions through business management practices, musicians continuously cross genre boundaries and, by extension, create new social relationships and solidarities.[90]

Classifying Techno Cities

The final discussion of this chapter presents a case study of Bandcamp Librarian focused on localities and location tags (signifying cities, countries, and, sometimes, nationalities). Such tags help put local music scenes on the map. In the case of particularly prolific or creative cities they can be connected to specific genres as well. Typically, they identify the city or country where the music label or the artist is based. Prominent electronic dance music producers tend to manage their own labels that are integral to promoting music and structuring scenes,[91] contributing to the burgeoning of independent music communities across the globe.

The case study draws on features extracted from thirty-six Bandcamp libraries. The libraries are those referred to in piece of music journalism addressing the Bandcamp libraries of 'underground' techno labels described by the author as 'non-commercial, ... jack-y and groovy, ... space-y and futuristic and dark and weird'.[92] Such *niche media* are particularly efficient in creating group identities[93] and enabling genre formation within groups.[94] Without claiming exhaustiveness, the collection used in this case study provides a brief insight into the sounds of a curated group of underground techno labels in which the geographic affiliation of the individual tracks is often indicated by their Bandcamp location tags.

The collection includes 14,198 tracks analysed by the Librarian. A total of 97,334 tags are attached to the tracks, 13 per cent of which refer to locations or nationalities. The majority of the location tags designate cities. The most influential cities in the collection, based on the number of techno labels that tagged them in their Bandcamp library, are: Berlin (tagged by eighteen labels); Detroit (tagged by ten labels); Chicago (tagged by six labels); London (tagged by three labels). The remaining cities were only tagged by one or two labels. Cities are usually tagged because they are label or artist locations, or influential reference points within the translocal techno circuit.[95]

By grouping the tracks that are tagged with the same city into a single cluster, the Librarian can be assigned to detect the overall sound(s) of the city. In the case of Berlin, the city that is tagged by the highest number of labels, this amounts to 2,350 tracks released between 1994 and 2021. Ninety-five per cent of these tracks appear on labels based in Berlin. Of course, a single stylistic cluster will not account for the sonic diversity of such an influential city. To provide more variety, the tracks associated with Berlin can be distributed into the following three clusters by means of the algorithm:

Cluster 1: Techno, Electro, and Minimal / Deep Tech

The first Berlin cluster includes 1,434 tracks, and is tentatively associated with three distinct genres: Raw /Deep/ Hypnotic Techno (7 per cent), Classic / Detroit / Modern Electro (7 per cent), and Minimal / Deep Tech (6 per cent). Track examples:

- DJ T-1000 / Detroitrocketscience – 'Sounds Like Space'[96] (2006; DJ T-1000; Bandcamp tags: Detroit techno; electronic; electro; minimal techno; Berlin)
- Toktok – 'Polka Dots'[97] (2003; Toktok Records; Bandcamp tags: electronic; house; slamjack; techno; Berlin)

- STRISC. – 'Staja'[98] (2018; Flash Recordings; Bandcamp tags: acid; acid techno; Berlin; Berlin techno; electronic; flash; Florian Meindl; infekt; insekt; STRISC.; techno; Tim Xavier; Berghain techno; electronic; industrial; techno)

DJ T-1000 is a Detroit-born techno producer based in Berlin since 2005. Produced under the *Detroitrocketscience* moniker, 'Sounds Like Space' conjures the dreamy textures of Detroit techno instrumentation. Described on the Bandcamp page as 'a very moody, hypnotic, late-night vibe', the track appeared on the 2006 album *The Art of Transformation*, which features other 'lowtempo' tracks and an electro track called 'Elektroberlin'.[99] The emergence of *Detroitrocketscience* within the Berlin collection reflects Detroit techno's Afrofuturist aesthetics and its historical alliance with Berlin.

'Staja' is a similarly spacious and atmospheric release, although it sounds more abstract in terms of its detachment from the classic drum machines and synthesisers of electronic dance music. Conversely, 'Polka Dots' delves further into the past by preserving the rhythms and melodies of a lively nineteenth-century folk dance of Czech-Polish origin,[100] representing the 'irreverant [sic], dirty, silly, raunchy [...] underground side of German techno'.[101]

The folksonomies used in this cluster range through a diversity of genres: techno and variations (169); experimental (168); Detroit techno (167); house (165); acid (164); electro (160); minimal techno (154). 'Techno and variations' seems to be a good expression for the heterogeneity of this cluster, which may indicate the need to define more clusters for better classification results.

Cluster 2: Raw Techno

Composed of 718 tracks, the second group is more confidently identified as raw, stripped-down techno: Raw / Deep / Hypnotic Techno (34 per cent), Peak Time / Driving Techno (12 per cent), and Hard Techno (9 per cent).

- Tommy Four Seven – 'X9'[102] (2015; 47; Bandcamp tags: electronic; techno; Berlin)
- Sylvie Maziarz – 'His Tension'[103] (2020; Flash Recordings; Bandcamp tags: acid; acid techno; Berlin techno; electronic; techno; Berghain techno; Berlin)
- D. Carbone – 'Irritating Collapse'[104] (2014; Mord Records; Bandcamp tags: electronic; acid; badabing; Berlin; distortion; dungeon; filthy; Italia; Mord; Repitch; rotterdam; techno; Rotterdam)

Tommy Four Seven's menacing industrial techno is characterised by reverberant soundscapes and heavily processed field recordings, while Sylvie Maziarz delivers an energetic, acid-influenced track that stays locked on its target. Acid is a frequent tag in the Bandcamp label folksonomies, referring to the genre-defining sound of the legendary Roland TB-303 bassline generator. The vibe of 'Irritating Collapse' is adequately captured by the 'distortion', 'dungeon', and 'filthy' tags. The latter two are also fitting descriptors for subterranean techno clubs where such tracks as 'Irritating Collapse' are often played.

Acid leads the way among the folksonomies of this cluster: acid (286); acid techno (264); Berlin techno (253); Berghain techno (232); techno (134); experimental (124); techno and variations (92).

Cluster 3: Ambient

Finally, ambient emerges as the defining genre for a smaller cluster of 198 tracks: Ambient (45 per cent), Melodic House & Techno (5 per cent), and Hard Techno (5 per cent). All of the track examples (from separate producers) were initially released on Avian, which may suggest that this label delivers a well-defined and influential sound:

- ZOV ZOV – 'Endless Lines'[105] (2014; Avian; Bandcamp tags: experimental; Berlin)
- Pris – 'Sunk'[106] (2016; Avian; Bandcamp tags: experimental; Berlin)
- 400 PPM – 'Evitandus'[107] (2013; Avian; Bandcamp tags: electronic; experimental; techno; New York)

These tracks are sonic experiments operating through harsh drones, distorted field recordings, and piercing textures; two of them ('Endless Lines' and 'Evintadus') are beatless. While the folksonomies indicate that they belong to the experimental genre, the Librarian's classifier is focused on dance music genres and does not include an 'experimental' class, with ambient falling closest to this category. Consequently, the classification result can be deemed as accurate.

The most frequent tags of this cluster are aligned with its classification as ambient/experimental: experimental (eighty-three); ambient (forty-three); Berghain (thirty-two); alternative (twenty-three); archive (twenty-one); Ostgut Ton (eighteen); acid (seventeen). The repeated appearance of an Ambient cluster in the Librarian's classification results reflects the prevalence of ambient and experimental tracks on techno releases.

The folksonomies detected during the classification of Berlin labels refer to music genres, geographical locations, and environments (Berlin; Rotterdam; Italia; New York; dungeon), label names (Ostgut Ton; Flash; Mord; Repitch), associations with dirt or disease (infekt; insekt; filthy), and the name of an influential Berlin club (Berghain).

Interestingly, from the 448 tags containing the word 'Berghain' only 146 are used by the label owned by the club (Ostgut Ton), and 285 occur as part of Berghain techno, tagged by a different label, Flash Recordings, to every track in its Bandcamp catalogue. Within the 2,350 tracks of the dataset, Berlin techno appears 307 times. As a genre indicator this tag is ambiguous; furthermore, it is attached to musically different tracks such as 'Staja' in the first cluster and 'His Tension' in the second cluster, which might suggest that it is used as a meta-genre indicator. However, 285 occurrences of 'Berlin techno' are attached, again, to the Flash Recordings releases. It is unlikely that within the Berlin dataset the Berghain techno tracks and the vast majority of Berlin techno tracks are released by a single label that is not affiliated with Berghain, which rather suggests that these folksonomies are used as marketing tools to reach wider audiences.

Conclusion

Two approaches to genre classification in electronic dance music have been discussed, with on the one hand the evaluation of historical narratives and, on the other hand, an algorithmic methodology. The hegemonic narratives of the development of techno illustrate how genre histories and categories are shaped by extra-musical contexts. It is my argument furthermore that genre formation in EDM crucially depends on interactions that occur between musicians, label owners, and audiences within sonic-cultural as well as virtual spaces, in addition to the business practices and management techniques of the music industry.

The dynamic of genre formation via online music services can be demonstrated in the subgenre stratifications within the Bandcamp libraries of underground techno labels. Employing an automatic classification algorithm trained on industry taxonomy in charting the genre affiliations of these labels, the classification exercises confirm the mutability of electronic dance music genres. While the subgenres detected by the classifier are aligned with the general musical directions of the investigated Bandcamp libraries, the taxonomy categories are inadequate to deal with diversity of the artist folksonomies. Capturing a range of subgenres, sonic aesthetics, locations and environments, legendary clubs, and labels, the interpretation of these narrowly targeted artist tags is reliant on the informal musical expertise of prosumer users. The interpretive and semantic diversity of these navigational signposts confirms Bandcamp's portrayal as 'anti-algorithmic'[108] in dance music journalism, as opposed to the dominant music streaming services regulated by AI recommendations.

The original formation of electronic dance music was fuelled by the direct interaction between DJ-producers and dancers. Within the digital ecosystem, the Bandcamp tags used by the artists and labels discussed in this chapter are meant to evoke the sonic affects that attract bodies and sustain dance floors.[109] Akin to Thornton's micro-media, they circulate on the ground level of electronic dance music scenes while being interconnected with a wider network of social and economic relations and employed as tools of direct marketing.[110] Although its folksonomical genre categorisation is not necessarily an extension of offline transactions, Bandcamp is ideologically and structurally aligned with earlier 'alternative' forms of cultural production and distribution tied to noncorporate institutions.[111]

Notes

1. Hesmondhalgh, David, Ellis Jones, and Andreas Rauh. 2019. 'SoundCloud and Bandcamp as Alternative Music Platforms'. *Social Media + Society* 5(4): 1–2.
2. McDermott, Matt. 2020. 'Anti-Algorithmic Music: How Bandcamp Is Helping Artists Beat the Odds'. *Resident Advisor*. 2 July. https://ra.co/features/3703 (accessed 15 April 2023).
3. Duffin, Clare, and Allan Dumbreck. 2016. 'Digital Music Distribution'. In *Music Entrepreneurship*, ed. Allan Dumbreck and Gayle McPherson. London and New York: Bloomsbury, pp. 201–02.
4. While the platform embraces a wide musical spectrum, the first genre listed on Bandcamp (<https://bandcamp.com/#discover>) is 'electronic' – further divided into twenty-four categories ranging from the cornerstones of electronic dance music (such as house, techno, and electro) to more obscure genres with limited danceability (such as downtempo, IDM, chillwave, or vaporwave).
5. McLeod employs the spelling 'electronic/dance music' to signify the inclusion of genres that are not produced for dancing.
6. Butler, Mark J. 2012. *Electronica, Dance and Club Music*. Farnham: Ashgate, p. xiii.

7. St John, Graham. 2013. 'Writing the Vibe: Arts of Representation in Electronic Dance Music'. *Dancecult: Journal of Electronic Dance Music Culture* 5 (1), Para 1.
8. Fabbri, Franco. 1982. 'A Theory of Popular Music Genres: Two Applications'. In *Popular Music Perspectives: Papers from the First International Conference on Popular Music Research, Amsterdam, June 1981*, ed. David Horn and Philip Tagg. Goteborg: IASPM, p. 59; Holt, Fabian. 2007. *Genre in Popular Music*. Chicago: University of Chicago Press, pp. 22–24.
9. Fabbri, 'A Theory of Popular Music Genres', p. 52.
10. Holt, 'Genre in Popular Music', p. 22.
11. Fabbri, 'A Theory of Popular Music Genres', pp. 60–63.
12. Negus, Keith. 1999. *Music Genres and Corporate Cultures*. London: Routledge, pp. 25–26.
13. McLeod, Kernbrew. 2001. 'Genres, Subgenres, Sub-subgenres and More: Musical and Social Differentiation Within Electronic/Dance Music Communities'. *Journal of Popular Music Studies* 13(1): 66.
14. Negus, *Music Genres*, p. 26.
15. McLeod, 'Genres, Subgenres, Sub-subgenres and More', pp. 59–60.
16. One possible illustration is provided on the popular webpage Ishkur's Guide to Electronic Music: https://music.ishkur.com (accessed 15 April 2023).
17. Thornton, Sarah. 1996. *Club Cultures: Music, Media, and Subcultural Capital*. Hanover: University Press of New England, pp. 151-60.
18. Rietveld, Hillegonda C. 2013. 'Introduction'. In *DJ Culture in The Mix: Power, Technology, And Social Change In Electronic Dance Music*, ed. Bernardo Alexander Attias, Anna Gavanas, and Hillegonda C. Rietveld. New York: Bloomsbury, p. 3.
19. Lindop, Robin. 2010. 'Re-evaluating Musical Genre in UK Psytrance'. In *The Local Scenes and Global Culture of Psytrance*, ed. Graham St John. London: Routledge, p. 116.
20. Thornton, *Club Cultures*; McLeod, 'Genres, Subgenres, Sub-subgenres and More', p. 72.
21. Shuker, Roy. 1998. *Key Concepts in Popular Music*. London: Routledge, p. 122.
22. Pachet, François, and Daniel Cazaly. 2000. 'A Taxonomy of Musical Genres'. In *Content-Based Multimedia Information Access – Volume 2* (RIAO 2000 Conference Proceedings), ed. Jean Mariani and Donna Harman. Paris: Centre de Hautes Études Internationales d'Informatique Documentaire. pp. 1238–45.
23. Lindop, 'Re-evaluating Musical Genre in UK Psytrance', p. 117.
24. Ibid., pp. 128–29.
25. Ibid., pp. 117–19.
26. Negus, *Music Genres*.
27. Negus, *Music Genres*, p. 28.
28. Reynolds, Simon. 1999. *Generation Ecstasy: Into the World of Techno and Rave Culture*. New York: Routledge; Brewster, Bill, and Frank Broughton. 2006. *Last*

Night a DJ Saved My Life: The History of the Disc Jockey. Updated ed. London: Headline; Sicko, Dan. 2010. *Techno Rebels: The Renegades of Electronic Funk*. 2nd ed. Detroit: Painted Turtle.

29. Butler, Mark J. 2006. *Unlocking the Groove: Rhythm, Meter, and Musical Design in Electronic Dance Music*. Bloomington: Indiana University Press, pp. 36–40.
30. Brewster and Broughton, *Last Night a DJ Saved My Life*, pp. 340–49.
31. Sicko, *Techno Rebels*, pp. 35–39; Pope, Richard. 2011. 'Detroit Techno and Dystopian Digital Culture'. *Dancecult: Journal of Electronic Dance Music Culture* 2 (1): 25–26.
32. Pope, 'Detroit Techno and Dystopian Digital Culture', p. 32.
33. Sicko, *Techno Rebels*, pp. 66–68.
34. Toffler, Alvin. 1980. *The Third Wave*. Toronto: Bantam Books, p. 153.
35. Kolioulis, Alessio, and Hillegonda C. Rietveld. 2018. 'Detroit: Techno City'. In *Sounds and the City, Vol 2*, ed. Brett Lashua, Stephen Wagg, Karl Spracklen, and M. Selim Yavuz. Cham: Palgrave Macmillan, pp. 40–41.
36. Brewster and Broughton. *Last Night a DJ Saved My Life*, pp. 356–57.
37. Kolioulis, Alessio, and Rietveld. 'Detroit: Techno City', p. 39.
38. Reynolds, *Generation Ecstasy*, pp. 219–20.
39. Sicko, *Techno Rebels*, pp. 131–32.
40. The demolition of the Berlin Wall in 1989 marked the end of the Cold War and the reunification of the country.
41. Robb, David. 2002. 'Techno in Germany: Its Musical Origins and Cultural Relevance'. *German as a Foreign Language Journal* 2(2): 144–46.
42. St John, Graham. 2009. *Technomad: Global Raving Countercultures*. London: Equinox, pp. 28–64.
43. Peter, Beate. 2014. 'Breaching the Divide: Techno City Berlin'. In *Poor, But Sexy: Reflections on Berlin Scenes*, ed. Geoff Stahl. Bern: Peter Lang, pp. 182–86.
44. Lücke, Martin. 2020. 'Club Culture and Electronic Dance Music in Berlin: An Economic, Social and Aesthetical Perspective'. In *The New Age of Electronic Dance Music and Club Culture*, ed. Anita Jóri and Martin Lücke. Cham: Springer, p. 56.
45. Mazierska, Ewa, and Tony Rigg. 2021. 'Challenges to British Nightclubs During and After the Covid-19 Pandemic'. *Dancecult: Journal of Electronic Dance Music Culture* 13(1): 71.
46. Garcia, Luis-Manuel. 2016. 'Techno-Tourism and Post-industrial Neo-romanticism in Berlin's Electronic Dance Music Scenes'. *Tourist Studies* 16(3): 89.
47. Kolioulis, Alessio, and Rietveld. 'Detroit: Techno City', p. 42.
48. Holt, *Genre in Popular Music*, p. 28.
49. Kolioulis, Alessio, and Rietveld. 'Detroit: Techno City', p. 40.
50. Rietveld, Hillegonda C. 2018. 'Dancing in the Technoculture'. In *The Routledge Research Companion to Electronic Music: Reaching Out with Technology*.

Sounds and the City, Vol 2, ed. Simon Emmerson. Cham: Palgrave Macmillan, p. 129.

51. Charles, Christopher. 2020. 'Genre in Practice: Categories, Metadata and Music-Making in Psytrance Culture'. *Dancecult: Journal of Electronic Dance Music Culture* 12(1): 42.
52. Hesmondhalgh, Jones, and Rauh. 'SoundCloud and Bandcamp as Alternative Music Platforms', p. 1.
53. 'Spotify—Company Info'. *Spotify*. 2021. https://newsroom.spotify.com/company-info/ (accessed 14 August 2023).
54. Graham, Stephen. 2016. *Sounds of the Underground: A Cultural, Political and Aesthetic Mapping of Underground and Fringe Music*. Ann Arbor: University of Michigan Press, pp. 115–16.
55. Ibid., pp.118–20.
56. Thornton, *Club Cultures*.
57. Holt, *Genre in Popular Music*, p. 24.
58. Tófalvy, Tamás. 2020. 'Niche Underground: Media, Technology, and the Reproduction of Underground Cultural Capital'. In *Popular Music, Technology, and the Changing Media Ecosystem*, ed. Tamás Tófalvy and Emília Barna. Cham: Palgrave MacMillan, pp. 69–71.
59. Graham, *Sounds of the Underground*, p. 143.
60. McDermott, 'Anti-Algorithmic Music'.
61. Hesmondhalgh, Jones, and Rauh. 'SoundCloud and Bandcamp as Alternative Music Platforms', pp. 6–9.
62. Caparrini, Antonio, Javier Arroyo, Laura Pérez-Molina and Jaime Sánchez-Hernández. 2020. 'Automatic Subgenre Classification in an Electronic Dance Music Taxonomy'. *Journal of New Music Research* 49(3): 269–84.
63. Holt, *Genre in Popular Music*, p. 26.
64. Holt, *Genre in Popular Music*, pp. 14–15.
65. Kroski, Elyssa. 2005. *The Hive Mind: Folksonomies and User-Based Tagging*. 7 December. https://web20bp.com/13s2a6019/wp-content/uploads/2013/03/The-Hive-Mind-Folksonomies-2005.pdf (accessed 15 April 2023).
66. Vander Wal, Thomas. 2007. 'Folksonomy Coinage and Definition'. *Off The Top*. 2 February. https://vanderwal.net/folksonomy.html (accessed 14 August 2023).
67. Lepa, Steffen, Anne-Kathrin Hoklas, Hauke Egermann, Stefan Weinzierl. 2015. 'Sound, Materiality and Embodiment Challenges for the Concept of "Musical Expertise" in the Age of Digital Mediatization'. *Convergence: The International Journal of Research into New Media Technologies* 21(3): 1–7.
68. Charles, Christopher. 2020. 'Genre in Practice: Categories, Metadata and Music-Making in Psytrance Culture'. *Dancecult: Journal of Electronic Dance Music Culture* 12(1): 27.
69. Gaffney, Michael, Pauline Rafferty. 2009. 'Making the Long Tail Visible: Social Networking Sites and Independent Music Discovery'. *Program* 43(4): 375–76.

70. Caparrini, Antonio, Javier Arroyo, Laura Pérez-Molina, and Jaime Sánchez-Hernández. 2020. 'Automatic Subgenre Classification in an Electronic Dance Music Taxonomy'. *Journal of New Music Research*, 49 (3): 269–84.
71. The following subgenres were borrowed from Beatport's 2021 Jan charts: Afro house; ambient; bass house; big room; breaks; dance / electro pop; deep house; drum & bass; dubstep; electro (classic / detroit / modern); electro house; funky / groove / jackin' house; future house; garage / bassline / grime; hard dance / hardcore; hard techno; house; indie dance; leftfield bass; leftfield house & techno; melodic house & techno; minimal / deep tech; nu disco / disco; organic house / downtempo; progressive house; psy-trance; reggae / dancehall / dub; tech house; techno (peak time / driving); techno (raw / deep / hypnotic); trance; trap / hip-hop / R&B.
72. The tags 'techno' and 'electro' were excluded from this frequency list.
73. The performance of the Librarian is limited by the accuracy of the subgenre classifier. The scores of the algorithm are similar to the model of Caparrini et al., which can be seen as fair results when taking into account the standard features extracted, the high number of subgenres, and subgenre proximities. Caparrini et al. offer a few suggestions for improving the classifier, much of which would involve structural analysis carried out, ideally, on full-length Beatport tracks (as opposed to the freely provided two-minute samples used in this project).
74. <https://github.com/bvitos/bandcamp_librarian>.
75. Kaul, Timor. 2017. 'Electronic Body Music'. In *Handbuch Popkultur*, ed. Thomas Hecken and Marcus S. Kleiner. Stuttgart: J.B. Metzler Verlag, p. 102.
76. 'Sonic Groove Records Biography'. Sonic Groove. 2017. www.sonicgroove.com/about.html (accessed 14 August 2023).
77. The percentage values in brackets require some explanation. When processing the individual audio files, the classification algorithm determines a class-membership probability value for each of the thirty-two classes (subgenres) the track might belong to. In the next step, the clustering algorithm attempts to establish groups (clusters) in which the tracks are as similar as possible to each other in terms of their class-membership probabilities, and as dissimilar as possible to tracks in other clusters. After defining the clusters, the algorithm calculates the class-membership probability values at the centre point of each cluster. Finally, the project output shows the subgenres with the three highest probability values at each centre point: in the case of Cluster 1, these values are 9 per cent, 7 per cent, and 7 per cent. In effect, this organises the tracks around an amalgam of genres – the higher the probability value, the more pronounced the influence of the associated genre is at the centre.
78. https://sonicgroove.bandcamp.com/track/catenary (accessed 14 August 2023).
79. Throughout this chapter, some of the tag examples were capitalised to ensure their correct spelling.

80. https://sonicgroove.bandcamp.com/track/negative-energy-density (accessed 14 August 2023).
81. https://sonicgroove.bandcamp.com/track/vanishing-point (accessed 14 August 2023).
82. Reynaldo, Shawn. 2016. 'Adam X Goes Down the Wormhole'. *Red Bull Music Academy*. August 4. https://daily.redbullmusicacademy.com/2016/08/traversable-wormhole-interview (accessed 14 August 2023).
83. https://blushresponse.bandcamp.com/track/instrumentality-2 (accessed 14 August 2023).
84. https://adamx.bandcamp.com/track/i-sit-alone (accessed 14 August 2023).
85. https://adamx.bandcamp.com/track/mitral-regurgitation-ancient-methods-mix (accessed 14 August 2023).
86. https://admx-71.bandcamp.com/track/uncompleted-remnants (accessed 14 August 2023).
87. https://sonicgroove.bandcamp.com/track/step-4 (accessed 14 August 2023).
88. https://orphx.bandcamp.com/track/walk-into-the-broken-night-2 (accessed 14 August 2023).
89. 'My track is in the wrong genre / How do I change the genre of my track?' *Beatport*. 2023. https://support.beatport.com/hc/en-us/articles/14763291379604 (accessed 14 August 2023).
90. Negus, *Music Genres*, pp. 178–84.
91. Charles, Christopher. 2019. 'Part of the Tribe: Crews, Residence, and Affiliation in Underground Dance Music Scenes'. *IASPM Journal* 9(2): 60–61.
92. Kirn, Peter. 2020. 'Underground Techno Labels: A Bandcamp Guide'. *CDM*. 1 May. https://cdm.link/2020/05/underground-techno-labels-a-bandcamp-guide/ (accessed 14 August 2023).
93. Thornton, *Club Cultures*, pp. 151–60.
94. Fabian. *Genre in Popular Music*, p. 21.
95. Bennett, Andy, and Richard A. Peterson. 2004. 'Introducing Music Scenes'. In *Music Scenes: Local, Translocal and Virtual*, eds. Andy Bennett and Richard A. Peterson. Nashville: Vanderbilt University Press, pp. 8–10.
96. https://djt1000.bandcamp.com/track/sounds-like-space (accessed 14 August 2023).
97. https://toktokrecords.bandcamp.com/track/polka-dots (accessed 14 August 2023).
98. https://flashrec.bandcamp.com/track/staja (accessed 14 August 2023).
99. https://djt1000.bandcamp.com/album/the-art-of-transformation (accessed 14 August 2023).
100. St. Pierre, Kelly. 2020. 'Polka'. In *Music around the World: A Global Encyclopedia*, 3 volumes, ed. Andrew R. Martin and Matthew Mihalka. Santa Barbara: ABC-CLIO, Vol. 2, p. 680.

101. Kirn, Peter. 2020. 'Underground Techno Labels: A Bandcamp Guide'. *CDM*. 1 May. https://cdm.link/2020/05/underground-techno-labels-a-bandcamp-guide/ (accessed 14 August 2023).
102. https://47x47.bandcamp.com/track/x9 (accessed 14 August 2023).
103. https://flashrec.bandcamp.com/track/sylvie-maziarz-his-tension-flash-recordings (accessed 14 August 2023).
104. https://mord.bandcamp.com/track/irritating-collapse (accessed 14 August 2023).
105. https://avianstore.bandcamp.com/track/endless-lines (accessed 14 August 2023).
106. https://avianstore.bandcamp.com/track/sunk (accessed 14 August 2023).
107. https://avianstore.bandcamp.com/track/evitandus (accessed 14 August 2023).
108. McDermott, Matt. 'Anti-Algorithmic Music'.
109. Goodman, Steve. 2010. *Sonic Warfare: Sound, Affect, and the Ecology of Fear*. Cambridge, MA: MIT Press.
110. Thornton, *Club Cultures*, pp. 141–42.
111. Hesmondhalgh, Jones, and Rauh. 'SoundCloud and Bandcamp as Alternative Music Platforms'.

Further Reading

Caparrini, Antonio, Javier Arroyo, Laura Pérez-Molina, and Jaime Sánchez-Hernández. 2020. 'Automatic Subgenre Classification in an Electronic Dance Music Taxonomy'. *Journal of New Music Research* 49(12): 1–16.

Graham, Stephen. 2016. *Sounds of the Underground: A Cultural, Political and Aesthetic Mapping of Underground and Fringe Music*. Ann Arbor: University of Michigan Press.

Hesmondhalgh, David, Ellis Jones, and Andreas Rauh. 2019. 'SoundCloud and Bandcamp as Alternative Music Platforms'. *Social Media + Society* 5(4): 1–2.

Negus, Keith. 1999. *Music Genres and Corporate Cultures*. London: Routledge.

Sicko, Dan. 2010. *Techno Rebels: The Renegades of Electronic Funk* (second edition). Detroit, MI: Wayne State University Press.

PART IV

Sonic Subjectivities

12 | Timbre and Gesture at the Threshold of Meaning

MARIA PEREVEDENTSEVA

Introduction

In both scholarly and journalistic writing on the genre, electronic dance music (EDM) has often been framed in unapologetically bodily terms. It is music for dancing, 'losing it', and for inducing ecstatic states of *'jouissance'* during which 'the parameters of one's individuality are broken down by the shared throbbing of the bass drum'.[1] Mark Butler writes that rhythm constitutes the *'raison d'être'* of the genre and that, 'in many ways, the beat *is* the music', while Luis Manuel Garcia attributes EDM's physicality to the tactility of those beats, which foster an affect of 'stranger-intimacy' by entraining dancing crowds to the groove.[2] The assumption underpinning many of these arguments is that by centring bodily feeling and affective resonance, EDM's beats elicit physical responses 'without being routed through representation' and symbolic, reflective thought.[3] In turn, this leads Jeremy Gilbert and Ewan Pearson to claim that EDM enacts a 'refusal of logocentric imperatives', with its physical immediacy offering dancers temporary relief from the symbolic constitution of their egos and access to primal, pre-individuated states.[4]

Lurking beneath Gilbert and Pearson's well-intentioned emphasis on EDM's physicality is the spectre of the 'old mind–body blues': a racialised trope that links rhythm with the body and an 'unshakeable primality' when compared to an unspecified 'music of the mind', and that pits the 'white logic' of music analysis against the 'feel' of Black popular music.[5] What is more, the discursive placement of EDM on the body side of this dualism creates a tension between EDM and electronic music more broadly. In Adam Harper's study of the discourse on embodiment in electronic instrument design, the acousmatic nature of electronic music is described in terms of a 'disconnect' between performers' gestures and the sounds that they create.[6] Contrary to Garcia's analysis of EDM, synthesised sound is thus often framed as 'a "loss" or "disconnection" of the body, "touch", or "feel"'.[7] Butler addresses this issue in his later work, where he describes the strategies employed by EDM performers to signal their connectedness to the sounds being created and make their physical performance gestures 'legible' to audiences.[8] However, it then becomes unclear how audiences can respond in an immediate and non-representational manner to the explicitly communicative gestures of EDM performers, which are themselves interpretative embodied representations of the sounds being transmitted. To my mind, the friction between these perspectives arises because the beats of EDM tend to be conceived of as primarily rhythmic and temporal devices, and because EDM audiences tend to be viewed primarily as dancers rather than listeners. In Butler's framework, 'reflective' 'listener orientation' is reserved only for producers and DJs, while fans are described as 'performing audiences' who creatively – though apparently without conscious mediation – respond through dance. If pushed to its logical conclusion, this division of musical labour resurrects a different facet of the mind–body blues in that it reserves reflexive intentionality for music creators while consigning audiences to mental passivity; in effect, their role is portrayed as simply vibrating along in synchrony with the beats. This stereotype recalls Theodor Adorno's 'jitterbug' caricature of popular music fans, and is one which EDM scholars including Butler have otherwise rightly worked to discredit.[9]

In light of the persistence of the mind–body blues in EDM scholarship, this chapter re-thinks established models of EDM participation by centring the activity of listening as it relates to both producers and EDM's (dancing) fans, with the aim of closing the gap between conceptions of predominantly-cerebral versus predominantly-bodily modes of musical engagement. After all, EDM as a culture extends beyond live events into record stores, bedrooms, and online fora, where opportunities for dancing may be limited but where listening – including but not restricted to the kind of reflective structural listening valorised in Western art music – is ubiquitous. The fact that EDM is not simply background music in these settings is evidenced by the impassioned comments users leave on tracks, mixes, and dedicated blogs, which often describe the experience of hearing certain sounds, argue over their relative value, and attempt to imaginatively reconstruct their composition.[10] For these reasons, I consider EDM fans and artists to be united at a fundamental level in how they orient to and process sound, and suggest that this listener orientation can be operative in both raves and settings removed far from the dance floor. More specifically, in what follows I probe *what* is being listened to, shifting focus away from rhythm onto the timbral and gestural underpinnings of EDM's beats. As Garcia notes, 'beats beat not only time, but [also] surfaces, bodies, listeners, dancers, and crowds', and it is worth acknowledging that – before they are perceived as rhythmic events – beats are sound events that are triggered by a movement (gesture) which activates an object into a characteristic mode of sounding (its timbre).[11] Both of these parameters bear on the ways that listeners may respond to those beats, and both rely on an intricate choreography of motor and cognitive processes which undermine characterisations of EDM as 'mindless' in interesting ways.[12]

To illustrate this point, compare Jovonn's track 'N.Y.N.J.' with Lucy's 'Vibrations of a Circular Membrane'.[13] Both are in 4/4 time, at 120 BPM, and feature bass-drum hits on every beat of the bar. However, the sonority of those beats is very different: Jovonn's is a deep, dry, and slightly gritty drum-machine kick which produces a distinct sense of rooted, downward motion. Lucy's, on the other hand, is a sample of an acoustic drum with a wide wooden body, thick skin, and some added noisy reverb. Despite its presumed size, the drum's timbre is shallow and seems to reside in the middle of the audio field. Rhythmically, and if thinking of these bass-drum parts in isolation, these beats and their affective properties should be indistinguishable. However, their differences in timbre promote distinct physical responses, with Jovonn's beats pulling the feet down into a relaxed stomp, while Lucy's conserve momentum for steadfast forward motion. In turn, the timbral-gestural qualities of these beats nudge their perceivers to orient in particular ways to the other musical features of these tracks, and to ultimately locate them in their cultural milieus of classic New York house and dark tribal techno respectively: a conjugation of movements, affects, thoughts, and affiliations that cannot be accounted for through rhythmic properties alone. A recent study of groove and micro-timing in EDM supports this line of argument, observing that 'sound-related aspects of rhythmic events, such as amplitude envelope . . ., intensity, and timbre . . . profoundly affect the feel of the groove and have implications for its appeal to bodily movement or engagement'.[14]

The fact that EDM, by definition, is synthesised and acousmatic, and thus does not typically involve the actual interaction of resonant objects to produce the sounds heard at the point of playback, does not weaken its gestural basis. The model of cognition I adopt is based on the '4E' (embodied, embedded, enacted, and extended) cognition paradigm and James Gibson's ecological theory of perception.[15] According to these theories, cognition is constituted in bodily action and premised on an underlying continuity between the perception of the everyday environment and the cognitive habits that are developed to make sense of it. In practical terms, this means that humans will accumulate exploratory embodied knowledge of the behaviours and properties of objects in diverse environments through 'perception-action coupling' via 'repeatedly executed sensorimotor routines'.[16] This habituated knowledge is then used to make sense of unfamiliar environments such as acousmatic music, supplemented with 'ideomotor simulation' that takes place 'at a virtual level of mental imagery'.[17] For the purposes of the present argument, this notion of continuity suggests that similar mechanisms will be active in the cognition of all forms of music, whether acoustic or electronic, and that the differences between them will reside in the balance of sensorimotor and ideomotor processing, and the cultural associations of specific musical forms.

Timbre and gesture represent useful parameters with which to explore the workings of the embodied mind because they invite a reconsideration of musical first principles, such as what constitutes a sound event, where in the body–mind–environment it resides, and what kinds of events make up a coherent musical environment. Timbre poses this challenge due to being largely 'preattentive' – that is, short-circuiting conscious decision-making about which of its perceived qualities are most significant, and instead relying on the evolutionarily advantageous habit of equating the sound heard to a known acoustic source.[18] In doing so, timbre problematises neat divisions between material reality and its conscious representation. Specifically, it forces the realisation that humans' biological and cultural habits selectively rework the 'given' material properties of the perceived source into a perceptual object that 'works in our world' at a specific moment, thereby highlighting the two-way traffic between embodied mind and environment in sense-making.[19] Musical gesture, on the other hand, constitutes a first principle in a pragmatic sense, being 'primordial' to individual tones as the event 'through which, at which point, and by means of which music happens'.[20] In effect, gesture can be thought of as a precondition for the creation of sound. However, especially in acousmatic electronic music like EDM, the responsibility for this creation arguably lies less with the producer than the listener. In the embodied cognition framework that I adopt, listeners' experiences of all music involve the physical and mental simulation of the actions implied by its sounds, through which newly formed 'gestural-sonorous objects' gain conceptual identity and become felt as well as thought.[21]

While the conception of listening articulated here is substantially different from the supposedly detached, analytical mode associated with the idealised Western art music listener, I want to leave open the possibility that EDM – like all music – can equally be listened to structurally, or not.[22] One of my core arguments is that timbral gestures play a fundamental role in structuring EDM listening. But, as Mariusz Kozak points out, the study of gesture itself has historically privileged the perspectives of performers and producers, while its role in listeners' experiences of music has received less attention.[23] Therefore, to lay the theoretical groundwork for thinking about the gestures of *listening*, I will first outline the mechanics of the interdependence of timbre and gesture in musical experience, and then explore how the synthesised timbral gestures of EDM afford listeners opportunities to experience supernormal ways of bodily being. I will argue that hearing EDM through a timbral-gestural lens can lead to a better understanding of the centrality of listeners' embodied agency in the construction of the musical environment to which they simultaneously respond, and that this, in turn, can enrich understandings of EDM's affectivity based on a causal model of imposed stimulus and automatic response. More broadly, it is hoped that the theory of timbral gesture that I put forward can provide new ways of thinking about how EDM listeners make sense of electronic sound, and how this process is guided by, and ultimately transforms, the social relations through which musical meaning-making arises.

Timbre and Gesture: First Principles

Definitions of timbre and gesture are entwined with the problem of musical metaphor, highlighting tensions between what is considered musically 'real' and part of 'the music itself' and the objects that music analysts (and listeners more generally) construct, describe, and theorise as part of their interpretative work. At its base, gesture is a metaphor for movement. Musical gesture can encompass everything from a single sound-producing action such as a finger depressing a key on a keyboard, to a more complex event that unites several actions in a single perceptual unit (e.g. the arrangement of parameters in a digital audio workstation). An example of this could be the first bass drop in Aho Ssan's 'Simulacrum II', which agglomerates into a discrete form from a seeming multitude of synthesised processes.[24] Furthermore, gesture is a movement that 'express[es] an idea or meaning' and provides a 'dynamic analogue' to expression such that, similar to the bodily gestures that accompany speech, new information is added that is not reducible to the sound signal alone.[25] For Lawrence Zbikowski, however, the fact that musical gesture exceeds a one-to-one translation of matter to mind does not render it extraneous. On the contrary, he argues that because 'sonic analogues are basic to musical grammar', musical gestures *as* metaphors actually constitute the 'essential materials of musical expression'.[26] A complicating factor is that there is no guarantee that a performer's gesture will align in movement or meaning with the gesture perceived by the listener, whether in a traditional instrumental setting or in electronic music performance. This remains true even if, as discussed by Butler and Harper, explicit efforts are made by equipment manufacturers to 'build in' opportunities for physical expression. An element of contingency remains because both the performance and interpretation of musical gesture are based on the 'culturally-enactive' nature of musical meaning which is derived from formal and personal learning, knowledge of particular cultural contexts, and individual bodily capabilities, habits, and life histories.[27]

Similar problems abound for timbre, which Stephen McAdams describes as an umbrella concept uniting multiple perceptual attributes based on the spectral (frequency), temporal (envelope), and spectrotemporal (frequency and amplitude flux) properties of sound waves.[28] Unlike pitch and amplitude, measured in hertz and decibels respectively, no single measure of an acoustic stimulus is responsible for timbral identity, though it is largely dependent on the nonlinear interaction of these features. Irrespective of this internal complexity, timbre functions as one of the primary perceptual vehicles for the recognition of sound sources and, during this process, it achieves a paradoxical unity despite being distributed along the productive, acoustic, and perceptual domains of sound.[29] For example, most listeners will be able to distinguish between the sounds of strings and brass, even if not necessarily identify them, based on the perception of their different material properties and modes of activation (i.e. metal, wood, string, plucking, blowing, bowing). Yet manipulating pitch, volume, and attack time can drastically blur the boundaries between these instrument families – a technique exemplified in the opening of Gérard Grisey's 'Partiels'. On the other hand, in the EDM world, listeners frequently claim to be able to distinguish between the 'acid' sound of the original analogue Roland TB-303 bass sequencer and its digital clones, despite the mathematical structure of the synthesis pathways and the gestural affordances of these machines being identical.[30] Therefore, despite ostensibly being determined by the physical properties of the sound source, the manifold cognitive processes required to achieve a unified timbral identity, which – like all extended acts of perception – are influenced as much by ingrained perceptual and cultural habits as the given stimulus, have led Cornelia Fales to suggest that 'in very real sense, timbre exists only in the mind of the listener'.[31] As with musical gesture, she argues that through the act of perceptual fusion, timbre often diverges from its originating source, constructing a sonic object 'that may not always coincide with the version existing in the physical world'.[32]

This purported divergence could explain why the language used to describe sound and timbre has historically been considered 'whimsical', 'subjective', and seemingly 'arbitrary'.[33] A piano timbre can be described as 'brilliant' despite the material properties of a piano and its playing technique having nothing to do with the transmission of light waves. The acid basslines of the 303 are often described as 'whistling' when the cut-off frequency and resonance are set to high, and 'squelching' when envelope modulation is high, while certain pads are referred to as 'keening' or 'icy', again despite the synthesis of these sounds having little in common with vocal production or the physical compression of wet matter. It appears that, as with extra-verbal and musical gestures, these linguistic devices carry more information than is contained in the sound alone, reflecting something of their speaker's cognitive idiosyncrasies and wider knowledge and habits. A new wave of research emerging in the 2010s has provided compelling evidence to suggest that this seemingly arbitrary language is, in fact, undergirded by perceptual schemata that are consistent between cultural groups and genre communities, and that timbre cognition may be a key mediator between musical embodiment and felt affect.[34] For example, in his corpus analysis of orchestration treatises, Zachary Wallmark observes that action words describing qualities of movement, words pertaining to material properties, and words articulating correspondences between different sensory domains together constitute the three overarching categories used to describe timbre.[35] My study of vernacular EDM discourse online uncovers a similar privileging of these types of metaphors, which are also often refracted through wider tropes specific to EDM culture and reflect the extremity and mind-altering 'unreality' of its synthesised sounds.[36] This is significant in the context of the present argument because the existence of stable genre-specific timbral terminology underscores the fact that both sonic and (sub)cultural factors play a role in timbre cognition, and that this is underpinned by the bodily affordances of the music in question. Taken together, these studies underline how fundamentally entwined timbre cognition appears to be with real or imagined movement, whether that movement is an intentional action that produces sound by encountering another object, or an exploratory movement that helps to situate the listener in relation to their environment and the other objects active within it.

Metaphor itself, conceived of as a transfer of information from one domain to enhance understanding of another, has occupied a central place in theories of embodied cognition since the 1980 publication of George Lakoff and Mark Johnson's *Metaphors We Live By*.[37] Their basic argument was that the rich variety of metaphors that characterise developed languages are underpinned by image schemata based on humans' everyday embodied experiences of motion, verticality, directionality, and so on, and that these schemata are habitually transferred between the sense modes to conceptualise different areas of experience. In the simplest case, many cultures employ the verticality schema to understand differences in sonic frequencies through the metaphor of pitch height. Laurence Barsalou developed this idea by arguing that the qualities and patterns of felt experience that underpin image schemata are encoded in the brain as 'perceptual symbols'.[38] He proposed that perceptual symbols capture patterns of activation of the various sensorimotor areas that were involved in the initial perception of an object, and that these areas can be re-activated to produce neural simulations that allow the perceiver to infer greater knowledge about a new object that may be given only partially to direct experience. In music psychology, these concepts have been supplemented with insights from emerging research into mirror neurons to explore the multi-modal nature of music cognition. Newer work in this field suggests that sound is processed in terms of 'intentional, hierarchically organised sequences of expressive motor acts behind the [sound] signal' which 'can be interpreted in terms of the expressive dynamics of personal vocal and physical gestures'.[39] In a different study, Wallmark and colleagues observed considerable functional overlap between the auditory and tactile sensory regions in the perception of timbre.[40] This led them to suggest that listeners process timbre simultaneously as sound and touch, and that the coupling of auditory and motor regions means that the mental simulation of timbre includes both the action required to produce the sound and how it would *feel* to carry out that action.[41]

The growing consensus in the field of embodied cognition therefore holds that sensory, motor, and cognitive processes are inseparable, with the feeling of the body's interactions with its environment generating conceptual structures that then guide future actions. The continuous involvement of different sense modalities, which have distinct sensory associations accrued over a lifetime of perceptual and cultural learning, precludes a deterministic understanding of how listeners embody musical gestures. That is, while a gesture such as an ascending scale may employ the same verticality schema as an ascending-frequency filter because both go 'up' through a portion of the frequency spectrum, this does not mean that listeners will necessarily simulate both through the same kind of (physical or imagined) 'upwards' action. This is because a scale may also be associated with stepwise movement, whereas a filter may be associated with rotary actions – each of which may have other motional, emotional, and conceptual associations that will result in distinct embodied responses. Importantly, these simulations will also be guided by cultural knowledge about the aptness of responses in specific musical environments. For example, physically raising one's hands to express the tension and anticipation of resolution as a filter sweep prepares for a bass drop would be more acceptable in a rave than the same interpretative gesture would be accompanying a scale run during a symphony finale in a concert hall.

To summarise, I argue that the feeling that accompanies timbre perception transforms the movement trajectories underpinning its cognition into gestures proper, as it gives them meaning that exceeds both the action and the sound as individual percepts by uniting them into a coherent new object. This process is metaphorical in the sense that it cross-modulates the sensorimotor information contained in both percepts, 'fleshing them out', and thereby allows listeners an expanded understanding of the sound-producing object simultaneously as its characteristic mode of sounding *and* the feeling of that sounding. What is more, the simulated gestures through which listeners come to grasp timbre help to enhance their understanding of their auditory environment more generally, as their dimensions help to establish the virtual space of the music and listeners' positions and bodily capabilities in relation to it. For example, the cognition of a resonant snare sound with a long reverb tail brings with it an embodied impression of a virtual space big enough to transmit those reverberations, as well as the physical force required to make this action fill that space. This embodied knowledge will then guide the choreography of future gestures to be commensurate with the sonic setting.

The working definition of a timbral gesture I carry forwards, therefore, is of a sonic event cross-modally united in perception through the felt projection of an action trajectory that accounts for its spectrotemporal character and localises it in the virtual musical environment constructed by the listener. Thinking through how the main mid-range synth in Ectomorph's 'Crawl of the Cthulhu' might be perceived provides a good example.[42] This instrumental line occupies a wide frequency range that might, in other circumstances, be separated into different perceptual streams based on register, and features automated filter effects asynchronously applied to different frequency bands. The trajectory of this line – at least to my ears – simulates the sensation of writhing, as discrete portions of the spectrum are variously brought into and out of focus in a cyclical fashion, and with associations of energy exertion brought about by the addition of noise elements. The internal consistency of this gesture, which prevents it from overtaking the entire sound spectrum, is reinforced by the ways it appears to recoil from the artificially sustained hi-hats and the periodicity of reverb and delay effects placed on the snare, which work to contain the synth within the spatial boundaries constructed by the percussion, thus discretising it as unified action trajectory in itself. Rather than a physical movement or fixed concept alone, this understanding of timbral gesture conceives of the agency of the listener as doing more than simply reacting to auditory stimulus by way of causal correspondence. Instead, the act of perception-action coupling itself constructs and expresses – via simulation – the tensions, emotions, and meanings ultimately attached to the timbral-gestural event. In other words, because the perception of timbral gesture involves an internal awareness of the body and the forms of touch and motion that go into the production of the sound, the 'hearing in' of meaning in the music is grounded by a bodily 'feeling in' which adds 'a latent expressivity to listening'.[43]

Seen in this way, perceiving timbral gestures 'secure[s] a human space of reflection and subjectivity', overtly exercising what Ingrid Monson has called 'perceptual agency', which she defines as the 'socioculturally mediated capacity to act'.[44] Monson is explicit about the motivation for this concept being the need to connect 'microprocesses of musical contemplation and experience with larger contexts of social and cultural life' and thereby narrow the gap between conceptions of musical engagement as either sensory, non-conscious *feeling* or conscious, reflective *knowing*.[45] My invocation of agency in the perception of timbral gestures in EDM is similarly concerned with articulating the coexistence and mutuality of these cognitive modes in all musical experience. I underline it here to challenge the emphasis on unconscious and unreflective modes of musical engagement in the EDM literature discussed in my introduction, and to suggest that the presence or absence of a dance floor does not in itself determine the quality of the musical experience that will be had. The concept of agency employed here thus brings with it an opportunity to consider the wider social and cultural conventions that guide individual embodied responses to sound. In turn, it sets the stage for analysing how those responses are communicated with others, via either coordinated movement in social EDM settings or verbal exchanges employing the elaborate scene-specific embodied metaphors described above. Understanding the embodied basis of these communicative strategies could ultimately serve to delineate the intersubjective space of musical experience that exists beyond and between individual EDM events and provides the scaffold upon which EDM culture's values are overlaid. Before exploring this potential for intersubjectivity further, however, it will be useful to consider how the ontology of synthesised sound extends the understanding of timbral gesture established so far.

Synthesised Timbre and Sonic Prosthesis

The enactment of timbral gesture becomes especially interesting in the case of music that is produced and manipulated via electronic means, and which therefore is not bound to the physical and mechanical constraints of a 'real' acoustic environment, natural sound sources, or human physiology. Using sound synthesis, the long reverb tail of the snare gesture described above can be superimposed onto an otherwise dry acoustic space; its attack can be attenuated, and the natural decay implied by the attack can be prolonged and granulated through various effects so that it appears to exist in a forcefield of its own. An example of this could be the snare in Drexciya's 'Gravity Waves'.[46] In more extreme cases, a synthesiser or DAW can create timbral-gestural objects that would be self-negating or simply impossible to produce through the manual interaction of physical objects. Electronic music thus productively challenges the tendencies of acoustic timbre cognition to mask potential slippages in the inferential chains involved in preattentively relating a heard sound to a source. In light of this, Simon Zagorski-Thomas suggests a conception of electronic timbres as 'sonic cartoons' – hyperreal schematic representations of real-world spaces and activities which may exaggerate some features and leave others out but which are still guided in part by embodied action.[47] An example he gives is of the gesture occurring at 3'31 in Aphex Twin's 'Bucephalus Bouncing Ball', which appears to merge a succession of highly processed metallic scraping actions into a unified mimetic approximation of the effect of gravity on a bouncing ball, while making no effort to conceal the implausibility of the conjunction of these materials, actions, and forces in a natural acoustic setting.[48]

This goes back to the point raised by Harper, discussed above, that electronic dance music can paradoxically appear to be less mappable onto the body than acoustic instrumental music, because it is less accessible through embodied simulation or the knowledge of instrumental gestures alone. This could explain why electronic timbres, despite their ubiquity in contemporary music of all stripes, continue to be used to represent nonhuman beings, activities, and spaces. Rashad Becker's *Traditional Music of*

Notional Species albums for PAN exploit this association to the full, making manifest in sound the behaviours and rituals of bodies that defy anthropomorphic understanding while still cohering on a conceptual level as unified entities.[49] This is because, despite their indubitable strangeness, his timbral gestures activate fragments of the neural codes of known objects and actions. For this reason, it is wise to avoid underestimating the ability of the human perceptual system to relate complex acousmatic or synthesised sounds to what Luke Windsor calls the 'higher order structures of the everyday acoustic environment'.[50] As an ecological theorist, Windsor subscribes to the principle of continuity underpinning the model of cognition adopted here, so the structures he describes should be understood to include the laws of physics and the learned expectations about object behaviours under particular environmental conditions that humans use to make sense of the world.

With reference to the acousmatic nature of electronic sound, Denis Smalley's theory of spectromorphology systematises the ways that both composers and listeners perceive what he calls 'sound-shapes' in a four-part taxonomy of 'gestural surrogacy'.[51] His scheme builds outwards from the most to the least life-like sound-gesture couplings, with the first order including sounds created by everyday gestures prior to their incorporation into a musical setting; the second including traditional instrumental gestures (acoustic or synthesised); the third involving inferred gestures due to ambiguity around the sound source or its mode of activation; and the fourth order concerning unknown and unknowable sources and causes.[52] Smalley ultimately asserts that even the most 'adventurous' electronic sounds can 'maintain a humanity' by retaining 'gestural vestiges' that are known to listeners.[53] This aligns with the ecological principle that human perceptual systems are rarely satisfied with ambivalence or incomplete information.[54] Smalley's insistence on traces of humanity in even the most otherworldly sounds thus supports the idea that listeners latch onto the vestiges encoded in past musical experiences to map out and extend their embodied understanding of otherwise alien timbral gestures.

Extending these ideas, Eric Clarke suggests that acousmatic listening – which, since the advent of music recording, arguably constitutes the norm for musical experience rather than an aberration – actually places more emphasis on a 'particularly intense' kind of 'reflective or contemplative' auditory attention.[55] He argues that, in acousmatic conditions, listeners have to work to make up for the lack of visual stimulus and 'make sense of perceptual events that seem to have no obvious practical motivation'.[56] Contrary to widely held beliefs about the nature of EDM participation, therefore, traditional EDM listening environments such as low-lit clubs with concealed loudspeakers and DJs stationed in booths could, in fact, actively promote precisely this type of attentive listening, as audiences strive to make sense of what is heard in relation to their existing knowledge of the world. The challenge to preattentive timbre cognition that this poses thereby creates an opportunity for perceptual learning. It requires listeners to adapt to new ways of imaginatively experiencing their bodies, which, in turn, relies on the metaphorical aspect of timbral gesture to enable the knowledge of one perceptual domain to transform and add meaning to another. Therefore, in moments of these exploratory extensions of corporeal capabilities, listeners' bodies inhabit a 'nexus of sometimes competing musical meanings and expressions'.[57] Moreover, given the timbral gestures of EDM often exaggerate the dimensions and trajectories of natural gestures, I argue that they effectively serve as virtual prostheses that allow experiential glimpses into ways of being beyond normative, bounded, individual corporeality.[58]

For example, in jungle, there is often a perceptible tension between the weighty basslines which act as an 'anchor' that pulls the body down and the 'frenetic, unpredictable multiplicities' of the breakbeats that, conversely, suggest an upwards momentum.[59] Together, these gestures invoke a kind of physical incommensurability that extends listeners' sense of their strength and bodily boundaries in what is (ideally) a pleasurable and cognitively stimulating manner. Similarly, anyone who has ever seen a footwork battle – a genre with similarly stratified bass and percussion gestures – will have noted the virtuosic contortions enacted by dancers as a way of creatively coping with the diverse movement trajectories suggested in the music, which go beyond simply articulating downbeats or rhythmic phrases and express a deeper level of engagement with the structures of sound. A stylised portrayal of this can be found in the video for Jlin's 'Carbon 7 (161)', whose choreography simultaneously responds to the conventions of footwork and contemporary dance.[60] Another example that further highlights the metaphorical aspect of enacting significance onto sound can be found in the opening of the Digital Mystikz anthem 'Anti-War Dub'.[61] Here, the two distinct lines contained in the sound signal – a sub-bass with 'wobbles' achieved by a filtered noise oscillator and a simple sine wave doubling the bassline's melodic contour a few octaves above – are perceptually streamed into one gesture that viscerally transforms the distributed acoustic stimulus into a unified percept, simulating the impression of a vast column of air that threatens to engulf the entire sensorium and propels the body forwards and outwards with a vigorous affective charge. From a listener's perspective, if heard on the powerful sound systems on which the UK dubstep scene was founded, the feeling of both being carried away by this charge and trying to resist it will require some degree of bodily and cognitive adaptation.

Significantly, if the enactive mimesis or simulation of timbral gestures makes possible the 'experience [of] music as the action of a dynamic organism similar to a human organism', then it could be argued that listening to music brings with it projected knowledge of how sound works: how sonic frequencies, periods, and onsets combine into a functioning whole, even if that knowledge corresponds only loosely to how the perceived sounds were actually produced.[62] Calling back to Clarke's notion of the reflective listening facilitated in acousmatic settings, this suggests that the imaginative embodiment of timbral gestures constitutes what Mark Reybrouck describes as 'epistemic interaction' with sound – a process that attempts to *make sense* of music and the listener's place in music, rather than merely react to it.[63] Therefore, despite the intricacies of the production of electronic sound being hidden in the 'black boxes' of synthesisers and DAWs, and in informal channels of knowledge dissemination, repeated exposure to electronic sounds can provide listeners with an elaborate virtual or inferred knowledge of the characteristic properties of electronic sound sources, such as the warm 'whomp' of a Roland TR-808 kick drum or the saturated kaleidoscopes of Serum basslines. This is all the more pronounced in the case of EDM, which, unlike some of the more esoteric fringes of experimental electronic music, frequently re-uses the same timbral gestures to the extent that they become symbolic of entire subgenres. In effect, this trans-historical repetition or 'nomadic memory' serves to reinforce listeners' habituated, embodied, and enculturated knowledge of its sounds.[64] The heightened degree of agency that this ascribes to listeners can help to remodel understandings of the social dynamics of EDM participation, as it decentres the roles of the DJ, producer, and the musical recording as the ultimate arbiters of musical meaning. As mentioned above, the metaphorical slipperiness of gesture – especially when paired with the even more slippery ontology of electronic timbre – means that there is no guarantee of an intentional alignment between a gesture programmed by a producer and its performative realisation by listeners. This has important implications for established theoretical accounts of EDM's affectivity which I address in the next, concluding section.

Conclusion: The Threshold of Meaning

At the beginning of this chapter, I observed that the distinctive characterisation of listener engagement with EDM in the literature relies on a conception of affect as a physical force that compels participants into ecstatic states through rhythmic entrainment. Group synchrony through entrainment has been extensively researched due to its apparent ability to strengthen social bonds between those involved in synchronous activity.[65] Briefly put, in entrainment, the perception of a periodic stimulus signal (such as a beat pattern) is said to 'drive' the perceiving organism into a temporally coordinated, or 'driven', response that can include physical movements like dance as well as imagined simulations.[66] The prosocial aspect of this has to do with the links between theories of entrainment and mirror neurons, which suggest that the autonomic imitation of observed actions is fundamental to developing the empathy that is required for the establishment of social relationships.[67] In music, Kai Tuuri and Tuomas Eerola suggest that mirror neurons serve as a basis for 'empathetic' listening, in which the attribution of intentionality to a musical 'other' is based on the embodied affordances of a 'gestural signature' which is inferred 'in terms of [listeners'] own ontology of emotions and intentions'.[68] Extending this into the sphere of intercultural understanding, Clarke, Jonna Vuoskoski, and Tia DeNora argue that 'empathic resonance' encourages listeners to enter into an 'empathic relationship' with the 'virtual person' of the music and the cultural materials through which they are constructed.[69]

In social settings like raves, Maria Witek argues that empathic resonance also involves other listeners on account of synchronisation between individuals' driven responses to the music and the gestures of others around them. For her, this social resonance constitutes an extended, embodied form of consciousness that is further amplified if those co-present have similar cultural norms and beliefs.[70] Ultimately, however, Witek relates this form of consciousness to affect, and attributes a 'smoothness and lack of differentiation' to the experience.[71] This smooth, pre-qualitative characterisation of affect is grounded in the philosophy of Gilles Deleuze, Félix Guattari, and Brian Massumi, which has dominated humanities scholarship since the mid-1990s (and been subject to robust critique by Ruth Leys and Brian Kane).[72] While this is certainly not Witek's intention, given her explicit invocation of the cultural, issues arise when this conception of affect is adopted in wider EDM discourse, as it allows affect and sound to be bundled into a binary opposition to the purportedly 'striated' character of language and culture.[73] This, in turn, can lead to the framing of listener responses to EDM as existing at a level 'autonomous' from or beneath consciousness proper.[74] As mentioned in my introduction, despite the emancipatory ideals underpinning affect's escape from the 'prison-house of language', this model of EDM's affectivity has led to characterisations of dance music engagement as lacking meaningful agency, reinstating the mind–body blues.[75] In this formulation, present in the writings of Gilbert, Steve Goodman, Rupa Huq, Tim Jordan, and others, EDM participants are merely synchronously driven by the supposedly pre-personal and non-symbolic force of sound waves and other stimuli.[76] However, this quasi-mechanistic conception of sympathetic resonance between music and listeners problematically sidesteps the frictions to this experiential smoothness that cultural and other differences can impose. Furthermore, it resurrects an outdated model of authorial intention and passive listening that recalls the industrial group Laibach's 'one transmitter, a multitude of receivers' satire of totalitarianism, effectively precluding the understanding of different qualities of experience that may prevent or negatively impact some listeners' experiences of resonance, empathy, and entrainment'.[77]

The theory of timbral gesture presented in this chapter challenges the passive, one-directional conception of EDM's affectivity through its emphasis on listener agency and intentionality as constitutive of the cognitive effort required to make embodied sense of the sounds of EDM. The metaphorical slippage inherent to timbre cognition as well as its expressive dimension in musical gesture, which presupposes expectations of shared cultural codes between producers and intended listeners, suggests that embodied responses to dance music lie at the intersection of affect and meaning, rather than anterior to, or autonomous from, meaning as a whole. That is to say, the experience and (internal or external) expression of timbral gesture requires working through a listener's socio-culturally mediated perceptual habits and capacities to act as they interact with the (equally socio-culturally mediated) interpretations of those gestures by others. This process thus creates opportunities to reconcile any differences present in their respective performances. While there can be no guarantee of this being smooth or undifferentiated, the empathic relationships fostered through communal participation in EDM's vibe, nevertheless, make the possibility of resolving any differences more forthcoming. It should also be noted that the potential for empathic resonance that the embodiment of EDM's timbral gestures enables is not exclusive to live, social consumption settings: the virtual agent onto whom listeners project music's intentionality can be located in recordings and experienced in web-based virtual worlds. However, it is likely that physical proximity to other listeners will lend a sense of intense immediacy to these acts of social mediation and make it possible for listeners to influence each others' performances of the music, actualising the mutual influence that distinguishes entrainment proper from mere resonance.[78]

Ultimately, this mediating process highlights the self-amplifying relays between the cultural and the material, and the body, mind, and other body-minds in musical experience. As such, it reconfigures affect away from being a pre-personal force that weaves indiscriminately around dancing bodies into an *inter*personal binding force that can facilitate intersubjective understanding. In this view, timbral gesture constitutes the embodied threshold that brings the physical irreducibility of affect into the cultural arena, actualising it, and enabling it to be communicated between co-participants in a musical event. In doing so, it leaves material traces that can be historicised and contextualised to aid understanding of the differing corporeal realities of EDM listeners throughout the genre's history. Granting music analysis access into this social space should not be seen as an act of reification that seeks to legitimate certain musical practices over others or impose difference for the sake of taxonomy. Instead, paying attention to how individual embodied realities are negotiated through the interpretative expression of musical materials can lead to a greater understanding of the material and cultural conditions that constrain them, in turn making it possible to think of affect's processes of becoming as *becoming otherwise*. Listening to the supernormal timbral gestures of EDM can therefore destabilise established regimes of being and knowing, and the expressive qualities inherent to their embodiment can make tangible the communal realisation of new social formations.

Notes

1. Kodwo Eshun, *More Brilliant Than The Sun: Adventures in Sonic Fiction* (London: Quartet Books, 1998), 99; Jeremy Gilbert and Ewan Pearson, *Discographies: Dance Music, Culture, and the Politics of Sound* (London: Routledge, 1999), 64–65.
2. Mark J. Butler, *Unlocking the Groove: Rhythm, Meter, and Musical Design in Electronic Dance Music* (Bloomington, IN: Indiana University Press, 2006), 4; Luis-Manuel Garcia, 'Beats, Flesh, and Grain: Sonic Tactility and Affect in Electronic Dance Music', *Sound Studies* 1 (1) (2015): 60, https://doi.org/10.1080/20551940.2015.1079072; Luis-Manuel Garcia-Mispireta,

Together, Somehow. Sound, Affect and Intimacy on the Dancefloor (Durham, NC: Duke University Press, 2023).
3. Garcia, 'Beats, Flesh, and Grain', 60.
4. Gilbert and Pearson, *Discographies*, 60.
5. Tom Perchard, 'New Riffs on the Old Mind-Body Blues: "Black Rhythm," "White Logic," and Music Theory in the Twenty-First Century', *Journal for the Society of American Music* 9 (3) (2015): 323, 340, https://doi.org/10.1017/S175219631500019X; See also Susan McClary and Robert Walser, 'Theorizing the Body in African-American Music', *Black Music Research Journal* 14 (1) (1994): 76, https://doi.org/10.2307/779459.
6. Adam Harper, 'Out of Touch? Challenges in Reconnecting Bodies with Instruments "Of the Future"', *Contemporary Music Review* 39 (2) (3 March 2020): 259, https://doi.org/10.1080/07494467.2020.1806629.
7. Harper, 'Out of Touch', 259.
8. Mark J. Butler, *Playing with Something That Runs: Technology, Improvisation, and Composition in DJ and Laptop Performance* (New York: Oxford University Press, 2014), 99.
9. Butler, *Playing with Something*, 106; Butler, *Unlocking the Groove*, 72–73; Theodor W. Adorno and George Simpson, 'On Popular Music', in *Essays on Music*, ed. Richard D. Leppert (Berkeley, CA: University of California Press, 2002), 465.
10. See Edward K. Spencer, 'Re-Orientating Spectromorphology and Space-Form through a Hybrid Acoustemology', *Organised Sound* 22 (3) (2017): 324–35, https://doi.org/10.1017/S1355771817000486; Thomas Brett, 'Autechre and Electronic Music Fandom: Performing Knowledge Online through Techno-Geek Discourses', *Popular Music and Society* 38 (1) (2015): 7–24, https://doi.org/10.1080/03007766.2014.973763.
11. Garcia, 'Beats, Flesh, and Grain', 61.
12. Gilbert and Pearson, *Discographies*, 71.
13. Jovonn, *Out All Nite E.P.*, 12" Vinyl (USA: Emotive Records, 1991); Lucy, *Self Mythology*, 2 x LP Vinyl (Germany: Stroboscopic Artefacts, 2016).
14. Ragnhild Brøvig-Hanssen et al., 'A Grid in Flux: Sound and Timing in Electronic Dance Music', *Music Theory Spectrum* 3 (2021), https://doi.org/10.1093/mts/mtab013; See also Hans T. Zeiner-Henriksen, 'The "Poum Tchak" Pattern. Correspondence Between Rhythm, Sound, and Movement in Electronic Dance Music' (Doctoral Dissertation, Oslo, Norway, University of Oslo, 2010).
15. Francisco J. Varela, Evan Thompson, and Eleanor Rosch, *The Embodied Mind: Cognitive Science and Human Experience* (Cambridge, MA: MIT Press, 1991); George Lakoff and Mark Johnson, *Metaphors We Live By* (Chicago, IL: University of Chicago Press, 2003); Mark J. Rowlands, *The New Science of the Mind: From Extended Mind to Embodied Phenomenology* (Cambridge, MA: MIT Press, 2010); James J. Gibson, *The Senses Considered As Perceptual*

16. Mark Reybrouck, 'Experience as Cognition: Musical Sense-Making and the "In-Time/Outside-of-Time" Dichotomy', *Interdisciplinary Studies in Musicology* 19 (2019): 58, https://doi.org/10.14746/ism.2019.19.4.
17. Reybrouck, 'Experience as Cognition', 58.
18. Cornelia Fales, 'The Paradox of Timbre', *Ethnomusicology* 46 (1) (2002): 59, https://doi.org/10.2307/852808.
19. Fales, 'The Paradox of Timbre', 58.
20. Rolf Inge Godøy, 'Gestural Affordances of Musical Sound', in *Musical Gestures: Sound, Movement, and Meaning*, ed. Rolf Inge Godøy and Marc Leman (London: Routledge, 2010), 110; Anthony Gritten and Elaine King, *New Perspectives on Music and Gesture* (Farnham: Ashgate, 2011), 2.
21. Rolf Inge Godøy, 'Gestural-Sonorous Objects: Embodied Extensions of Schaeffer's Conceptual Apparatus', *Organised Sound* 11 (2) (2006): 149, https://doi.org/10.1017/S1355771806001439.
22. Western art music, often abbreviated to WAM, is used in musicology as shorthand to describe the European classical music tradition and its associated values and discourses.
23. Mariusz Kozak, 'Listeners' Bodies in Music Analysis: Gestures, Motor Intentionality, and Models', *Music Theory Online* 21 (3) (2015): Section 1, Paragraph 5 https://mtosmt.org/issues/mto.15.21.3/mto.15.21.3.kozak.html.
24. Aho Ssan, *Simulacrum*, FLAC Album (Subtext, 2020).
25. Rolf Inge Godøy and Marc Leman, eds., *Musical Gestures: Sound, Movement, and Meaning* (London: Routledge, 2010), 5; Lawrence Zbikowski, 'Musical Gesture and Musical Grammar: A Cognitive Approach', in *New Perspectives on Music and Gesture*, ed. Anthony Gritten and Elaine King (Farnham: Ashgate, 2011), 84.
26. Zbikowski, 'Musical Gesture and Musical Grammar', 84.
27. Ian Cross, 'Musicality and the Human Capacity for Culture', *Musicae Scientiae* 12 (1) (2008): 156, https://doi.org/10.1177/1029864908012001071.
28. Stephen McAdams, 'Musical Timbre Perception', in *The Psychology of Music*, ed. Diana Deutsch, Third Edition (Amsterdam; London: Academic Press, 2013), 35.
29. Cornelia Fales, 'Short-Circuiting Perceptual Systems. Timbre in Ambient and Techno Music', in *Wired for Sound. Engineering and Technologies in Sonic Cultures*, ed. Paul D. Green and Thomas Porcello (Middletown, CT: Wesleyan University Press, 2005), 157.
30. Mark Smith, 'Roland – TB-03 Bass Line · Tech Review · RA', Resident Advisor, 18 January 2017, https://ra.co/reviews/20571.
31. Fales, 'Short-Circuiting Perceptual Systems', 163.

32. Fales, 'The Paradox of Timbre', 58.
33. Zachary Wallmark, 'A Corpus Analysis of Timbre Semantics in Orchestration Treatises', *Psychology of Music* 47 (4) (2019): 588, https://doi.org/10.1177/0305735618768102.
34. Zachary Wallmark et al., 'Embodied Listening and Timbre: Perceptual, Acoustical, and Neural Correlates', *Music Perception* 35 (3) (2018): 332–63, https://doi.org/10.1525/mp.2018.35.3.332; Asterios Zacharakis, Konstantinos Pastiadis, and Joshua Reiss, 'An Interlanguage Study of Musical Timbre Semantic Dimensions and Their Acoustic Correlates', *Music Perception* 31 (4) (2014): 339–58, https://doi.org/10.1525/mp.2014.31.4.339; Asterios Zacharakis, Konstantinos Pastiadis, and Joshua Reiss, 'An Interlanguage Unification of Musical Timbre: Bridging Semantic, Perceptual, and Acoustic Dimensions', *Music Perception* 32 (4) (2015): 394–412, https://doi.org/10.1525/mp.2015.32.4.394.
35. Wallmark, 'A Corpus Analysis of Timbre Semantics in Orchestration Treatises', 601.
36. Maria Perevedentseva, 'Electronic Dance Music and the Discursive Web: Interpreting Value, Sociality and Knowledge Construction on Boomkat.com', in *Music and the Internet: Methodological, Epistemological, and Ethical Orientations*, ed. Christopher Haworth, Danielle Sofer, and Edward K. Spencer (Routledge, in press).
37. Lakoff and Johnson, *Metaphors We Live By*.
38. Lawrence W. Barsalou, 'Perceptual Symbol Systems', *Behavioral and Brain Sciences* 22 (4) (1999): 577–660, https://doi.org/10.1017/S0140525X99002149.
39. Overy and Molnar-Szakacs (2009, see note 67) cited in Zachary Wallmark et al., 'Embodied Listening and Timbre: Perceptual, Acoustical, and Neural Correlates', *Music Perception* 35 (3) (2018): 334, https://doi.org/10.1525/mp.2018.35.3.332.
40. Wallmark et al., 'Embodied Listening and Timbre'.
41. Wallmark et al., 'Embodied Listening and Timbre', 355.
42. Ectomorph, *Stalker*, 2x12" (Vinyl) (USA: Interdimensional Transmissions, 2018).
43. Deniz Peters, 'Touch: Real, Apparent, and Absent. On Bodily Expression in Electronic Music', in *Bodily Expression in Electronic Music: Perspectives on Reclaiming Performativity*, ed. Deniz Peters, Gerhard Eckel, and Andreas Dorschel (London: Routledge, 2012), 21, 25.
44. Kozak, 'Listeners' Bodies in Music Analysis', Section 4, Paragraph 6; Ingrid T. Monson, 'Hearing, Seeing, and Perceptual Agency', *Critical Inquiry* 34 (2) (2008): 37.
45. Monson, 'Hearing, Seeing, and Perceptual Agency', 57.
46. Drexciya, *Grava 4*, 2xLP (Vinyl) (Netherlands: Clone, 2002).
47. Simon Zagorski-Thomas, 'The Spectromorphology of Recorded Music. The Shaping of Sonic Cartoons through Record Production', in *The Relentless*

Pursuit of Tone. Timbre in Popular Music, ed. Robert Fink, Zachary Wallmark, and Melinda Latour (New York, NY: Oxford University Press, 2018), 349.

48. Zagorski-Thomas, 'The Spectromorphology of Recorded Music', 56–57; Aphex Twin, *Come to Daddy*, 12" EP (Vinyl) (UK: Warp Records, 1997).
49. Rashad Becker, *Traditional Music of Notional Species, Vol. I*, LP (Vinyl) (Germany: PAN, 2013); Rashad Becker, *Traditional Music of Notional Species, Vol. II*, LP (Vinyl) (Germany: PAN, 2016).
50. Luke Windsor, 'A Perceptual Approach to the Description and Analysis of Acousmatic Music' (Doctoral Dissertation, London, City, University of London, 1995), 88–89.
51. Denis Smalley, 'Spectromorphology: Explaining Sound-Shapes', *Organised Sound* 2 (2) (1997): 107–26, https://doi.org/10.1017/S1355771897009059.
52. Smalley, 'Spectromorphology', 111–12.
53. Smalley, 'Spectromorphology', 112.
54. Gibson, *The Senses Considered As Perceptual Systems*, 303.
55. Eric F. Clarke, 'The Impact of Recording on Listening', *Twentieth-Century Music* 4 (1) (2007): 50, 68, https://doi.org/10.1017/S1478572207000527.
56. Clarke, 'The Impact of Recording on Listening', 68.
57. Kozak, 'Listeners' Bodies in Music Analysis', Section 6, Paragraph 1.
58. For an article that substantially develops this argument, see Maria Perevedentseva, 'Timbre and the "Zone of Entanglement" in Electronic Dance Music: Re-Thinking Musico-Sociol Ontologies with the Mycelial Turn', *Dancecult* 15 (1) (2023): 41–60. https://doi.org/10.12801/1947-5403.2023.15.01.03.
59. Paul C. Jasen, *Low End Theory: Bass, Bodies and the Materiality of Sonic Experience* (New York: Bloomsbury Academic, 2017), 179.
60. Jlin – *Carbon 7 (161)*, Music Video, 2017, https://youtu.be/cxPBqUh3kSU.
61. Digital Mystikz, *Haunted / Anti War Dub*, 12" (Vinyl) (UK: DMZ, 2006).
62. Marc Leman, 'Music, Gesture, and the Formation of Embodied Meaning', in *Musical Gestures: Sound, Movement, and Meaning*, ed. Rolf Inge Godøy and Marc Leman (London: Routledge, 2010), 147.
63. Mark Reybrouck, 'Musical Sense-Making and the Concept of Affordance: An Ecosemiotic and Experiential Approach', *Biosemiotics* 5 (3) (2012): 391.
64. Hillegonda C. Rietveld, 'Disco's Revenge: House Music's Nomadic Memory', *Dancecult Journal of Electronic Dance Music Culture* 2 (1) (2011): 4–23.
65. Joshua Bamford, Birgitta Burger, and Petri Toiviainen, 'Turning Heads on the Dance Floor: Synchrony and Social Interaction Using a Silent Disco Paradigm', *Music & Science* 6 (2023): 1–13, https://doi.org/10.1177/20592043231155416; Martin Clayton et al., 'Interpersonal Entrainment in Music Performance: Theory, Method, and Model', *Music Perception* 38 (2) (2020): 136–94, https://doi.org/10.1525/mp.2020.38.2.136; Patrick E. Savage et al., 'Music as a Coevolved System for Social Bonding', *Behavioral and Brain Sciences* 44 (2021), https://doi.org/10.1017/S0140525X20000333; Ragnhild

Torvanger Solberg and Alexander Refsum Jensenius, 'Group Behaviour and Interpersonal Synchronization to Electronic Dance Music', *Musicae Scientiae* 23 (1)(2019): 111–34, https://doi.org/10.1177/1029864917712345; Maria G. Witek, 'Feeling at One: Socio-Affective Distribution, Vibe, and Dance-Music Consciousness', in *Music and Consciousness 2: Worlds, Practices, Modalities*, ed. Ruth Herbert, David Clarke, and Eric Clarke (Oxford: Oxford University Press, 2019), 93–112.

66. Hans T. Zeiner-Henriksen, 'The Poum-Tchak Pattern. Correspondence Between Rhythm, Sound, and Movement in Electronic Dance Music' (Doctoral Dissertation, Oslo, Norway, University of Oslo, 2010), 63.

67. Vittorio Gallese, Morris N. Eagle, and Paolo Migone, 'Intentional Attunement: Mirror Neurons and the Neural Underpinnings of Interpersonal Relations', *Journal of the American Psychoanalytic Association* 55(1) (2007): 131–75, https://doi.org/10.1177/00030651070550010601; Marco Iacoboni, 'Imitation, Empathy, and Mirror Neurons', *Annual Review of Psychology* 60 (1) (2009): 653–70, https://doi.org/10.1146/annurev.psych.60.110707.163604; Katie Overy and Istvan Molnar-Szakacs, 'Being Together in Time: Musical Experience and the Mirror Neuron System', *Music Perception* 26 (5)(2009): 489–504, https://doi.org/10.1525/MP.2009.26.5.489.

68. Kai Tuuri and Tuomas Eerola, 'Formulating a Revised Taxonomy for Modes of Listening', *Journal of New Music Research* 41 (2)(2012): 142, https://doi.org/10.1080/09298215.2011.614951.

69. Eric F. Clarke, Tia DeNora, and Jonna Vuoskoski, 'Music, Empathy and Cultural Understanding', *Physics of Life Reviews* 15 (2015): 76–79, https://doi.org/10.1016/j.plrev.2015.09.001.

70. Witek, 'Feeling at One', 97.

71. Witek, 'Feeling at One', 99.

72. Gilles Deleuze and Félix Guattari, *A Thousand Plateaus. Capitalism and Schizophrenia*, trans. Brian Massumi (New York, NY: Bloomsbury Academic, 2013); Brian Massumi, 'The Autonomy of Affect', *Cultural Critique* 31 (1995): 83–109, https://doi.org/10.2307/1354446; Brian Massumi, *Parables for the Virtual: Movement, Affect, Sensation, Post-Contemporary Interventions* (Durham, NC: Duke University Press, 2002); Ruth Leys, 'The Turn to Affect: A Critique', *Critical Inquiry* 37 (3) (2011): 434–72, https://doi.org/10.1086/659353; Brian Kane, 'Sound Studies without Auditory Culture: A Critique of the Ontological Turn', *Sound Studies* 1 (1) (2015): 2–21, https://doi.org/10.1080/20551940.2015.1079063.

73. Deleuze and Guattari, *A Thousand Plateaus*, 559.

74. Massumi, 'The Autonomy of Affect'.

75. Fredric Jameson, *The Prison-House of Language: A Critical Account of Structuralism and Russian Formalism* (Princeton, NJ: Princeton University Press, 1972).

76. Gilbert and Pearson, *Discographies*; Jeremy Gilbert, 'Signifying Nothing: "Culture", "Discourse" and the Sociality of Affect', *Culture Machine* 6 (2004), https://culturemachine.net/deconstruction-is-in-cultural-studies/signifying-nothing/; Steve Goodman, 'Speed Tribes: Netwar, Affective Hacking and the Audio Social', in *Cultural Hacking: Kunst Des Strategischen Handelns*, ed. Thomas Düllo and Franz Liebl (Vienna: Springer, 2005), 139–55; Steve Goodman, *Sonic Warfare: Sound, Affect, and the Ecology of Fear* (Cambridge, MA: MIT, 2010); Rupa Huq, 'Raving, Not Drowning: Authenticity, Pleasure and Politics in the Electronic Dance Music Scene', in *Popular Music Studies*, ed. David Hesmondhalgh and Keith Negus (London: Arnold, 2002), 90–102; Tim Jordan, 'Collective Bodies: Raving and the Politics of Gilles Deleuze and Felix Guattari', *Body & Society* 1 (1)(1995): 125–44, https://doi.org/10.1177/1357034X95001001008.
77. Laibach quoted in S. Alexander. Reed, *Assimilate: A Critical History of Industrial Music* (New York, NY: Oxford University Press, 2013), 130.
78. Andrea Schiavio, Maria Witek, and Jan Stupacher (2023) 'Meaning-Making and Creativity in Musical Entrainment', *Frontiers in Psychology* 14: 2 (DOI: https://doi.org/10.3389/fpsyg.2023.1326773).

Further Reading

Clarke, Eric F., 'The Impact of Recording on Listening', *Twentieth-Century Music* 4 (1) (2007): 47–70.

Danielsen, Anne, Ragnhild Brøvig, Kjetil Klette Bøhler, Guilherme Schmidt Câmara, Mari Romarheim Haugen, Eirik Jacobsen, Mats S. Johansson et al., 'There's More to Timing than Time: Investigating Musical Microrhythm Across Disciplines and Cultures', *Music Perception* 41 (3) (2024): 176–98.

Godøy, Rolf Inge, and Marc Leman, eds., *Musical Gestures: Sound, Movement, and Meaning* (London: Routledge, 2010).

Schyff, Dylan van der, Andrea Schiavio, and David J. Elliott, *Musical Bodies, Musical Minds: Enactive Cognitive Science and the Meaning of Human Musicality* (Cambridge, MA: MIT Press, 2022).

Wallmark, Zachary, Marco Iacoboni, Choi Deblieck, and Roger A. Kendall, 'Embodied Listening and Timbre: Perceptual, Acoustical, and Neural Correlates', *Music Perception* 35 (3) (2018): 332–63.

13 | Pulse Trains

An Autoethnography of Techno Production in Berlin

NICOLAS BOUGAÏEFF

Introduction

With reference to examples from my techno productions, this chapter describes and analyses the experience I gained as a music producer during ten years in Berlin, the German capital that I moved to in order to immerse myself in its buoyant techno music scene. Involvement as an artist in the techno scene operates through many modalities: releasing records, performing DJ and live sets, collaborating with other artists, and developing an online presence. I strove to apply these with a particular focus on record production.[1] The focus of this chapter will be particularly on production processes in electronic dance music, particularly techno music, and as such aims to answer the following questions: What are the different stages of studio production and how do they operate? What techniques and mindsets can be effective to produce successful records within this specific genre? What rhythmic principles might underpin techno music?

Techno may be understood as an up-tempo genre of approximately 120 to 150 beats per minute (BPM) focused on repetitive, hypnotic groove layers that together constantly animate its sixteenths grid (sixteenth note rhythmic divisions), which is emphasised as what I term a 'pulse train', which plays out within a four-to-the-floor framework. Techno works by creating a tight relationship between rhythm, sound design, and mixdown. Although the four-to-the-floor groove is ubiquitous, a minority of tracks do have syncopated kick drum patterns. The tempo can depend on the artist and trend, and outlier trends or tracks can be found beyond this range. The timbres and arrangement can be stripped back and minimal, sophisticated and atmospheric, raw and distorted, or anywhere in between. Although short vocal samples or spoken word fragments occasionally appear, the instrumentation prioritises electronic sources, be they synthesised or sampled. The music is often focused on additive and gradual processes:[2] stacking and transforming loops, the latter often with different lengths resulting in polymetric structures. These processes are most often applied to rhythm and timbre rather than melody or harmony. Harmony is often static if not entirely absent. Tonal harmony is generally avoided, except for cases where influences from other subgenres, such as trance, for example, are incorporated. Parallel harmony is common, an example is a house music-influenced trope in which a single chord is chromatically transposed in quick sequence. Melody, sometimes entirely absent, sometimes modal, will often favour dissonant intervals and a relatively small pitch-class set. Techno offers a broad umbrella of subgenres that each focus on a narrow set of aesthetic codes. DJs who are focused on an underground vibe might typically prefer to create a seamless and hypnotic mix, whereas commercially oriented festival DJs might include tracks with vocals, dramatic build-ups, and drops. While the global techno scene has many niches, each with distinct aesthetics, for the purpose of this chapter I will consider the genre in a broad sense and describe production techniques in a way that can apply to minimal, industrial, melodic, dub, or other variants of techno.

The main research method that underpins the discussion is analytic autoethnography, an approach to research 'in which the researcher is (1) a full member in the research group or setting, (2) visible as such a member in published texts, and (3) committed to developing theoretical understandings of broader social phenomena'.[3] Following these guidelines, I describe how I became a member of a global techno scene with Berlin as focal point; I write in the first person to make myself visible and to show my presence in the setting; and finally, I draw links between my experience and techno music in general. I moved to Berlin in 2008 with the intention of becoming a professional techno artist. One of my first opportunities was developing controllers for Richie Hawtin's 'Plastikman Live Tour' and subsequently co-founding music technology company Liine with Hawtin and others, a project that took time away from music production but which helped me get more deeply involved in the scene. I released my first solo records on German techno label Trapez in 2013, started releasing records on NovaMute (and later Mute) in 2017, and played my first DJ gig in 2018 in Berlin's flagship club Berghain, a world-famous techno club situated in the cavernous and labyrinthine industrial building of a disused power plant.[4] Between these milestones, I released records on many other techno labels; toured in Europe; played a live audio/visual show with visual artist Itaru Yasuda at London nightclub Fabric; collaborated with more experienced music artists, such as Daniel Miller, Marcus C. Maichel, and Max Cooper; mentored younger Berlin-based artists Narciss and Shaleen; and exchanged remixes with international artists, including Nicole Moudaber and Chris Liebing.

The discussion will first establish my position within the techno scene and the existing research context of techno production. Three sections then follow, each with one of my tracks as its focus, respectively, 'Ellipse',[5] 'Pulse Train',[6] and 'Cognitive Resonance'.[7] The first section, 'Ellipse', discusses the value of collaboration with an established artist in the scene, as well as the importance of recognising idiomatic conventions of a genre. The second section, 'Pulse Train', discusses the importance of using embodied knowledge as part of the creative process once sufficient production techniques have been acquired and internalised. Embodied knowledge is my body's response to dance music, built through years of listening and dancing to techno music, which I can use as a gauging mechanism in the production process. Till calls this, in the context of songwriting, 'engaging with unconscious processes'.[8] A similar process occurs when I listen to my body for direction on a techno production. The third section, 'Cognitive Resonance', proposes a set of rhythmic principles that underlie the genre of techno.

Context

Techno music is a global phenomenon and Berlin is one of its focal points. The development of techno in Berlin in the 1980s and the early 1990s came about through a melting pot of musical influences and political circumstances. Early electronic influences included synthpop, EBM (electronic body music), and industrial bands such as New Order, Depeche Mode, Cabaret Voltaire, Suicide, Front 242, Skinny Puppy, and Ministry. A televised Kraftwerk concert from 1970, where they arguably played repetitive proto-techno, was attended by Dimitri Hegemann, who, after experimenting with various event formats in Berlin throughout the 1980s, including Atonal, as well as Fischbüro and its basement club UFO, would subsequently found Tresor club in 1991, dominated by forms of techno. Kraftwerk was also highly influential on the first wave of Detroit techno musicians, Juan Atkins, Derrick May, and Kevin Saunderson, who in turn inspired several generations of musicians in the USA and abroad.[9] Throughout the decade of the 1980s, house and techno records quickly made their way over from the US and UK, and West Berlin clubs like Turbine were soon focused on these emerging genres. Until the fall of the Berlin Wall at the end of 1989, East Berlin did not have a free DJ culture; rather, one needed state-sanctioned sound engineer qualifications for organising and playing at discos. Records from the West were difficult to obtain in the GDR.[10] The fall of the Berlin Wall accelerated electronic music cultural development during the 1990s. Acid house had a surge of popularity around this time, echoing the UK second summer of love. Disused spaces were soon used for illegal parties, many of these eventually becoming legitimate operations such as Tresor club. Techno quickly evolved, with harder and faster aesthetics eventually giving way to a contrasting minimal style, which was reduced and slower.[11] The 2000s were marked by electroclash, a short-lived but intense revival of 1980s aesthetics, as well as the massive popularity of minimal techno as epitomised by Minus label of Canadian expat Richie Hawtin (aka Plastikman). The 2010s saw a revival of 1990s aesthetics, with fast and harder sounds, often mixed with trance influences, becoming a leading trend by the early 2020s. While techno is 'a vast genre with a myriad of subgenres',[12] certain constants tend to remain, such as electronic sounds, an instrumental approach with few or no vocals, and that techno is music for dancing. To date, the influence of Berlin on the global techno scene has remained undisputed.

A number of studies exist about electronic dance music production. Butler provides a survey of rhythm, metre, and metric displacement.[13] Zeiner-Henriksen offers research on the morphology of bass drums in dance music.[14] Kühn provides an account of techno production from an ethnographic perspective.[15] A number of commercial publications, going back to the 1990s, provide insights on electronic music production techniques and the creative process, for example Snoman,[16] Brett,[17] and DeSantis.[18] Few academic studies are published specifically about techno production by established producers in the scene. Bergemann analyses techno groove production through the lens of his own vinyl releases in his PhD thesis.[19] Online platforms such as Aulart, Echio, Seedj, and Home of Sound currently offer, as of 2023, video content from active techno producers. While my own thesis focused on Richie Hawtin's Plastikman project, specifically the technical approach behind the 2010 live tour,[20] this chapter takes my own recordings as case studies of techno production.

Success for an artist within the techno scene can be related to 'scene-specific popularity capital'[21] and is dependent not only on the popularity of their tracks and DJ mixes, but also on the size of their following on social media, and the level of their integration in the scene. The latter can be measured through a range of modalities: releases on renowned labels; remixes for and by established artists; performances at significant venues and events; mixes published on recognised platforms; and interaction with peers and fans on social media. Richie Hawtin used a single word, 'traction',[22] to describe a successful application of these modalities.

Successful integration can generate what Thornton calls 'subcultural capital'[23] such as gaining recognition and a sense of belonging, which in turn can be leveraged for one's career. Gaining the recognition of respected peers can translate into new opportunities such as invitations for gigs, releases, and remixes. A sense of belonging can translate into effective new behaviours with colleagues, such as a comfortable, relaxed demeanour when interacting in written communications as well as in person in professional settings.

In 2012, five years after my first visit to Berlin, I did not feel I had reached my goal of gaining recognition as an electronic musician. In the frame of the aforementioned modalities, I was convinced that getting signed to established labels would help confirm my integration into the techno scene and would, by extension, provide recognition as a techno artist. However, despite producing electronic music since I was a teenager, I could not get signed to renowned labels, a position that may be familiar to many electronic musicians. In my case, beyond the usual challenge of producing tracks to a professional level and finding a supportive label, my creative output oscillated between producing tracks that fitted the genre of techno music, on the one hand, and seeking innovative composition techniques on the other hand. The boundaries between my roles as artist and researcher have been porous. The resultant inner conflict is a common challenge inherent to autoethnography, one I had to face because of my attempt to provide an account of techno production, to map rhythmic and stylistic principles of the genre while simultaneously putting these into practice as an artist in the scene. There is a tension between outsider and insider. I believed that successful integration also held broader value, that mastering a popular music genre, while not necessarily a commitment to pursue a career within a scene, was part of a comprehensive education as a composer and a necessary part of a professional skillset for a musician specialising in popular electronic music. Despite these challenges, my autoethnographic research approach ultimately proved successful. It granted me the opportunity to explain, from the unique perspective of first-hand experience in the Berlin scene, the technical detail of the various composition and production techniques behind a successful techno track. The following sections provide such understanding of three different tracks, 'Ellipse' (2013), 'Pulse Train' (2014), and 'Cognitive Resonance' (2017), presented in their chronological order of production. The emergence of rhythmic principles, including pulse trains and others, is documented as they appeared throughout the research.

Ellipse

In 2013, I collaborated with established artist Max Cooper on two tracks, 'Ellipse' and 'Fracture', on *Movements EP*, a digital and 12" vinyl record released on Traum Schallplaten.[24] The creative process, composition and production techniques, and stylistic distinctions behind the tracks will be discussed here, while reflecting on how collaboration can foster artistic development.

The first track, 'Ellipse', was initially created through a back-and-forth process where I sketched out a melody using Operator, a synthesiser plug-in included with Ableton Live. I was inspired by Mathew Jonson's approach to melody, such as on 'Marionette',[25] which often features implied polyphony,[26] a technique where a single instrument line creates the illusion of a polyphonic texture by quickly jumping between registers. The melody I created relied on this technique by introducing octave jumps independently of the pitch sequence. The pitch sequence is a short two-beat loop. Loops in techno tend to be short, very often two or four beats. Longer phrases are often created by repeating short loops with slight variations. I sent this initial material to Cooper, and he sketched out a track.

We met up at my Berlin home studio a few weeks later when he was in town for a performance, and we worked together on the track for a few hours. Our work consisted of creating and editing new materials, with little time spent on mixing. I noticed that sometimes when I proposed a new sound or pattern, Max remarked that it sounded perhaps too 'minimal' in the sense of mid-2000s minimal techno cliché. We did not establish a vocabulary to define what we were looking for. Rather, the palette of sounds was narrowed down through trial and error, and resolved to fitting with the melodic techno subgenre that Traum Schallplatten was pushing. Max was tightly associated with the label at the time. Other examples of melodic techno could include work by Swedish duo Minilogue, or Âme's classic 'Rej'.[27] Melodic techno is usually modal, somewhat melancholic or yearning, filled with light snappy percussions, and padded with deep drones to fill the bass and sub frequencies.

Back at his own studio in London, Cooper wrapped up the track by adding melodic details (occasional embellishments or transpositions inserted unpredictably in a long eight-bar cycle); audio micro-edits (often created with Ableton's Beat Repeat effects plug-in placed in series, various other effects, and manual edits of resampled audio); tightening up the mixdown (an important area of focus is usually on the balance of the kick drum (kick) and bass pattern, relative to each other and to the rest of the track); and sending over versions for my feedback.

The second track, 'Fracture', was created through a similar process although here I took more initiative, taking the 'Ellipse' project file as a starting point, initially keeping the instrument, effect, and mix settings intact, and making incremental changes. A major change was to switch from swing to straight groove. I varied the main riff by removing octave displacements and by shrinking intervals while conserving the melodic shape. These changes resulted in a melody with increased drive. I reduced the density of the drum patterns and reduced the amount of ornamental glitch sounds. I sketched out a structure for the track and sent my work over to Cooper. As with the first track, he once again made major contributions by creating new sounds, generating new glitches and micro-edits, and balancing the mix. Particularly attention was once again paid to the balance between kick and bassline.

The other tracks on the EP, 'Walls' and 'Meadows', were written solely by Max. The digital release also included three remixes. Of these, the label commissioned two and I approached my colleague NYMA for the third. I was not privy to the business details of the two remixes commissioned by the label. The NYMA remix was delivered for no fee as a personal favour. Remixes are often commissioned without paying a fee. The work is implicitly done as a favour, a remix exchange, for the intrinsic artistic value of participating in a record, in the hope of advancing one's career through the subcultural capital of being active in the scene, or a combination of the above.

The impact of *Movements EP* was immediate and resulted in a breakthrough, and a few months later I released my solo EP *Decompress EP*,[28] the first of three solo records that I would release were with Trapez, a renowned techno sub-label of Traum Schallplatten. Riley Reinhold, the owner of Traum and Trapez, became generally much more receptive to new music I sent his way. The demos I had sent in the past, up to five years earlier, had not elicited any response. The work I was delivering now intersected with Reinhold's interests for Trapez. He changed his perspective on my work, certainly because he now knew my name through my collaboration with Cooper but also because my approach to techno genre-based music production, through the collaboration, had considerably grown. I became more cognisant of stylistic details appropriate to minimal techno, more comfortable with incorporating its genre conventions, better aware of common tropes to consider avoiding, and more attentive to a highly detailed level of production quality.

'Pulse Train'

'Pulse Train'[29] appears on my second solo record on Trapez, titled *Pulsar Nite*. As a techno track it is relatively slow at 125 BPM, yet it maintains a driving four-to-the-floor groove with a solid kick sampled from a track by techno producer Johannes Heil, drums created with an MFB Tanzbär analog drum machine, and a short two-beat motoric bassline. Dreamy sustained chords slowly fade in and out throughout the track. I was inspired by Vangelis and sought a way to combine expressive synths with techno. The chords, inspired by movie soundtracks by Philip Glass and Jerry Goldsmith, rely on neo-Riemannian theory,[30] a technique that affords a rich palette of connected triads while avoiding cadences associated with tonal harmony.

Here I address the creative process of the recording, its composition techniques, the interplay behind creativity and industry success, and the emergence of a rhythmic principle within these activities. The creative process behind 'Pulse Train' began as an effort to embrace extra-musical inspirations and bodily engagement rather than composing with a predominantly intellectual or technical approach. Both the track and its title were inspired by an imaginary sensation of travelling through floaty and euphoric mental spaces. This sensation came to me in the studio a few minutes before the production session when I challenged myself to translate a feeling into music. I specifically chose this creative process as an attempt to distance myself from theoretical approaches. After taking a few moments to dwell within the imaginary scene, I created a small collection of musical elements, chose a duration and shape for the track, arranged the elements into a structure matching the duration and shape, and improvised a series of chords overtop. I worked quickly; the production process took about 45 minutes. I slept on it and took only a few hours to polish the mixdown the next morning.

The bassline (Figure 13.1) relies on modal ambiguity to avoid the sensation of a clear tonal centre. The melody, played on a TAL VST emulation of a Roland SH-101, generally outlines a G Dorian mode. The two accidentals, D♯ and B♮, emphasise major-minor ambiguity.

Fig. 13.1 'Pulse Train' bassline

Fig. 13.2 'Pulse Train' chords

The sustained chords (Figure 13.2), improvised on a Nord Lead 2 (a virtual analogue synthesiser), rely on chromatic modulations that play around the mode and ambiguities suggested by the bassline. The chords were specifically chosen to create feelings of otherworldliness, in combination with a synth timbre that slowly pulses in and out. The waves of sound, the crescendos and decrescendos, are created with a volume envelope and real-time manipulation of the Nord's low-pass filter.

'Pulse Train' can be recognised as techno by the tempo, the choice of electronic sounds, the driving four-to-the-four groove, and the emphasis on slight variations within repetitive patterns through the application of effects such as filter, reverb, and delay, as well as through the omission and reintroduction of elements. The track is structured with a stripped-back opening and ending to aid DJ mixing. Its sound is balanced in such a way to create equal loudness of the kick, bass, chords, and drums. I take into consideration loudness, the human ear's tendency to perceive different frequency bands more easily than others.[31] For example, high frequencies between 2,000 and 4,000 Hz are easily audible so it is important to make sure these are not too loud, otherwise the recording could be overbearing or painful to hear in a club environment. Conversely, frequencies below 200 Hz are harder to perceive, so they need to be relatively loud in the mix to feel equally balanced. Loudness is a phenomenon so important as to merit its own international standard[32] and its consideration applies for any dance club track, not only techno.

The positive response I received for the track during the months following its release influenced my creative process. It was released in June 2014, and Maceo Plex – an established international house and techno DJ – included 'Pulse Train' in a *Boiler Room* performance in October that same year.[33] Eric Estornel, the artist behind the Maceo

Plex pseudonym, invited me to produce new material for a release on his label Ellum. I wanted to find out how I could build on the success of this one track, and produced a handful of new recordings in which I applied a similar production style and composition techniques as I did for 'Pulse Train' and submitted these to Estornel. Although this did not lead to a long-term working relationship, one of the tracks I submitted, 'The Ecstasy of Gold', was eventually released four years later as part of an Ellum compilation.[34] Both tracks, 'Pulse Train' and 'The Ecstasy of Gold', remain in my top streamed tracks on Spotify, and 'Pulse Train' remains in the top 10 downloads for Trapez on Beatport. The 'Pulse Train' experience confirmed that I had interiorised the techno tropes of a solid four-to-the-floor groove; an atonal bassline in a short two beat loop; a careful balance of repetition and variation; and a structure amenable to easy mixing by a DJ. I combined a successful application of these techno tropes with some of my own compositional ideas in the chords. The experience with 'The Ecstasy of Gold' showed me that there is potential value, in terms of building on an initial success, in producing more tracks in a relatively narrow and focused style.

An important rhythmic principle, pulse trains, first emerged in embryonic form as the track's title 'Pulse Train'. I propose the use of the term 'pulse train' to describe the prominent articulation of a steady pulse, most commonly following the quarter notes, eighth notes, and sixteenth notes grid. In my track 'Pulse Train', the 4/4 kick articulates the quarter note pulse train, an open hi-hat articulates the eighths pulse train, and the bassline articulates the sixteenths pulse train. Each pulse train is twice as fast as the previous. Pulse trains are a rhythmic feature that seems quasi-omnipresent in techno music. In a vast majority of techno tracks, an uninterrupted stream of sixteenths is articulated either with a single sound or created as a composite between different elements.

Techno is music focused on materialising, beautifying, and groovifying pulse trains, especially the sixteenths grid. Microtiming, the short displacement of a sound relative to a perfect temporal grid, is an important technique for creating groove[35] which I subtly applied to each drum sound besides the kick. In the context of creating 'Pulse Train', despite the attention I gave to the harmonic materials, the underlying groove is an essential part of what makes the track work on the dance floor. The sustained chords work partly because they are supported and contrasted by rigidly quantised rhythmic elements: the rolling bassline, the hi-hats, the backbeat, and the 4/4 kick. All these elements, together or individually, articulate and emphasise the sixteenths grid. In other words, these elements materialise a pulse train.

Yet, pulse trains are so ubiquitous in techno and related forms of electronic dance music as to be unnoticed. It took years of production experience before I could point out their existence. Naming the track was a first step taken unaware of the significance, followed years later by explicitly naming the rhythmic concept. The correspondence between initial track title and later theoretical construct is not a coincidence. I found that analytical insight often appeared first in embryonic form in my production practice before later becoming clear as a music theory concept. In this case, the term 'pulse train' was on my mind years before I became aware of, and articulated, its importance as a rhythmic principle in techno. This process of practice preceding analysis was, in hindsight, a core aspect of my approach to analytic autoethnography. Such insights into rhythmic principles of techno are further explored in a discussion that follows on producing the track 'Cognitive Resonance'.

'Cognitive Resonance'

In 2017, I released the *Cognitive Resonance* 12-inch[36] that marked a significant leap forward in my techno production career. The three tracks on the EP were taken from my album *Principles of Newspeak*, where my creative process was focused across three intensive months on structural and aesthetic parameters. Inspired by harder approaches to techno, I began to use distortion more prominently. The discussion here focuses on creating the polyrhythms and the sound design that combine to give 'Cognitive Resonance' its powerful industrial sonic palette. Boomkat, a record shop specialising in electronic music, describes the track as 'a peak time steamroller with incessant alarm sounds wrapped around murderous kicks and swarming sound designs'.[37] I set out to explore rhythmical principles of techno through the eight tracks of *Principles of Newspeak*. The futuristic optimism of techno innovators seemed at odds with hyper-repetition[38] and the rigid conventions of genre producers. In the hope of gaining insight, I set the following constraint: each of the eight tracks would be in a different time signature based on an integer from one to eight. This experiment put basic rhythmic structures under a microscope, an approach that provided clarity and shed light on the following rhythmical principles of techno: a pulse train of sixteenths is articulated; a kick (drum) articulates 4/4 beats; groupings in powers of two predominate; polymetricity enables non-binary groupings. I was hoping that exploring these principles would help me better map out structural boundaries in techno and push beyond them in the future.

Rhythmic relationships of powers of two are simple because they merely halve or double the speed of a pulse train. This ratio is analogous to an octave, the simplest interval in the pitch domain. I quickly discovered that time signatures in one, two, four, and eight are very similar. To provide variety, one compositional solution is to keep some sounds at tempo and slow others down. Accordingly, the time signatures for title track 'Principles of Newspeak', 'Truthful Hyperbole', and 'Room 101' are respectively 1/2, 1/1, and 2/1; this allowed me to emphasise the tempo halving by including ever fewer kicks and focusing on sounds that articulate the quicker pulse train.

Rhythmic relationships of prime numbers beyond two are interesting because they yield, from the combination of a pair of loops, a complex pattern that resolves over a duration longer than either loop. You get more out of it than you put in. 'Cognitive Resonance' features a single-note synth riff in 7/16 over a 4/4 kick (Figure 13.3) thus creating a polymetric relationship as the synth and kick are in phase with each other after four notes and seven kicks. Furthermore, while both the synth and kick share the 16ths grid as a base unit, each instrument articulates a different pulse train and thus implies a different tempo.

Rhythmic independence could be inspired by the industrial spaces typical of techno clubs, where one can imagine various machines working simultaneously, each clacking, spinning, or grinding away at its own rhythm. The distortion and high-energy urgency of the sound design can suggest the propulsive energy of turbines in a power plant. After spending so much time in Berlin and Berghain, I was able to absorb the atmosphere of the industrial spaces, resonating these in the sound and rhythms of my techno productions.

The 2+2+2+1 closed hi-hat accent pattern supports the same part of the polymetric pattern as the synth, while the upbeat open hi-hat supports the

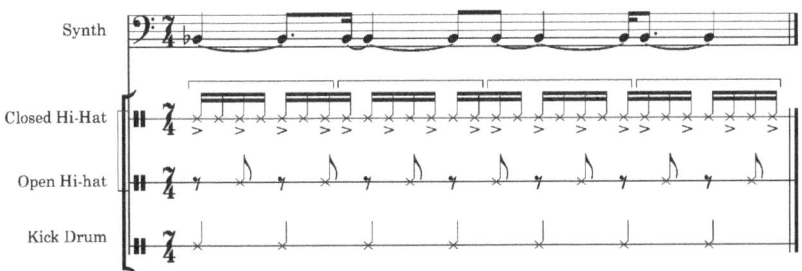

Fig. 13.3 'Cognitive Resonance' rhythmic structure

same part as the kick. Alluding to two different parts of a polymetric pattern within a single instrument, as demonstrated here with the hi-hats, is a powerful rhythmic technique akin to implied polyphony.

The structure of the track was created early in the process by asking myself a few key questions: how long will the track need to be, what arc will the track follow, and how many sections are necessary? The specifics of the answers do not matter, they can be arbitrary or follow artistic whim. Asking the questions helps to define a structure. Defining a draft structure, early in the creation process, can be effective. Following my answers, I sketched out a structure for 'Cognitive Resonance' in the Arrangement View of my digital audio workstation (DAW) production software, Ableton Live. I used dummy audio clips when I did not yet have a suitable sound. This process yielded a skeletal outline that I could use as a framework for the production phase. Another approach could focus first on fully producing and mixing a stack of loops, and then dragging out these loops to improvise a structure.

The production phase followed four steps: jam, edit, collage, refinement. The first step was focused on jamming. While the rhythms of *Principles of Newspeak* were carefully thought out, each sound began as improvisations in the hopes of capturing a techno feeling of immediacy. I created a large amount of material by recording improvisations a couple hours a day over a few days. In addition to Ableton Live, I used the equipment I had at that time: an Endorphin.es modular synthesiser, a Metasonix F-1 distortion pedal, as well as an Erica Synths Tube Delay and a Vermona reTubeVerb spring reverb unit, the latter two both on loan from a friend.

The next step of the production phase was focused on selecting and editing the sounds that match the industrial techno style I was listening to and aiming for. I spent two weeks editing the recordings of my improvisations down to a sound library (a collection of curated sounds) organised in loops, one-shots, and textures. The editing process followed five steps: 1) listen to the recordings until a sound jumps out at me; this was an exercise in aesthetic appraisal and trusting my emotional and bodily response, asking myself is this a ferociously exciting sound, how does it make me move?; 2) crop the sound into a loop, a one-shot, or a longer texture; 3) give the sound a relevant tag, for example 'blaring alarm' or 'metal pot', and copy the sound to the Ableton Live Session View; 4) delete the portion of the recording that I had so far auditioned and rejected, which was important to develop my decisiveness; 5) continue listening until the next sound caught my attention, or until the end of the recordings. During the editing step I would often get caught up in a sound and start further processing it. I embraced this process and recorded the newly generated material. These new recordings would themselves be subject to the same editing process described above.

The collage step of the production phase consisted of assembling the track by combining and developing various materials from the sound library I had created. The process for choosing sounds relied on my immediate emotional response, and if a sound or loop made me want to move or dance. In most cases I chose the first sound that caught my attention as I browsed the curated sound library. I already had an affinity for a particularly bright and insistent metallic one-shot stab created with a Furthrrrr Generator Eurorack synth module by Endorphin.es, a Buchla-style complex oscillator. Looping and processing this particular sound became the main element of 'Cognitive Resonance'. I was inspired by Rrose's track 'Waterfall',[39] where a short synth sample is looped and filtered throughout, a technique confirmed and described by the artist a few years later.[40] My aim was to apply a similar technique to the lead sound in my own track. I also chose a few short sounds, again from the library, to mark turnarounds at the end of sections. For example, the end of 16-bar phrases in 7/4 (112 beats) are marked by various loud and distorted banging and swooshing sounds (see the 'Vermona Rev' row in Figure 13.4). This has the effect of re-energising a groove by 'turning around' and giving dancers the feeling of a new beginning. Turnarounds are a standard feature of electronic dance music and they are particularly useful in a repetitive techno context. Between the low-end, the hi-hats, the lead, and the turn-arounds, all elements necessary to complete the track were now collected. A techno track can be effective with only a small number of sounds that are well produced and fitting together. Sound quality and appropriateness is ultimately appraised through emotional response and embodied knowledge: I note how the sounds and their combinations make me feel and make me move. I took a few moments to sketch out a structure by laying out the elements in sections of 16 bars (see Figure 13.4). While a structure could also be improvised, in this case the approach was more cerebral. I chose a simple and symmetrical structure with a long central break to redirect and focus the audience's attention on other musical parameters: rhythm and timbre.

The next step consisted of three types of audio refinement: spectral, corrective, and expressive. Audio refinement can apply to electronic music production in general, with the added considerations, in the context of electronic dance music and techno production, of club sound systems,

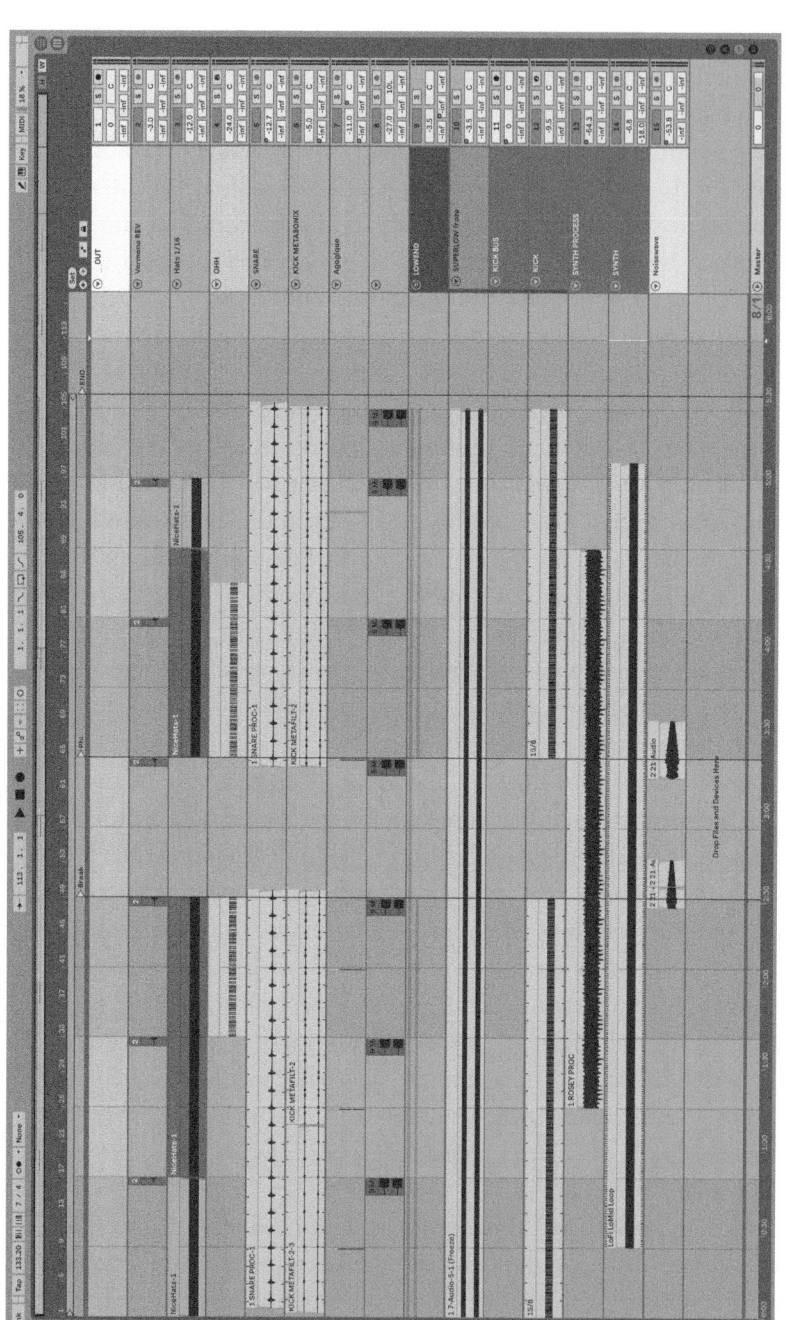

Fig. 13.4 'Cognitive Resonance' track structure

playback volume, and genre-specific stylistic conventions. The goal of spectral refinement is to both beautify a sound and make sure that it will remain pleasant at loud volume. Sounds with few prominent resonances seem to be more tolerable at loud volume than sounds with sharp resonances, and I grew to equate tolerability at loud volume with pleasantness. Through trial and error, relying on emotional response and embodied knowledge, I found that sounds with a flatter spectrum, tending towards equal power across the spectrum, seem generally more pleasant than sounds with distinctive resonances. Sonic pleasantness is all the more important to address when the palette is made of aggressive, whirring, thundering machine sounds. The technical steps taken through spectral refinement greatly contribute to achieving this type of colour, through EQ (equalisation) and various other tone shaping tools. The broad strokes of shaping the spectrum can be achieved with high- and low-pass filters. For example, sounds that do not contribute to the low-end frequencies typically do not need anything below 100 Hz, and the high frequencies of any sound can be reduced anywhere from 3 kHz to 12 kHz for a warmer sound. Finer transformations are achieved with static and dynamic peak EQs. I listen carefully to a sound and pay attention to which spectral components I deem important and which I deem obtrusive. This is a 'reduced listening' mode,[41] where I pay attention to different aspects of a sound in isolation. I trust my physical response to decide which components are obtrusive or important. In the case of the lead sound in 'Cognitive Resonance', a single note recorded with the Furthrrrr Generator, a sound generator that creates very rich tones, I spent most of my time scanning through the audio spectrum and considering the volume of individual harmonics. The workflow is as follows: I listen for resonances that are too loud, single tones in the harmonic spectrum that seem to stick out and call too much attention to themselves. I reduce loud resonances with a narrow peak EQ. I often use a dynamic EQ to apply the effect only when the resonance is loudest. I am careful to reduce the obtrusive harmonics by only the minimum amount necessary. Too much reduction itself brings a new, often unwanted, colour to the sound. Identifying obtrusive harmonics conversely helps identify other, more important, components of the spectrum which I might choose to gently emphasise with a broader EQ boost.

The goal of corrective refinements is to maximise the impact of the sound by adjusting various parameters which may include the duration in accordance to the groove, the dynamic profile of the sound for power and impact, stereo width for a feeling a fullness, where the audible spectrum is purposefully filled with energy. A full sound enhances impact and has a powerful and compelling effect on the dance floor, something I know from my own experience dancing and listening, and that I can assess in the studio through my own response. A fuller sound feels good; it works well on the dance floor. These adjustments, such as trimming, transient shaping, compression (or expansion), limiting, loop crossfading, stereo widening (or narrowing), are applied as necessary rather than as matter of course. I usually made a point of committing to each refinement decision by recording a sound and all its real-time transformations – whether the result of fades, edits, or plug-ins – to a new audio file ('bouncing the sound') after each step and, again, removing previous iterations from the project. This prevented me from second-guessing previous decisions and helped me to move forward.

Expressive refinements act as phrasing, they consist of transformations to a sound over time. They are particularly effective when the initial sound is free of blemishes. Further processing tends to magnify any unwanted components of a sound, hence the usefulness of the preceding refinement steps. Expressive refinements are often called automation because the process in a digital audio workstation (DAW) typically consists of automating changes in effect plug-ins. Expressive refinements can be meticulously programmed as DAW automation, or they can be performed live. In the case of 'Cognitive Resonance', they were created by performing and recording transformations in real time with software and hardware effects. I played back the looping one-shot from the DAW, Ableton Live. A MIDI controller was mapped to the filter and resonance of a low-pass filter. The sound was then sent to a Return channel, itself going out to an individual hardware output distinct from the main output. The signal could now be sent through the hardware effect units, before going back into the computer to be monitored from within Ableton Live. This allowed me to create feedback by sending the monitored signal back to the Return channel. A common issue with this approach is that monitoring sound in real time through software creates latency. I found that the latency added a short delay, a microrhythm, as an additional effect in the chain, which I experienced as very pleasant. I could appraise the effectiveness of this microrhythm on the groove by my bodily response, giving a sense of increased drive and entrainment. I inserted additional effects on this delayed sound, mapped these effects to the MIDI controller, and further expressively shaped this additional trailing delay. The combination of software and hardware controls allowed me to perform a swell of effects that slowly developed around the original sound.

I produced *Principles of Newspeak*, including its second track, 'Cognitive Resonance', during the first three months of 2017. Shortly after its completion, I sent the album to Daniel Miller, founder of Mute Records. I was already in contact with Miller through my previous involvement, years earlier, in music technology venture Liine. At the time, he had on occasion invited me and colleagues to send him music for his DJ sets. I eventually took him up on the invitation and sent him my productions once or twice a year. 'Cognitive Resonance' elicited a positive response from Miller and he proposed to release a three-track 12-inch EP on NovaMute, effectively relaunching the Mute sub-label following a decade-long pause.[42] A limited number of white-label vinyl copies[43] were manufactured and sold exclusively through Hard Wax, a renowned Berlin record shop. The 'Cognitive Resonance' release on NovaMute directly led to a first Berghain gig as the track both significantly raised my profile and fits the austere and cavernous techno aesthetics the venue is known for. Berghain offered me an opening slot, midnight to four a.m., during a Klubnacht in 2018. Klubnacht is the main Berghain event, every week from Saturday 23:59 to Monday mid-morning. This performance opportunity was enabled by a confluence of circumstances: the release of 'Cognitive Resonance', its inclusion in performances by high-profile techno DJs, including Chris Liebing[44] and long-time Berghain resident Boris, and the buzz around the relaunch of NovaMute. More opportunities across Europe followed the Berghain gig. Sustaining this influx of gigs necessitated releasing more records, releasing mixes, and preparing new performances, typical activities for a professional electronic dance music producer.

Conclusions

Through a discussion of three case studies of techno production processes, this chapter has aimed to give an insight into techniques and creative processes that are involved, through which stylistic characteristics of techno music could be identified, in terms of rhythm and timbre. The discussion of the collaborative recording of 'Ellipse' shows that stylistic distinctions, in this case between minimal techno and melodic techno, are as important as they can be subtle. Distinctions between minimal techno and melodic techno, in this case foregoing bongo sounds typical of late 2000s minimal in favour of synth melody ornaments, were determined through discussions and choices made as part of a collaborative production process. Collaboration can also foster artistic development and open doors to new professional opportunities.

The analysis of the production of 'Pulse Train' gave the insights into how embodied knowledge, gained through listening and dancing, is a significant component in the creative process of producing techno, in particular regarding techno's rhythmical principles. Having already interiorised production techniques and immersed myself in techno scene-specific aesthetic codes, I could shift from a cerebral to a more emotional or embodied approach. The concept of a 'pulse train' emerged as an important insight into a rhythmic principle to describe the prominent articulation of a steady pulse in techno music. Finally, 'Cognitive Resonance' enabled a discussion of how rhythmic complexities can be produced. It also gave insight into how a new sonic palette may be produced within the constraints of the techno genre. Several rhythmical principles that I observed during my experience as a producer in Berlin hold true for how I create a techno track: a pulse train of sixteenths is prominently articulated; a kick articulates beats; groupings in powers of two predominate; polymetricity enables non-binary groupings. Pulse trains are central to techno music and polymetric groupings of prime numbers create rich relationships within a pulse train.

Three insights emerged from the comparative analysis: pulse trains as central rhythmic structure of techno music; interiorising production techniques and immersing oneself in scene-specific aesthetic codes are essential components of the learning process; and embodied knowledge, gained through listening and dancing, is a significant component of an effective creative process for producing techno. Overall, the discussion shows the importance of aesthetic decision-making: interiorising production techniques, cultivating a sensitivity to scene-specific aesthetic codes and sonic signatures, and drawing on embodied knowledge acquired through listening and dancing. This approach may apply more generally within electronic dance music and enable one to add a distinct and personal aesthetic[45] to a track while sufficiently acknowledging the aesthetics of a specific dance music scene.

Notes

1. See, for example, my discography here: www.discogs.com/artist/3234510-Nicolas-Bouga%C3%AFeff.
2. Steve Reich, *Writings on Music, 1965–2000* (New York: Oxford University Press, 2002).

3. Leon Anderson, 'Analytic Autoethnography', *Journal of Contemporary Ethnography* 35 (4) (1 August 2006): 373–95.
4. Mats Wurnell (6 October 2016). The Berghain Backstory: Building Berlin's Most Legendary Nightclub. *Medium*. https://medium.com/cuepoint/the-berghain-backstory-building-berlins-most-legendary-nightclub-87ad2d901ee9.
5. Max Cooper and Nicolas Bougaïeff, *Movements EP*, Vinyl 12" 33 1/3 RPM, Digital Audio, TRAUM V162 (Germany: Traum Schallplatten, 2013), https://open.spotify.com/album/1lhb2dVezO7JIeaojcdSQF?si=02HRvOK1R02Rh0nena9F7w.
6. Nicolas Bougaïeff, *Pulsar Nite*, Digital Audio, TRAPEZ 155 (Germany: Trapez, 2014), https://open.spotify.com/track/2h34pP7c8258reGzpbUr5M?si=92333d6714d24516.
7. Nicolas Bougaïeff, *Cognitive Resonance*, Vinyl 12" 33 1/3 RPM, Digital Audio, 12NOMU179 (UK: NovaMute, 2017), https://open.spotify.com/track/3gUyLZUXeXFXWgYMIbooNw?si=20a61ae5cfa74639.
8. Rupert Till, 'Singer-Songwriter Authenticity, the Unconscious and Emotions (Feat. Adele's "Someone Like You")', in *The Cambridge Companion to the Singer-Songwriter*, ed. Katherine Williams and Justin A. Williams (Cambridge: Cambridge University Press, 2016), 291–304.
9. Dan Sicko, *Techno Rebels: The Renegades of Electronic Funk* (Detroit: Wayne State University Press, 2010).
10. Felix Denk and Sven von Thülen, *Der Klang Der Familie: Berlin, Techno and the Fall of the Wall* (Berlin: BoD – Books on Demand, 2014).
11. Sean Nye, 'Minimal Understandings: The Berlin Decade, The Minimal Continuum, and Debates on the Legacy of German Techno: Minimal Understandings', *Journal of Popular Music Studies* 25 (2)(June 2013): 154–84.
12. Suade Bergemann, 'Composition Portfolio : Producing Techno Grooves' (Doctoral Thesis, Newcastle University, 2011), http://theses.ncl.ac.uk/jspui/handle/10443/1283.
13. Mark Jonathan Butler, *Unlocking the Groove: Rhythm, Meter, and Musical Design in Electronic Dance Music* (Bloomington: Indiana University Press, 2006).
14. Hans T. Zeiner-Henriksen, 'Moved by the Groove: Bass Drum Sounds and Body Movements in Electronic Dance Music', in *Musical Rhythm in the Age of Digital Reproduction*, ed. Anne Danielsen (Routledge, 2010), 121–40.
15. Jan-Michael Kühn, 'Focused Ethnography as Research Method: A Case Study of Techno Music Producers in Home-Recording Studios', *Dancecult: Journal of Electronic Dance Music Culture* 5 (1) (2013): 1–16.
16. Rick Snoman, *Dance Music Manual* (New York: Routledge, 2019).
17. Thomas Brett, *The Creative Electronic Music Producer* (New York: CRC Press, 2021).

18. Dennis DeSantis, *Making Music: 74 Creative Strategies for Electronic Music Producers* (Berlin: Ableton, 2015).
19. Bergemann, 'Composition Portfolio'.
20. Nicolas Bougaïeff, 'An Approach to Composition Based on a Minimal Techno Case Study' (Doctoral Thesis, University of Huddersfield, 2013).
21. Kühn, 'Focused Ethnography as Research Method'.
22. Richie Hawtin, Conversation with the author, 2015.
23. Sarah Thornton, *Club Cultures: Music, Media, and Subcultural Capital* (Cambridge: Polity, 1996).
24. Cooper and Bougaïeff, *Movements EP*.
25. Mathew Jonson, *Marionette*, Digital Audio, WAG002 (Wagon Repair, 2005), https://open.spotify.com/track/0LG0XwV3KdCgHsGrqN1u4u?si=b54f10a76ab54817.
26. Stacey Davis, 'Implied Polyphony in the Solo String Works of J. S. Bach: A Case for the Perceptual Relevance of Structural Expression', *Music Perception: An Interdisciplinary Journal* 23 (5)(2006): 423–46.
27. Âme, 'Rej', Digital Audio, INNERVISIONS02 (Germany: Innervisions, 2005), https://open.spotify.com/track/5l3TZLe5uEk7vdXbHghZZW?si=62dab6cb744f4850.
28. Nicolas Bougaïeff, *Decompress EP*, Digital Audio, TRAPEZ 148 (Germany: Trapez, 2013).
29. Nicolas Bougaïeff, 'Pulse Train', Digital Audio, TRAPEZ 155 (Germany: Trapez, 2014), https://open.spotify.com/track/2h34pP7c8258reGzpbUr5M?si=b216bf0fc1364ff6.
30. Richard Cohn, 'Introduction to Neo-Riemannian Theory: A Survey and a Historical Perspective', *Journal of Music Theory* (1998): 167–80.
31. Harvey Fletcher and Wilden A. Munson, 'Loudness, Its Definition, Measurement and Calculation', *Bell System Technical Journal* 12 (4) (1933): 377–430.
32. International Organization for Standardization, 'ISO 226:2023', ISO www.iso.org/standard/83117.html.
33. Maceo Plex Boiler Room Berlin DJ Set, 2014, https://www.youtube.com/watch?v=5vHRUsP20dQ.
34. Coccolino Deep, Nicolas Bougaïeff, and Gauthier DM, *Asteroid Matter, Vol 1*, Digital Audio, ELL044D (Ellum Audio, 2018).
35. For further reading on microtiming, see the many outputs of the RITMO Centre for Interdisciplinary Studies in Rhythm, Time and Motion: www.uio.no/ritmo/english/.
36. Nicolas Bougaïeff, 'Cognitive Resonance', UK: NovaMute, 12NOMU179. 2017.
37. Nicolas Bougaïeff, 'Cognitive Resonance', Boomkat https://boomkat.com/products/cognitive-resonance.

38. Bougaïeff, 'An Approach to Composition Based on a Minimal Techno Case Study'.
39. Rrose, Merchant of Salt, Vinyl 12" 33 1/3 RPM, Digital Audio, SD19 (Sandwell District, 2011).
40. Mark Smith, 'The Art Of Production: Rrose · Feature / RA', *Resident Advisor*, 10 March 2020, https://ra.co/features/3619.
41. Michel Chion, *Guide to Sound Objects. Pierre Schaeffer and Musical Research*, Trans. John Dack and Christine North, 1983, http://ears.pierrecouprie.fr/spip.php?article3597.
42. Editor, 'Artist To Artist: Nicolas Bougaïeff & Daniel Miller', Ransom Note, 1 October 2017, www.theransomnote.com/music/interviews/artist-to-artist-nicolas-bougaieff-daniel-miller/.
43. Vincent Jenewein, 'White Label', *Journal of Popular Music Studies* 33 (3) (1 September 2021): 78–80.
44. Chris Liebing is an internationally known German techno DJ active since the early 1990s.
45. Jan-Michael Kühn, 'Working in the Berlin Techno Scene: Theoretical Sketch of an Electronic Music "Scene Economy"', *Journal Der Jugendkulturen* (2011), 9.

Further Reading

Butler, Mark J. (2006) *Unlocking the Groove: Rhythm, Meter, and Musical Design in Electronic Dance Music*. Bloomington, IN: Indiana University Press.

Brøvig, Ragnhild & Danielsen, Anne (2016) *Digital Signatures: The Impact of Digitization on Popular Music Sound*. Cambridge, MA: MIT Press.

D'Errico, Mike (2022) *Push. Software Design and the Cultural Politics of Music Production*. New York: Oxford University Press.

Danielsen, Anne (ed.) (2010) *Musical Rhythm in the Age of Digital Reproduction*. London: Routledge.

Strachan, Robert (2017) *Sonic Technologies. Popular Music, Digital Culture and the Creative Process*. London: Bloomsbury Academic.

14 | EDM's Secret Technologies

ROBERT FINK

'How Many Articles Are There about DJ Pierre?' (The Secrets of Black Technology)

It is no exaggeration to claim that the appropriation of Black creativity has driven the commercial music industry, especially in the development of electronic dance music.[1] While some tributaries flow through Europe, the mainstream of dance music can be firmly linked to the Black Atlantic,[2] from its polyrhythms through the Afro-diasporic innovations of rhythm & blues, funk, disco, garage, house, techno, jungle, UK garage, and dubstep *seriatim* to whatever dance floor innovation galvanises the club scene on the day you read this. While the electronic aspect of EDM, its distinctive relation to audio and computer technology, may seem an exception, a coherent discourse based in Afro-futurism sees Black appropriation of technologies usually coded 'white' as itself creative, a form of bricolage that repurposes obsolete or deprecated technologies through transformative misuse.[3]

This much is uncontroversial. Yet, music history struggles when attempting to seek out detailed traces of what Erik Davis calls the 'Black Electronic'[4] in the documentary record: one generally can discover much more about white *re*-appropriations of Black technological appropriations than about those original generative moments of creative misuse. Some of this is the discursive racism and heterosexism that DJ-producer Moby, an unwilling beneficiary, called out in 1995, as the cultural framework around EDM was just coming into focus:

> Homophobia and racism. Yeah, if you look at house culture, which was basically ignored for a long time, it was only when white kids started making house music that journalists could start taking it seriously. There are lots of articles about Aphex Twin and Orbital, because they're all white guys you can understand. But how many articles are there about DJ Pierre?[5]

The survey in this chapter will also have more to say about Orbital than DJ Pierre: have I fallen prey to the same myopia? Maybe – although I have tried to give both their proper respect in what follows. However, I will also take seriously the counterclaim registered by South African journalist and DJ Julian Jonker that the distinctive sonic power conjured up through the systematic abuse of electronics in the Black Atlantic diaspora was (and remains) a Black technology *meant to be kept secret*:

Black secret technology is taking white technology apart and not putting it back together properly. Black secret technology is discovering the mis-uses of the Roland TB-303, a machine originally intended to help rock guitarists practice over synthesized basslines, but tweaked in order to create acid house and all its subsequent variations. Black secret technology is the manifestation of what William Gibson famously predicted: the street finds its own use for things.[6]

Thus a hint of privilege inheres in Moby's well-intentioned request that journalists pay less attention to him and more to dance music's Black innovators, as if a 'mad scientist' like DJ Pierre would happily give away all his lab secrets to the first white person with a notebook who asked nicely.

It seems that nobody in the *Social Text* symposium where Moby spoke out was yet aware that a perspicacious Dutch observer of sonic culture, Hillegonda Rietveld, had already interviewed Pierre Jones three years earlier, along with Larry Sherman and Earl 'Spanky' Smith Jr., his collaborators in the pioneering Chicago house collective Phuture, regarding their genre-defining recording 'Acid Tracks'.[7] Rietveld noted Smith's account of telling Jones about 'something crazy' coming from his second-hand Roland TB-303 Bass Line synthesiser: 'I called him on the phone to come and listen to it, and he got to it and he started turning the knobs changing my frequency [settings of the EQ] on it, and that's what it started from . . . . But the funny thing is when the batteries ran out the same exact *acid* was coming back in.'[8] It's a good story, as far as it goes – but as the key to the secrets of a powerful Black technology, it feels inadequate.

I offer a deeper dive into the intricacies of the 303's nested control surfaces below. Smith recalled his friend DJ Pierre messing around with multiple knobs and effecting a 'change of frequency', which may seem as though he was referring to some kind of parametric EQ requiring multiple settings to function. But the TB-303, built around a monophonic analogue synthesiser, neither had nor needed a full-blown equalisation circuit.[9] Smith didn't specify that changing 'frequency' really meant turning two controllers, the RESONANCE knob in combination with the CUT OFF FREQ knob. The latter is the second in a row of six near the top edge of the device in what Roland called the 'tone control section'.[10] As its name implies, the cutoff freq(uency) knob applies a low pass filter to the 303's single oscillator; Roland suggested starting at twelve o'clock and turning the pot gradually counter-clockwise to 'shave off the upper harmonics of the sound, making the tone softer and reducing the volume'.[11] Jones' secret was to *do the opposite:* he twisted the cutoff pot all the way to the right – something you were not expected to do – giving the maximum possible boost to upper harmonics and making the 303's tone louder and more strident. Smith didn't mention this, but the treble could be sharpened even more by turning the next knob hard right as well, maximising the RESONANCE of the filter circuit itself.

In 1992, it seems Smith wanted outsiders to believe that there was something uncanny about this harsh acid sound. How else could it survive, a veritable ghost in the machine, even after the batteries died and all other settings were lost? The explanation for this 'mystery' is so simple that one is tempted to assume self-protective mystification on his part. Pitch and rhythm patterns input into the TB-303's built-in sequencer were stored in RAM, and thus disappeared like any other computer data when the power was cut off.[12] The tone control section, on the other hand, used old-fashioned rotary potentiometers whose physical position encoded the filter settings for the acid house sound – and a potentiometer at rest tends to remain at rest, until somebody sets it in motion.[13]

As elder statesmen of house, Smith and Jones are now happy to recount the legend of the TB-303 and the acid sound to anyone who asks. The story has become a myth, and has been, for better or worse, mixed up in their minds with deeply held stereotypes of Black spontaneity and creativity. Speaking to *DJ Mag* in 2014, DJ Pierre recalled the primal knob-twisting scene not as secret experimentation with technology, but as a spontaneous hour-long 'jam session', and once *that* discursive door was opened, some very familiar cliches of jazz appreciation could rush in: 'We knew there was nothing out there like what we were coming up with, and we knew what it did for us on the inside. We knew that there was something there that spoke. We all knew, man. It was natural and pure.'[14] The squelchy high-resonance filter sweeps of acid house may have signified many things in their time, but 'natural and pure' was surely not one of them. Observers of Black culture have come to recognise this defensive use of language – a way to keep one's secrets while telling (white) people what they want to hear – as its own kind of linguistic technology, often called 'signifying' in the Black vernacular.[15] Signifying, whether self-conscious or intuitive, allows African-American music makers to talk openly about Black technology while keeping its secrets safe.

It's usually the white kids who spill the beans. So that's who we have to talk about.

'Exactly what the 303 was Intended for, and Exactly the Wrong Use of It.' (Roland TB-303)

Nobody has been asked more about their relationship to secret technologies than the Hartnoll brothers of Sevenoaks, Kent. As Orbital, they helped bring the sound of acid house to the top of the UK pop charts with their 1990 breakthrough hit 'Chime'.[16] After the track became famous, a picture was staged of Phil and Paul leaning over the closet space under the living room stairs in their family home, where Paul had built a small, constantly shifting collection of second-hand electronics over the previous twelve months.[17] Hartnoll, an impecunious and aspiring producer still in his first course at art school, was trying to approximate what he thought was the most exciting sound in dance music, one accessible even on a strict budget: both Chicago-style acid house and Detroit techno were dominated by the raw sound of the previous generation of low-fi samplers and synths run directly into an inexpensive four-track cassette tape recorder, with no money wasted on studio mixing or fancy effects.[18]

Only two of the devices in Hartnoll's signal chain would have been considered 'professional-level' gear in 1989: an insurance settlement had just allowed him to buy a two-year-old Akai S700, a 12-bit digital sampler with integrated sequencing; and he also had a relatively up-to-date standalone eight-track sequencer from Alesis, the MMT8. But the backbone of his set-up was obsolete hardware from the early 1980s: Roland's TR-909 Rhythm Composer, a hybrid digital-analogue drum machine; and the even older, fully analogue TB-303.

Hartnoll knew what he was getting with the 909 and the 303, as these were the sonic staples of acid house. He could afford them because few British musicians had made the connection between the 'acid' sounds on 12-inch records from Detroit and Chicago and the actual Roland hardware used to make them. The typical British owner of a TB-303, had, like the semi-pro keyboard player who eventually sold his to the Hartnolls for £100, been using it to provide automated basslines for contemporary UK pop hits:

'He'd programmed the whole bass-line arrangement of West End Girls by the Pet Shop Boys', explains Hartnoll. 'This is exactly what the 303 was intended for, and exactly the wrong use of it. My brother had to stand there and listen to it knowing full well we were going to use it to make acid house.'[19]

Let's spare a moment of respect for this anonymous journeyman slaving away at the 303's notoriously terrible user interface in the manner its designers intended. The founder of the Roland Corporation, Ikutaro Kakehashi, was a self-taught engineer with no formal musical training who imprinted on his employees the goal of creating simple, inexpensive electronic musical instruments that anyone could play.[20] The first generation of integrated microprocessors, into whose limited memory dozens of musical patterns could be programmed and then recalled at the touch of a button, was immediately pressed into the service of this noble ideal. But Roland's engineers consistently overestimated the ability and desire of musicians to learn the complex, non-intuitive data-input protocols required to interact with their first generation of 'computer-controlled' electronic instruments.

The difficulties inherent in talking musically to the primitive pattern sequencer of the TB-303 can be traced to a form of parametric thinking native to 1970s computer circuit design. Faced with the technical problem of storing a musical pattern efficiently in very limited memory – the TB-303's three UPD444 1024 x 4-bit RAM chips gave it a scant 3KB of digital storage, barely enough to store an ASCII character representation of the page you are currently reading – Roland's engineers proceeded algorithmically, parsing the information to be stored not note by note, the way humans do, but parameter by parameter. Pitch information was stored in one data structure, durations in another, accents and slides in a third, and so on.[21] Doing it this way allowed for some elegant programming tricks. Having successfully (in Roland-speak) 'memorised' a musical pattern, a user could, in theory, build up the bassline for a complete song using a simple recursive algorithm: COPY the opening pattern to a new memory location; SWAP out the pitch data; LEAVE the other parameters untouched; CONCATENATE and REPEAT. This procedure could be executed up to 64 times before the 303 ran out of memory, and the device could be programmed to play the stored patterns back in any order.

In practice, it was devilishly hard to get musical ideas into that little silver box. Perhaps the most deceptive aspect of Roland's interface for the 303 was the miniature keyboard represented on its button-littered top surface.[22] This is not a keyboard you can 'play' in any meaningful sense, because the interface is relentlessly *modal*: most of its buttons, even those that look like piano keys, have two or even three functions which depend on a series of nested decisions, registered by twisting knobs or pressing other buttons, about the 'mode' the device is in.

Its cluttered modal interface and parametric data-entry process makes programming 'normal' music into the TB-303 totally counter-intuitive. According to the 303's fifty-page (!) owner's manual, after putting the device into 'pattern write' mode (twist knob), choosing a memory location (twist knob and press two buttons, one of which will be amongst the white keys on the virtual keyboard), and activating the nested sub-mode for writing pitch (press button), you are ready to start entering a musical pattern on the 303's default 16-beat grid. But in pitch writing mode, you can *only* enter pitch information, which means you must choose from the pitch buttons on the virtual keyboard exactly sixteen times, *no matter how many actual notes are in the pattern*. Repeatedly tapping the 'write' button will allow you to review this sequence of pitch data. Press another button to shift into 'time' mode, and you can now add durations. Each of the sixteen pitches you just entered must individually be set either not to sound (this is how you write a rest), to sound with an attack (a note), or to sound without an attack (a tie), and in this mode, you must remember to tap the 'write' button to advance to the next pitch in the pattern after each three-way choice. The 'write' button also has a *third* modal function, which is to allow you to add information about articulation; if you return to pitch mode and hold the 'write' button down rather than just tap it, you can add accents (using the button that in time mode was used to turn a note off) and note-to-note slides. It should go without saying that this is not the way musicians think. After all, who imagines a semibreve as the result of sixteen separate decisions not to stop or retrigger it? Roland's manual concedes the point by recommending that users transcribe basslines into a written representation of the TB-303's internal data structure (a series of circles and dashes called a 'writing table') before even trying to program them.[23]

It also goes without saying – because Hartnoll himself said it in print, repeatedly – that the bass parts in 'Chime' were never going to be programmed in this labour-intensive way, because he wasn't using the 303 to play bass at all. The bassline of 'Chime' came from Hartnoll's Yamaha DX100, a cheap but effective digital synth which had a physical keyboard for easy note entry and whose default patch was a chunky 'analogue bass' sound. For the first draft of 'Chime', a four-minute version recorded direct to the six inputs of a Yamaha four-track, Hartnoll played bass notes on the DX100 under cascades of pitched-up piano triads from the Akai sampler, while the TR-909 and HR16 drum machines running on their own internal sequencers contributed short percussion loops. Once it was clear the track had promise, Hartnoll remixed and extended it to twelve minutes and re-recorded the whole thing, turning over responsibility for the drums, bassline, and sampled chord riffs to the MMT8 sequencer so that he could 'jam' over them. As the sequenced tracks spooled out onto tape, Hartnoll moved back and forth between the TR-909 and the TB-303, one right behind the other in his closet,[24] using the 909's internal mixer to switch parts of the drum groove on and off while twisting knobs and pressing buttons to coax elegant, burbling patterns of real-time figuration from the 303.

Our long detour through the TB-303 owner's manual – which one can imagine was carefully handed over by its previous owner only to be tossed aside by the Hartnolls as useless – is necessary to understand how brazenly acid house pioneers like Phuture and Orbital disregarded the key assumption Roland's engineers had made about how their bassline synthesiser would be used. These users were not at all concerned with mastering the elaborate process of using the memory banks to store coordinated patterns of pitch, duration, accent, and articulation to be played back as musical 'phrases'. They were going to use the 303 for a style of electronic dance music that had little to do with the Roland Corporation's initial dream of affordable, traditional music-making for the masses. Phuture and Orbital were going for something much more disruptive and innovative.

As Rietveld established early on, the 303-based 'acid' sound was made possible within a mostly African-American and sexually explorative, underground house scene that enabled producers like DJ Pierre to introduce a new sonic palette. Yet, the Hartnolls are an example of the first generation of British rave artists to figure out how to appropriate and deploy it with a degree of technical authenticity. Acid was a subset of the stripped-down style of Chicago house associated with the queer club dance called 'jacking', a hard, physical set of movements that involved slamming the upper body forward and down violently to the beat while jack-knifing at the waist so that the pelvis moved back and forth in the same rhythm. Plenty of late 80s 'jack tracks' employed nothing but a pair of MIDI-coupled 808 and 909 drum machines played live to tape – no chords, no vocals, no distractions, just disciplined submission to a four-on-the-floor beat.[25]

Jack became 'acid' when you added the textures of a melodic 303 to the mix. Early adopters in the Chicago dance music scene never used the TB-303 for basslines; there was already enough low-range content in the analogue kicks they sequenced from their 808s and 909s. House music producers took advantage of the fact that the 303 was not designed to be used as a deep bass instrument: its default frequency range was 130–260 Hz, already at the top of the 'bass' range, and by using the octave transpose button and tuning knob, they could push its output squarely into the middle of the audio spectrum, where the synth's tone-shaping controls, designed by Roland to approximate the sound of an acoustic upright bass or an electric bass guitar, could work their wonky magic.[26] As Phuture's Earl

Smith didn't precisely reveal above, with the cut-off frequency and resonance knobs turned all the way up, the 303's cheap and cheerful low-pass ladder filter emphasised a mess of harmonic overtones several octaves above its fundamental pitches, giving it a corrosive buzz which the house community metaphorically dubbed 'acid'.[27]

The pitch content of acid house riffs was generated by taking the path of least resistance through the complicated note entry protocol for the 303: since you *had* to enter a pitch for each of the sixteen slots in a pattern, and inexperienced users were unclear on how to use 'time mode' to create a rest or a sustained tone, acid house was defined by endlessly cycling loops of exactly sixteen notes. The pitch collections for the loops were assembled more or less at random, since house producers were not trained keyboardists and cared more about textures than the West European classical tonal implications of jumping around the fully chromatic set of pitch buttons located across the 303's virtual black and white keys. Quasi-random patterns of accents and slides, created inadvertently when a user dropped out of pitch or time mode while pressing buttons, could give the constant sixteen-beat looping a twisty, syncopated feel. Modern software emulations of the TB-303 often include a 'randomise' button which instantly fills up a pattern with these kinds of serendipitous interactions. Acid house thus offered a brilliant remapping of the TB-303's interface: Roland's intent was that users would adjust the analogue tone section once, to emulate the bass sound they wanted, and then forget it, while spending the bulk of their time and energy mastering the intricacies of entering, storing, and recalling dozens of patterns to choreograph and phrase a bassline. Instead, acid producers tended to build an entire track around a single, fortunately found pattern, using the resonance and cut-off frequency knobs as tone control devices to execute complex transformations of its sound characteristics, in real time, while recording.

Orbital did not invent this bag of tricks ('Chime' simultaneously pays homage to, and appropriates, previous innovations by underground Black producers in Chicago and Detroit) but they did decode and then inject Black secret technology into the mainstream of both British popular music and Japanese instrument design. Performing live on the first generation of sound samplers and analogue-digital electronics became their calling card at raves and festivals, which ironically actualised Ikutaro Takehashi's original intent, that relatively affordable electronic instruments like the TB-303 democratise popular music making, by disregarding every intention he and his engineers had formulated about how those devices should be used.

I hope the preceding discussion justifies writing about *both* Orbital and DJ Pierre: remember that there is no visual documentation of how Phuture's electronics were set up in 1985 when the first version of 'Acid Tracks' was dubbed direct to cassette tape, no picture that shows us where their 303 and 909 were placed, no first-hand descriptions of how Earl Smith and Pierre Jones came across the acid sound more illuminating than 'we let the machine run and kept twisting knobs'.[28] The record of Black secret technology, as is so often the case with subaltern narratives, must be read where it is (eventually) written.

Have you Found the Doubled-Up Key Group Phasing Trick Yet?' (Akai S950)

Close listening to the original 1990 under-the-stairs recording of 'Chime' reveals a strange digital glitch coming from the Akai S700 sampler, which for much of the track was being asked to play two stuttering riffs, both derived from the same ricocheting pair of sped-up piano chords, at the same time.[29] As Hartnoll tells it, he deliberately made this happen, taking advantage of his sequencer's inability to trigger the multiple overlapping samples in precise synchronisation: 'One of the things I did like about it was having [the main riffs] next to each other on the MMT8 and then, for extra oomph at any point, I could put the two on together and it phased. You know, where the same notes hit, I'd get this nice sort of sample phase, the machine being unable to handle playing the same thing twice.'[30]

What Hartnoll here calls 'sample phase' happens when the same digitised sound is being played back from two different memory locations at the same time – or, rather, at not precisely the same time, thanks to unpredictable hardware interactions between the sequencer's MIDI clock and the corresponding one in the sampler it is trying to control. As sampled audio content goes slightly out of phase, interference patterns arise, akin to the temporal blurring of echoes in a large reverberant space ('chorus') or the high-range filter sweep produced when two tape recordings of the same material fall out of alignment thanks to an engineer's thumb on one of the reels ('flanging').

Sample phasing was endemic to the first generation of breakbeat hardcore, a UK genre even more lo-fi than the most homemade acid house. Consider the spartan set-up of bedroom producer DJ Seduction (*aka* John Kalkan of Highgate, North London), in 1992: one sampler (Akai S950), one synth (Roland JD-800), and a four-track mixer.[31] Kalkan didn't even own a drum machine. Hardcore experiments like 'Sub Dub' and 'Drop the Bass' were driven by multiple layers of breakbeats triggered directly, in real time, from a single overworked S950. Pervasive chorusing from the always ever so slightly out of phase beat collages gave a watery, 'sampledelic' sound to what critics would later hail as a new species of dance floor avant-gardism.[32]

Inadvertent phasing and flanging caused by simultaneous but imprecise triggering of identical breakbeats is one of the reasons 80s-vintage Akai samplers like the S700 and S950 are still valued today by experienced drum and bass producers with retro tastes. Witness a 2013 discussion (edited for length) that broke out around the Akai S950 sampler on the UK fan site dogsonacid.com:

[DWARDE] Got one of these the other week . . . had never used hardware before. Well enjoying this as a process as opposed to doing everything in the box . . .

[JACK_YGGDRASIL] Got a really raw upfront sound to those, 950 working well for ya! What are you sequencing on?

[DWARDE] Sequencing in Renoise. :)

[JACK_YGGDRASIL] Another Q Dwarde, are you processing your samples before going into the 950? Or straight in and tweaked on the desk?
Oh and have you found the doubled up keygroup phasing trick yet ;)?

[DWARDE] Yeah, all about the phasing effects, can get well mad with different filter envelopes on each group too! Enjoying using the Renoise delay column (and same sample on different key-groups and outputs) to get that fat phase/flange effect on breaks, can hear it in this tune. It's the first thing I made a couple of days after getting the Akai, just as an experiment to get to grips with it all.[33]

A short dip into the S950 owner's manual will be necessary to decode this exchange.[34] The basic data structure of an Akai hardware sampler like the 950 was the 'program', a mapping of an arbitrary number of digital audio samples onto an equally arbitrary number of 'keygroups', which could be any size, and either discrete or overlapping. Akai's engineers were proud of this system's flexibility: it could mimic a single keyboard instrument with a wide range, like a piano (one sample per keygroup per octave, with overlaps to smooth out the transition); it could function like a small combo (bass sample mapped to the lower octaves, overlapping slightly with a slightly foreshortened version of the keyboard layout above); it could even be arranged like a set of traps, with individual drum and percussion sounds mapped to small ranges of adjacent keys for easy two-handed playing.

However, using the 950 to 'drum' on the keyboard meant defeating the basic purpose of a sampler, which is to turn a finite collection of digital audio files into an infinitely extensible virtual instrument with variable pitch. The Akai S950's default mode for mapping a sample onto a keygroup modulates the sample to each key, using its internal clock to speed up or slow down playback and thus change the pitch level. However, buried deep on the fifteenth page of program settings lives a parameter called 'const[ant] pitch', off by default, which instructs the sampler to assign samples to keygroups without modulating their pitch. This setting was useful for creating virtual drum sets; it was also a key step in using the sampler to construct the looping breakbeats which defined the sound of early-90s rave and jungle.

Here's the recipe: (1) use the Akai's line input to record a short percussion break from an LP or 45rpm single into memory (when in doubt, try the famous 'Amen' break);[35] (2) use the Akai's sample editing capabilities to adjust the start and end points of the sample, creating a tight loop that repeats without arrhythmia; (3) rename and then edit multiple copies of the sample, setting new start-end points to capture both regular and irregular spans of the original break, defined by the interaction of kick and snare; (4) create a custom program in which the original full sample and its chopped subsets are assigned to a small range of keys using constant pitch; (5) while recording from the sampler's line out(s), 'drum' creatively within this keygroup, triggering the original break and its constituent pieces in varied patterns to create a complex, fast-moving stream of irregular and angular rhythms, *aka* 'breakbeat science'.

As the owner of a vintage Akai S950 which (*pardon my flex*) once belonged to our interlocutor Moby above, I have more than once executed exactly these steps as a demonstration for students in my History and Practice of EDM class at UCLA. Thus, I discovered for myself how a simple slip of the fingers might well have opened up a new palette of sampledelic sonic possibilities for early rave producers. Once you have sampled a break, naturally you want to hear it. Although there is a 'playback' button on the face of the device, since you are going to end up creating keygroups anyway, why not map the sample to one of your program's existing keygroups and trigger it from your keyboard? Unless you have already made the non-intuitive choice to define your first keygroup as the range from a given key *to itself* (i.e., one single key), you're going to end up with multiple adjacent keys triggering the same sample at the same pitch, and it is quite possible, even probable, that you will do what I did, which is strike two adjacent keys in the keygroup at the same time.

Or, rather, not *precisely* at the same time, since a finger accidentally striking two adjacent keys is inevitably going to land on them slightly out of phase.

The result is a distinctive, heavily phased sound: two identically pitched iterations of the sampled breakbeat, triggered a few fractions of a second apart, interfering with each other to create an impromptu filter sweep. It's cool, but non-reproducible since no human can generate the same keyboard mistake twice. But breakbeat producers quickly figured out that it was possible to make a sampler stumble this way on purpose. Anyone who read through to the advanced applications section of the Akai S950 manual would discover how easy it was, and still is, to 'layer' keygroups. A single program could contain multiple copies of the same keygroup, with the same samples attached; a single keystroke would then trigger the sample multiple times, and the inability of the sampler's clock to trigger them exactly in phase would mass-produce the 'phased breakbeat' sound. This is the 'doubled-up keygroup effect' that user jack_yggdrasil refers to in the exchange quoted above. If you wanted the 'fat phase/flange' effect that 950 user dwarde was after, the manual went on to explain how slight detuning of up to four keygroup layers using Akai's 'fine tune' setting would do the trick.[36]

'First, Gavin Puts in a Four-Bar "Click Track" at the Start of the Song.' (Amiga 500/MED 3.0)

By 1992, even hardware sampling was going out of style. Inexpensive software running on second-hand mid-1980s PCs like the Atari ST could now talk to and even replace rackmount samplers like the Akai S950. (The Atari, released in 1985, was the first – and for a long time *only* – personal computer with a built-in MIDI interface.) Not only was this software much easier to use, thanks to the Atari's graphic interface and mouse; the precision of its MIDI clock, synced directly to the CPU, became legendary within the dance music world: 'I just remember I'd hook up my S950 sampler [to the Atari], put a loop in there, listen to it, and it would so rock. I could listen to it for 10, 15 minutes, and it wouldn't shift at all. Something about the ST was militant in its sequencing.'[37]

Some hardcore rave and jungle producers preferred an even cheaper 80s alternative, the Commodore Amiga, which by 1990 was shipping with free audio sampling software and a mod-tracker-style sequencing program called the MED (Music EDitor). Urban Shakedown's 1991 recording 'Some Justice',[38] with its jittering, phased breakbeats, was one of the first major dance hits built entirely on a personal computer, as the enthusiast magazine *Amiga Format* giddily noted in its August 1992 issue, featuring Amiga enthusiasts Gavin King and Claudio Giussani on the cover.[39] Inside, the Urban Shakedown duo shared details of their production process, which relied on two Amiga 500s running MED 3.0 in tandem, yielding eight simultaneous software tracks which they, in tried-and-true acid house fashion, mixed directly to tape in a bedroom studio. The Amiga's audio chipset was so robust, its clock timing so precise, that the two machines had no trouble triggering studio-quality samples in perfect unison forever, once they were coaxed into synchronisation. But the sync itself was tricky – unlike the Atari ST, the Amiga had no MIDI ports, and the solitary commercial attempt to implement a MIDI driver in software using its serial port was still two years in the future. For the lads in Urban Shakedown, the only substitute was an unbelievably low-tech trick from EDM's distant past:

> First, Gavin puts in a four-bar 'click track' at the start of the song. This is a simple series of bleeps in a 4/4 pattern. Claudio puts a similar three-bar track at the start of the sequence on his machine. Gavin then starts his sequence and Claudio starts his on the second bar of the click track. It's then just a matter of Claudio adjusting the timing until the two machines are perfectly in sync. A single-bar gap after the clicks allows them to start the tape running to record the final output.[40]

Anyone who has heard Giorgio Moroder tell the story of making Donna Summer's 1977 'I Feel Love' in the Daft Punk track that bears his name will recognise this 'click track' as EDM's original technological secret, the improvised control pulse that allowed Moroder to sequence dance floor beats on an ancient Moog from the analogue 1960s: 'I didn't have any idea what to do, but I knew I needed a click. So we put a click on the 24-track, which then was synced to the Moog modular. I knew that could be a sound of the future.'[41] Fifteen years into that sonic future, Urban Shakedown had to reinvent the (secret) wheel. The Amiga ran on digital software; there was no way to force it to respond directly to pulsed control voltages like the old Moogs did. Instead, Giussani turned to an even older Afro-diasporic technology: he lined up the two Amigas by ear, in real time, like a club DJ beatmatching grooves on two turntables. Giussani had just twelve beats – at 140 BPM, that's only a little over five seconds – to get his timing spot on. How many false starts there must have been – and how much accidental phasing, if even one of the sampled drum loops was doubled between the machines!

If 'Some Justice' is any guide, Giussani and King loved the 'swoosh-y' effect of sampled breaks phased by hand. Like most breakbeat hardcore and jungle producers, they were mimicking one of the deepest secret technologies of Jamaican reggae. Dub mixers like King Tubby and Lee 'Scratch' Perry didn't have samplers or sequencers, of course; but they were past masters at using their studio's parametric EQ as a timbral modulator:

In order to achieve the most effective filter 'swoosh' sound you need to reduce the Q to near its narrowest setting then crank up the boost to at least +12 dB before then sweeping the frequency control smoothly up and down for that King Tubby-like effect. Try routing your hi-hat, snare and cymbals solely to a group and then apply your EQ sweep to that! Better still, route your snare spring reverb to the same group and you will *be* King Tubby![42]

By now we're in on some of the secret ways in which the Black Electronic propagates around the Black Atlantic: from dub in Jamaica to Chicago house, where DJ Pierre got his own 'swoosh' experimenting with the frequency and resonance knobs on a second-hand TB-303's tone control section. Then from Chicago over to UK hardcore and jungle, whose London-based producers happened on yet another way to get that acid sound, zeroing in on the sweep-filtering effect created when identical breakbeat samples were inadvertently triggered out of phase. The musicians surveyed in this chapter were engaged in a collective game of transatlantic leapfrog, using accidents for innovation, spurring engineers to codify their missteps into new devices with elaborate instruction manuals, which the next microgeneration happily spurns.

There are those within dance culture who believe that these paths of creative misuse are open to any electronic artist of any race who sincerely seeks *techgnosis*, the hidden knowledge necessary to wield the power of Black technology: ' ... the virtual logic of the Black Electronic is not rooted in ethnic facts but rhizomatically spreads through the increasingly open-ended and hybridized zones of electro-acoustic cyberspace'.[43]

It's not clear that the racial problematic inherent in electronic dance music culture, the tension between Black roots and silicon-coloured off-shoots, can be resolved quite as airily as Erik Davis, deploying the theory-laden vernacular of a powerful (and white) techno-utopian counterculture, claims here. But it does seem that anybody, Black or white, can make a mistake. Sometimes those mistakes are productive, and the most productive mistakes do tend to spread like weeds, rhizomatically, losing in the process some of their rootedness.

To err, after all, is neither Black nor white. It is simply human.

Notes

1. The musicological bibliography on this topic is extensive, but the most recent historical treatment is Matthew Morrison's definitive summary in *Blacksound: Making Race and Popular Music in the United States* (Berkeley: University of California Press, 2024).
2. See Paul Gilroy, *The Black Atlantic. Modernity and Double Consciousness* (Cambridge, MA: Harvard University Press, 1993).
3. The crucial texts here are Marc Dery, 'Black to the Future', in Marc Dery, ed., *Flame Wars: The Discourse of Cyberculture* (Durham, NC: Duke University Press, 1994), 179–222; and Kodwo Eshun, *More Brilliant than the Sun: Adventures in Sonic Fiction* (London: Quartet Books, 1998). Both authors provide extensive readings of Black musical texts within the ambit of electronic dance music culture.
4. Eric Davis, 'Polyrhythmic Cyberspace and the Black Electronic', in Paul D. Miller, ed., *Sound Unbound* (Cambridge, MA: MIT Press, 2008). https://techgnosis.com/polyrythmic-cyberspace-and-the-black-electronic/ (accessed 24 April 2024).
5. Moby (Richard Melville) as quoted in 'The Cult of the DJ: A Symposium', *Social Text* 43 (Autumn 1995): 76.
6. Julian Jonker, 'Black Secret Technology (The Whitey on the Moon Dub)', *ctheory.net*, 4 December 2002 https://journals.uvic.ca/index.php/ctheory/article/view/14571/5418 (accessed 21 April 2024).
7. Phuture (1987) 'Acid Tracks'. USA: Trax Records.
8. Smith 1992 cited in Hillegonda C. Rietveld, '(Dis)placing Musical Memory: Trailing the Acid in Electronic Dance Music', in Ed Montano and Carlo Nardi, eds., *Situating Popular Musics* (IASPM 16th International Conference Proceedings, 2012), p. 354. www.academia.edu/24717739/_Dis_placing_musical_ memory_Trailing_the_acid_in_electronic_dance_music (accessed 11 June 2024). Emphasis, brackets, and ellipses in original.
9. An equalisation (EQ) circuit controls the amount of energy routed to an arbitrary number of frequency 'bands' (usually equally spaced) in a device's audio output. An EQ circuit is parametric if the bands can be controlled individually.
10. See Roland 'The 303 Story', 2025, for an illustration of the Roland TB-303 Bassline: www.roland.com/us/promos/303day/#:~:text=The%20TB%2D303%20Bassline%20Synthesizer,time%20with%20the%20drum%20beat.
11. *Roland TB-303 Owner's Manual*, 1981, p. 34.
12. RAM, as Daft Punk remind us, stands for 'random access memory'. Pattern information in the TB-303 was stored in three UPD444C RAM chips which were designed to be *static*, able to go into low-power hibernation when not actively in use. These static chips still required a small amount of power to

function, so removing the TB-303's battery put the user at risk of losing or (more likely) scrambling their stored patterns, thus, as we'll see, allowing the randomness of *acid* back in.

13. A potentiometer (often abbreviated as 'pot') is an infinitely adjustable analogue device designed to change the differential in electric charge – the 'potential' – across a circuit, thereby changing the amount of current flowing through it. Pots can be linear, like the sliders on mixing equipment, or rotary, like the control knobs on the Roland TB-303. Sometimes a rotary pot modifies the *relationship* between two circuits, as with the 303's 'resonance' knob, which controls a circuit that boosts the frequencies adjacent to a linked filter's cutoff to create what engineers call a 'knee', a clearly audible resonant peak. If both cutoff and resonance are pushed as high as possible, the resulting circuit path will be maximally bright and edgy.

14. Andrew Whitehurst, 'Game Changers: Phuture, "Acid Tracks"', *DJ Mag,* 9 July 2014. https://djmag.com/content/game-changers-phuture-acid-tracks (accessed 22 August 2023). This quote has been condensed from two of Jones's quotes in adjacent paragraphs of the article.

15. The definitive study of this practice is Henry Louis Gates, Jr., *The Signifying Monkey: A Theory of African American Literary Criticism* (New York: Oxford University Press, 2014); a direct application to Afro-diasporic music is at the heart of Samuel A. Floyd, *The Power of Black Music: Interpreting Its History from Africa to the United States* (New York: Oxford University Press, 1995).

16. Orbital (1990) 'Chime'. UK: FFRR.

17. The brothers Paul and Phil Hartnoll are illustrated in the linked article in their studio closet where 'Chime' was recorded, ca. 1991, Paul resting his arm next to the Roland TB-303, with above the TR-909 drum machine, in April Clare Welsh 'Orbital Will Tour Their 1991 Debut Album "The Green Album" 2024'. *DJ Mag.* 16 October 2023. https://djmag.com/news/orbital-will-tour-their-1991-debut-album-green-album-2024.

18. Orbital's 'Chime' has become a canonic EDM track, and its production has been the subject of much detailed technical reminiscence by Hartnoll. The following discussion is particularly indebted to: Richard Buskin, 'Classic Tracks: Orbital, "Chime,"' *Sound on Sound,* Dec 2006 (www.soundonsound.com/techniques/classic-tracks-orbital-chime, accessed 19 August 2023); Smith, Matt, 'Landmarks: "Chime" by Orbital', *Electronic Sound,* n.d. (www.electronicsound.co.uk/landmarks/chime-by-orbital/, accessed 17 August 2023); and Stuart Aitken, "Mistletoe and Chime: The Story of Orbital's Acid House," *The Guardian,* 16 December 2013 (www.theguardian.com/music/2013/dec/16/chime-orbital-acid-house-dance-music, accessed 15 August 2023).

19. Aitken, 'Mistletoe and Chime'.

20. See Ikutaro Kakehashi (with Robert Olsen), *I Believe in Music: Life Experiences and Thoughts on the Future of Electronic Music by the Founder of Roland Corporation* (Wisconsin: Hal Leonard, 2002), pp. 33ff.
21. Figure 1 on page 5 of the *Roland TB-303 Owner's Manual* (1981) shows a representation of parametric data structure for a bassline as it is stored in the Roland TB-303: 'Each "pattern" can remember various musical factors, such as "pitch," "length of note," and "accent," individually. After memorizing several patterns, these patterns may be joined to produce the Bass line of a musical piece.' For the illustration, see: https://ia802805.us.archive.org/23/items/synthmanual-roland-tb-303-owners-manual/rolandtb-303ownersmanual_text.pdf#:~:text=and%20consequently%20it%20is%20a%20difficult%20thing,on%20the%20rhythm%2C%20chord%20progression%2C%20style%20of</color_Yellow.
22. Again, see Roland (2025) 'The 303 Story' for an illustration of the Roland TB-303 Bassline: www.roland.com/us/promos/303day/#:~:text=The%20TB%2D303%20Bassline%20Synthesizer,time%20with%20the%20drum%20beat.
23. *Roland TB-303 Owner's Manual* (1981), pp. 9–15.
24. Recall the image of brothers Paul and Phil Hartnoll in their studio closet where 'Chime' was recorded, ca. 1990–91. Welsh, 'Orbital Will Tour Their 1991 Debut Album "The Green Album." 2024.'
25. On jacking and Chicago's queer Black house culture, see Micah Salkind, *Do You Remember House? Chicago's Queer of Color Undergrounds* (New York: Oxford University Press, 2019), pp. 230ff. The key theoretical statement about gay dance music and bodily discipline is still Walter Hughes, 'In the Empire of the Beat: Discipline and Disco', in Andrew Ross and Tricia Rose, eds., *Microphone Fiends: Youth Music and Youth Culture* (New York: Routledge, 1994), pp. 147–58.
26. At the centre of the tone stack was an unusual low-pass filter with a four-pole diode ladder, interacting with an equally temperamental envelope modulator and the unpredictable tonal effects of the TB-303's 'accent' circuit to create results which many audio experts believe are too complex to be modelled digitally. See 'The TB-303 Confusion Cleared Up Once and For All', *electro-music.com*, 24 April 2006 (https://electro-music.com/forum/viewtopic.php?highlight=303&t=11244, accessed 27 August 2023). For an extremely technical discussion of the TB-303's low-pass filter see www.timstinchcombe.co.uk/index.php?pge=diode.
27. 'Do you know why it is so difficult to emulate the sound of this little gem which sells today for around 5,000 F? Answer: it is impossible to find the poor quality components that gave the 18 dB/octave filter its special character.' D. Korn, quoted in Olivier Julien, 'La technologie de la French Touch: Les Paul ou Pierre Schaeffer?', *Musurgia* 9:2 (2002), p. 80. Translation by the author.

28. Whitehurst, 'Game Changers'. For the original 1992 interview, see Hillegonda C. Rietveld, *This is Our House: House Music, Technologies and Cultural Spaces* (London and New York: Routledge, 2020).
29. Hartnoll has always been cagey about the source of these chords, but the consensus of trainspotters on the web is that all the samples in 'Chime' can be found somewhere on an easy listening album called *Sleepy Shores* by Johnny Pearson and his Orchestra (Pennyfarthing, 1972). See www.whosampled.com/sample/617879/Orbital-Chime-Johnny-Pearson-Sleepy-Shores/ (accessed 6 September 2023).
30. Buskin, 'Classic Tracks: Orbital, Chime'.
31. Kalkan detailed his first production setup in a Facebook post from 5 April 2019 (www.facebook.com/DJSeductionJohn/photos/a.10157702563093356/10158261466178356/?type=3, accessed 21 September 2023).
32. Simon Reynolds, *Generation Ecstasy: Into the World of Techno and Rave Culture* (London: Little, Brown, 1998), pp. 136–41.
33. www.dogsonacid.com/threads/tunes-akai-s950.752827/ (posted 29 March 2013; accessed 6 September 2023). Renoise is a software DAW built on a 'mod tracker' framework. Mod trackers, whose simple numerical interface closely 'tracks' MIDI data, are favoured by producers who need to drive multiple hardware synths and samplers, because they are fast and accurate when triggering samples.
34. For an illustration of the basic sampling architecture of 12-bit sampler Akai S950, showing that samples are arranged into key groups mapped out across the keyboard range within a program, see Figure 1 on page 8 of Akai's owner's manual, *S950 Midi Digital Sampler*, 1988: https://manuals.fdiskc.com/flat/Akai%20S-950%20Owners%20Manual.pdf.
35. The 'Amen' break is named for its source, a soul-jazz instrumental called 'Amen, Brother', recorded in 1969 as a B-side by the Winstons, an American soul group. It appeared on the first LP of *Ultimate Beats and Breaks* (SBR 501), issued by Street Beat Records in 1986 as a resource for hip-hop DJs and producers. It is one of the most sampled breakbeats in modern popular music. The best discussion of the 'Amen' break remains Nate Harrison's recording, 'Can I Get an Amen', a 2004 art installation in the form of a custom-pressed LP that is preserved on video at https://archive.org/details/NateHarrisonCanIGetAnAmen (accessed 17 September 2023).
36. 'For example, with a simple string program with just one keygroup, to thicken the sound, simply make a copy of that keygroup in Page 03 and then detune it in Page 06. In a more complicated multi-sample program that has, for example, four keygroups, copy KG1 to create a new keygroup, KG5, copy KG2 so that you create another new keygroup, KG6, copy KG3 so that you create another keygroup, KG7 and copy KG4 to create KG8. Now detune keygroups 5-8 slightly.' Akai S950 Owner's Manual, n.d., p. 66.

37. Producer Trevor Jackson *aka* Underdog, quoted in Matt Annis, 'Instrumental Instruments: Atari ST'. www.daily.redbullacademy.com (6 October 2017, accessed 18 September 2023).
38. Urban Shakedown, feat. Mickey Finn (1991) 'Some Justice'. UK: Urban Shakedown.
39. Maff Evans. & Gary Lord, 'Hitting the Big Time, or: "How Your Amiga Can Make You Rich and Famous"', *Amiga Format* 37 (August 1992): 26. For the cover-page illustration, with Gavin King (front) and Claudio Giussani (back) see: https://amr.abime.net/issue_193#:~:text=Amiga%20Format%2037%20(August%201992)%20%2D%20Amiga%20Magazine%20Rack&text=Everybody%20shake%20down!
40. Ibid.
41. Daft Punk, 'Giorgio by Moroder', *Random Access Memories* (Columbia, 2013).
42. Description from user 'noiseboy' on the *Dub Discussion Board*, 1 July 2003, in answer to the question, 'Did Tubby use a parametric EQ?' (www.interruptor.ch/Php5/dubboard/viewtopic.php?t=438, accessed 14 May 2024). The variable 'Q' indexes the width of an electronic filter's frequency passband; in this case it refers to the width of the resonant peak that produces the familiar swoosh when a filter sweeps across the audio spectrum.
43. Davis, 'Polyrhythmic Cyberspace'. Davis's first exploration of these ideas, *TechGnosis: Myth, Magic, and Mysticism in the Age of Information* (New York: Crown, 1998), came early enough to become a part of EDM's technocultural history, not merely a commentary on it.

Further Reading

Mark Butler, *Playing with Something that Runs* (New York: Oxford University Press, 2014).
Marc Dery, ed., *Flame Wars: The Discourse of Cyberculture* (Durham, NC: Duke University Press, 1994).
Paul D. Miller, ed., *Sound Unbound* (Cambridge, MA: MIT Press, 2008).
Matthew Morrison, *Blacksound: Making Race and Popular Music in the United States* (Berkeley: University of California Press, 2024).
Micah Salkind, *Do You Remember House? Chicago's Queer of Color Undergrounds* (New York: Oxford University Press, 2019).

15 Dance Music and Flow

TAMI GADIR

The concept of flow can be used to capture the affective state of moving to electronic dance music. The flow state or flow experience can describe several possible phenomena, including the fluid movements of bodies to dance music and bodily sensations that result from encountering the sonic qualities of dance music, possibly enhanced by dance drug experience. This chapter offers an analysis that links flow states on dance floors from the micro level, to the socioeconomic operations of club cultures at the meso level and the larger neo-liberal capitalist structures that underpin them at the macro level. Other scholars have offered examples of this interplay. For example, in the context of creative industries, Angela McRobbie argues that club cultures act as a structural model (not a mere metaphor) for the broader embrace of flexibility (insecurity) and informal networking.[1] In addition, ideas of creativity may be understood through the concept of 'flow' in the work of Mihalyi Csikszentmihalyi, an unself-conscious sense of 'being in the moment' that can be experienced during dancing, meditation, or creativity.[2] The catch-all, plural (and positive) quality of the concept of flow makes it easy to apply to many things and hard to argue with. However, using Augustine Sedgewick's critique of flows,[3] the discussion in this chapter aims to take McRobbie's position a step further. It connects real-life dance floor flow experience and discourse, which leak into and inform each other, with neo-liberal conceptualisations and applications of flow in the wider world.[4]

Ideas of flow are used by dance music scholars in different ways to express some of these affective states. Ben Malbon, for example, uses Csikszentmihalyi's theory of flow to articulate how it feels to dance with others in a club, particularly at peak collective moments of euphoria, when music and dance can combine with the enhancing effects of dance drugs for a roomful of people simultaneously.[5] Kai Fikentscher's ethnography of the New York underground dance floor engages the concept of vibe to describe the feeling that results from the synchronicity between music and dance, and the 'interdependence' of clubbers and DJs.[6] Although he does not directly use the term 'flow' to describe this phenomenon in this study, one of his interviewees uses it to describe the peak moment on dance floors as a time when 'everything and everyone flows together, a moment where time seems erased'.[7] Overall, there is also a continuity between Fikentscher's terminology of 'the vibe' to describe the nexus between music, dance, and dancer that relates to Csikszentmihalyi's flow theory.

For Fikentscher, the flow comes from an ideal balance of effort and skill, which is achieved through the DJ's deliberate moderation of the energy of the dance floor with a musical ebb and flow. Rather than maintaining a constant state of high energy that would encourage consistent dancing, a musical choice made by a skilled DJ may follow a high-energy or familiar track with a more laid-back or unfamiliar track. This contrast can push some people off the dance floor, but is ultimately part of the bigger musical journey that mixes moods and energy levels. David DePino, a DJ quoted by Fikentscher, likes to experiment with tunes both to hear them in a club sound system and to gauge how people respond to them, and in doing so, challenging clubbers to be open to new music.[8] In addition, the dance music scholar's fieldwork can document dance floor flows and interact with them in unique ways. Alice O'Grady illustrates this in an analysis of how immersion in dancing can be experienced as flow by those that she has observed in her fieldwork, as well as by herself. However, as a researcher, she is compelled to reflect on, and eventually write about, the observations and experiences. This means there is an intrinsic state of tension in the role of the 'ethnographer of the flow experience', as attempting to capture this experience necessarily constitutes a disruption to the flow state.[9] Such examples show how flow can provide an appealing frame for a phenomenology of clubbing and of electronic dance music culture and practice.

As a concept used outside of dance music studies, flow acts as an anthropological, economic, or sociological metaphor for the virtual flow of money, so-called workflows, and resources, music, language, and culture. All these are subsumed within the multiscalar flows of globalisation, as articulated and critiqued in the work of Arjun Appadurai.[10] The metaphorical or virtual flows denote, or at least imply, organicism and inevitability, which is to say that they naturalise a political process rather than acknowledging deliberative construction.[11] Among others, Deleuze and Guattari have used the term to describe the motion of their 'lines of flight'.[12] In addition, research on education and pedagogy, some of which intersects with psychology and neuroscience, applies the concept to music, dance and dance improvisation, and sports or exercise.[13] One of the farthest-reaching cross-disciplinary applications has resulted from the work of Csikszentmihalyi, whose positive psychology theories of flow have accommodated and been absorbed into the language and theory of management, as a framework for improving workers' positivity, and by extension, performance and productivity.[14]

Far from remaining in the order of the abstract, flow in such contexts feeds a different, larger-scale kind of flow: that of the movement of capital and labour.[15] The work of the Flow Research Collective epitomises this, as it uses 'the most powerful elements of executive coaching [and] scientific research' to address the lack of productivity of 'the average knowledge worker'.[16] The work of the collective has been featured in the *Harvard Business Review*, *Entrepreneur*, CNN, *National Geographic*, *TIME*, and *Forbes*. One of the striking promises it makes is 'on-demand flow states'. It has been used to train people in the elite university sector, government departments, and the biggest corporations. Significantly, it has endorsements from Ray Kurzweil (Google's director of engineering), Elon Musk (CEO of Tesla, X, SpaceX, etcetera), Michael Dell (CEO of Dell), Bill Clinton (former US president), Anousheh Ansari (CEO of XPRIZE), Pharrell Williams (successful music producer), and Tony Robbins (entrepreneur and motivational speaker). Of course, none of this means that flow is a bad idea in and of itself, or that it should be discarded completely.

On the contrary, flow can be a helpful analytical and exploratory tool for some of the slipperiest phenomena, such as music and its affects/effects. Furthermore, it is used in myriad ways across different theoretical traditions by Facebook, Accenture, Audi, and the San Francisco Police Department; not all of which set out to celebrate flow as a means to 'peak performance'.[17] Nevertheless, just as it is important to underscore the ways that political and social justice discourses are cynically bent to the goals of capital (rather than to those of actual political and social justice),[18] so too should it be highlighted that flow science lends itself to being adapted and deployed for the neo-liberal, individualising ideologies that uphold these very same goals. If flow research now takes the form of 'neuroscience based training to help you accomplish more, in less time, with greater ease',[19] then any potentially radical intentions of flow analysis, say within the context of dance floors, should be rigorously and unambiguously disarticulated from such corporate-technocratic applications. This should not be confused with a denial of the inextricable relationship between dance floors and their political economic structures. Rather, it calls for a conscious ideological position to be taken where it is possible to draw attention to, contest, and oppose these structures.

Flow is well suited to describe the experience of dance music genres such as techno, house, and trance because of the music's looping, repetitious form, the common practice of DJ sets as continuous, the tendency in such music to maintain a consistent tempo across hours-long flows of music without pause, and the way that, as a result of these features, time itself becomes a flow of music, dance, and perpetual motion. The end of a dance music track flows seamlessly into the beginning of another.[20] For people who only ever hear DJ sets in their totality, whether from dance floors themselves, or, as is becoming increasingly common, through online live streams, or pre-recorded podcasts, there is no distinction between beginning and end: only one long, flowing line, which may feel more like an infinite spiral. The precise sameness of the repetitive beats, characteristic of electronic dance music and a particularity of machine-made rhythms, helps the dancer to experience a state of flow. The repetition of sound anchors the anticipation of patterns and allows the body to move without hesitation or deliberation.[21] The bodily coherence of repetition in dance music lends itself to flow.[22] These work together with other features of dance music spaces that are also described in Csikszentmihalyi's account of 'rock dancing', such as loudness and low light, which facilitate flow because they 'eliminate distractions and focus attention', allowing people to 'merge with the music'.[23]

Shifts in musical tension constitute flow too. Sound undulates in the unfolding form of dance music – building, peaking, resolving, and rising again. The variation in density and intensity happens at the macro-scale of the musical structure in order to be conducive to flow, rather than detracting from it. A 'breakdown' is where the texture of the track or DJ set is thinned out temporarily, often, though not always, by a removal of bass and kick drum or other sounds from the rhythm section. For example, in Tommy Four Seven's 'Surma' (Speedy J Dub Tool), there is hardly a breakdown, but the variation is provided by techniques such as filtering, reverb, sweeps, and other sound effects.[24] By contrast, 'Trummerfeld' by Extrawelt (Oliver Huntemann Remix) has an extraordinarily long breakdown, including a section where all senses of rhythm and direction temporarily cease, giving way to an aimless swirl of sound.[25] Even such moments may be seen not as ruptures to the flow but rather moments in a recording where it recedes – a low tide, or a period of stasis within the flow. The kinds of breakdown where regular metre is removed are also the kinds that can facilitate change in the flow of bodily movement. Where the bass and beat, which normally anchor dancing in the body's bottom half, are removed, attention can turn to arms and the upper body. Expressive and fluid movements incorporating wrists and fingers in response to upper frequencies may temporarily supplant what may otherwise have been heavier, jerky movements of the body's feet, legs, and core.[26]

EDM scholar Mark Butler writes about the concept of flow as emergent from the ongoing interplay between the DJ, their performing technologies (laptop, turntables, or other DJ gear), and a dancing crowd or listening audience. He draws on understandings of flow by non-music scholar Csikszentmihalyi as mental absorption during challenging tasks; by hip-hop scholar Tricia Rose as circularity and motion in African American cultural and musical practice; and by musicologist Robert Fink regarding parallels and continuities between minimalist music and contemporary media. According to Butler, the continuous character of a dance music performance – in the form of consecutive DJ sets that may last for several hours (sometimes even days, at festivals) – lends itself to flow. The dynamic relationships between DJs, technologies, and dancers are brought about by the unfolding flow-like qualities of improvisation and responses by the DJ to what is happening on the dance floor. Flow is used in a positive sense to describe an open-endedness of function and form.[27]

There is a scholarly legacy of mid-twentieth-century scholars such as Adorno, who saw the political effect of the mass reproduction of music as dystopian.[28] As Garcia-Mispireta notes, there is a multiscalar denigration of repetition across Adorno's work: from the macro, in the form of whole musical works as they relate to industry and culture, to the micro, such as repetition within the internal form of a piece.[29] Horkheimer and Adorno argued that 'unending sameness' (standardisation and repetition) in contemporary art, music, and other culture of the 1940s was a replication of the kind of conformity that allowed a total subjugation to late capitalism, actual authoritarianism, and fascism to proliferate.[30] Garcia-Mispireta's work on repetition and pleasure helps to show the relevance of Adorno's historical position on cultural reproduction to flow in dance music. Adorno, influenced by a psychoanalytic tradition, understood repetition as a kind of lack (of direction, progression, or development) which disregards the processual value that people derive from repetitive musical elements.[31] Flow can therefore be found within this processual space where repetition is allowing music to unfold rather than 'develop'. For Butler, the cultural baggage of reproduction as lack can be constructively abandoned in favour of embracing the affordances of sound reproduction and its musical and social interplay. As he argues, DJs shape their sets through the 'creative transformation of recorded musical objects' (in this case, dance music tracks), which, together, can 'constitute an energetic field of possibility'. Butler and Garcia-Mispireta's work are examples of the generative ways that the concept of flow can be deployed to describe some of the seemingly mystifying aspects of dance music's sound and practice.[32]

Recreational drugs are often used in dance music spaces to enhance flow experiences. Although a variety of psychoactive substances, painkillers, and stimulants may be used for this purpose, MDMA ('ecstasy') is among the more commonly known drugs in post-disco dance music cultures since the late-1980s.[33] Its effects include an increase in feelings of connectedness, empathy, and sensory intensity, as well as possessing stimulant effects that allow people to remain alert and dance all night. An amplified musical, sensory, and social experience is sometimes additionally accompanied by a loss of ego and ego-related anxieties and 'defences'.[34] The relationship between MDMA and late-1980s to early-1990s rave-related dance music cultures in the UK has been characterised by Simon Reynolds as inextricable: the drug experience is 'programmed' into the very character of the music, and vice versa. On this point, Hillegonda C. Rietveld notes that house music, one of the electronic dance music genres where ecstasy was first most commonly used in Europe, has, due to its repetitive phrases and messages of hope, compatible sonic and social qualities to enable the freeing experience of MDMA (ecstasy).[35] The loss of self or ego described in many of the scholarly and journalistic accounts (and their interviewees) is similar to the loss of self-consciousness that Csikszentmihalyi, Abuhamdeh, and Nakamura describe as taking place when a person is 'completely involved in something to the point of forgetting time, fatigue, and everything else but the activity itself'.[36] For Csikszentmihalyi, absorption in, and enjoyment of, an activity such as dancing can only take place when a degree of effort or 'challenge' is countered by some degree of 'mastery':

The list of challenges included releasing energy, lacking self-consciousness, looking good, building up energy, dancing to songs that the subject has not heard before, feeling motion, feeling comfortable, losing the self, feeling in control of the social situation, relaxing, exercising, putting a lot of thought into the dancing, having people watch the subject's dancing, merging with the music, feeling in control of the relationship with the partner, controlling body movements, concentrating, having variety in body movements, feeling tired, attracting people sexually, repeating the same movement(s) many times, coordinating body motion with the music, being different from the way the subject usually is, communicating nonverbally, meeting people, seeing self as one with the universe, feeling high on drugs, communicating with the partner, and feeling drunk.[37]

While 'the partner' implies a different social context than DJ-driven dance floors, where people generally dance independently or in groups, the majority of the attributes he describes are identifiable with dance music practices and suggest the ideals that inform conceptions of flow states on dance floors. Csikszentmihalyi's analysis of rock dancing also shows that the interpersonal aspects of social environments are essential components of viscosity for experiencing states of flow. As illustrated by Fikentscher, Malbon, and Butler regarding the interactions between dancers and other dancers, DJs and dancers, and the sound of music and dancers, similar processes are at work in electronic dance music culture.

Flow, used in this way, is also used in the positive psychology popularised in self-help culture, which is consistent with, and helpful to, the component of neo-liberal ideology that encourages individuals to direct their goals and aspirations inwardly.[38] Dance music emerged as a culture both defined by, and in defiance of, a newly neo-liberal world in the 1970s.[39] The electronic dance floor is, by extension, a space where connection and atomisation coexist in dynamic tension. Most people cannot meet the expectations of success as defined for them by neo-liberal dogma. While music and MDMA can temporarily offset the brutality of this world by eliciting feelings of connection, empathy, and flow states, these are, at their core, about pleasurable experiences and feeling good on the inside. In this sense, the flow state is itself a form of self-help, and much like other kinds of self-help, it can act as a way to manage the brutality as it is. It is a stand-in for, or diversion from, the form of struggle required to combat the very issues for which help is being sought. There is a point of comparison here with Csikszentmihalyi's idea that fulfilment is contingent on how individuals *interpret* externalities or material realities. When framed in this way, flow, and the 'challenge–skill' balance, is part of a continuum of beliefs that hold that people can overcome material struggle by manifesting their desires and thinking positively.[40] It is the capacity to gain 'control over the contents of our consciousness' and even, as his research leads him to conclude, a psychological process that seems beyond 'cultural differences':

The flow experience was not just a peculiarity of affluent, industrialised elites. It was reported in essentially the same words by old women from Korea, by adults in Thailand and India, by teenagers in Tokyo, by Navajo shepherds, by farmers in the Italian Alps, and by workers on the assembly line in Chicago.[41]

Csikszentmihalyi and his contemporaries' perspective that flow or the right 'challenge-skill' balance is the key to unlocking fulfilment is now the prevailing wisdom required for any twenty-first-century creative, recalling

McRobbie's argument that club cultures are an example of how culture industries and other workplaces approach business.[42] Overall, there is an ideological consistency between what the experiential flow state on dance floors offers, the socioeconomic practices of club cultures, and the larger neo-liberal apparatus that shapes it all.

One of the senses of flow that is worth briefly turning to, given that it is one that is crucial to the production and performance of electronic dance music, is that of electronic technology and its dependence on electricity. While a continuous flow of electricity is relied on, however, it is not inevitable or guaranteed. On the contrary, it is contingent and fragile. As Gavin Steingo argues through his research on electronic music production practices in Soweto, South Africa, this is a political issue.[43] Factors on whether music can be produced at all include whether 'gear' actually works or can be powered, reflected in the distinctly non-flowing aesthetics effects of involuntary 'digital malfunctioning', such as 'gaps, glitches and "speed bumps"', which are produced by technological failure rather than by the fetishisation of glitch. They also relate to whether electronic music technologies are available, based on the social and material conditions of those who wish to make it. In short, people cannot always obtain music technologies, these technologies do not always work effectively or smoothly even when they are obtained, and the infrastructural technologies, such as the electrical grid, on which electronic creative processes depend can break down. In some locations, and for some classes of people, this is a familiar and regular experience. Such a reality illustrates that flow is a helpful framework only if it is understood as contingent, subject to disruption, and vulnerable to the potential malfunctioning of any of the infrastructures from and to which music flows.[44]

Another critical intervention into the idea of flow can be found in the work of Sedgewick. While not about music, Sedgewick's thesis resonates with the overarching concern of this chapter with the purposes for which the concept of flow is used. Sedgewick conveys the abstract, uninterrupted movement of processes that '[submerges] ... the individual will within a social abstraction ... an endorsement of mechanised industrial processes as inevitable, natural, and indeed desirable'.[45] Importantly, he also alludes to the countercultural recent history of the instructive phrase 'go with the flow', where the aspiration is 'relinquishing contrary impulses, ideas, and intentions and submerging yourself in that course of events'.[46] Sedgewick passes over the counter cultural comparison, stating that to comment on it at length it would be 'unforgivably square'. I will relieve him of this burden: flow is transferable to the experiences that hippies and post-hippie ravers in their respective summers of love have sought out. For those who believe in the ways that music, or music's social environment, can facilitate flow, music and dance are communal spaces that invite a loss of self and ego. The 1960s counterculture is culturally and historically the closest musical culture where such an ethos was prioritised.[47] Subgroups of this culture sought self-discovery and consciousness through music, new technologies, art, and psychedelic drugs.[48]

In North America, such countercultures blended their interpretations of Native American cultural practices and symbols with notions of the self as a lifetime improvement project. As they have matured and started to retire, members of these countercultures have used this blend of ideas to influence broader popular culture, as well as media, self-help industries, and corporate wellness culture. The symbols and practices that are now associated in hindsight most overtly with this section of the hippie movement have, in some senses, endured in psychedelic trance culture, where nostalgia for the past and links with a notion of nature and the earth are blended with Indigenous and tribal cultural symbols in ways that are reductive, exoticised, and suited to Western fantasies of escape. Rietveld highlights that the musical aesthetic and culture of psychedelic trance (or psytrance) is distinctly 'technologised' even as it engages with these earthy symbolisms.[49] Moreover, many contemporary commercial EDM festival settings have adopted and augmented the carnivalesque features of psychedelic trance culture, combining them with aesthetics identifiable with late 1980s and early 1990s rave scenes, such as pacifiers, glow sticks, fluorescent clothes, child-like and feminine-coded costumes, theme park rides, and fantastical stage sets. The overarching themes in this context are escape, going with the flow, and choosing your own adventure.

These elements can be traced back to one particular dance music environment, which is known as the home of psytrance, namely the coastal area of the Indian province Goa. In the unique historical, geographical, and cultural attributes of this setting, flow – especially the rapid, globalised neoliberal kind that enables Westerners to let go of their urban lifestyles – has a multitude of effects that include buttressing inequalities between the property-owning class and the rest, forcing mobility of tourist migration flows on Indigenous and poor populations. Arun Saldanha's longitudinal ethnographic work and analysis of a Goa psytrance community makes possible an interpretation of flow that suggests it 'is not always liberating'.[50]

In addition, flow is embedded in the operational histories of capitalism, even as it describes embodied knowledge and the attainment of higher consciousness. As Sara Ahmed points out, helping people be the best versions of themselves also helps them to be the most productive, in a capitalist sense:

> We make ourselves happy, as an acquisition of capital that allows us to be or to do this or that, or even to get this or that ... Positive psychology becomes the instrumentalization of happiness as a technique ... Happiness becomes, then, a way of maximizing your potential of getting what you want, as well as being what you want to get. Unsurprisingly, positive psychology often uses economic language to describe happiness as a good.[51]

There is a continuity between the flow articulated in the positive psychology of Csikszentmihalyi and the contemporary promotion of happiness as analysed by Ahmed. They both paradoxically – or perhaps not – provide frameworks through which to understand processes and systems that serve the ideologies of capitalism. Sedgewick notes that flow does so through the illusion of choice and the reality of compliant productivity. It is used to prescribe the management of work and finance (workflow, flow chart, cash flow) and to dictate the direction or directions that processes will take within a system. Flow is deployed as a metaphor for the inevitability of top-down decisions about the flows of ideologies and of exploitable resources, people, and capital across international borders. The idea of flow normalises and naturalises a specific political economy.[52] Its deployment has been extraordinarily successful – ideologically speaking. In the end, flow, as a concept both in and out of dance music, may be elusive for those who seek it. Far from an innocent idea, it may also be debatable in what it offers as either a prescriptive ideological agenda or as a conceptual framework for understanding existing social, cultural, aesthetic, political, and historical processes.

Conclusion

Flow is a flexible metaphor. It takes many forms and has many functions. There is an ease with which flow can be adapted to positive psychology and the self-help discourse used by corporate management culture, while also seamlessly being applied to electronic music dancing. At first glance, it may seem incongruous that flow should be embraced by these different ways of understanding the world at once, especially since the underground ethos of dance music culture, in particular the hippie-derived versions that reject normative ways of being, is decidedly anti-corporate and anti-establishment. The very idea of dancing for hours, without an express purpose, is radically unproductive in the capitalist sense. However, continuity can be found across these frameworks and philosophies. In this context, I agree with Sedgewick's argument that flow, as a concept, works to naturalise processes, ideologies, and actions that are, in fact, deliberative and constructed.[53]

In short, flow in electronic dance music is constitutive of a positive dance floor experience, but this also configures a social environment where people are having a good time while they look inward (rather than to external power structures) for action and change, and view that as empowerment. Certainly, flow can be an appealing, even liberating, idea and experience. But it would be better if removed from its positive psychology associations and consciously reframed in the service of collectivist, transformative ends. If flow could be redirected from its neo-liberal utilitarian and self-help uses to instead nourishing an anti-establishment, noncompliant collective spirit focused on turning utopian experiences into social aspirations, only then might dance floors model, enact, and mobilise such a potential.

Notes

1. Angela McRobbie, 'Clubs to Companies: Notes on the Decline of Political Culture in Speeded up Creative Worlds', *Cultural Studies* 16(4), 2002: 516–31.
2. See also: Fred Turner, 'The Arts at Facebook: An Aesthetic Infrastructure for Surveillance Capitalism', *Poetics* 67, 2018: 53–62; Fred Turner, *From Counterculture to Cyberculture: Stewart Brand, The Whole Earth Network, and the Rise of Digital Utopianism* (Chicago: The University of Chicago Press, 2006); Fred Turner, 'Burning Man at Google: A Cultural Infrastructure for New Media Production', *New Media Society* 11(1 & 2), 2009: 73–94.
3. Augustine Sedgewick, 'Against Flows', *History of the Present* 4(2), 2014: 143–70.
4. Howard S. Becker, 'Becoming a Marijuana User', *American Journal of Sociology* 59 (3), November 1953: 235–42; Augustine Sedgewick, 'Against Flows', *History of the Present* 4(2), 2014: 143–70.
5. Ben Malbon, *Clubbing: Dancing, Ecstasy and Vitality* (London: Routledge, 1999), 139–43; Kai Fikentscher, *You Better Work! Underground Dance Music in New York City* (Hanover: Wesleyan University Press, 2000), 79–84.
6. Fikentscher, *You Better Work!*, 80.
7. Fikentscher, *You Better Work!*, 41.
8. Fikentscher, *You Better Work!*, 83.

9. Alice O'Grady, 'Interrupting Flow: Researching Play, Performance and Immersion in Festival Scenes', *Dancecult: Journal of Electronic Dance Music Culture* 5(1), 2017: 31.
10. Arjun Appadurai, 'Disjuncture and Difference in the Global Cultural Economy', *Theory, Culture and Society* 7 (2–3), 1990: 295–310; H. Samy Alim, 'Straight Outta Compton, Straight aus München: Global Linguistic Flows, Identities, and the Politics of Language in a Global Hip Hop Nation', in *Global Linguistic Flows, Hip Hop Cultures, Youth Identities, and the Politics of Language*, ed. H. Samy Alim, Awad Ibrahim, and Alastair Pennycook (New York and London: Routledge, 2009), 1–22.
11. Sedgewick, 'Against Flows', 143–70.
12. Gilles Deleuze and Felix Guattari, *A Thousand Plateaus: Capitalism and Schizophrenia* (Minneapolis & London: University of Minnesota Press, 1987).
13. Lucy Green, *Music, Informal Learning and the School: A New Classroom Pedagogy* (Aldershot and Burlington: Ashgate, 2008), 56–59; Rebecca J. Lloyd and Stephen J. Smith, 'Interactive Flow in Exercise Pedagogy', *Quest* 58(2), 2006: 222–41; Michele Biasutti and Katarina Habe, 'Teachers' Perspectives on Dance Improvisation and Flow', *Research in Dance Education* (June 2021): 1–20; Michele Biasutti and Luigi Frezza, 'Dimensions of Music Improvisation', *Creativity Research Journal* 21(2–3), 2009: 232–42.
14. Mihalyi Csikszentmihalyi, *Beyond Boredom and Anxiety* (San Francisco & London: Jossey-Bass Publishers, 1985); Mihalyi Csikszentmihalyi, *Good Business: Leadership, Flow, and the Making of Meaning* (New York: Penguin, 2003).
15. Sedgewick, 'Against Flows', 143–10.
16. Flow Research Collective, www.flowresearchcollective.com/ (accessed 11 September 2023).
17. Flow Research Collective, www.flowresearchcollective.com/ (accessed 11 September 2023).
18. Nancy Leong, *Identity Capitalists: The Powerful Insiders Who Exploit Diversity to Maintain Inequality* (Stanford, CA: Stanford University Press, 2021), 6–12.
19. 'Training', Flow Research Collective, www.flowresearchcollective.com/training.
20. Mark Butler, *Unlocking the Groove: Rhythm, Meter, and Musical Design in Electronic Dance Music* (Bloomington: Indiana University Press, 2006), 53–55, 242.
21. Eugene Montague, 'Moving to Music: A Theory of Sound and Physical Action', (PhD diss., University of Pennsylvania, 2001), p. 40.
22. Luis-Manuel Garcia, 'On and On: Repetition as Process and Pleasure in Electronic Dance Music', *Music Theory Online* 11(4), 2005: 1–14.
23. Csikszentmihalyi, *Beyond Boredom and Anxiety*, 104–06.
24. Tommy Four Seven (2009) *Electric Deluxe* (edlx.005), Netherlands.

25. Extrawelt (2009) 'Trummerfeld (Oliver Huntemann Remix)'. *Dark Side of My Room / Trümmerfeld (Remixes)*. Cocoon Digital (CORDIG009), Germany.
26. An interviewee, former psytrance DJ Warren, has pointed out that lower-frequency sounds tend to afford movements from lower body parts and the body's centre of gravity, while the mid- and high-frequency sounds bring on the so-called finer movements of body parts such as the arms.
27. Mark Butler, *Playing with Something that Runs: Technology, Improvisation, and Composition in DJ and Laptop Performance* (Oxford: Oxford University Press, 2014), 225–28.
28. Butler, *Playing with Something that Runs*, 176–78.
29. Garcia, 'On and On'.
30. Max Horkheimer and Theodor W. Adorno, 'The Culture Industry: Enlightenment as Mass Deception', in *Dialectic of Enlightenment: Philosophical Fragments*, ed. Gunzelin Schmid Noerr, trans. Edmund Jephcott (Stanford: Stanford University Press, 2012), 94–136.
31. Garcia, 'On and On'.
32. Butler, *Playing with Something that Runs,* 174–75.
33. Malbon, *Clubbing*, 106–11; Simon Reynolds, *Energy Flash: A Journey Through Rave Music and Dance Culture* (London: Picador, 2008), xxxii; Bill Brewster and Frank Broughton, *Last Night a DJ Saved My Life: The History of the Disc Jockey* (London: Headline, 2006), 380.
34. See, for example, Jerome Beck and Marsha Rosenbaum, *Pursuit of Ecstasy: The MDMA Experience* (Albany: State University of New York Press, 1994); Push and Mireille Silcott, *The Book of E: All About Ecstasy* (London: Omnibus Press, 2000), 8; Malbon, *Clubbing*, 116–32.
35. Simon Reynolds, 'Rave Culture: Living Dream, or Living Death?', in *The Clubcultures Reader: Readings in Popular Cultural Studies*, ed. Steve Redhead, Derek Wynne, and Justin O'Connor (Oxford: Blackwell, 1997), 87–88; Hillegonda C. Rietveld, *This is Our House: House Music, Cultural Spaces and Technologies* (London: Ashgate, 1998), 147–48.
36. Mihalyi Csikszentmihalyi, Sami Abuhamdeh, and Jeanne Nakamura, 'Flow', in *Flow and the Foundations of Positive Psychology: The Collected Works of Mihalyi Csikszentmihalyi*, ed. Mihalyi Csikszentmihalyi (Dordrecht: Springer, 2014), 230–31.
37. Csikszentmihalyi, *Beyond Boredom and Anxiety*, 111.
38. See, for example, Heidi Rimke, 'Self-Help, Therapeutic Industries, and Neoliberalism', in *The Routledge International Handbook of Global Therapeutic Cultures*, ed. Daniel Nehring, Ole Jacob Madsen, Edgar Cabanas, China Mills, and Dylan Kerrigan (London: Routledge, 2020), 37–50.
39. Richard Dyer, 'In Defence of Disco', *Gay Left* 8 (Summer, 1979): 20–23.
40. See, for example, Norman Vincent Peale, *The Power of Positive Thinking* (Old Tappan, NJ: Touchstone, 2003); Napoleon Hill, *Think and Grow Rich*

(London: Vermillion, 2019); Rhonda Byrne, *The Secret* (New York: Atria/ Hillsboro: Beyond Words, 2018).
41. Mihalyi Csikszentmihalyi, *Flow: The Psychology of Optimal Experience* (New York: Harper Collins, 1990), 4.
42. Angela McRobbie, *Be Creative: Making a Living in the New Culture Industries* (Cambridge: Polity Press, 2016).
43. Gavin Steingo, 'Sound and Circulation: Immobility and Obduracy in South African Electronic Music', *Ethnomusicology Forum* 24 (1) (March 2015); see also Alan Durant, 'A New Day for Music? Digital Technologies in Contemporary Music-Making', in *Culture, Technology and Creativity in the Late Twentieth Century*, ed. Philip Hayward (London: John Libbey, 1990), 193–95.
44. Steingo, 'Sound and Circulation', 102–23.
45. Augustine Sedgewick, 'Against Flows', *History of the Present* 4 (2) (Fall 2014): 146–47.
46. Sedgewick, 'Against Flows', 152–53.
47. Tim Lawrence, *Love Saves the Day: A History of American Dance Music Culture, 1970–1979* (Durham, NC: Duke University Press, 2003), 9–10. See also A. Kabil (14 July 2017) 'This Magical Drug Mansion in Upstate New York Is Where the Psychedelic '60s Took Off'. *Timeline*. https://timeline.com/drug-mansion-psychedelic-60s-5116867d5041.
48. Turner, *From Counterculture to Cyberculture*, 31–38.
49. Hillegonda C. Rietveld, 'Dancing in the Technoculture', in *The Routledge Research Companion to Electronic Music: Reaching out with Technology*, ed. Simon Emmerson (London: Routledge, 2018), 121–24.
50. Arun Saldanha, *Psychedelic White: Goa Trance and the Viscosity of Race* (Minneapolis: University of Minnesota Press, 2007), 51–52. See also Arun Saldanha, 'Psychedelics Under Catastrophe: Reflections on the October 7 Rave Massacre', *The South Atlantic Quarterly* 124(2) (2025): 375–97.
51. Sara Ahmed, *The Promise of Happiness* (Durham, NC: Duke University Press, 2010), 10.
52. Sedgewick, 'Against Flows', 144, 151–52.
53. Sedgewick, 'Against Flows,' 147.

Further Reading

Csikszentmihalyi, Mihalyi. *Flow: The Psychology of Optimal Experience*. New York: Harper Collins, 1990.

Garcia-Mispireta, Luis Manuel. *Together, Somehow: Music, Affect, and Intimacy on the Dancefloor*. Durham, NC: Duke University Press, 2023.

McRobbie, Angela. *Be Creative: Making a Living in the New Culture Industries*. Cambridge: Polity Press, 2016.
Sedgewick, Augustine. 'Against Flows'. *History of the Present* 4 (2), Fall 2014: 143–70.
Wark, McKenzie. *Raving*. Durham, NC: Duke University Press, 2023.

Discography

Extrawelt (2009) *Trümmerfeld* (Oliver Huntemann Remix), Trümmerfeld Remixes. Cocoon Recordings. CORDIG009. Available at: http://boomkat.com/downloads/216987-extrawelt-trummerfeld-mixes (Downloaded: 29 August 2009).

Tommy Four Seven (2009) *Surma* (Speedy J Dub Tool), *Surma EP*. Electric Deluxe. EDLX005. Available at: http://boomkat.com/downloads/207651-tommy-four-seven-surma-ep (Downloaded: 20 July 2009).

PART V

Dance Floor Identities

16 | Feminine Subjectivities

Gender in Electronic Music Production and Performance

SAMANTHA PARSLEY

Drawing on empirical data, this chapter shows how women artists navigate the gendered complexities of working in a highly male-dominated occupation. The discussion addresses six subjectivities enacted by women producing and performing electronic dance music, showing the impacts these subject positions have on their careers. I conclude the chapter by showing how women's collectives are challenging the status quo within the industry by providing public and visible action through the 'safety and strength in numbers' of collective activism. 'Producer' here refers to artists who self-produce their own music at home, rather than those producing other people's music in a professional studio setting. Despite some similarities, there are different gender dynamics at play in such settings with some excellent texts devoted to exploring them.[1] In addition, although 'production' is sometimes used to denote remixing/ mashing-up music on the fly during DJ sets or playing improvised music with live set-ups, none of my interviewees used the term in this way.[2]

Theoretical inspiration is taken from two sources in order to recognise gender as a socio-historical construct that shifts over time, and which is performed in response to political, power-laden, and situational factors. First, McRobbie understands feminine subjectivities as arising from 'cultural forms and interpellations (or dominant social processes) [that] call women into being, produc[ing] them as subjects'.[3] This view of subjectivity emphasises the role of context and culture beyond the individual in making up selfhood, following a social constructivist view of the world where we primarily learn who we are – and who we aspire to be – through intersubjective social relations.[4] Secondly, I resonate with Thomas' emphasis on the 'interrelation of power and subjectivity in identity formation',[5] recognising that social forces are neither neutral, nor experienced as independent from one another. Here, this translates into a commitment to recognising the intersectionality of these women's experiences[6] within an overall investigation of identifying as a woman electronic dance music DJ/producer. These ideas are foundational to the field of Critical Management Studies[7] from which I write. They also underpin my choice to use the term 'woman' in what follows – rather than the more biologically deterministic 'female'. Being a woman is something that the artists in my study 'do' rather than something they 'are'.[8] Avoiding the term 'female' also supports my intention to be trans-inclusive, although to my knowledge all the artists whose voices appear below are cis-gendered. Several were queer and/or working in environments that challenged heteronormativity.

As this is a chapter that deals with subjectivity, I first offer some background to my own position. I am a white, UK-born-and-based academic working in a business school. At the time of writing I am in my early fifties, a long-time lover of electronic music, and regular clubber for the past twenty-three years. I taught myself to DJ in 2015 and perform at grass roots level a few times a year. I am a co-organiser of a small community multi-genre dance festival[9] and work alongside industry as a co-chair of the Association of Electronic Music's diversity working group. I began researching the careers of women (self)producers of electronic music in 2017[10] and around the same time began to learn music production myself,[11] which developed into a source of auto-ethnographic data in its own right[12] alongside the programme of interviews from which this chapter draws.[13]

Gender Imbalance in Electronic Dance Music Production

Largely on account of its technology-dependent character, producing and performing electronic music has historically been regarded – and written about[14] – as a male domain, in Anglo-Euro-American contexts at least.[15] This is despite some of the field's most important pioneers being women, for example Wendy Carlos, Suzanne Ciani, Pauline Oliveros, and Daphne Oram's compositions with tape and modular synthesisers, popularising electronic sounds across film and TV, which influenced early electronic popular music in the UK, America, and Europe, Globally, early women electronic music artists include Mieko Shiomi (Japan) and Iris Sangüesa from Chile.[16] The over-emphasis on men's contributions to electronic music, such as household names Frankie Knuckles, Marshall Jefferson, Tiesto, and so on, is perhaps the first instance of power-laden dynamics that we can discern as having an impact on feminine subjectivities in this field. When immersing themselves, and learning about music production and performance, women do not see themselves represented *as* women practitioners, experts, or pioneers of the craft.[17] This immediately signals 'Oh, I'm different' to women at the start of their career (or before) with important consequences as I discuss further below.

At the time of writing, women[18] make up less than 6 per cent of the producers of US Billboard chart songs,[19] and are estimated to be only 9 per cent of the members of the Audio Engineering Society in the UK.[20] According to the most recent figures, girls make up a small proportion of enrolments on UK music technology A-levels[21] and degree courses.[22] Similarly, women artists remain a low-key presence at electronic music festivals: at 104 UK festivals in 2022, only 18 per cent of the headline acts were women[23] and women comprise 27 per cent of festival acts across Europe.[24] The situation is worse in nightclubs with the numbers of women playing globally in 2019 ranging between 6 per cent in 150 large iconic 'A-list' venues to 11 per cent in smaller-capacity grassroots clubs.[25] Inequality also goes beyond representation in numbers with surveys repeatedly revealing the electronic music industry as rife with discrimination,[26] sexual harassment, and microaggressions[27] towards women who work in it.

A more gender-balanced electronic music industry matters because women have as much right to follow a creative music career as men, yet are prevented from entering because they do not see people 'like them' in that world.[28] Once women do join the industry, a lack of role models translates into isolation, stunted networks, and limited career opportunities, as they can find themselves the only woman on the line-up at the club, struggling to be taken seriously in the 'bro culture'[29] that particularly characterises underground and grassroots electronic dance music scenes. Initiatives working towards increasing representation of women in the industry[30] can only be successful if women feel *included* as well as admitted – and as the findings I present in this chapter show, we still have a long way to go – although we are undoubtedly making progress.[31]

An Ethnographic-Feminist Methodology

The findings presented below are drawn from a feminist ethnography of women, technology, and cultural production within the electronic music industry.[32] I refer to this as a feminist methodology because it explicitly champions and raises the visibility of women electronic artists, but also because I have used methods to generate my data that foreground reflexive rapport with participants[33] and pay close attention to the small, everyday details of their and my own lives.[34] I have formally interviewed a range of industry stakeholders and women producers (n=63), had countless conversations with others, and followed posts and dialogues on social media. I have produced regular podcasts, and the project has also been featured in a number of music media outlets.[35] I have taken part in industry conferences and panels, maintained social media platforms and a website, and compiled a Producer Directory to raise the visibility of women, trans, and non-binary artists.[36] In addition, I have worked with a leading industry body for electronic music, taking part in industry conferences and panels, and shaping strategy. I have also taught myself to DJ and produce music as already noted.

From my research with women who work creatively in electronic dance music, it is possible to draw six subject positions. These insights emerged especially from a series of formal semi-structured interviews with artists producing and performing a range of electronic dance music genres, from drum and bass and hard techno to house and downtempo chill. These are combined with my ethnographic and autoethnographic observations as an artist, activist, industry advisor, and electronic music fan, as well as an academic researcher.[37] Analysis was undertaken concurrently with data collection[38] in order to refine propositions and emerging themes in what Silverman calls an 'intensive/ extensive' manner.[39] In the initial stages of analysis this means a small number of interviews (in my case twelve) are analysed in-depth to identify patterns which then serve as a template for deductively coding the remaining data. Subject positions developed from the first stage analysis were used as the template for subsequent interviews. New data that emerged were incorporated into the template as analysis and further data collection proceeded in tandem. It was also possible to probe for further data on the emerging subject positions as new interviews were conducted, and informal conversations took place. This approach proved fruitful for strategically managing a large and complex dataset to ensure usable outcomes, whilst remaining open to new data arising as the project progressed. The discussion that follows details the six subject positions, which can be summarised as follows: the intersectional artist; the genderless artist; visible woman as invisible artist; shrinking violets versus tough cookies; one of the boys; and bringers of 'divine feminine energy'. This will be followed by a consideration of whether women-only learning spaces and teamwork may be a possible way to resolve marginalisation in a male-dominated industry.

The Intersectional Artist

Any attempt to talk about feminine subjectivities must first recognise the 'maze' of intersectionalities that make up lived experience – and in particular the lived experience of oppression and marginalisation.[40] When the women in my study talk about being a woman, they are also talking about the kind of woman they are at the intersection of many other identity characteristics – including – but not limited to – race, colour, age, sexuality, weight, socio-economic background, and parental status. Several participants told me how they were refused entry to the DJ booth, clubs, and festival stages, and had their presence questioned because (usually male) security staff assumed they were 'groupies'. When I asked Nelly if the particular microaggression she had encountered was on account of her gender and her racial appearance she responded:

Yes, and size as well, At the time I was much larger than [I am now], so race, gender, size, just everything. Like, I wasn't a traditional-looking DJ . . .

As Nelly's words suggest, attempting to write an intersectional account of one's data is complex, particularly when it comes to actually theorising what those compound systems of oppression (or indeed advantages) mean in terms of the operation of power and the production of subjectivities.[41] Although this is not an explicitly intersectional chapter, I nonetheless wish to recognise that not all the women in my study experienced their gender in the same way even *within* intersectional categories, as India explains:

I understand that even as a Black woman I have a privilege 'cos I have fairer skin, I'm not a dark-skinned Black woman.

Similarly, other artists talked about looking younger than their age as a source of privilege, while at the same time recognising the 'sell-by date' stamped on women in the music industry. Others remarked that they hid their age and vigilantly edited their photos so as to appear 'ageless' as a strategy to avoid this. The issue of age was also bound up with maternity and motherhood, with younger participants expressing anxiety around when, and if, to have children and how to manage any absence from their career:

I would want to make sure there's a lot of things to promote, for example I'd make sure I've got [music] releases scheduled . . . I've got this fear like if you come out of gigs for five months people think you've stopped the career, or you don't want to do it anymore, cos they're not seeing things going on. (Naomi)

It is of note that very few of the older, more experienced producers I interviewed for this study were mothers, with those who were explaining how difficult, expensive, and exhausting it is to combine motherhood with touring and producing responsibilities, or recounting stories of outright discrimination:

[T]hings were going really well, and then I got pregnant with my son ... and basically as soon as they found out it was like a hot rock being dropped ... (Carmen)

However, there was also recognition by some mothers of the increasing opportunities offered by festivals and 'day parties' that might allow them to work less anti-social hours.

With the above in mind, the rest of the data presented in this chapter inherently involves a range of intersections that I cannot do justice to here. However, where other identity characteristics are implicated I aim to 'complicate gender'[42] as the sole category at play in the accounts that follow. However, having made that commitment I move to a subject position that seemingly removes gender from the equation altogether.

The Genderless Artist

Conceiving of themselves as 'genderless' was experienced by the producers in this study in a variety of ways. First, there were reports that until a certain point in their career, some of the artists had never noticed, or really thought about the fact that they *were* women, and by extension they had taken for granted that the landscape they operated in was so heavily male dominated.

At that point I was like the only female DJ [in my hometown scene]. So, I never thought about it, like I didn't even think 'it's hard for girls or it's hard because I'm a girl and I'm pretty'. No, I never like even thought about that, [I guess] I just was so focused on my own thing. (Celene)

This 'gender-blindness'[43] was underlined by the sentiment that gender should be irrelevant to career success and this was reported with varying degrees of conviction and indignation. There were those who merely wished for this as a desirable future state of a utopian music industry: for example, Suzie – a new producer who felt that 'the end goal is for no one to notice what gender, or colour, or whatever you are, right?', through to those who expressed annoyance at the fact music might not be the sole criteria on which women were being judged:

I don't want to focus on [gender], I just want to focus on it being art, I never ever tag anything that's female DJ, female producer, cos I want to avoid that whole thing. (Alice)

I wouldn't purposely be like 'I need more females in my playlist', I'm like, if there's good music there's good music, [doesn't matter] if it happens to be by a man or a woman. (Naomi)

In this vein, several artists declined my invitation to be interviewed because they avoided practices that associated them with their gender. Likewise, a (male) festival organiser I interviewed remarked that a gender-expansive artist they had booked to perform had asked to be removed from all promotional materials where they would be associated with the festival's goal of increasing representation of minoritised genders.

These data evidence wider discourses of perceived meritocracy in the electronic music industry and creative industries more generally.[44] Comments along the lines of 'I don't care what gender, race or anything else the DJ-Producer is, I'm only interested in good music' are commonplace – indeed, almost *guaranteed* – in response to any positive action initiative posted on social media in a mixed-gender space for example.[45] This means that women in this industry are constantly reminded that their gender *shouldn't* matter and that any desire to contest this or push back against such assumptions leads to difficult feelings to be reconciled. For example, responding to comments on social media that 'the music is all that matters' was recounted to me during interviews as being infused with anxiety about how best to respond, because it is so entrenched in societal discourse. I was told of personal and of misogynistic online abuse, or feelings of guilt and shame for not speaking out. My own experience of posting on a festival's Facebook page to question why the line-up was 80 per cent white men supports this. Early on in my data collection and not yet confident in my identity as a gender researcher, I crumbled under the pressure of upsetting comments attacking me, my research, and the idea of positive action. Others I interviewed also reported the exhaustion they experience almost daily as they engage in the work of 'calling out' inequality when they see it, or the guilt they feel if they don't.[46]

Visible Woman, Invisible Artist

However, the impossibility of becoming 'genderless' can be seen in the insights I present below. Almost everyone I spoke to noted how their gender made them hyper-visible. This manifested itself in every sphere – from classroom to DJ booth and in spaces related to production:

[T]hey told me it's only 10 per cent [women] in the whole school, so just imagine ... you're surrounded by a lot of boys, and they're all younger than you. (Heather)

I was their only ever main room female resident, and there was animosity up there I fucking tell you. It wasn't nice up there. (Jenny)

[P]retty much always it's assumed that I'm going to be the singer cos I'm a woman, so then I have to go through the process of 'no, I'm a producer', and then already you've got a weird disadvantage cos you kind of have to like prove yourself. (Hayley)

Through my own immersion in the industry I have observed the overwhelming maleness in magazine articles,[47] YouTube tutorials, memes, cartoons, music conference panels, and in music technology stores – both in front of and behind the counter. Women stand out because they are unusual bodies that 'don't fit' the somatic norm.[48] On more than one occasion I have noticed official photographers taking pictures of me when I'm twiddling knobs in the gear labs at music conferences – no doubt to later show how inclusive and diverse their users are. Yet beyond the photo-frame, every other person in the room is a man. Given growing attention to gender inequality in the electronic music industry in recent years[49] there is pressure on organisations to demonstrate their commitment to diversifying their rosters and line-ups, which some saw as leading to tokenism, or 'box ticking' as Loretta described it.[50] Grace also noted – with disdain – how her 'marketable' appearance was often commented on before her music. However, others saw potential tokenism more positively as an opportunity to shine despite being given the gig under questionable circumstances. One of the teachers on a women-only DJ course I attended told us her aim as an early-career artist warming up for bigger (male) acts:

Everyone's gonna *expect* the headliner to be good, but I want them to walk away thinking 'Wow! That warm-up girl was amazing' because they're not expecting much so it's easy for me to blow them away. (Teacher at Female DJ course)

Being visible as a woman was also expressed as a moral imperative, with some artists seeing it as their duty to be extra visible, to the point that they considered themselves ambassadors or role models for their gender.

I was the only woman [on my course] with 250 men, so that was probably the first time that I was like 'Oh. Wow'. And I thought this is really hard for me and this isn't natural and actually I'm having a really difficult time of this ... but because there [were] no women there I was like *fuck this*, I have to learn this. (Hayley)

I always say I bring the glamour to the geek, but I think of myself as a geek first and then a glamorous kind of person ... if I encourage just one [attractive] woman to do this, not just be an Instagram model ... I'll be like *yeah!* (Carmen)

... yes it's like, I dress in a sexual way or a sexy way when I DJ but I also have an engineering degree and I also am a sick DJ don't tell me what I can and cannot do. (Mona)

Mona's words above hint at how women are scrutinised and policed for their appearance in physical and online spaces in ways that men are not. Further impacts are discussed in the sections below, but here, the fact that they are women in a 'male space' marks these artists as different, as outsiders, with all the connotations of hyper-visibility, not-belonging, and exclusion (intentional or not) that brings. Even if everyone is friendly on a one-to-one basis, in a group setting difference is magnified and it's hard not to feel excluded.[51]

Observing the dynamics behind the decks at events showed this in action. As the guys back-slap, high-five, hug, and fist-bump each other during DJ change-overs, they all but ignore a woman when she takes to the stage. I doubt the men I watched were even aware they were doing this. More conscious exclusionary tactics were also reported to me with artists telling stories of equipment sabotage and, more commonly, having the equipment explained to them, or tampered with during their set.

I was forced to play 'back to back' with this guy, and he just took over. I got to play two records in an hour. (Angelica)

This was reported as getting worse the more 'feminine' you look, and the more attractive you are, which blinded others to their skill and legitimacy – particularly around technical skill and competence. We see this in Hayley's account above, feeling at a 'weird disadvantage' because she felt she had to prove herself.

Regularly being doubted as not having the correct technical skills in DJing and especially music production was universal across the interviewees:

[W]hen you mention to people you *produce* music, a lot of them actually can't believe it, like 'really? *really*? you a woman . . . no this is a man's thing' . . . 'we need to listen [to your music], we need to prove it['s you]', and yes, normally they are amazed – nobody can believe it's me. (Katarina)

[O]ne bloke [was] . . . like literally showing me how to use a mixer before my set . . . mate, I've been DJing for 15 years, you don't need to show me how. (Tess)

I have also experienced this when I've been DJing. Having my space invaded by a drunk guy trying to 'party with me' behind the booth.[52] On other occasions, men have come behind the decks 'trying to help', sometimes from the crowd, but also sound engineers assuming I don't know what I am doing.[53] As Tyla summarises here, men demonstrate a sense of entitlement around the DJ booth space and the equipment through this behaviour:

You've obviously got to feel more powerful than the person that you're interrupting, you know to lean across me and do [touch/ adjust] something? that's certainly dominance. (Tyla)

The impact this subtle and not-so-subtle undermining has on one's self-belief and esteem leads to not speaking up, asking questions, getting involved, networking, reaching out to collaborators, and so on.

[W]hen I was a student I would wait till all the guys left the room and I would be the last person with my professor to feel comfortable to ask him questions. (Liz)

I was the only woman and person of colour in this group. I don't know what the [tech] does, it just makes a lot of noise, which is cool, but *everyone else seems to know*, so I'm not going to ask any questions, I just can't be bothered to feel stupid and look stupid. (Emma)

This 'reluctance' is then cast as women having a lack of confidence, or that they are 'suffering' from imposter syndrome, which individualises the problem as a 'pathology' to be fixed rather than a systemic and structural issue to be addressed.[54]

Shrinking Violets and Tough Cookies

The assumption that 'women lack confidence' is a taken-for-granted discourse throughout the industry, and commonly espoused by the women themselves as a reason why they were so under-represented. as Tara explains in relation to finding female-produced music for her radio show:

[T]here isn't enough music *by* women and I don't know what that reason is, but I think a lot of it's down to confidence. (Tara)

Often this manifested itself as an imperative to 'step up' and 'put yourself forward' even when faced with anxiety-provoking situations. For example, Tess explained how she hand-delivered mixtapes to club promoters in her home town when she was starting out,[55] and Suzie spoke of not being afraid of 'going out and grabbing opportunities'. Likewise, Alyson underscores the importance of 'having the courage of your convictions' and being assertive in the face of poor treatment. To *not* do so was seen as a failing or sign of weakness:

... it's still, like I'm not pushing myself enough, I know that. (Helen)

[W]e're awesome but we're not just shouting about it enough and we sometimes think we're not ready enough, [well] lady, I'm sorry but you will never, *ever* be ready and if you don't get out there then that's where you'll stay, you're not going to move forward. (Alice)

Other areas where a lack of confidence is taken unquestionably as the reason why women decline invitations are conference panels or studio demonstration and track deconstructions (both offline and online). As such, well-meant effort is channelled into initiatives that 'help' women feel more empowered and gain the bravery required to 'step up' to such opportunities. There have been many instances throughout the research where I have been asked for advice, or to speak at workshops and seminars aimed at helping women gain the confidence to submit their music, contact promoters, or network. However, whilst these initiatives are valuable for many, and provide a strong source of support, peer development, and connections for the women who attend them, they nonetheless position women artists' exclusion as their own fault and something for them to fix.[56]

Furthermore, as Olive wryly remarks:

A lot of women are *more* than confident enough to walk into a room full of men and hold their own. We're not a bunch of shrinking violets. (Olive)

Yet 'holding their own' in male-dominated public spaces is harder to do than it first appears, often requiring considerable effort beyond the norm, and nerves of steel:

[I] just had this insane drive to just show all of those men that no, no I can do this just as good, if not better than you, and I'm going to do it my way and I do not care what you say about it. (Kate)

This kind of 'toughening up' takes a psychological toll with the emotional fallout and exhaustion such constant battling brings. It even threatens physical safety with women often expected to place themselves in hostile, or dangerous situations. More than one participant told me about serious sexual assault either they or women known to them had suffered, with other stories referring to drinks being spiked, or being 'hit on' by so-called collaborators. Less extreme but perhaps even more commonplace among grass-roots artists is the assumption that to get gigs in the first place you need to go to other DJs' parties, which throws up particular challenges for women:

> I don't feel comfortable going to an all-night gig on my own where I know no one, at the other end of the country, just to meet a promoter who might – or probably won't – book me anyway. (Esther)

This was echoed in a story told to me by an artist playing at an event run by a well-respected record label. Despite this being a professionally run, well-known global brand, she was still left to walk three miles alone to a train station at 4 a.m. after her gig. It was during the 'petrol crisis' that hit the UK in 2021 and there were no taxis available, and the promoters were 'so wasted on booze and coke' that they were unable to drive her.

This unwelcoming and sometimes hostile environment is not only confined to physical encounters. Three examples (of many) from my online observations include a well-established techno producer playing live using drum machines while dancing in her seat, ridiculed in the comments beneath the video for 'bouncing on a dildo' under her desk, another who was challenged that half her equipment wasn't plugged in and accused of 'trying to be one of the cool boys' because she was wearing a beanie hat, and yet another accused of 'attention grabbing' while playing her set because she wasn't wearing a bra under her vest. These comments aimed at women performers are often shockingly hostile, and as Jenny summarises here, caused her to withdraw from online music spaces altogether:

> I suffered a severe amount of abuse at the hands of some of these – quite reputable – DJs, really like hateful, sort of like online slagging, so I won't join any of the ones that aren't exclusively women. (Jenny)

Interestingly, despite earlier describing herself as a 'tough cookie' during our conversation, Jenny still felt the need to minimise her experiences here with the words 'sort of like' to describe behaviours that she clearly found upsetting and damaging.

Unsurprisingly this kind of experience results in an unwillingness on the part of women artists to accept invitations to do this kind of work. This in turn makes women artists even more invisible, and means that record labels, tech companies, streaming platforms, and so on find it hard to be more representative in their communication materials. As Mary Beard[57] reminds us, censoring women's speech and public appearance has been a technique to eviscerate women's power since antiquity, and social media offers a particularly effective modern form of this violence.

An alternative reading of this situation, therefore, could be that 'putting yourself out there' is extremely challenging unless the environment is welcome and receptive. This has certainly been borne out by bespoke campaigns to attract women artists to record labels, remix competitions, and women-only development events:

[We] didn't think we were going to get many demos but after about 24 hours we had 90 demos, and it was amazing . . . I don't know if it's because we've actively said look girls we want you, we're listening, send us your music? (Adeline)

Every time we do a new contest, we get usually you know 50 to 100 new members in the group. (Angelica)

they sent us a bunch of synthesisers and we had a few hundred women come to this awesome space [. . .] and we had different rooms set up with different synthesisers and we taught them to all these women. We had to turn people away we were completely full. (Leah)

In summary then, being confident to 'put yourself out there' requires constant vigilance as artists operate outside their comfort zone for a lot of their working life. It is much easier to exhibit 'confidence' when assured of a safe space in which to do so.

One of the Boys

The above accounts of surviving outside one's comfort zone are all the more notable when we take into account the backgrounds of many of the artists I spoke to. A historical or current sense of 'maleness' in behaviours, and to some extent identity, was mobilised by about two-thirds of the artists I interviewed. They explained to me how their childhoods were 'boyish', either because they hung out with boys, enjoyed 'male' pursuits, or had parents who actively encouraged them to engage in activities that transgressed traditional gender norms, perhaps contributing to a sense of being 'genderless' (or at least less traditionally feminine) given that masculinity is regarded as the norm in a patriarchal context.

I feel like I've always been into quite male stuff, I'm a bit of a tomboy in that sense, I've always been into sport, my dad he's really into motor sports, so when I was growing up we were always out on motorbikes, just always involved in more male stuff. (Naomi)

I think part of my story I can thank my dad a lot for, my dad kind of brought me up in way where he treated me as though I was his son, which is probably why I ended up studying [electrical] engineering. (Genevieve)

> I was not classified as a normal girl back then at all, they wouldn't see me as a girl for some reason, I didn't look anything like a boy but they just didn't treat me like other girls... people still nowadays say to me that I'm different than other girls, I'm not your typical girl, and I still don't understand it. (Katarina)

Gaming, DIY, early computing, and engineering were cited as enabling greater comfort around music technology in later life, meaning that for women who had not been socialised around such things the difficulties described in the previous section might be seen as even more daunting. As noted in the introduction to this chapter, the technological world of electronic music production and performance is culturally coded as 'masculine' and while being proficient in it may affirm masculine identity (albeit perhaps as 'geeks or nerds') it actively transgresses feminine identities.[58] Thus, it is perhaps not surprising that around 40 per cent of my dataset includes women who recounted a 'boyish' history and preferences for 'men's pursuits' since they would have experienced lower psychosocial barriers to participation than women with more traditional gender identities. This has important implications for how to tackle gender imbalance, as Olive observes:

> the fact that computers have traditionally been gendered as boys' toys and girls have been separated from that, that playing on computers is a boys activity from that primary age, I think *that's* the thing that needs to be addressed. (Olive)

Given that gendered occupational stereotypes generally form as young as seven years old,[59] efforts to empower women to become and remain electronic music artists probably need to start at a very young age.

Being 'one of the boys' – or at least trying to be – was also enacted through everyday practices aimed at 'fitting in' or 'passing',[60] most noticeably through dress. The 'DJ uniform' of cool t-shirt and jeans was repeatedly labelled by participants as 'androgynous', yet clearly echoes male norms of dress. This corresponds to subject positions found in a study of EDM DJs undertaken in the mid 2000s in the US that women DJs were stereotyped as either 'Sex kittens', 'T-Shirt DJs', or 'dykes', and it appears that not much has changed.[61] Given that we have already seen how some artists deliberately reject this pressure, dressing in overtly feminine and sexualised ways, for example Carmen's 'glam in the geek' and Mona's self-described provocativeness. However, more of the artists in my study or that I have observed more broadly framed their self-presentation in 'DJ uniform' as chosen for 'comfort' or as an effective strategy for being taken more seriously as an artist. Emily told me how she only received negative comments on her livestreams when she wore a party dress while DJing instead of her more usual 'DJ uniform' of baggy t-shirt and jeans. Recounting the accusation from the troll that she was copying 'Paris Hilton' and was a sad indictment of what DJing these days had come to, Emily was visibly upset as we talked, telling me how she would never again wear anything 'pretty' to DJ. Likewise, Kate went to extreme lengths to disguise her gender to avoid backlash:

I was just like I *hate* this, I hate that I have to deal with this, so I would literally dress like a boy, like I covered every part of my body, like there was nothing you could really tell, I had long hair but I didn't wear makeup ... it was like I was just doing everything in my power ... to draw attention away from the fact that I was a woman, and it's kind of heart-breaking. (Kate)

The result of such practices is an attempt to be genderless, but it has the effect of literally dressing the role of 'electronic music artist' as a man, reinforcing masculine traits as inherently part of the job, and subtly alienating women from aspiring to be one. Ashcraft speaks firmly to this idea using the metaphor of Cinderella's 'glass slipper'[62] to explain how affective and sensory cues give rise to the 'naturalisation' of occupations as stereotypically embodied. These everyday subtleties are in part constituent of 'implicit bias',[63] which means we do not question how and why some occupations just 'naturally' seem to fit certain groups and not others.[64]

Bringers of 'Divine Feminine Energy'

In contrast to being 'one of the boys', requiring women to assimilate into a male identity and downplay femininity as an ethic of sameness, an alternative subjectivity – of difference – was mobilised by some of the artists I interviewed. At the core of this idea was a concern for 'feminine energy' that was either uniquely valuable by itself, or a refreshing balance to the qualities men bring.

it's not a bad thing to be more feminine ... we're not trying to be the men, we're trying to have our own space in the music industry overall, which is going to look different to what the men look like in their roles. (Olga)

In relation to appearance, some artists spoke of deliberately dressing up to perform, as we saw in the case of Carmen and Mona above, to show that technical prowess and skill is not at odds with feminine physical attractiveness. Other ways women were seen as different were attributed to biological and other essentialist factors:

> [W]omen are a little bit more emotional . . . a lot more emotional, and there's only one reason for that, it's because of the hormonal cycle, which is something the men [don't] have, and I think this biological difference between us makes us behave differently and approach life a little bit differently. (Ruby)

> [It's] feminine energy . . . we bring the beauty, we bring like the truth, we bring the kind of like aesthetics of things, we kind of like do our hair or put makeup on and all this kind of stuff [. . .] So it takes us longer to just really focus in and just almost like drill into learning this stuff [music production]. (Evelyn)

This feminine energy was mobilised to justify why women were less confident as we have seen above, but also used by some to suggest differences in the actual music that women make with women being seen to make music that has more 'soul', less 'bang', and so on. Given that 'deep house' is one of the genres where women are least represented[65] and some of the artists I interviewed make and play the hardest 140+ BPM techno imaginable, I am doubtful that this is actually the case. What is significant, however, is that women believe they are doing something special and different in order to earn their right to be there – it is not enough to demand acceptance and respect on the same terms as men.[66]

However, one area where I have consistently noticed that women do behave differently is behind the decks. Smiling, making eye contact, dancing, and generally being a 'conduit of joy' as Hayley delightfully put it, women truly perform as they play, unlike many male DJs. This is likely to be because women are socialised to be looked at. Initially as the object of the male gaze, but then internalised as a seemingly neutral imperative to please anyone who looks on.[67] As noted above this can draw unwanted comments and sexualised remarks, but nonetheless it can also be a very positive element of difference. I am regularly complimented on the infectious happy energy I convey when I DJ and know that this is a reason I have been booked to play. Notably, while performing an afternoon set to a packed festival crowd recently I noticed that many of the people at the front of the crowd were young girls, smiling and waving to me in safety – delighted to be seeing a woman up there on the stage (even if I was easily old enough to be their mother!). I like to think that seeing a woman having fun and loving what she's doing sent a positive message to those young girls. Likewise, when attending gigs that have all-women line-ups there seems to be an aesthetic of fun that is off the scale, compared to the sober seriousness of men who may not even make eye contact with the crowd as they play. This was often recognised by male allies who remarked to me how having women performing alongside them brought a less hyper-masculine, toxic vibe to events:

the men want us there, they really, they're like it's a fresh breath of air that you girls are coming along because it's a sausage fest over here. (Alice)

Stronger Together?

We have seen how women electronic music artists enact a range of subjectivities that allow them to stand out, fit in, hide, or hold their own in ways that have varying implications for their careers. What unites almost all the stories presented above, however, is that they are individualistic tales of coping alone, or fending for oneself. Very often the women I interviewed expressed interest and relief when I told them that others had told me of similar incidents or experiences to theirs. Very few of the artists, and none of those with longer career histories, spoke of using or even being aware of women's support networks. Many struggled to even name many other women artists. Battling alone was recounted almost as a badge of honour – clawing oneself up and living to tell the tale. But happily this is changing and with it, I argue, comes greater potential for systemic change.

At the time I started the research, women's groups were forming across the music space to facilitate safe spaces for women to come together to learn, mentor, play gigs as a collective, organise parties and conferences, and generally form networks of like-minded people to support one another.[68] Although some have been around for several years – for example, Female:pressure in Berlin, Discwoman (now DW Artists) in NYC, and Psy-sisters in the UK,[69] – the emergence of these collectives accelerated after the 'Me too' campaign went viral in 2017 when women across all sectors in the creative industries started to share their experiences and speak out against misogyny, sexual violence, and discrimination.[70] I have witnessed these groups proliferate both offline and online, have had conversations with several founders, and been an active member of one myself.

They are vital wellsprings of camaraderie and social and emotional support as well as vehicles for sharing skills, and developing career networks, as Zara explains about the group she founded:

the guys all go football together ... they have boxes at Arsenal and that's where deals get cut and things like that, and they move up and down the high street, one person loses their job here and before you know it six months later he's working at [company name], whatever, and I just thought that we don't really have that for our generation of women. (Zara)

All-women initiatives are also formed for teaching music and related courses to women,[71] where there is a general sense across my interviewees and ethnographic observations that tuition away from men can be vital in encouraging women to ask questions and feel empowered to learn – as we saw in Liz's and Emma's words above about not wanting to speak out when in a minority. Collectives are also associated with record labels to specifically platform women artists,[72] and others assist record labels to diversify their roster of artists.[73] They raise the visibility of minoritised genders, sometimes focusing on particular genres,[74] and they act as lobbying forces on issues of women's safety in the industry.[75]

However, even this more organised activism is a double-edged sword – most collectives are run by volunteers, providing largely free (or very cheap) services to their members, and as such the work of redressing gender imbalance falls as an extra, unpaid, burden on the shoulders of the very constituencies they are aimed at helping, while dominant groups remain free to focus on the 'real' work of their music careers. Another potential tension is the corralling of women into exclusive spaces where 'women talk to other women about women' – as I have expressed it at several panels and talks – something which has questionable power for change. Although global groups like She Said So have had success in placing diversity issues on the agenda of mainstream conferences, such as IMS Ibiza 2019,[76] my experience is that attendance at 'gender' panels at such events is almost exclusively by women. As part of my work with a leading industry body for electronic music, I have also found it hard to receive public buy-in and support from male gatekeepers in promoting our research and initiatives, even when individuals will privately claim they are allies.

Conclusion

Throughout the research I have repeatedly faced questions about why gender imbalance is a problem in electronic dance music and continued to receive push back.[77] Why does it matter who makes the music we listen to, or who performs it for us to dance to in clubs? As one festival participant remarked, 'I don't listen to music with my eyes so why should I care who's up there performing?' These are words spoken from a position of privilege – when you are able to enter a career and not face barriers, exclusion, or harm simply because you are a certain gender, race, or sexuality. Through my presentation of the six subjectivities enacted by participants in my study, I hope to have shown that women's career experiences in this industry are seriously impacted by unequal treatment on the basis of gender. They simply have to work harder, expending more physical, emotional, and financial resources than their male counterparts in order to succeed. In short, a forceful discourse of meritocracy underpins the creative industries, which can disadvantage marginalised identities, and electronic dance music is no exception.

Notes

1. See Marie, K. (2022) *Conversations with Women in Music Production: The Interviews*, Essex, CT: Backbeat; Reddington, H. (2021) *She's at the Controls: Sound Engineering, Production and Gender Ventriloquism in the 21st Century*, Sheffield:Equinox; Wolfe, P. (2020) *Women in the Studio: Creativity, Control and Gender in Popular Music Sound Production*, London: Ashgate.
2. See Butler, M. (2014) *Playing with Something That Runs: Technology, Improvisation, and Composition In DJ and Laptop Performance*, Oxford: Oxford University Press.
3. McRobbie, A. (2009) *The Aftermath of Feminism*, London: Sage: p. 13.
4. I am particularly influenced here by the classic ideas of Berger, P. and Luckmann, T. (1967) *The Social Construction of Reality: A Treatise in the Sociology of Knowledge*, New York: Doubleday.
5. Thomas, R. (2009) 'Critical Management Studies on Identity: Mapping the Terrain' in M. Alvesson, T. Bridgman, & H. Willmott (eds.) *The Oxford Handbook of Critical Management Studies*, Oxford: Oxford University Press, p. 167.
6. Crenshaw, K. (1989) 'Demarginalizing the Intersection of Race and Sex: A Black Feminist Critique of Antidiscrimination Doctrine, Feminist Theory and Antiracist Politics', *Chicago Law Journal*, Issue 1 Article 8.
7. See Tadajewski, M, Maclaran, P, Parsons, E, Parker, M. (2011) *Key Concepts in Critical Management Studies*, London: Sage for an introduction to these ideas.
8. West, C., & Zimmerman, D. (1987) 'Doing Gender', *Gender & Society*, 1: 125–51; see also Nentwich, J., and Kelan, E. (2014) 'Towards a Topology of "Doing Gender": An Analysis of Empirical Research and its Challenges', *Gender, Work and Organization*, 21 (2): 121–33.

9. See www.deevstock.com for details.
10. Kindly funded from 2019–2021 by a Research Fellowship from The Leverhulme Trust (2019-598-7).
11. For more info see Resident Advisor https://ra.co/dj/dovetail/biography and for music, https://soundcloud.com/dovetail_uk.
12. Parsley, S. (2022) 'Feeling Your Way as an Occupational Minority: The Gendered Sensilisation of Women Electronic Music Artists', *Management Learning*, 53 (4): 697–717.
13. Findings from the full research project can be found in Parsley, S. (2025) *Minor Keys: Gender, Inequality and Work in Electronic Music*, Bristol: Bristol University Press and Parsley, S. and Johansson, M. (2025) 'A Slog, a Push, and a Labour of Love: How Women Electronic Music Artists Navigate Gendered In/Visibility in a Creative Industry through "Ameliorative Work"', *Organization*. Online first doi.org/10.1177/13505084251348689.
14. For example, see Introduction to Rodgers, T. (2010) *Pink Noises*, Durham, NC: Duke University Press.
15. Armstrong, V. (2011) *Technology and the Gendering of Music Education*, London: Ashgate; Prior, N. (2018) *Popular Music, Digital Technology and Society*, London: Sage, pp. 88–89.
16. See Merrich, J. (2021) *A Short History of Electronic Music and its Women Protagonists*, Rome: Arcana:, for an impressive history of women's contributions to electronic music from around the world.
17. See Armstrong, *Technology and the Gendering of Music Education*, and also www.wiswos.com for Linda O'Keefe's project 'Women in Sound, Women on Sound' aiming to redress gender imbalance in music education.
18. Due to the 'hidden', freelance, and quasi-amateur character of producing electronic dance music, demographic statistics about this precise population do not yet exist, so here I present a range of indicators from neighbouring fields such as popular music, DJing, audio-engineering, and education.
19. Stacey, S. Pieper, K, Hernandez, K, Wheeler, S. (2025) Inclusion in the Recording Studio? Gender & Race/ Ethnicity of Artists, Songwriters & Producers across 1,200 Popular Songs from 2012 to 2024, USC Annenberg Inclusion Initiative, https://assets.uscannenberg.org/docs/aii-inclusion-recording-studio-2025-01-29-2.pdf.
20. Brereton, J., Daffern, H., Young, K., Lovedee-Turner, M. (2020) 'Addressing Gender Equality in Music Production: Current Challenges, Opportunities for Change, and Recommendations' in R. Hepworth-Sawyer, J. Hodgson, L. King, and M. Marrington (eds.) *Gender in Music Production*, London: Routledge, pp. 219–50.
21. Brereton et al., *Addressing Gender Equality*.
22. Born, G., & Devine, K. (2015). 'Music Technology, Gender, and Class: Digitization, Educational and Social Change in Britain', *Twentieth-Century Music*, 12 (2): 135–72

23. Dunford, S. Keay, L. & Peplow, G. (2023) 'Why female headliners are still too big a "risk" for top festivals like Glastonbury' *Sky News,* https://news.sky.com/story/why-are-only-17-of-uk-festival-headliners-female-in-2023-12854240.
24. FACTS 2022, available at https://femalepressure.wordpress.com.
25. DJanemag (2019) 'Sad Statistics of Gender Equality in Club and Festival Line-ups' https://djanemag.com/news/sad-statistics-gender-equality-club-and-festival-lineups.
26. AFEM (2021) 'AFEM Gender Diversity in the Electronic Music Industry Report', *Association for Electronic Music,* https://associationfor electronicmusic.org/2021/12/20/afem-diversity-inclusion-working-group-present-the-gender-diversity-in-the-electronic-music-industry-report/.
27. Available via In the Key resources at https://inthekey.org/resources/commentary-facts-and-figures/.
28. For an explanation of when, how and why role models are effective see Morgenroth, T., Ryan, K., Peters, K. (2015) 'The Motivational Theory of Role Modeling: How Role Models Influence Role Aspirants' Goals', *Review of General Psychology,* 19 (4): 465–83.
29. For an overview of this phenomena from a US perspective see Khawaja, J. (2016) 'What Do Coachella's EDM Bros Think About EDM Bros?: An Anthropological Study' *Vice* www.vice.com/en/article/9avdbp/what-do-coachellas-edm-bros-think-about-edm-bros.
30. For example, Keychange's 50/50 – the UK Performing Rights Society's programme intended to increase representation of women on line-ups www.keychange.eu.
31. The proportion of female acts at festivals worldwide has risen from 9.2 per cent in 2012 to 30 per cent in 2023. FACTS (2024) available at https://femalepressure.net/FACTS2024-femalepressure.pdf.
32. 'In the Key' www.inthekey.org funded 2019–2021 by The Leverhulme Trust; Parsley, *Minor Keys.*
33. Parsley, 'Feeling your Way'.
34. Bartow, A. (2021) 'Feminist Methodologies and Intellectual Property', in M. Calboli and M. Montagnini (eds.) *Handbook of Intellectual Property Research: Lenses, Methods, Perspectives,* University Press Scholarship Online. https://doi.org/10.1093/oso/9780198826743.003.0048
35. Shukla (2022) 'In The Key of She is a new directory of women, trans and non-binary electronic producers', *Resident Advisor,* https://ra.co/news/77261; Warren, S. (2021), 'Why representation still matters for minorities in the dance music', *Beatportal,* www.beatportal.com/features/why-representation-still-matters-for-minorities-in-dance-music/. *Audio Media International* (2021) 'In The Key of She: Prof Samantha Warren on her research project on experiences of women in EDM' https://audiomediainternational.com/key-of-she-prof-sam-warren-on-her-research-project-on-experiences-of-women-in-edm/.

36. www.inthekey.org/directory.
37. It is, of course, somewhat difficult and perhaps futile to try to make these distinctions between facets of identity when conducting ethnographic work.
38. Miles, M., Huberman, M., & Saldaña, J. (2020) *Qualitative Data Analysis: A Sourcebook*, London: Sage, p. 63.
39. Silverman, D. (2019) *Interpreting Qualitative Data*, London: Sage, p. 118.
40. Gottardello, D. (2023) 'The Maze: Reflections on Navigating Intersectional Identities in the Workplace', *Gender, Work and Organization*, 30 (5): 1839–54. DOI: 10.1111/gwao.13030.
41. Davis, K. (2016) 'Intersectionality as Critical Methodology' in A. Petö, L. Sissel, K. Davis, A. Brewster, N. Lykke, R. Koobak (eds.) *Writing Academic Texts Differently: Intersectional Feminist Methodologies*, London: Routledge DOI: 10.4324/9781315818566-1.
42. Davis, 'Intersectionality as Critical Methodology'.
43. For a definition see the UN Statistics wiki 'Glossary of Terms' https://unstats.un.org/wiki/display/genderstatmanual/Glossary+of+terms.
44. Eikhof, D., and Warhurst, C. (2013) 'The Promised Land? Why Social Inequalities are Systemic in the Creative Industries', *Employee Relations*, 35(5): 495–508.
45. See Gadir, T. (2017) 'Forty-Seven DJs, Four Women: Meritocracy, Talent, and Postfeminist Politics', *Dancecult: Journal of Electronic Dance Music Culture*, 9 (1): 40–72.
46. Elsewhere I conceptualise this more fully as 'ameliorative work' – see Parsley and Johansson 'A Slog, a Push, and a Labour of Love'.
47. This is now far less apparent than when I began the research, as magazine editors have made huge strides in balancing the gender and race of the artists they feature; see, for example, *DJ Mag, Mixmag, Resident Advisor*.
48. Ashcraft, K. (2013) 'The Glass Slipper: "Incorporating" Occupational Identities in Management Studies', *Academy of Management Review*, 38 (1): 6–31.
49. For example, the Keychange initiative noted above, Toolroom Records 'We Are Listening' campaign started in 2018, Primavera Festival's commitment to 50/50 gender-balanced line-ups (see www.bbc.co.uk/news/newsbeat-48484558) and the IMS Ibiza 2019 music conference being co-run with global gender diversity organisation She Said So (see www.youtube.com/watch?v=I7JEyGV7fs8&list=PL-K2OtvqhGqXN_xg4fb_iw1Kaie4d1XYu&index=6).
50. This practice is becoming known as 'femwashing' where organisations derive reputational benefit from practices that emphasise gender diversity or women's empowerment, whilst the reality of their commitments to gender diversity are less positive – see, for example https://theconversation.com/feminism-washing-are-multinationals-really-empowering-women-120353.
51. Abtan, F. (2016) 'Where Is She? Finding the Women in Electronic Music Culture', *Contemporary Music Review*, 35 (1): 56.

52. The bar owner laughed, dismissively suggested I should feel 'grateful' at my age, but I'm pleased to say that the offending man was nonetheless removed from the premises by security.
53. I note that sound engineer interference is a common occurrence for all DJs, but the level of 'advice' given to me as a woman was quite staggering – for example having the waveform on the CDJ pointed out to me.
54. Tulshyan, R. and Burey J-A. (2021) 'Stop Telling Women They Have Imposter Syndrome', *Harvard Business Review,* 11 February 2021; Warren, S & Khan, N (2021) 'Confidence, imposter syndrome and jobs that "aren't for us"' PPL/Women in Ctrl Webinar Series www.youtube.com/watch?v=JZHdpnbNym0.
55. This is no different than is required of all DJs regardless of gender but, as we see later in this section, it carries gendered risks.
56. See for example, 'Confidence, imposter syndrome and jobs that "aren't for us"'.
57. Beard, M. (2017) *Women and Power: A Manifesto*, London: Profile Books.
58. Armstrong, V. (2011) *Technology and the Gendering of Music Education*, London: Ashgate. p. 63 and Doubleday, V (2008) 'Sounds of Power: An Overview of Musical Instruments and Gender', *Ethnomusicology Forum,* 17(1); 3–39
59. This is remarkably consistent across the world. Based on a study replicated globally – Chambers, N. Kashefpakdel, E., Rehill, J., and Percy, C. (2018) *Drawing the Future: Exploring the Career Aspirations of Primary School Children from around the World.* Available here www.educationandemployers.org/drawing-the-future/.
60. See for example Rydzik A., and Ellis-Vowles V (2018) 'Don't Use "the Weak Word"': Women Brewers, Identities and Gendered Territories of Embodied Work', *Work, Employment and Society,* 33(3): 483–49.
61. Farrugia, R. (2012) *Beyond the Dance Floor: Female DJs, technology, and Electronic Dance Music Culture*, Bristol:Intellect.
62. Ashcraft, K. (2013) 'The Glass Slipper', and Ashcraft, K. (2020) 'Senses of Self: Affect as a Pre-Individual Approach to Identity at Work' in A. Brown (ed.) *Oxford Handbook of Identities in Organizations*, Oxford: Oxford University Press, pp. 848–63.
63. See for example 'Project Implicit' www.projectimplicit.net/.
64. In relation to gender and 'ideal' organisational bodies see Meriläinen, S. C., Tienari, J., & Valtonen, A. E. (2015) 'Headhunters and the "Ideal" Executive Body', *Organization,* 22 (1): 3–22.
65. Based on my periodic, non-scientific, counting up of women artists who appear in the 'deep house' Top 100 chart on Beatport.com.
66. Also invoked by studio producers in Jagger, S., and Turner, H. (2020) 'The Female Music Producer and the Leveraging of Difference', in R. Hepworth-Sawyer, J. Hodgson, L. King, and M Marrington (eds.) *Gender in Music Production*, London: Routledge, 251–68.
67. The classic text on this is Mulvey, L. (1989) *The Visual and Other Pleasures*, London: Macmillan, and for an example of a contemporary application in

music see Karsay, M. J. K. Platzer, P., and Plinke, M. (2018) 'Adopting the Objectifying Gaze: Exposure to Sexually Objectifying Music Videos and Subsequent Gazing Behavior', *Media Psychology*, 21 (1): 27–49.
68. Wei, W. (2019) 'All-woman collectives have instigated real, positive change in the music world', *Mixmag*, http://mixmag.net/feature/all-woman-collectives.
69. Female Pressure www.femalepressure.net/ DW Artists www.discwoman.com/roster Psy-sisters https://psysisters.com/.
70. See https://metoomvmt.org/.
71. A few examples: MPW https://musicproductionforwomen.com/; Saffron https://saffronmusic.co.uk/; Femme House www.thisisfemmehouse.com/.
72. Lady of the House www.ladyofthehouse.org.uk/releases/; DW Artists www.discwoman.com/roster; and Boudica are three examples of many.
73. For example see Sydney Blu's Change the Beat (formerly 23by23) initiative www.changethebeat.ca.
74. For example, Boudica for hard techno and Dynamics for dnb/ jungle.
75. For two specifically related to electronic music, see Rebekah's 'For the Music' www.metoo-music.com/ and Eve Horne's 'We Are the Unheard' https://wearetheunheard.com/.
76. Although SSS have now rescinded their involvement with IMS after Beatport became a shareholder in the company – a music organisation that has suffered from several reports of racist bullying and harassment, for example see www.shesaid.so/blog/2023/4/10/on-beatport-and-workplace-toxicity-ims-updates.
77. Parsley, S. (2022) 'Leaving "Identities" out of Electronic Music is not an Option: Here's Why' https://inthekey.org/leaving-identities-out-of-electronic-music-is-not-an-option-heres-why/.

Further Reading

Armstrong, V. (2011) *Technology and the Gendering of Music Education*, London: Ashgate

Farrugia, R. (2012) *Beyond the Dance Floor: Female DJs, Technology, and Electronic Dance Music Culture*, Bristol: Intellect.

Parsley, S. (2022) 'Feeling Your Way as an Occupational Minority: The Gendered Sensilisation of Women Electronic Music Artists', *Management Learning*, 53 (4): 697–717.

Reddington, H. (2021) *She's at the Controls: Sound Engineering, Production and Gender Ventriloquism in the 21st Century*, Bristol: Equinox.

Wolfe, P. (2020) 'A Studio of One's Own' in *Women in the Studio: Creativity, Control and Gender in Popular Music Sound Production Ashgate*, London: Routledge, pp. 93–123.

17 | The Divisiveness of the Bass Music Drop in the North American Festival Setting

ED KATRAK SPENCER

During the 2010s, massive EDM festivals in North America foregrounded a sensationalised musical meme known as 'the drop': that moment when the tempo of a track halves as powerful sub-bass frequencies, filthy bass sounds, and new 'debased' sonic materials suddenly take hold within the soundscape of a DJ set. Popularised by producer-DJs such as 12th Planet and Skrillex in the United States, the drop is central to the 'bass music' genres of dubstep and trap,[1] where it functions less as a return to a rewarding and steady musical framework[2] and much more as a trigger for feelings of rupture, shock, and ritualised disgust.[3] In this context, an early example of a US dubstep drop section can be heard between 0.54 and 2.16 in the 2012 track 'MMXXII' by 12th Planet, while a trap drop section can be heard between 0.37 and 1.05 in the 2014 track 'Drop (Get Silenced)' by Mr. Carmack.[4] Pre-drop vocal samples are often used to maximise a sense of hiatus before the drop, an indicative example being the 2017 track 'The Drop' by Gammer (0.48 ff.). Significantly, the drop often articulates a sense of aggression or one-upmanship through sonic weaponry references, as emphasised by the rain of bombs on the cover of Gammer's 2017 EP.[5]

During my fieldwork at Spring Awakening festival in Chicago (2017) and Lost Lands festival in Ohio (2017 and 2018), it became clear that the experience associated with the bass drop in dubstep and trap is often far removed from the feeling of continuity that can be heard in canonical electronic dance music genres such as house, trance, and techno.[6] As Tiger (from Southern California) put it, 'the drop became a thing. Listen to old techno – there's no drops, it's just transitions.' North American 'Headbangers' (as fans of the dubstep producer Excision are known) are intensely aware that these groove-based models of EDM have existed in the past and persist in the present through genres such as psytrance, yet they are sometimes shunned as an unwelcome Other against which true fans of 'bass music' define themselves. At the Cave of Souls stage on the final day of the inaugural Lost Lands, this idea of bass music breaking away from conventional dance music experience became especially marked when Jeff (from Denver) explained through pursed lips, 'I don't like music that sounds like it's trying to hypnotise me' – he despised EDM that was 'too trancey'.

A clear indication of the paradigm shift embodied by the bass music drop arrived during an incongruous set at Spring Awakening. Mija (one of only two female acts performing at the festival) took to the Equinox Stage (the second stage) and announced that she was thrilled to be back having 'played here two years ago'. She then explained that she was 'going to play something a little different, take you back to my roots' – we were about to hear the music she 'grew up on'. The set began with spoken-word samples from what sounded like a documentary about The Warehouse and the genesis of Chicago house in the late 1980s. Over a four-to-the-floor house groove, Mija then pronounced 'I'm gonna take you on a journey'. The house odyssey that ensued was met with confusion. Its slow-burning timbral continuity and perpetual four-to-the-floor pulse appeared to afford stasis and suspicion rather than the moving and grooving it was supposed to choreograph. Put simply, the crowd did not know what to do. These impressions were confirmed when Alistair, who was standing beside me, shouted 'this set sucks, boring as fuck!' His friend Tyson, with whom I had been conversing online prior to the festival, then added – pleadingly – 'We want bangers!' With 'bangers', Tyson was alluding to a series of short, discrete, condensed tracks featuring drops. He did not want to be taken on Mija's journey.

Why not, one might well ask. The analysis within this chapter offers two broad perspectives on the conundrum presented by the bass music drop in recent years. It begins by considering the significance of bass music's discursive mediation and behavioural affordances, showing that the sense of rupture delivered by the drop is enmeshed with social and musical disputes (especially in online festival groups). Drawing upon both digital ethnography and on-the-ground fieldwork, I demonstrate that fans of so-called 'hard' bass music occasionally troll supposedly less authentic fans of 'soft' bass music before considering how vernacular terms such as 'chads' and 'wooks' are used to describe different festivalgoer stereotypes. Second, the chapter explores the gendered dimensions of the bass music drop by drawing on interview and focus group material, qualitative data in the form of 'bass music diary' entries completed by festivalgoers, and thick description of festival experience. Notwithstanding female participation, UK bass music has been associated with a specific kind of androcentric masculinity,[7] and within the context of the United States there exists a similar phenomenon that is commonly named through a vernacular shorthand: 'brostep' (a portmanteau of 'bro' and 'dubstep'). The chapter ends by considering North American bass music's #MeToo moment of reckoning regarding alleged sexual misconduct by Datsik (an influential 'brostep' producer second only to Excision). In doing so, the chapter suggests that despite previous and ongoing associations with unity, transcendence, and escapism, EDM is sometimes unable to escape the divisions and ills of the world as it is. This scenario is significant in terms of the future of EDM studies. Rather than downplaying the dark sides of EDM culture through affirmative scholarship, our field would benefit from a critical turn and methodological innovation.

From Mosh Pits to Militaristic MDMA Consumption

The bass music drop's involvement in the production of dis/unity is something that defines its role in the Midwestern festival setting: through the very act of bringing people together, the drop can sow discord and ill-feeling. One of the most striking examples of this paradox is the practice of moshing, which takes place at the onset of certain drops. Rather than being an inherently spontaneous kind of crowd behaviour, moshing is often a premeditated activity. During the breakdown and build-up sections of the mix, a circular space opens up as members of the crowd gradually move outwards – backing away from each other, as it were. This circular gap is known as 'the pit'. Crowd members must not enter the pit until the drop. Some use their arms to police others and enforce this unspoken rule, while others rebel and enter the pit prematurely to gain attention. At the onset of the drop, festivalgoers charge into the pit, violently pushing and elbowing others in their way as they attempt to reach the opposite side. Others try to avoid the melee by staying on the edge of the pit or by hurriedly moving away from it. The intensity of the mosh pit is short-lived. After twenty seconds or so it usually starts to peter out after the first wave of people have traversed the space, although subsequent entries into the pit may occur in an attempt to trigger a second wave of moshing.

As a prominent way of territorialising the drop, moshing is characterised by a tension between individual and collective motivations. Charging into a mosh pit is at once a selfish way of venting one's pent-up frustrations as well as a selfless ritual that brings about a kind of collective catharsis. Yet the very existence of the practice at EDM festivals is also controversial and gives rise to deliberately provocative statements and arguments online. One of the contributing factors to the controversial status of moshing is the sheer diversity and disparity of hybrid genre histories as well as music fandoms (and anti-fandoms) in the festival setting. On the one hand, as a genre within the meta-genre of EDM, North American bass music is firmly tethered to the mythology and rhetoric of Peace, Love, Unity, Respect (PLUR) associated with dance festivals,[8] yet as I discovered during my fieldwork, many festivalgoers initially became fans of dubstep due to its entanglements with a musical tradition centred on hard rock, hardcore punk, and metal. Though denounced by hardcore dubstep fan Stacy (from New Jersey) as something fake and sugary ('almost like Splenda'), the idea(l) of PLUR is an incredibly important set of values for festivalgoers such as Gilly who seek to nurture and preserve it. As she reflected despairingly at the end of Lost Lands 2018, many festivalgoers 'don't understand the idea of PLUR ... And that's what this was supposed to be about!' Alluding to moshing and the genre's affinities with hard rock, she reasoned that 'dubstep is just such a grungy, hard style of music and I feel like dubstep fans are the same kind of people – they're hard and grungy'.

Similarly, debates about specific artists often result in the exacerbation of divisions between 'hard' and 'soft' bass music fans. In between the first two iterations of Lost Lands, a version of the 'I don't care that you broke your elbow' meme[9] was shared via social media to troll followers of Illenium, an artist associated with melodic, emotive, 'soft AF [as fuck]' bass music that 'doesn't belong at Lost Lands'. There were further layers of sardonicism in this meme. The choice of meme template was itself reminiscent of the popular Excision & Space Laces anthem 'Throwin' Elbows',[10] a track which frequently prompts the formation of a mosh pit when played in the festival setting. In one version of the meme, an additional caption stresses that the only appropriate place for crying at Lost Lands is in the mosh pit following serious injury, not in response to a beautiful and tear-jerking Illenium track.

More broadly, socio-musical divides within the online–offline festival setting are articulated with reference to different practices of drug use and different festivalgoer stereotypes. During my fieldwork in Chicago, Milo explained that knowledgeable, 'heady' aggregations of festivalgoers such as Excision's 'Headbangers' mainly smoke marijuana – understood as the archetypal and most authentic bass music drug. In contrast, the 'Wook' stereotype (millennial hippies that resemble the shaggy wookies in *Star Wars*) is more associated with psychedelic drugs and the music of Bassnectar. Critically, Milo described MDMA as a typical 'bro drug' beloved of 'the Chads' (Chad being regarded as a typical bro name). This emphasis on MDMA as a (pejorative) marker of distinction and dis/unity is out of step with conventional perspectives on this prominent party drug.

Discussing the very different context of house music, Stan Hawkins notes that MDMA consumption serves to ensure that the 'individual's sexuality and gendered identity fades into insignificance', a phenomenon that gives rise to the 'idea of abandoning the restrictions of traditional and patriarchal "states of being"'.[11] Yet perversely, for Milo, MDMA consumption was a marker of obnoxious male heteronormativity. The 'Chads' are often regarded as an ignorant and unsympathetic type of festivalgoer who are driven by a quasi-militaristic motivation on the festival field – an arena suitable for taking excessive amounts of drugs and showing off their physiques. As AJ lamented on the final night of Lost Lands 2018:

I feel like these people are just there to get fucked up. It was a whole other level of drugs that people were taking. Maybe the people that are sitting there and watching Illenium or something like that are getting kinda emotional, but the people out there going hard are just crazy – I dunno the word for it but it's not PLUR ... They're like 'house music sucks – we don't wanna see any of that we just wanna see the hard stuff'. It's like 'man, there's other music out there than just bass'.

The Bro Circle

If excessive MDMA consumption complicates and problematises the idea(l) of PLUR, then how exactly does this drug-fuelled bro behaviour relate to the bass music drop during a festival set? And how does the drop choreograph togetherness and antipathy simultaneously? On the Saturday of Spring Awakening 2017, I walked over to the Solstice Stage (the main stage) and positioned myself towards the back of the large crowd that had gathered to watch the set by Yellow Claw (a prominent duo known for producing what they call 'Amsterdam Trap Music'). A topless alpha male – the ringleader of a group of bros – noticed that I was standing alone and struck up a conversation. They soon discovered that I was from the UK (they were all from Chicago). The exchanges offered were phatic: though trivial, they were intended to establish and maintain a social bond, being as it were part of an untold invitation to join the group.

Although this welcome was certainly generous, the subsequent gift of a wide-armed embrace from the ringleader seemed to say, 'you're with us now' and ensured that I became indebted and conscripted, having had little choice in the matter. As with a fieldwork encounter in Berlin's famous Berghain nightclub described by Luis-Manuel Garcia, it was clear that the bros were on MDMA (known as 'molly' in the USA), and this was a key contributor to their 'insistent friendliness'.[12] Yet the situation resembled a *forged* and *enforced* togetherness rather than the seamlessness of the vague-yet-meaningful belonging that Garcia conceptualises through his notion of social liquidarity. Another important distinction can be made. Following Garcia's reading of Elias Canetti's crowd theories, one might regard the group of bros as a 'crowd crystal', namely 'a group of already-intimate friends' who had the effect of 'catalysing intimate behaviours around them' – a 'kernel' around which others like me could coalesce.[13] But this was not the case, since the forged togetherness was explicit, edgy, and gendered. Instead, the circle of bros resembled Canetti's throbbing or rhythmic crowd, because these 'men wanted to be more, *then* and *there*... they *wished* to be large, and they expressed this in a specific state of communal excitement'.[14] This was a territorial performance: the throbbing hub of bros were concerned with appearance and display – they wanted to be seen. Moreover, the 'membrane' between the bros and the rest of the crowd was selectively permeable, to use a biological metaphor. Once I had been enlisted, I stood with the bros and in opposition to everyone else around us. The forged togetherness was simultaneously a form of exclusion, therefore, something that would soon become clear.

After the topless alpha male (henceforth TAM) exclaimed 'Ohh, third molly just kicked in!' his desire to discipline his band of followers began to increase. I had been recruited to a tightly controlled unit of bros and was expected to act in a certain way as instructed. For the TAM (and thus all of us), Yellow Claw's music was 'the hardest trap shit' – going hard and 'turning up' was thus non-negotiable.[15] During a breakdown, the TAM gathered the circle closer together to form a huddle. Arms were placed firmly around my shoulders, our heads were brought together, and we came into close contact with each other's body odour and sweat. This was a team talk. Our instructions were as follows: 'on this next drop we are going hard as fuck!' During the build-up, the huddle started to oscillate up and down and a chant of 'For the Boys!' took hold in time with the half-step pulse. At the onset of the drop itself, the volatile male compound suddenly transformed straight from its solid state into chaotic Brownian motion – they had become *gassed up*.[16] This was a violent sublimation (in the scientific sense of the term). Any liquid-like relationality had been bypassed completely, and the confrontational pushing that was now happening meant that we were exerting unwanted pressure on the rest of the crowd around us. We were impinging upon and territorialising their space, resulting in dirty looks. Moreover, the gaseous male particles were now competing among themselves, each trying to go harder than anyone else. In conjunction with the bass music drop, the 'bro drug' of MDMA engendered hunger and rivalry rather than universal and unconditional happiness.

However, the most revealing moment of the set arrived during another huddle during a breakdown section, whereupon a small brunette girl approached the ring and put her arms around the shoulders of two bros. What was happening here? Perhaps she was trying to buy in to the male monopoly of turned-up musical experience (wanting some of what we had, as it were); or maybe she was entering the circle due to spontaneous communitas or social liquidarity; she may even have been trying to pacify our bro lattice through the power of PLUR so that we might dissolve into the rest of the crowd (putting to an end our sublimations). But in any case, the lone brunette girl did not realise that our compound was male and socially inert. It was exclusively 'For the Boys!' and would not form bonds with others. After several awkward seconds, the girl realised that she had misjudged her gesture and retreated into the anonymity of the crowd.

This episode illustrates the divisiveness and gendered dimensions of the bass music drop in the North American festival setting, which is not limited to mainstage trap sets but also dubstep sets at smaller stages. As well as being excluded through the enforcement of male togetherness, women can also suffer in more physical ways during the onset of the drop. Reflecting on Black Tiger Sex Machine's set at Lost Lands 2017, Naomi's bass music diary entry describes a painful experience of moshing:

Honestly, it was almost horrific. I thought that I enjoyed dubstep, but I was at this set and couldn't figure out how to move/dance. The music felt very forced and violent. There were multiple mosh pits that broke out and as a woman I got shoved around too much.

The subject of women suffering in or being excluded from mosh pits was also something that Tiger and Angelo reflected on during our focus group session. As Tiger explained, the phrase 'no clit in the pit' 'is an actual thing', while in festival Facebook groups there are calls for women-only mosh pits 'because males dominate the scene'. As Tiger – and many others – have pondered, 'what's the correlation between testosterone-fuelled males and dirty bass music?'[17] In some ways, this correlation is fallacious. For Stacy, a bass music set is an intensely personal sonification of her own life as well as something that renders audible the experience of the world as it is:

When you listen to music from my generation, you had the Spice Girls, the Backstreet Boys, and it was all bubbly and about love – but that's not what the world is. The world is a disgusting place and humans are the real filth, you know, and that is the one true thing that we can accept, because it's our human nature ... Everyone has shit they've dealt with in their life that you know no human being knows how to register or process ... I resonate with this music because it's so chaotic and unpredictable and so heavy and deep. I think that's why I love it so much: because finally, someone put my thought process in a musical setting. If you can put someone's mind process in beats, that's what it's like. So it feels very comforting for me, to be in that madness. I only know how to be myself in chaos because I've lived in chaos my whole life.

Yet at the very same time as being so enraptured with the bass music drop, Stacy was also intensely aware of the power that male producer-DJs have over their devoted female followers:

Most of these DJs have power. There's people that will send them nudes [via SnapChat] and will dress up in their attire and go all out fangirl. I myself bought a sponsored sweatshirt ... I support the vision that a lot of that money goes towards and what they [the artist] want to accomplish – with that I have no problem – but I don't want to buy everything in one shot like a lot of people do. That would take up my whole paycheck ... To have that kind of power when all you do (I'm not saying it's all you do – I see what DJs do and it's complicated, but in a sense it's not) is go on a computer and just distort the sounds. A lot of people can do it. But to establish a fan base to that extreme is quite scary. It's very weird, and it's enough to alter someone's mental state.

The strange relationship between producer-DJs and fans that Stacy alludes to here is part of a broader trend whereby festival performers are elevated to a god-like status through a kind of branded love.[18] Her concerns also hint at a dark, sexual underside of North American dubstep that came to light in 2018.

Bass Music and #MeToo: For a Critical Turn in EDM Studies

On 14 March 2018, less than six months after his back-to-back headline set with Excision at the inaugural Lost Lands festival, Datsik (Troy Beetles) was accused by several women via social media of multiple sexual assaults. The accusations coincided with the wider #MeToo movement and concerned Datsik's predatory behaviour after shows. Female web users recalled being given special access passes with 'TUL$A' written on them, a mirror word that marked them out as 'A SLUT' so that they could be easily identified and ushered onto the tour bus after Datsik's performances. Once on the bus, the alleged victims claimed to have been pressured into drinking alcohol or tricked into taking ketamine so that they were no longer able to give sexual consent or resist, at which point Datsik was said to have raped them before leaving them on the street.[19] The allegations were widely shared online, triggering a flame war across social media platforms such as Facebook, Twitter, and Reddit. A hastily written statement posted by Datsik on Twitter, in which he cast himself as a 'vibe reader',[20] only served to fuel the online flame war. The remainder of Datsik's 'Ninja Nation' tour was swiftly cancelled, and he was sacked by his management, Deckstar, by his agency, Circle Talent, and by his own label, Firepower Records. He was not booked to perform at Lost Lands 2018 or 2019, and he has not appeared at any other festival since the allegations.

When I spoke to Stacy a few weeks after the allegations surfaced, she reasoned that the episode had revealed a side of the dubstep scene that people did not normally talk about. On the one hand, she stressed that male bass music DJs are akin to rock stars in North America, and their powerful allure now seemed to be something toxic and dangerous rather than life-affirming. But on the other hand, she was critical of some women who were now making use of social media's inflammatory potential in a narcissistic manner. When I asked Stacy whether she was still listening to Datsik's music in the wake of the allegations, she said that she was because regardless of what had happened and what might happen, his music was still good. She was also sure, however, that no DJ would dare to play his music until his innocence was proven. More broadly, while some social media users were inclined to make light of the accusations and champion Datsik because of his incredible drops (his bass music becoming a source of absolution, as it were),[21] others were inclined to believe the admittedly unproven claims based on brostep's wider reputation as male-oriented and misogynistic audio porn. Significantly, the track 'Too Late to Say No' from Datsik's 2013 EP *Coldblooded* became a point of reference during the flame war and was presented as proof of his latent criminality. The drop in 'Too Late to Say No' is prefaced by an introduction in which Datsik raps. For several online commenters, these lyrics were prophetic in what they suggest:

Just follow the bottle, take you there
Snuck in the house with a full blank stare
Nowhere to go so you go with the flow
Too early to stop but too late to say no
[Drop]

How are we to hear the drop in 'Too Late to Say No' considering Datsik's subsequent fall? As a musical event disconnected from the world as it is? Or as the sound of rape? Blaming everything on the behavioural affordances of the North American bass music drop is just as problematic and dangerous as claiming that it is autonomous and absolute – something wholly disconnected from its god-like creators and various kinds of 'bro' behaviour.

Holistically, the North American bass music drop is often as divisive as it is unifying, since it brings people together while sowing discord and ill-feeling. The paradoxes introduced in this chapter problematise certain perspectives on more canonical or 'orthodox' electronic dance music, which has been variously associated with female, queer, and kinky kinds of sexual pleasure;[22] selflessness and oneness (to the point where thinking in terms of differentiation is eliminated);[23] and the dissolution of gendered differences.[24] As such, the North American bass music drop is a key site for further inquiry[25] and one that necessitates a critical turn in EDM scholarship.

Before envisioning the scope of this critical turn, it is worth rewinding. The 'first generation' scholarly work on EDM during the 1990s and early 2000s arguably needed to be advocative in its conceptual orientations in order to justify its inclusion within academe. Alternatively, it may well be the case that radical forms of togetherness and cultural politics (for the time) did exist (albeit fleetingly) during this halcyon era of the so-called long 1990s – a period of history that ended with the global financial crisis in 2008. But today, as Stacy's remarks suggest, EDM generally and the drop in particular are often the powerful sonification of a damaged world and our present societal operating system,[26] being as it were both a symptom of these ills and a prescription drug that one can use as a coping mechanism through self-medication. Its epistemological and emotional value can be found more in this sobering practice of self-medication than in established associations with intoxication and mind alteration.

Shortly before this book went to press, I was asked to provide an expert comment on the viral hit 'Planet of the Bass',[27] a parody of 1990s Eurodance that triggered much amusement and anemoia among Gen-Z web users (anemoia being sardonic nostalgia for a time that one did not personally experience or that never existed). When the track's co-star DJ Crazy Times exclaims 'Oh I've got an idea / World peace!' as the beat drops, the sheer absurdity of history can be felt to gyrate awkwardly. As Kate Fowler notes in the resulting feature article, the vibe of 1990s dance music seems 'so far [removed] from the post-pandemic, post-Trump, post-climate deadline pessimism that Gen-Z are growing up in'.[28] One of the aims of a critical turn in EDM studies must be to investigate Gen-Z's (post-)ironic consumption of 'old-skool' dance music and the ways in which their cultural politics differs from that of the original rave generation. The spectre of Theodor Adorno could haunt this task, since listening to 'Planet of the Bass' on repeat may well prompt 'the happiness of knowing that one is unhappy ... [and] the awareness that one has missed fulfilment'.[29] By critically listening to and studying EDM, we will be able to better contemplate what it is like to be human in an era of increasing cultural and societal division and significant technological developments, including the dawn of the artificial intelligence era.

Alongside matters of history and generational proclivities, questions of race and racism also surround the case study introduced in this chapter and the future of our field. Significantly, the whiteness of the 2010s North American festival setting was often sustained through a 'vision of a White utopia' in official promotional videos – a utopia in which it appears that 'there are no people of colour at all'.[30] More broadly, the history of electronic dance music is littered with idealistic colourblind rhetoric, which means that racism often exists unseen in an arena where it is supposed to be absent, as Arun Saldanha's critical study of Goa trance demonstrates.[31] This *Cambridge Companion* arrives in the wake of 2010s social justice movements, and it will be important for EDM Studies to heed the words of BBC Radio 1 DJ Clara Amfo following the murder of George Floyd in 2020. In response to colourblind rhetoric and the white consumption of Black dance musics, Amfo stressed that 'people want our culture, but they do not want us ... you cannot enjoy the rhythm and ignore the blues'.[32] Similarly, it could be argued that EDM studies can no longer just enjoy the rhythm through affirmative work but must address more troubling issues concerning race, gender, political weaponisation, and the flow of capital in the age of music streaming. In addition to interrogating our own conceptual pieties and positionalities through a greater degree of reflexivity, this prospective endeavour will also require methodological innovation.

A first strategy for the future might be to do EDM research not as individual researchers, but rather collaboratively within diverse teams. This may also attenuate the limitations of grounded theory approaches, since the 'bottom-up' sentiments emerging from dominant participant demographics could be more rigorously scrutinised during the research team's 'top-down' discussions of these data. Second, as evidenced by the innovative work of Maria Perevedentseva,[33] Jenessa Williams,[34] and other colleagues, it will be important to develop critical online–offline research methods that are appropriate to the age of social media and the so-called culture wars.

In hindsight, the story of electronic dance music is in many ways also the story of the internet. Contrary to the early 1990s hope that rave culture and the World Wide Web would usher in a more connected and egalitarian society,[35] we are now dancing in the age of selfie-consciousness and digital division. In order to cope, we variously embrace the filth of the bass music drop or the fictive past future of 'Planet of the Bass', all while music streaming pollutes the sky[36] and bombs fall from it.

Notes

1. UK dubstep initially evolved from dub versions of 2-step garage records (hence the name) in South London during the early–mid 2000s. By the mid-2010s, the dubstep derivative popular in North America centred around heavily modulated and distorted bass drops and a 'half-step' tempo of 150BPM (that feels like 75BPM). The single word 'trap' will be used to refer to EDM trap throughout this chapter – a bass music genre that also settled on 150BPM half-step during the mid-2010s. As Justin Burton notes, 'the bulk of the writing dedicated to defining trap shows up in the midst of the confusion between EDM trap and trap rap', and while it is important to maintain a clear distinction between the two, it is also the case that trap rap's 'huge brass and string sounds would be incredibly influential on EDM trap', as would the use of the characteristically booming bass sound of the Roland TR-808 kick drum, offbeat 'hey!' samples, sprinkler hi-hats, and machine-gun snares. J. Burton, *Posthuman Rap* (New York: Oxford University Press, 2014), 100.
2. R. Solberg, '"Waiting for the bass to drop": Correlations between Intense Musical Experiences and Production Techniques in Build-Up and Drop Sections of Electronic Dance Music', *Dancecult*, 6(1) (2014), 66.
3. E. K. Spencer, 'Music to Vomit to: The Dubstep Drop, the Bass Face, and the Sound of the Social Web', in *Cultural Approaches to Disgust and the Visceral*, ed. M. Ryynänen, H. Kosonen, & S. Ylönen (London: Routledge, 2022) www.taylorfrancis.com/chapters/oa-edit/10.4324/9781003205364-17/music-vomit-edward-spencer.
4. 12th Planet (2012) 'MMXII', in *The End*. Smog Records (United States) SMOG023; Mr. Carmack (2014) 'Drop (Get Silenced)', in *Bang, Vol. 3*. Lightsleepers / Self-released (United States).
5. Gammer (2017) 'The Drop', in *The Drop*. Monstercat (Canada) MCEP124.
6. For a classic theoretical perspective on groove-based continuity in canonical EDM, see L-M. Garcia, 'On and On: Repetition as Process and Pleasure in Electronic Dance Music', *Music Theory Online*, 11 (4) (2005) https://mtosmt.org/issues/mto.05.11.4/mto.05.11.4.garcia.html.

7. C. Stirling, '"Beyond the dance floor"? Gendered Publics and Creative Practices in Electronic Dance Music', *Contemporary Music Review*, 35 (1) (2016), 130–49.
8. The first use of the acronym PLUR is often attributed to New York DJ Frankie Bones, but its spread across the globe during the 1990s and 2000s was accelerated by various mailing lists for ravers (run via hyperreal.org) and an associated newsgroup, alt.Rave. Hyperreal.org featured a series of raver testimonials that sought to preach about the power of PLUR. See M. A. G. Witek, 'Feeling at One: Socio-Affective Distribution, Vibe, and Dance-Music Consciousness', in *Music and Consciousness 2: Worlds, Practices, Modalities*, ed. R. Herbert, D. Clarke, & E. Clarke (Oxford: Oxford University Press, 2019), 93. In the North American festival setting of the 2010s, bracelets made from plastic beads ('kandi') were often traded between festivalgoers through a wordless ritual known as the 'PLUR handshake'. For a perspicacious perspective on PLUR and its racial discontents in the North American festival setting, see J. S. Park, 'Searching for a Cultural Home: Asian American Youth in the EDM Festival Scene', *Dancecult: Journal of Electronic Dance Music Culture*, 7 (1) (2015), 15–34.
9. See 'You Know What? I'm Just Gonna Say It', *Know Your Meme*, https://knowyourmeme.com/memes/you-know-what-im-just-gonna-say-it.
10. Excision & Space Laces (2016) 'Throwin' Elbows', in *Virus*. Rottun (United States). ROTD191.
11. S. Hawkins, 'Feel the Beat Come Down: House Music as Rhetoric', in *Analyzing Popular Music*, ed. A. F. Moore (Cambridge: Cambridge University Press, 2003), 100.
12. L-M. Garcia, '"Can you feel it, too?": Intimacy and Affect at Electronic Dance Music Events in Paris, Chicago, and Berlin' (Ph.D. thesis, The University of Chicago, 2011), 132.
13. Garcia, '"Can you feel it, too?"', 207.
14. E. Canetti, *Crowds and Power* (London: Phoenix, [1962] 2000), 31, original emphasis.
15. It should be noted that Yellow Claw's music is strongly associated with the gym as well as with the dance floor or festival field. Yellow Claw tracks have been featured in Spotify's curated 'Hype' playlist, for instance, which is described as 'Aggressive trap and bass for the gym'.
16. The idea of being 'fully gassed' or 'gassed up' is an important vernacular metaphor in transatlantic bass music culture, indicating a state of crazed or hyperactive (over)excitement. See, for instance, Subtronics & Zeds Dead feat. Flowdan (2022) 'Gassed Up', in *Fractals*. Cyclops Recordings (United States). CR023. Though the idea of being 'gassed up' is especially prominent in UK bass culture, it is also used in the US festival setting alongside alternatives such as 'hyphy', a slang term for being hyperactive coined by the West Coast rapper Keak da Sneak.

17. Speaking in 2014, the UK dubstep pioneer Skream expressed several regrets about the ever-increasing hunger for the bass music drop and its gendered overtones: 'It just got to the point where [he pauses] it was all about drops ... But originally it wasn't ... It [dubstep] was almost a vibe and almost meditation at one point ... it was zoning out and actually listening to what's going on rather than such impact and such testosterone-fuelled music.' In THUMP, 'Skream – Come With Me (Documentary), *YouTube* (2014), www.youtube.com/watch?v=JUrde21uRPc, 2.44 ff., my transcription.
18. Graham St John shrewdly highlights the 'gulf' between artists and fans at corporate EDM festivals, but fails to acknowledge that this division is in fact carefully obfuscated through the maintenance of a spurious unity whereby festivalgoers become branded 'lovemarks' for powerful producer-DJs. See G. St John, 'Introduction to Weekend Societies: EDM Festivals and Event-Cultures', *Dancecult: Journal of Electronic Dance Music Culture*, 7 (1) (2015), 4. As Fabian Holt contends, festival brandscapes such as Tomorrowland do not exist outside the sphere of commercial interests as a countercultural vacuum, but rather exist '*within* modern consumer culture' and can be understood as microcosmic arenas for late capitalist logics. F. Holt, 'New Media, New Festival Worlds: Rethinking Cultural Events and Televisuality Through YouTube and the Tomorrowland Music Festival', in *Music and the Broadcast Experience: Performance, Production, and Audiences*, ed. C. Baade & J. A. Deaville (New York: Oxford University Press, 2016), 280, original emphasis. One interesting logic concerns the way that powerful producer-DJs exploit anti-fandom through collaborations that are virtually guaranteed to generate social media furore. Key examples are the Excision and Illenium collaboration *Gold (Stupid Love)* as well as *Worst of Both Worlds* by Caine, Dodge & Fuski, and GPF (a track that plays on antipathy between dubstep fans and hardstyle fans).
19. See M. Meadow, 'Datsik Accused of Multiple Instances of Sexual Abuse, Deletes Incriminating Tweets', *Your EDM* (2018), www.youredm.com/2018/03/14/datsik-accused-of-multiple-instances-of-sexual-abuse-deletes-incriminating-tweets/ (accessed 21 August 2025).
20. M. Meadow, 'Datsik Responds to Accusations of Sexual Misconduct', *Your EDM* (2018), www.youredm.com/2018/03/14/datsik-responds-to-accusations-of-sexual-misconduct/?fbclid=IwAR1uMPpBmDp4iYSPxxUmr19wNL8srbe5Ix1K9LiPDKXawAj1rWtQIqhGLfs (accessed 21 August 2025).
21. To put it another way, this defence of Datsik was 'clothed in logics of aesthetic utilitarianism', an irrational rationality that sighs '*just think of all the beautiful music we will miss out on now*'. W. Cheng, *Loving Music Till It Hurts* (New York: Oxford University Press, 2019), 19, original emphasis.
22. T. Young, 'La Petite Mort: Techniques of Orgasm in Electronic Dance Music', *Transposition: Music et Sciences Sociales*, 9, (2021), https://journals.openedition.org/transposition/6024?lang=en.

23. H. C. Rietveld, 'Ephemeral Spirit: Sacrificial Cyborg and Communal Soul', in *Rave Culture and Religion*, ed. G. St John (London: Routledge, 2004), 46. See also Witek, 'Feeling at One'.
24. G. St John, 'Trance Tribes and Dance Vibes: Victor Turner and Trance Dance Culture', in *Victor Turner and Contemporary Cultural Performance*, ed. G. St John (New York: Berghahn, 2008), 157–58, after T. Olaveson, '"Connectedness" and the Rave Experience: Rave as New Religious Movement?', in *Rave Music and Religion*, ed. G. St John (London: Routledge, 2004), 93.
25. A fascinating recent development is the queering of 'brostep' by nonbinary hyperpop artists, some of whom weaponise brostep timbres in order to troll the heteronormative masculinity with which it has been associated. See E. Spencer, 'Backtrolling Brostep? On the (Sub)Cultural Politics of Dubstep Memes in the Oeuvre Of Dorian Electra and Other Hyperpop Artists', *Internet Musicking: Popular Music and Online Cultures* (Online: University College Cork, 2022), available at https://youtu.be/h6rgaDGeXno?t=1900.
26. For a complementary perspective on this sonification of damage, see the discussion of the drop and the soar in R. James, *Resilience and Melancholy: Pop Music, Feminism, Neoliberalism* (Winchester: Zero Books, 2015).
27. kylegordonisgreat, 'Kyle Gordon – Planet of the Bass (feat. DJ Crazy Times & Ms. Biljana Electronica) [Official Video]', *YouTube*, www.youtube.com/watch?v=S-OgkNgxm3k.
28. K. Fowler, 'The Nostalgia of Hyperpop and Why It's Probably Here to Stay', *Off-Chance*, www.off-chance.com/blog/hyperpop-music-popularity, 2023.
29. T. W. Adorno, 'On Popular Music', in *Essays on Music*, ed. T. W. Adorno, R. D. Leppert, & S. H. Gillespie (London: University of California Press, [1941] 2002), 462.
30. D. L. Brunsma, N. G. Chapman, & J. S. Lellock, 'Racial Ideology in Electronic Dance Music Festival Promotional Videos', in *Race and Contention in Twenty-First Century US Media*, ed. J. Smith & B. K. Thakore (New York: Routledge, 2016), 157–58.
31. A. Saldanha, *Psychedelic White: Goa Trance and the Viscosity of Race* (Minneapolis: University of Minnesota Press, 2007).
32. In E. K. Spencer, 'Review of Joe Muggs and Brian David Stevens, "Bass, Mids, Tops: An Oral History of Soundsystem Culture" (MIT Press, 2019)'. *Dancecult: Journal of Electronic Dance Music Culture*, 12(1) (2020), 85–88.
33. M. Perevedentseva, 'Digital Approaches to Musical Discourse Analysis: A Case Study of Boomkat.com', in *Music and the Internet: Methodological, Epistemological, and Ethical Perspectives*, ed. C. Haworth, E. K. Spencer, & D. S. Sofer (New York: Routledge, in press).
34. J. Williams, 'The Metaethics of Online Fan Studies: Recruiting Music Interviewees from within the (Cancel) Culture Wars', in *Music and the*

Internet: Methodological, Epistemological, and Ethical Perspectives, ed. C. Haworth, E. K. Spencer, & D. S. Sofer (New York: Routledge, in press).
35. See, for instance, F. Turner, *From Counterculture to Cyberculture: Stewart Brand, the Whole Earth Network, and the Rise of Digital Utopianism* (Chicago: University of Chicago Press, 2006).
36. M. Brennan & K. Devine, 'The Cost of Music', *Popular Music*, 39 (1) (2020), 43–65.

Further Reading

C. Stirling, '"Beyond the Dance Floor"? Gendered Publics and Creative Practices in Electronic Dance Music', *Contemporary Music Review*, 35 (1) (2016), 130–49.

E. K. Spencer, 'Music to Vomit to: The Dubstep Drop, the Bass Face, and the Sound of the Social Web', in *Cultural Approaches to Disgust and the Visceral*, ed. M. Ryynänen, H. Kosonen, & S. Ylönen (London: Routledge, 2022), 160–74.

J. S. Park, 'Searching for a Cultural Home: Asian American Youth in the EDM Festival Scene', *Dancecult: Journal of Electronic Dance Music Culture*, 7 (1) (2015), 15–34.

W. Cheng, *Loving Music Till It Hurts* (New York: Oxford University Press, 2019).

F. Holt, 'New Media, New Festival Worlds: Rethinking Cultural Events and Televisuality Through YouTube and the Tomorrowland Music Festival', in *Music and the Broadcast Experience: Performance, Production, and Audiences*, ed. C. Baade & J. A. Deaville (New York: Oxford University Press, 2016), 275–92.

18 | Ageing Provocateurs

Responding to Older People's Participation in Electronic Dance Music Culture

ALICE O'GRADY AND ALINKA GREASLEY

In the middle of a psytrance set, two young men in their early twenties approach my friend. She is dancing alone, lost in the music on the dance floor. They crowd round her and interrupt her flow to ask a question. They are smiling, laughing, waving a mobile phone. She struggles to hear them over the noise, leans in and asks them to repeat the question. They laugh louder and shout, 'Can we take your photo? We just want to get a shot of you, you know, because . . . ' She looks up at them quizzically. 'Why? Why do you want to take my photo?' She raises an eyebrow, looks directly at them and waits for an answer. The laughing continues but is less self-assured. The young men begin to stutter. 'Because, you know, you're so . . . you're so . . . you're a legend! We just want . . . we hope we're still partying when we're that . . .' My friend looks up at them and finishes their sentence for them, "Old?"   (Fieldnotes, February 2022)

Introduction

Electronic dance music culture (EDMC) encompasses a broad range of musical genres, including house, techno, drum and bass, electro, dub, and psychedelic trance. These genres and sub genres attract different audiences with different motivations for attending.[1] Whilst each subgenre is likely to come with its own set of norms and practices, one trend that can be seen across participation is the rise in the number of older attendees. Industry figures show that whilst most attendees at electronic dance music events are young adults, people are continuing to participate in EDM scenes into their thirties, forties, fifties, and beyond.[2] However, club culture is not homogenous and patterns of participation vary according to genre, geographic location, and localised practice. The increased prevalence of older clubbers in some contexts indicates a changing demographic that destabilises conventional readings of a culture hitherto associated with youth. It also sheds light on the shifting priorities and expectations of older people in relation to (sub)cultural participation. Our research investigates the impact of this emerging trend on EDMC and seeks to understand the role clubbing plays in the lives of older participants. For the purpose of this chapter, we refer to the social and cultural practices centred on dancing to beat-based electronic music in a variety of settings such as clubs, raves, free parties, and festivals.

Our work draws on the perspectives of attendees, promoters, producers, and artists who remain involved in the scene beyond the age of forty to give an insight into the contradictory attitudes that circulate around the topic of club culture and ageing. Despite being founded on the ethos of Peace, Love, Unity, and Respect (PLUR) and long-established claims of being inclusive, negative attitudes to age prevail within EDMC. Older people's participation in the scene provokes polarised views even from those with 'insider' status, and notions of belonging in the scene can be undermined by concerns about fitting in, appearance, and feeling 'othered'. Older people's presence within club culture can cause conflicting reactions amongst younger club goers, within the industry, and even for the older participants themselves. In this chapter, we describe these older clubbers as 'ageing provocateurs'. The aesthetic of ageing in the context of club culture runs contrary to the representation of nightclubs as 'youth-focused' places[3] and clubbing as 'youth cultural activity'[4] despite the sustained participation of older people in specific scenes such as Goa psytrance,[5] jazz,[6] and gay nights.[7] Our research exposes the ageism that runs through EDMC and highlights the internal ageism that even those involved in the scene can embody. We attempt to foreground these tensions and contradictions and, in doing so, explore the ways in which older people's participation in club culture is forcing change. In what follows, we draw on current literature and a set of in-depth interviews we carried out with UK and EU promoters and producers aged over fifty. In addition, we draw insights from a survey investigating experiences of EDM attendance for 130 women aged over forty.[8] Our work is also informed by our own active participation in the electronic dance music scene for a combined total of fifty-five years.

Challenging the Norm of 'Youth Culture'

EDMC is generally represented as an expression of youth style, taste, and sensibility. Early scholarship theorises clubbing as a rite-of-passage activity that marks the transition into adulthood[9] resulting in an emphasis on the conceptual paradigm of youth culture as a tool for analysis. Participation in clubbing is at its height between the ages of eighteen and twenty-five[10] with involvement dropping off by the age of thirty-five as work and family commitments increase.[11] It is important to recognise that clubbing is not a homogenous activity and there may be different trends of participation according to different subgenres and localities.[12] Underneath these headline statistics, another picture emerges: as with other leisure trends such as skateboarding,[13] older people continue to participate in EDM scenes well beyond the category of youth. As Bennett argues, the very concept of 'youth culture' has become increasingly ambiguous,[14] its boundaries contested and in flux. Early literature represents clubbing as being predominantly the preserve of the young, with Sarah Thornton claiming, 'going out dancing crosses boundaries of class, race, ethnicity, gender and sexuality, but *not* differences of age'.[15] Although this narrative ignores the participation of older adults in the foundational years of acid house and rave culture, it was largely accepted as part of the emerging discourse on sub- and clubcultures. Today's perspective is rather different. Although quantitative demographic data by age is difficult to obtain, a widening of participation in club cultural activity is apparent on many dance floors. Participation in EDM by 'post-youth' individuals is having an impact not only on our understanding of what constitutes youth culture but also on the shifting expectations, values, and priorities of older people who sustain their involvement alongside adult commitments and responsibilities. Despite these shifts, ageist attitudes prevail and the presence of older people on dance floors and behind the decks can provoke negative responses that call into question the values of unity and respect enshrined within the PLUR ideal.

Dating back to the emergence of acid house in the mid-1980s, the current EDM scene includes participants who have been involved since its inception over thirty-five years ago. Young people who participated in the free party or rave scene in the UK at that time are now in their fifties and sixties. As Bennett points out, 'memories and cultural resonances of the dance parties of the early 1980s continue to have a significant impact on many of those individuals who were involved. Indeed, for many the attraction of the dance party has never faded, resulting in myriad strategies among ageing individuals to remain active in particular scenes.'[16] These individuals enjoy a certain 'veteran' status within the scene by virtue of the longevity of their involvement and stamina. They are respected and revered for their cultural capital and often adopt positions of authority either as promoters, event organisers, club owners, or DJs. This level of respect is not always extended to older clubbers on the dance floor. As well as being admired and celebrated by some, older clubbers can also be subjected to derision and ageist attitudes from younger participants and even, at times, door staff and security. Why does the presence of older clubbers provoke such polarising perspectives and what does it tell us about the prevailing attitudes to ageing in this specific cultural context?

Challenging the Narratives of Ageing

Decline-oriented approaches to age and ageing are common. Ageing is associated with an accumulation of deficits over time, including reduction in cognitive abilities, sensory perception, and daily activity, alongside an increased susceptibility to illness and frailty. Physical decline can be accompanied by negative psychosocial consequences such as depression, isolation, and loneliness.[17] The ageing process is characterised negatively, and the ageing population is often represented pejoratively.[18] As Madden says, 'narratives of decline operate on both individual and collective consciences, shaping our responses to ageing populations and the scripts that circumscribe our behaviour'.[19] Although older people clearly have a right to access and participate in culture and cultural activity, their participation in *club* culture seems to be particularly provocative because it challenges our deeply held beliefs about age-appropriate behaviour. Although clubbing is conventionally associated with a period of hedonistic youthfulness that might involve sexual experimentation or illegal activity such as recreational drug-taking, the emergence of the 'conscious clubbing movement', which includes day raves, sober raves, and wellness events, suggests millennial youth are finding alternative patterns of engagement.[20] Placing an older person within the frame of pleasure-seeking hedonism causes a cultural clash or a jarring of expectations and assumptions about what it is to be old. A type of cultural incongruity is produced which is hard to resolve. Despite this, some older people are reluctant to give up an aspect of their lifestyle that they report as having positive benefits on their physical and mental wellbeing.[21] It is well known that people are living longer and have different expectations of old age. There is an increased focus on 'ageing well', with a rise in terms such as 'successful ageing', 'active ageing', and 'healthy ageing'. Research has shown that avoidance of illness, mental and physical activity, and active involvement with life are factors that predict successful ageing.[22] Group activity and physical activity, in particular, are strong predictors of successful ageing over time.[23] Social dancing, which combines group activity with physical exercise, has been found to have significant health benefits for older adults[24] but studies tend to focus on those styles more commonly associated with ageing populations, such as ballroom or Scottish country dances. Among young adults, dancing to EDM can contribute to wellbeing[25] but how that plays out for older populations within the context of 'successful ageing' is yet to be fully explored.

Researching EDM and Ageing

Despite growing interest in shifting approaches to ageing from a cultural perspective, there is limited scholarship on the topic of EDM and ageing. Existing scholarship tends to investigate the experiences of older participants and uses qualitative methodologies to draw conclusions about the role clubbing plays, or has played, in the lives of those who might be characterised as being 'post-youth'. Research tends to explore how and why individuals continue to participate in a culture more usually associated with young people and how they reconcile their ageing identities with their clubbing personae. Attention is often paid to those behaviours considered to be at odds with 'responsible' adulthood such as recreational drug use.[26] While interest in this topic has persisted, driven by both moral panics in the popular press and health-related funding priorities from research councils, substance use by older people in this context presents something of a cultural conundrum. Voluntary risk-taking behaviour in the name of hedonism and the pursuit of pleasure runs counter to the conventional narratives associated with ageing and prompts us to re-evaluate cultural attitudes to growing old. Framed by the lens of youth culture and identity, Andy Bennett's work on dance parties, ageing, and lifestyle outlines how older participants, particularly those with professional backgrounds, develop and adopt strategies for engaging in 'sustainable fun'.[27] His interviewees do not express any regret at being older participants in EDM and claim that age brings benefits to participation. Similarly, our own research reveals older people experience a wide range of physical, social, and emotional benefits. Participants refer to attendance at electronic dance music events as a form of 'therapy' which keeps them physically active, releases stress and tension, and plays a key role in the affirmation of community. Despite the positive effects so passionately articulated, our respondents also reported challenges associated with being an older clubber, such as wear and tear on the body, lingering tiredness, slow recovery.[28] Although Bennett's informants do not perceive any problems or contradictions inherent in combining their lives as older adults with their clubbing activity, he states, 'the relationship between work and clubbing embodies an obvious, and in many ways precarious, series of contradictions'.[29] For those with significant commitments and responsibilities, a set of adjustments is made in order to manage and maintain two potentially competing lifestyles. These include moderating recreational drug use, allowing for greater recovery time after an event, and actively coordinating work and party schedules alongside other commitments. This aligns with our own research where a need to find balance is a key theme that emerges from our respondents.

Conversely, Julie Gregory's work focuses on desistance and 'post-scene narratives'.[30] She explores the identities of female clubbers who have moved away from participation in Toronto's rave scene who view their bodies as no longer appropriate sites for displaying an active 'raver' identity.[31] Investigating (non)rave participation, she retrospectively assesses the impact participation in rave culture has on identity formation and how that is carried forward into later life. Although the women ceased participation in rave as they no longer understood or experienced their ageing bodies as matching that of the 'ideal' raver, neither had they completely disconnected from it. They described their participation in the rave scene as providing them with self-esteem, confidence, non-judgemental attitude, and an ability to connect with others which they were able to transfer and apply in their post-rave lives, including within the professional sphere.

In 2019, *Dancecult: Journal of Electronic Dance Music Culture* published a special issue on EDM and ageing featuring articles on the experiences of older women,[32] the queer temporality of ageing performers such as the Pet Shop Boys,[33] and the concept of 'fluid multigenerationality' as characterised by the emergence of 'baby raves'.[34] For O'Grady and Madill, contributors to this special issue, what is or is not 'age appropriate' behaviour in a club becomes a site of playful resistance to entrenched cultural norms that operate in the world.[35] Their analysis reveals that older female clubbers are intentionally tactical about their involvement in the scene, paying attention to how they navigate the risks and pleasures of engaging in late night activity, sustained physical exercise, and recreational drug use, in order to sustain their 'actively engaged hedonism'.[36] In the same year and arising from the *Lapsed Clubber Project*, Beate Peter and Lisa Williams published findings from an online survey conducted three years earlier to ascertain how and to what extent ageing ravers continue to participate in club culture. Their research set out to investigate the life journeys of the original ravers of the late 1980s and early 1990s and to see how adult life events impact upon persistence or desistance in the scene. Their findings suggest that frequent attendance in young adulthood determines persistent participation in later life, whilst life course events such as relationships and caring responsibilities constrain participation in older adulthood. They demonstrate that such activities are not adolescence-limited and that the industry itself is adapting to its ageing market.[37]

Despite these adaptations, Harold Heath writing in *DJ Mag* suggests there are 'strands of ageism' running through club culture that impact the dance floor as well as the workplace.[38] Focusing on the experience of older female DJs, Kamila Rymajdo's work explores the intersection of ageism and sexism within the specific context of Manchester's club scene where masculine heritage is celebrated and female narratives all but erased. Describing club culture as being rife with 'unchecked ageism', Rymajdo highlights the continued underrepresentation of BAME women and older women within EDM and argues that the male-centric music industry is still 'plagued with inequalities' around race, gender, and age.[39] In her examination of the male-dominated programming of Norway's Musikkfest in 2016, Tami Gadir suggests women in the music industry have an 'expiry date' imposed upon them in a way that their male counterparts do not and that older women who DJ are 'not the idealised norm'.[40] While ageism might feel 'a little like the last acceptable prejudice',[41] older people's persistent presence on the scene and the scene's longevity itself mean that it is time for this position to shift.

Age as Provocation

The presence of older people in clubs provokes a range of reactions including admiration, amusement, ridicule, antagonism, prejudice, and derision. Previous research has explored the reactions and responses, both positive and negative, of younger clubbers when confronted by the presence of older women on the dance floor.[42] In our survey, one woman, aged forty, who attends bass and dub nights, reports:

I've been out several times where groups of young lads have asked to take selfies of me because they are amazed that I'm still out at my age and when they find out I am a mother, they are also amazed. They've said things like, 'Wow! I hope I'm still out getting fucked when I'm your age' and have called over more mates to look at me and tell them how old I am.

Male clubbers also attract attention. One of our male informants talks of being at a psytrance night and having 'a ring of youngsters, eighteen, nineteen-year-olds, all with their cameras on me' reproducing a type of quasi-celebrity status for the older person which is not always welcome. Similarly, older clubbers are represented as curiosities in the popular press.[43] Notable stories recounting older people stumbling unwittingly into clubs have been known to go viral.[44] Surveys circulate in the media which claim anyone clubbing over the age of thirty-seven is officially 'sad'.[45] Given these attitudes, is it any wonder that older clubbers are themselves conflicted about their participation in the scene?

Ambivalent Identities

Being conspicuous in a club by virtue of age can provoke contradictory responses from older clubbers themselves and produces a type of internalised ageism. Given what we know about the intersection between ageism and sexism in this context, it is not surprising that the bodies of older women in club spaces can be especially challenging to cultural norms associated with age. The physical appearance of older women in a club – how they dress, how they behave, and how they present themselves – takes on particular significance in a culture predicated on the celebration of youth, vitality, and play.[46]

In our study, women express contradictory views about their physical appearance within the club space. While dressing for comfort is important, they do not want to appear dowdy or outdated. Some describe enjoying dressing up in a playful or performative way, but this is tempered by concerns about being too outrageous or drawing unwanted attention to themselves. They both care and do not care what other people think. To some extent, age liberates, with many informants saying that they dress for themselves rather than others. Alternatively, others take great care in choosing an outfit that fulfils the competing demands described above. There is a strong sense that there is heavy lifting to be done in navigating the choices between what works well on a personal level, and what is acceptable or appropriate for the environment and the other people in it. For example, one woman, aged forty-two, who has been clubbing for over twenty years says:

I don't really know what to wear and find that I'm very concerned with fitting in, which is probably impossible to achieve (I don't have the body of a twenty-year-old) and frustrating as I don't think fitting in is what clubbing should be about, but I also don't want to feel self-conscious.

The presentation of age in the club is described differently by men. Some worry about feeling out of place, self-conscious, or uncomfortable as an older person, with concerns about their presence being treated with suspicion or being read as predatory. Even those with decades of involvement in the scene, both personally and professionally, express conflicting views about their participation. One man, aged fifty-four, speaks of wanting to 'let go' on the dancefloor but keeps himself in check through fear of ridicule. Another, aged forty-nine, describes 'squatting' within a culture that he believes should belong to young people. Their accounts highlight the ways in which their continued involvement in the scene is not straightforward and that their clubbing activity pushes at the cultural norms associated with age in ways that are not always comfortable.

An Ageing Industry

It perhaps goes without saying that the electronic dance music industry is not a homogenous entity. Different genres, venues, cities, and countries will have varying perspectives on and attitudes to older clubbers' participation and the impact of that involvement. While the peak of clubbing activity occurs between the ages of eighteen and twenty-five, the scene itself is ageing. With a history spanning four decades, it is not surprising that there are more older people participating in a culture with which they identify on a deep level. The industry is responding in a variety of ways. Promoters are hosting different types of nights to appeal to an older market. Retro nights are increasingly common as are daytime and family-orientated events which improve accessibility and accommodate multigenerational participation. The promoters we spoke to talked of the business strategies they adopt to cater for an older crowd, including offering flexible spaces, additional seating, and the provision of different types of drinks stocked at the bar.

One venue owner and promoter who has been in the business for over twenty years told us:

Heritage DJs are now starting at eight o'clock so their crowd are getting down there early, having some cocktails, having a nice pint in a glass, being able to sit down, chill out, get into the mood. And then they're coming upstairs and having a rave. And that kind of, that doesn't happen for the teenage nights. They get there at twelve o'clock, they go straight into the venue, they're already drunk or whatever, and they just rave till three o'clock and go home. So you can see the trends.

There is a growing awareness from event organisers that the presence of older people has a positive impact on the behaviour of younger clubbers and vice versa. Promoters talked of the calming effect older clubbers have on the younger crowd, with fewer instances of fighting reported, and a more considerate dance floor etiquette in operation when generations mix. One event organiser with thirty years' experience describes the effect of running nights where the demographic includes people in their twenties and thirties, right the way through to 'old hippies' in their sixties and seventies:

It keeps the older people a bit younger and it doesn't just feel like a retro night, for want of a better term, but the flipside is the younger people, it almost gives them a bit of a guidance. Despite the nature of the night, it's very rare we get casualties, you know, the people that overdo it. Generally speaking people tend to be reasonably sensible, and maybe just having people around who know what they're doing steadies things a bit. If there's a bunch of student lads who come in and they might be a bit, I don't know, slightly lairy, when they realise that everyone else is just being friendly and relaxed and stuff, they quickly soon relax, so it probably works well for both sides. I think it calms down the younger end, but the flipside is it sort of livens up the older end.

Despite the positive social and economic impacts of older people's participation, interestingly the promoters we spoke to revealed that they do not market specifically to an older audience. An exception to this would be retro nights, which are promoted as an opportunity for people to relive the glory days of raving from the 1980s and 1990s. However, these nights tend to be spoken about in fairly negative terms and are associated with heritage rather than contemporary culture. It seems that the industry is caught in a double bind. It wants to celebrate its history and acknowledge the legends of a bygone era but, at the same time, wants to keep the culture fresh, vibrant, and moving forwards. As one forty-nine-year-old music producer and DJ says:

Whether it's in the clothes that we're sold, the lifestyle that we're sold and you know, people no longer feel as old as a previous generation would have when they got to that age. When you go out to clubs, there's still loads of older people. But the real culture is owned by the youth, you know, and if it's not, I think it's really hard for a culture to have vibrancy.

So, do older people belong or do they not? Is it the responsibility of the industry to ensure all nights are open and inclusive of older people or not? The promoters we spoke to appear to be ambivalent about the presence of older participants. Having a defined, professional role within the scene as an older person provides some level of 'protection' from prejudice as their status within the club setting is commensurate with their age and seniority. However, even those involved in a professional capacity have told us 'clubs aren't places for old people'. Clubbers themselves also feel this ambivalence. They have a strong sense of belonging and yet experience public micro-aggressions as well as unbridled ageism that can make them feel simultaneously out of place. They feel they belong but there are caveats. Older clubbers choose carefully the type of night, the venue, the genre of music, and the demographic that supports their participation and fosters a sense of belonging. This degree of selectivity on the part of the older clubber is a strategy deployed to avoid discrimination and maximise enjoyment, camaraderie, and safety.

However, there are global and local differences. As one of our respondents noted:

Living in Europe, it's so much easier to be in the clubbing environment at an older age than in other countries like US, Australia and the UK. People are definitely more accepting and it's not unusual. Just depends on the party, type of event and genre. (Female EDM attendee, forty years old)

The experience of finding it 'easier' to be in a club space as an older person tells us not only about attitudes within certain venues, musical styles, and scenes but also about the wider, cultural context within which the club exists. What is deemed 'appropriate' behaviour for older people can vary and this has a significant impact on people's sense of belonging in club spaces.

Conclusion

EDM, as a broad musical style, is over thirty years old. It is a scene that has persisted over time and, as well as attracting new audiences, has brought many of its long-standing devotees along with it. Over this period there has been a proliferation of styles, genres, and sub genres that attract different audiences with different characteristics. Dance floors are by no means homogenous and local scenes can produce different patterns of participation according to gender, sexuality, ethnicity, and age. However, despite local differences and advances in musical and technological innovation, the overarching experience of going out dancing to electronic music has not changed significantly for over three decades. For some people in their forties, fifties, sixties, and beyond, EDM is still very much 'their scene' and they feel a deep sense of connection and belonging to the music and the community it fosters. At the same time, many young people entering the scene for the first time are keen to mark it out as their territory and are often surprised to find older people present in a context they had assumed belonged to youth. The question of who belongs (and who decides who belongs) in club culture has been a matter of concern for EDM scholars such as Malbon and Thornton, but is rarely discussed along the lines of age.

In this chapter, we have chosen to conceptualise older clubbers as 'ageing provocateurs' as their presence in the night-time economy is inherently provocative. It challenges what we think we know about older people as well as what we think we know about club culture. Limiting and restrictive attitudes about ageing and what is considered to be age-appropriate behaviours are deeply engrained and have, to a certain extent, been absorbed even by those who defy cultural norms through their own involvement in EDM. Older clubbers say that participation benefits their lives, providing 'emotional wealth' and 'physical therapy' that they are reluctant to relinquish, yet they also express concern that their involvement is somehow at odds with what is expected at their time of life. Clearly there are some club spaces that are more accepting of a wide generational demographic than others, though when intergenerational mixing occurs it can have positive impacts on all involved. Promoters are actively carving out such spaces to enable continued participation. Many clubbers refuse to be defined or constrained by their age. Nonetheless, ageing provocateurs play an important role in challenging negative stereotypes and in expanding our understanding of what inclusive dance music culture looks like.

Notes

1. Reynolds, S. *Generation Ecstasy: Into the World of Techno and Rave Culture*, New York: Routledge (1999); Stirling, C. '"Beyond the Dance Floor'? Gendered Publics and Creative Practices in Electronic Dance Music', *Contemporary Music Review*, 35(1) (2016), 130–49.
2. Penciu, A., Rawcliffe, S., Rea, T., and Mermiri, T. *State of Play: Dance Music. UK and Spain Report*, http://discover.ticketmaster.co.uk/stateofplay/dancemusic.pdf, 2015 (accessed 2 April 2023).
3. Rymajdo, K. 'A Barrier to Being Seen: Ageism and Sexism Intersect on the Dance Floor', https://ra.co/features/3930, 27 October 2021 (accessed 22 May 2022), 215.

4. Chatterton, P., and Hollands, R. *Urban Nightscapes: Youth Cultures, Pleasure Spaces and Corporate Power*, London: Routledge (2003), 68.
5. D'Andrea, A. '"The Decline of Electronic Dance Scenes"', in St John, G. (ed.), *The Local Scenes and Global Cultures of Psytrance*, New York: Routledge (2010), 40–54.
6. Oakes, S. 'Profiling the Jazz Festival Audience', *International Journal of Event and Festival Management*, 1(2) (2010), 110–19.
7. Bennett, A., and Taylor, J. 'As Time Goes By: Music, Dance and Ageing'. *Popular Music*, 31(2), (2012), 231–43.
8. Greasley, A. E., O'Grady, A., and Stapleton, S. E. 'Age Is Just a Number: Persistent Participation in Electronic Dance Music by Women over 40 Years'. *Psychology of Music*, 0(0) (2025). https://doi.org/10.1177/03057356251329229.
9. Malbon, B. *Clubbing: Dancing, Ecstasy, Vitality*, London: Routledge (1999); Thornton S. *Club Cultures: Music, Media and Subcultural Capital*, Cambridge: Polity (1995), 55.
10. Dinev, K. 'Nightclubs in the UK. Pent-up demand from consumers for going out is expected to support industry revenue growth'. IBISWorld.com, Industry Report I56.301, 2022.
11. Peter, B., and Williams, L. 'One Foot in the Rave: Ageing Ravers' Transitions to Adulthood and their Participation in Rave Culture', *Leisure Sciences: An Interdisciplinary Journal*, 44(7) (2019), 808–26.
12. Takahashi, M., and Olaveson, T. 'Music, Dance and Raving Bodies: Raving as Spirituality in the Central Canadian Rave Scene', *Journal of Ritual Studies*, 17(2) (2003), 72–96.
13. Willing, I., Bennett, A., Piispa, M., and Green, B. 'Skateboarding and the "Tired Generation": Ageing in Youth Cultures and Lifestyle Sports', *Sociology*, 53(3) (2019), 503–18.
14. Bennett, A. 'Dance Parties, Lifestyle and Strategies for Ageing', in Bennett, A., and Hodkinson, P. (eds.), *Ageing and Youth Cultures: Music, Style and Identity*, London: Bloomsbury (2012), 1.
15. Thornton, *Club Cultures*, 15.
16. Bennett, 'Dance Parties', 95.
17. Tani, M., Cheng, Z., Piracha, M., and Wang, B. 'Ageing, Health, Loneliness and Wellbeing', *Social Indicators Research*, 160(2–3) (2022), 791–807.
18. Wright-Bevans, K., and Murray, M., 'Resisting Negative Social Representations of Ageing', in Peel, E., Holland, C., and Murray, M. (eds.), *Psychologies of Ageing*, Cham: Palgrave Macmillan (2018), 253–81.
19. Madden, D. 'Introduction to Ageing with EDMC', *Dancecult: Journal of Electronic Dance Music Culture*, 11(1) (2019), 3.
20. Davies, E., Smith, J., Johansson, M., Hill, K., and Brown, K. 'Can't Dance Without Being Drunk? Exploring the Enjoyment and Acceptability of Conscious Clubbing in Young People', in Conroy, D., and Measham, F. (eds.), *Young Adult Drinking Styles*, Cham: Palgrave Macmillan (2019), 233–52.

21. Greasley et al., 'Age is Just a Number'.
22. Sowa, A., Tobiasz-Adamczyk, T-M, Poscia, A., and Ignazio la Milia, D. 'Predictors of Healthy Ageing: Public Health Policy Targets', *BMC Health Services Research*, 5 September; 16 Suppl 5 (2016), 289.
23. Moreno-Agostino, D., Daskalopoulou, C., Wu, Y. T., et al. 'The Impact of Physical Activity on Healthy Ageing Trajectories: Evidence From Eight Cohort Studies', *International Journal of Behavioral Nutrition and Physical Activity*, 17 (92) (2020).
24. Keogh, J. W. L., Kilding, A., Pidgeon, P., Ashley, L., and Gillis, D. 'Physical Benefits of Dancing for Healthy Older Adults: A Review', *Journal of Aging and Physical Activity*, 4 (2009), 479–500.
25. Cannon, J. W., and Greasley, A. E. 'Exploring Relationships between Electronic Dance Music Event Participation and Well-Being', *Music & Science*, 4 (2021), 1–17.
26. Green, R. '"I Wonder What Age You Grow Out of It?": Negotiation of Recreational Drug Use and the Transition to Adulthood Among an Australian Ethnographic Sample', *Drugs: Education, Prevention and Policy*, 23(3) (2016), 202–11.
27. Bennett, 'Dance Parties', 98.
28. Greasley et al., 'Age Is Just a Number'.
29. Bennett, 'Dance Parties', 98.
30. Gregory, J. 'Ageing Rave Women's Post-Scene Narratives', in Bennett, A., and Hodkinson, P. (eds.), *Ageing and Youth Cultures: Music, Style and Identity*, London: Bloomsbury (2012), 37–54.
31. Gregory, 'Ageing Rave Women's Post-Scene Narratives', 37.
32. O'Grady, A., and Madill, A. 'Being and Performing "Older" Woman in Electronic Dance Music Culture', *Dancecult: Journal of Electronic Dance Music Culture*, 11(1) (2019), 7–29.
33. Wodtke, L. 'The Irony and the Ecstasy: The Queer Aging of Pet Shop Boys and LCD Soundsystem in Electronic Dance Music', *Dancecult: Journal of Electronic Dance Music Culture*, 11(1) (2019), 30–52.
34. Armour, Z. 'Baby Raves: Youth, Adulthood and Ageing in Contemporary British EDM Culture', *Dancecult: Journal of Electronic Dance Music Culture*, 11(1) (2019), 53–71.
35. O'Grady and Madill, 'Being and Performing "Older" Woman', 23.
36. O'Grady and Madill, 'Being and Performing "Older" Woman', 25.
37. Peter and Williams, 'One Foot in the Rave', 16.
38. Heath, H. 'Raving is for Everyone: The Problem with Ageism in Dance Music', https://djmag.com/longreads/raving-everyone-problem-ageism-dance-music, 3 July 2019 (accessed 22 May 2022).
39. Rymajdo, 'A Barrier to Being Seen', 212.

40. Gadir, T. 'Forty-Seven DJs, Four Women: Meritocracy, Talent and Postfeminist Politics', *Dancecult: Journal of Electronic Dance Music Culture*, 9(1) (2017), 59.
41. Heath, 'Raving is for Everyone'.
42. O'Grady and Madill, 'Being and Performing "Older" Woman'.
43. Crummy, C. '"Afterparties? That would hurt": the older clubbers who won't stop dancing', *The Guardian*, www.theguardian.com/music/2019/dec/13/older-clubbers-who-wont-stop-dancing-ibiza-psytrance-colin-crummy 13 December 2019 (accessed 22 May 2022).
44. Gayle, D. 'DJ searches for elderly couple who tore it up at Fabric nightclub', *The Guardian*, www.theguardian.com/music/2016/may/17/dj-searches-old-couple-fabric-nightclub, 17 May 2016 (accessed 22 May 2022).
45. Bowman, L. 'No, it's not 'tragic' to go out clubbing past the age of 37', *Metro*, https://metro.co.uk/2017/07/08/no-its-not-tragic-to-go-out-clubbing-past-the-age-of-37-6762874/ 8 July 2017 (accessed 22 May 2022).
46. Malbon, *Clubbing: Dancing, Ecstasy, Vitality*, 3.

Further Reading

Bennett, A. 'Dance Parties, Lifestyle and Strategies for Ageing', in Bennett, A., and Hodkinson, P. (eds.), *Ageing and Youth Cultures: Music, Style and Identity*, London: Bloomsbury (2012), 95–104.

Gregory, J. 'Ageing Rave Women's Post-Scene Narratives', in Bennett, A., and Hodkinson, P. (eds.), *Ageing and Youth Cultures: Music, Style and Identity*, London: Bloomsbury (2012), 37–54.

Madden, D. 'Introduction to Ageing with EDMC', *Dancecult: Journal of Electronic Dance Music Culture*, 11(1) (2019), 3–6.

O'Grady, A., and Madill, A. 'Being and Performing "Older" Woman in Electronic Dance Music Culture', *Dancecult: Journal of Electronic Dance Music Culture*, 11(1) (2019), 7–29.

Peter, B., and Williams, L. 'One Foot in the Rave: Ageing Ravers' Transitions To Adulthood and their Participation in Rave Culture', *Leisure Sciences: An Interdisciplinary Journal*, 44(7) (2019), 808–26.

Index

Please note that the professional names of DJs have been rendered intact as single entities, rather than artificially split as though they consist of a surname and given name (e.g. Roni Size appears as 'Roni Size, not, 'Size, Roni').

+8, 210
12th Planet, 337

Adam X, 214
Adorno, Theodor, 232, 299, 347
Afrofuturism, 168, 174, 177, 209
ageism. *See* EDM, older people's participation in
Ahmed, Sara, 303
Alex Patterson, 193
Amado, Tony, 114–16
Amfo, Clara, 347
anemoia, 346
Angola
    carga. *See* DJs and producers, audience, interaction with, liveness
    independence, 112–13
    kuduro. *See* EDM, kuduro
    Luanda, 109, 112–14
    música de intervenção, 113
Aphex Twin, 194, 241, 276
Audio Engineering Society, the, 315

Barthes, Roland, 41–43
Becker, Rashad, 241
Bedlam, 4
Belleville Three, the, 209
Black Atlantic, the, 109–23, 276–77, 289
Black Tiger Sex Machine, 343
Böhme, Gernot, 37
Bovell, Dennis, 56
Butler, Mark, 231–32, 299–300

Cage, John, 185, 188–89, 190
Caldini, Carlo, 30–32
Canetti, Elias, 342
chill out (ambient), *xii*, 182, *196*, 216–17, 220–21
China
    Beijing, 137

guangchangwu, 129
Hong Kong, 43
karaoke. *See* clubbing and raving, klubbing
Mandopop. *See* EDM, Mandopop
mic-shouting. *See* EDM, mic-shouting
Shanghai, 137
clubbing and raving
    belonging. *See* EDM, belonging, secrecy
    definitions of, 4, 18–20, 32–33
    early, 101
    illegal. *See* legislation
    inner city (London). *See* EDM, drum and bass; UK, London
    'jacking', 282
    klubbing (karaoke), 129, 136–37
    moshing, 339–40, 343
    Peace, Love, Unity, Respect (PLUR), 168, 340–41, 354–55
    'rave moment', the, 25
    raves. *See* raves, festivals, teknivals and free parties
    Selbstbezüglichkeit, 19
    Selbstzweckhaftigkeit, 19
    Temporary Autonomous Zone (TAZ), 92
    'youth-focused', 354, 362, *see also* EDM, older people's participation in
clubs and venues
    Amnesia (Ibiza), 192
    architecture and design, 44
    AREA (New York), 34, 77
    Art House Tacheles (Berlin), 95
    Bar 25 (Berlin), 99
    Berghain (Berlin), 255, 271, 341
    boundaries, 354
        ageism. *See* EDM, older people's participation in
        bouncers, 21–23
        cost, 97, 135
        dress code, 21–23, 324–27, 360

opening hours, 4, 18, 24
Bunker (Berlin), 85, 94
C'est la Vie (Blackburn), 24
Cafe am Hochhaus (Munich), 75
Café Del Mar (Ibiza), 192
Canton Disco (Hong Kong), 43
Club Equinox (virtual), 147
Crackers (Blackburn), 24
dancefloors, 44, 192, 361–64
Danceteria (New York), 34
Eimer (Berlin), 95
Electric Circus (New York), 36–38
Fabric (London), 255
Fischbüro (Berlin), 84
Haçienda (Manchester), 35
Hardcore Techno Club, the (Berlin), 102
Heaven (London), 193
Horst Krzbrg (Berlin), 84
hostesses, 133–37
'inexistent' spaces, 44
Land of Oz (London), 193–94
Le Palace (Paris), 42
Mensch Meier (Berlin), 98
MGM Club (Beijing), 137
Ministry of Sound (London), 134
Music Institute, the (Detroit), 73
Palladium (New York), 35–37, 44
Pandemôneo (Luanda), 113–15
Paradise Garage (New York), 209
Piper (Rome), 32–33
Piper (Turin), 33
Red Cross Club (Rot-Kreuz-Club, Berlin), the, 102
Roaring Twenties, The (London), 61
Shoom (London), 193
Space Electronic (Florence), 31–38
Spectrum (London), 193
Studio 54 (New York), 44
Tresor (Berlin), 84–85, 100, 210, 256
Trip, the (London), 193
Turbine (Berlin), 84, 256
UFO (Berlin), 84
Warehouse, the (Chicago), 73, 209, 338
Whisky à Gogo (Paris), 37
Count Suckle (Wilbert Campbell), 54
Covid-19, 35, 138, 146
Coxsone Dodd, Clement Seymour, 52–54
Csikszentmihalyi, Mihalyi, 295, 298, 300–2

Danny Krivit, 75
Datsik (Troy Beetles), 339, 344–46
David DePino, 296

Deejays, 52, 63–65, 121
Digital Mystikz, 243
DJ Balli, 92
DJ Carlos Pedro, 113
DJ Crazy Times, 346
DJ Krust, 59
DJ Mad, 96
DJ Optical (Mark Quinn), 60
DJ Pierre (Pierre Jones), 276–78
DJ Seduction (John Kalkan), 284
DJ T-1000, 219
DJ Tanith, 84
DJ Warren, 307
DJ Znobia, 110, 116
DJs and producers. *see also* clubs and venues
  audience, interaction with, 155, 208, 232, 328
  animação, 118–20
  antiphony, call and response, 50, 138
  antisociality, 169
  carga, 110–11, 117–21
  flow, vibe, nowness, 156, 353
  liveness, performance, spectacle, 8–9, 110–11
  virtual, 11, 146
  courses, 319–21
  record archive of, 2, 6, 57, 71–75
  technology. *See* technology
  women. *See* EDM, gender imbalance
Doderer, Yvonne, 100
Dröhner, Alexandra, 100
drugs
  amphetamines, 182
  cannabis, 182
  cocaine, 41, 324
  ecstasy (MDMA, molly)
    dancing, relationship with, 27, 87, 140, 174, 192–93, 300
    masculinity of ('bro drug'), 340–42
    physical effects of, 28, 182
  ketamine, 345
  marijuana, 340
  'psychotropic technologies', 37
Duke Vin (Vincent Forbes), 54
economic matters
  capitalism and post-capitalism, 172, 304
  clubbing, cost of. *See* clubs and venues, boundaries
  cost; EDM, belonging, commodification of
  Covid-19. *See* Covid-19
  deindustrialisation, 167

economic matters (cont.)
  deterritorialisation, 172–74, 177
  gentrification, 11, 66, 84, 92–94, 99
  gig labour, 151
  neo-liberalism, 99, 173, 297, 301
  night-time economy, the, 129–30, 135
  social mobility, lack of, 172–74, 178
  Thatcherism, 88

Ectomorph, 239
electronic dance music (EDM)
  acid, 83, 207, 277–84, 355
    house parties. *See* raves, festivals, teknivals and free parties
  affectivity. *See* EDM, timbre and gesture
  Angolan. *See* Angola
  axé, 109–10
  belonging, 77, 100, 342, 364
    commodification of, 161
    communitas, 10, 67, 93, 153, 174, 346, 357
    cosmopolitanism, 3, 114
    drug-taking, collective. *See* drugs, ecstasy
    'gassed up', 349
    moshing, 339–40
    secrecy, 20, 23, 27
    shared experience (vibe, nowness), 118, 148, 154, 186, 206, 295, 300
    virtual, 146
  breakdown, 197, 298
  brostep, 338, 345
  carga. *See* DJs and producers, audience, interaction with, carga
  chill out. *See* chill out (ambient)
  Chinese. *See* China
  clubs. *See* clubs and venues
  collaboration, 259–60, 272
  definitions of, 1, 71
  distortion and reverb, 214–16, 239, 264, 266
  drum and bass (jungle), 167–78, 243, 285
  dubstep, 64, 121, 244, 340, 348
  electroclash, 257
  electronic body music (EBM), 84, 214–17
  electronica, 71, 85, 314
  festivals. *See* raves, festivals, teknivals and free parties
  footwork battle, 243
  funk (funkiness, funk carioca), 116, 169
  gabber, 96–97, 173
  garage, 1, 5, 7, 51, 209
  gender imbalance, 313, 343–44, 359
  genre and classification, 205–22, 258, 328, 353
  globalisation of, 128, 210
  grime, 51, 58, 65, 121, 175
  house, 170, 209, 233, 328, 338
  industrial, 85
  kuduro, 123
  Mandopop, 136, 140
  mic-shouting, 128, 142
  Nazism and neo-Nazism, relationship with, 96–97
  older people's participation in, 361–64
  phenomenology of, 184–87, 231, 296
  raves. *See* raving
  sound systems. *See* technology, sound systems
  spirituality, relationship with, 183, 184–87, 192, 197
  techno, 170, 208–11, 214–16, 218–20, 254–72
    Berlin, 219, 221
    CzechTek, 92
    Detroit, 4, 6, 85, 174, 209, 219, 256
    hardcore, 101, 328
    old, 337
  technology. *See* technology
  tempo, 1
    accelerated, 85, 167
    bass music drop, 337
    continuous, 298
    decelerated, 7
    high. *See* EDM, techno
    low. *See* EDM, chill out
    pulse trains, 261–64, 272
  timbre and gesture, 231–32
  trance, 347
    Goa, 347–48
    psychedelic trance (psytrance), 208, 303, 353
  trap, 337, 342
  'versioning', 63
  whiteness of, 347, 359
Eno, Brian, 190–91
Excision, 337
Extrawelt, 298

Fabbri, Franco, 207
Fikentscher, Kai, 295
Fisher, Mark, 177
folk music, 219
folksonomies. *See* EDM, genre and classification
Frankie Bones, 349
Frankie Knuckles, 6, 72, 170
Franziska Brems, 72
free party movement, the. *See* raves, festivals, teknivals and free parties

Freed, Alan, 73
future shock, 176–78

Gammer, 337
Garcia (Garcia-Mispireta), Luis-Manuel, 299, 341
Germany
  Berlin
    Atonal Festival, 85
    Berlin-Detroit axis. See EDM, techno, Detroit
    clubs. See clubs and venues
    Fuckparade (Hate Parade), 93, 101
    Kurfürstendamm, 84
    Love Parade, 84–86
    techno scene. See EDM, techno, Berlin
    Tekknozid, 84
    Wall, fall of, 83, 99, 210, 256
  Munich, 75
Gilroy, Paul, 53, 120–21
Glass, Philip, 261
Goa. See EDM, psychedelic trance, Goa
Goodman, Steve, 100
Graeme Park, 87
Gruppo 9999, 32
Gutmair, Ulrich, 97, 101
Guy called Gerald (Gerald Simpson), 58

Harrison, Harry, 88, 92, 99
Harrison, Mark, 89–92
Heartless Crew, 58

Ibiza, 191–93
  clubs. See clubs and venues
  ecstasy. See drugs, ecstasy
Illenium, 340
Isozaki, Arata, 35
Italian clubs. See clubs and venues

Jamaica
  Kingston, 50–51
  Rastafari, 55
  war, impact on, 50–51
  Windrush generation, the, 54, 60
Jammer, 58
Jimmy Cauty, 193
Johannes Heil, 261
Johnnie Stieler, 84
Johnson, Roy, 52
Jones, Hedley, 52
jouissance, 169, 173, 178, 231
Jovonn, 233

Kakehashi, Ikutaro, 280

King Tubby, 63, 289
KLF, The, 185, 193–94, 197
Kool DJ Herc (Clive Campbell), 53
Kraftwerk, 189–90, 209, 256

Land, Nick, 172
legislation
  Assembly Act. See raves, festivals, teknivals and free parties, Fuckparade
  bans (Chinese), 135–39, 141
  Criminal Justice and Public Order Act (1994), 18, 24, 88, 210
  drugs. See drugs
  Entertainment (Increased Penalties) Act (1990), 25
listening. See EDM, timbre and gesture
Long, Richard, 62
Lucy, 233

Maceo Plex (Eric Estornel), 262
Max Cooper, 259–60
McRobbie, Angela, 313
Mija, 338
Mille Plateaux, 210
mind-body blues. See EDM, timbre and gesture
Moby (Richard Melville), 276, 286
Moog_t, 94–97
Mr. Carmack, 337
Museum of Modern Electronic Music (MOMEM), 72
music journalism, 30, 176, 207–9, 217, 276, 320
  Crack magazine, 177
  Dancecult, 358
  DJ Mag, 278, 359
  Frontpage magazine, 86
  i-D magazine, 169
  Vogue Hommes, 42
Mutoid Waste Company, the, 85

Norman Jay, 56–57
NYMA, 260

O'Grady, Alice, 296
Orb, The, 185, 193–94, 197
Orbital, 276, 279–84, 291
parasociality, 149, 152–56
Paul Oakenfold, 193

Pet Shop Boys, the, 279, 358
Phuture, 277
Plastikman (Riche Hawtin), 255–57
punk, 85, 340

queerness, 346
  gay scene(s), local, 84
  gender norms, challenges to, 314, 325,
    See also EDM, gender imbalance
  homophobia, 276
  inclusivity. *See* EDM, belonging
  'jacking', 282
  queer spaces, 39, 77, 148

racial identity, 231
  Afrofuturism. *See* Afrofuturism
  Black Atlantic. *See* Black Atlantic, the
  Black technology. *See* technology, mis-use of
  creativity, racial coding of (appropriation), 276–89
  inclusivity. *See* EDM, belonging
  racial features, 317
  whiteness. *See* EDM, whiteness of

raves, festivals, teknivals and free parties, 4, 91–93
  Acid House Flashback Archive, 18
  acid house parties, 18, 83–84, 210, 256
  Atonal Festival, 85
  AWOL ('A Way of Life'), 171
  belonging. *See* EDM, belonging
  Big Chill, the, 194
  Blackburn Parties, the, 17
  Castlemorton Common (1992), 88–90
  CzechTek Festival, 95
  dancings, 113
  free party movement, the, 83, 86–89
  Fuckparade (Hate Parade), 93–97, 101
  Glastonbury Festival, 88
  Hate Parade. *See* raves, festivals, teknivals and free parties, Fuckparade
  Lost Lands (Ohio), 337–38
  Love Parade (Berlin), the, 84–86
  maratonas, 115
  Mayday (Berlin), 86
  Movement Electronic Music Festival (Detroit), 211
  Musikkfest (Norway), 359
  Notting Hill Carnival, 57, 90
  Reading Festival, 88
  Spring Awakening (Chicago), 337–38, 341–43
  Tekknozid, 84
  virtual. *See* DJs and producers, audience, interaction with, virtual
raving. *See* clubbing and raving
Reid, Duke, 52–54
Reinhold, Riley, 260

research projects
  Cybernetic Culture Research Unit (CCRU), 172–76
  Flow Research Collective, 297
  Lapsed Clubber Project, the, 18, 358
Reynolds, Simon, 30, 90, 175, 300
Riley, Terry, 189
Roni Size, 59–60
Rosner, Alex, 62
Rotterdam. *See* EDM, gabber

Satie, Erik, 187
Sedgewick, Augustine, 302
Sherwood, Adrian, 59
Skrillex, 337
Smalley, Denis, 242
Smith, Earl "Spanky", 277
So Solid Crew, 58
Sonic Groove, 214–17
Soweto, 302
Space Laces, 340
Spiral Tribe, 4, 85, 89–91, 210
Stahl, Geoff, 98
Stieler, Johnnie, 86, 97
Stockhausen, Karlheinz, 189
Strauss, D., 99
Sven Väth, 72

Takehashi, Ikutaro, 283
Tangerine Dream, 189
technology
  accelerationism, 173–78
  affordable, 129, 279, 302
  Bandcamp, 205–6, 213–22
  Beatport, 213–14
  digital audio workstation (DAW), 5, 173, 235, 266, 270
  distortion and reverb. *See* EDM, distortion and reverb
  drum machines, 214, 324
    Ableton, 259, 266
    MFB Tanzbär, 261
    Roland HR16, 281
    Roland TB-303, 236, 277–84, 291
    Roland TB-808, 244
    Roland TR-808, 6, 348
    Roland TR-909, 6, 279, 291
  Furthrrrr Generator, 267–69
  internet radio (Icecast), 147
  masculinity of, 314, 321, 326
  MED (Music Editor), 287
  military origins of, 171

mis-use of (Black, secret), 276–78, 284
mixers, 284
Moog, 288
musical instrument digital interface (MIDI), 6, 270, 287
Operator, 259
projectors, 38
radiograms, 55–56
remediation, 116, 146, 153, 155
Roland SH-101, 261
samplers, 7, 8, 167, 284–87
  Akai A700, 281
  Akai S700, 279
  Akai S950, 293
  Atari ST, 288
  Commodore Amiga, 287
sequencers, 214, 281
set-up, speed of, 22
social media platforms, various, 137, 149, 319
sound systems, 50–67, 121–23, 244
  DiY, 87–91
  Hekate Sound System, 92
  Mutoid Waste Company. *See* Mutoid Waste Company, the
  Spiral Tribe. *See* Spiral Tribe
  Studio 17, 59
Spotify, *xii*, 182, 187, *196*, 212
synthesizers, 281, 325
  Nord Lead 2, 262
  Roland JD-800, 284
techgnosis, 289
turntables, 37, 74, 175
Twitch, 146
teknivals. *See* raves, festivals, teknivals and free parties, 4
Terry T, 58
Toffler, Alvin. *See* future shock
Tommy Four Seven, 298

Trauma XP (Martin Kliehm), 93–95
travellers (nomads, squatters), 87–88, 91

Underground Resistance, the, 210
United Kingdom
  Blackburn, 17
  Bristol, 59
  Castlemorton Common, 88–90
  clubs. *See* clubs and venues
  Glastonbury, 88
  London, 57, 61, 90, 134, 167, 193, 255
  Manchester, 359
  Reading, 88
United States
  Chicago, 337–38, 341–43, *See* EDM, house
  clubs. *See* clubs and venues
  Detroit. *See* EDM, techno, Detroit Movement EDM festival, 211
  New York, 34, 295
  Ohio, 337–38
  San Francisco Disco Preservation Society, 73
Urban Shakedown, 288

Virilio, Paul, 172

Wild Bunch, The (later Massive Attack), 59
Witek, Maria, 245
Wong, Tom, 52–54

XOL DOG 400, 96

Yellow Claw, 341–43
Young, Lamonte, 188
'youth culture'. *See* clubbing and raving, 'youth-focused'

Zagorski-Thomas, Simon, 241
Zylberberg, Régine, 37

Printed in the United Kingdom by TJ Clays Ltd.